THEORY AFTER 'THEORY'

This volume argues that theory, far from being dead, has undergone major shifts in order to come to terms with the most urgent cultural and political questions of today. Offering an overview of theory's new directions, this groundbreaking collection includes essays on affect, biopolitics, biophilosophy, the aesthetic, and neoliberalism, as well as examinations of established areas such as subaltern studies, the postcolonial and ethics.

Influential figures such as Agamben, Badiou, Arendt, Deleuze, Derrida and Meillassoux are examined in a range of contexts. Gathering together some of the top thinkers in the field, this volume not only speculates on the fate of theory but shows its current diversity, encouraging conversation between divergent strands. Each section highlights new areas of theoretical exploration and stages a comparison between different but ultimately related ways in which key thinkers are moving beyond poststructuralism.

Jane Elliott is Lecturer in the Department of English and Related Literature at the University of York, UK. She is the author of *Popular Feminist Fiction as American Allegory: Representing National Time* (2008), and her essays have appeared in *Cultural Critique, Modern Fiction Studies, Novel,* and the *PMLA.* She is currently at work on a project on neoliberalism, choice and the novel.

Derek Attridge is Professor in the Department of English and Related Literature at the University of York, UK. Among his books are *Peculiar Language: Literature as Difference from the Renaissance to James Joyce* (1988), *The Singularity of Literature* (2004), *J. M. Coetzee and the Ethics of Reading: Literature in the Event* (2004) and *Reading and Responsibility: Deconstruction's Traces* (2010). His edited and co-edited volumes include *Post-structuralist Joyce: Essays from the French* (1984), *Post-structuralism and the Question of History* (1987) and *Acts of Literature* by Jacques Derrida (1992).

THEORY AFTER 'THEORY'

Edited by Jane Elliott and Derek Attridge

Routledge
Taylor & Francis Group

LONDON AND NEW YORK

First edition published 2011
by Routledge
2 Park Square, Milton Park, Abingdon, Oxon OX14 4RN

Simultaneously published in the USA and Canada
by Routledge
270 Madison Ave, New York, NY 10016

Routledge is an imprint of the Taylor & Francis Group, an informa business

Typeset in Bembo by
Book Now Ltd, London
Printed and bound in Great Britain by
TJ International, Padstow, Cornwall

British Library Cataloguing in Publication Data
A catalogue record for this book is available from the British Library

Library of Congress Cataloging-in-Publication Data
Theory after 'theory'/edited by Jane Elliott and Derek Attridge.
       p. cm.
Includes bibliographical references and index.
1. Literature—History and criticism—Theory, etc. 2. Literature—Philosophy.
I. Elliott, Jane, 1969–. II. Attridge, Derek.
PN441.T445 2011
801'.95–dc222010033268

ISBN13: 978–0–415–48418–3 (hbk)
ISBN13: 978–0–415–48419–0 (pbk)
ISBN13: 978–0–203–83116–8 (ebk)

CONTENTS

Notes on contributors   viii
Acknowledgements   xiii

Introduction: theory's nine lives   1
Jane Elliott and Derek Attridge

PART I
Assessing the field   **17**

1 Philosophy after theory: transdisciplinarity and the new   19
   Peter Osborne

2 Theory as a research programme – the very idea   34
   Cary Wolfe

3 Theory after critical theory   49
   William Rasch

4 Extinct theory   62
   Claire Colebrook

PART II
Between theory and practice: judgement, will, potentiality 73

5 Perception attack: the force to own time   75
   Brian Massumi

6 The will of the people: dialectical voluntarism and the
subject of politics   90
Peter Hallward

7 The persistence of hope: critical theory and enduring in
late liberalism   105
Elizabeth A. Povinelli

8 The practice of judgement: Hannah Arendt's
'Copernican revolution'   120
Linda M. G. Zerilli

PART III
Rethinking the politics of representation   **133**

9 When reflexivity becomes porn: mutations of a modernist
theoretical practice   135
Rey Chow

10 The canny subaltern   149
Eva Cherniavsky

11 Theory after postcolonial theory: rethinking the
work of mimesis   163
Simon Gikandi

PART IV
Biopolitics and ethics   **179**

12 After life: swarms, demons and the antinomies of immanence   181
Eugene Thacker

13 Inclining the subject: ethics, alterity and natality   194
Adriana Cavarero

14 The person and human life   205
Roberto Esposito

PART V
Renewing the aesthetic   **221**

15 The wrong turn of aesthetics   223
Henry Staten

16 Literature after theory, or: the intellective turn   237
    Laurent Dubreuil

17 The liberal aesthetic   249
    Amanda Anderson

PART VI
Philosophy after theory   **263**

18 The arche–materiality of time: deconstruction, evolution
    and speculative materialism   265
    Martin Hägglund

19 Concepts, objects, gems   278
    Ray Brassier

20 Pharmacology of spirit: and that which makes
    life worth living   294
    Bernard Stiegler

Index   311

NOTES ON CONTRIBUTORS

Amanda Anderson is Caroline Donovan Professor of English Literature at The Johns Hopkins University and Director of the School of Criticism and Theory (at Cornell University). She is the author of *The Way We Argue Now: A Study in the Cultures of Theory* (Princeton University Press, 2006), *The Powers of Distance: Cosmopolitanism and the Cultivation of Detachment* (Princeton University Press, 2001) and *Tainted Souls and Painted Faces: The Rhetoric of Fallenness in Victorian Culture* (Cornell University Press, 1993). She has also co-edited, with Joseph Valente, *Disciplinarity at the Fin de Siècle* (Princeton University Press, 2002).

Ray Brassier is Associate Professor of Philosophy at the American University of Beirut. He is the author of *Nihil Unbound: Enlightenment and Extinction* (Palgrave, 2007). He is currently working on a book that proposes to conjoin historical with eliminative materialism.

Adriana Cavarero is Professor of Political Philosophy at the University of Verona. Her publications include *Relating Narratives: Storytelling and Selfhood* (Routledge, 2000), *Stately Bodies: Literature, Philosophy and the Question of Gender* (University of Michigan Press, 2002), *For More than One Voice: Toward a Philosophy of Vocal Expression* (Stanford University Press, 2005) and *Horrorism: Naming Contemporary Violence* (Columbia University Press, 2008).

Eva Cherniavsky is Andrew R. Hilen Professor of American Literature and Culture and affiliated faculty in Women's Studies at the University of Washington. She is the author of *That Pale Mother Rising: Sentimental Discourses and the Imitation of Motherhood in Nineteenth-Century America* (Indiana University Press, 1995) and of *Incorporations: Race, Nation, and the Body Politics of Capital* (University of Minnesota

Press, 2006). Her current research considers the changing contours of the political in the context of neoliberal governance with an emphasis on the reimagination of citizenship in popular culture.

Rey Chow is Anne Firor Scott Professor of Literature at Trinity College of Arts and Sciences, Duke University. Since 1991 she has authored seven books, including *Writing Diaspora* (Indiana University Press, 1993), *Ethics after Idealism* (Indiana University Press, 1998), *The Protestant Ethnic and the Spirit of Capitalism* (Columbia University Press, 1992), *The Age of the World Target: Self-Referentiality in War, Theory, and Comparative Work* (Duke University Press, 2006) and *Sentimental Fabulations, Contemporary Chinese Films: Attachment in the Age of Global Visibility* (Columbia University Press, 2007). Her writings have been widely anthologized and translated into multiple European and Asian languages. *The Rey Chow Reader*, ed. Paul Bowman, is available from Columbia University Press.

Claire Colebrook is Edwin Erle Sparks Professor of English at Pennsylvania State University. She has published books on contemporary European philosophy, literary theory, feminist theory, literary history and poetry. Her two most recent books are *Milton, Evil and Literary History* (2009) and *Deleuze and the Meaning of Life* (2010).

Laurent Dubreuil is a Professor of Romance Studies and Comparative Literature and the Director of the French Studies Program at Cornell University. His main research has to do with philosophy, literary criticism and theory, and the epistemology of the disciplines. He is the author of several books, including, *À force d'amitié* (Paris: Hermann, 2009), *L'État critique de la littérature* (Paris: Hermann, 2009) and *Empire of Language* (Ithaca: Cornell University Press, forthcoming in 2011). The editor-at-large of the French interdisciplinary journal *Labyrinthe*, Dubreuil is currently assembling a special issue of *Diacritics* on 'Negative Politics'. A Mellon Fellow in the New Directions Program, Laurent Dubreuil is also working more and more on neuroscience, evolutionary theory or animal behaviour from a 'theoretical' and 'experimental' perspective.

Roberto Esposito teaches Theoretic Philosophy at the Istituto Italiano du Scienze Umane in Naples and in Florence. His main works, which have been translated into a number of different foreign languages, are *Categorie dell'impolitico* (Il Mulino, 1988, 1999), *Nove pensieri sulla politica* (Il Mulino, 1993), *L'origine della politica* (Donzelli, 1996), *Communitas: Origine e destino della comunità* (Einaudi, 1998), translated as *Communitas: The Origin and Destiny of Community* (Stanford University Press, 2010) and *Immunitas: Protezione e negazione della vita* (Einaudi, 2002). His most works are *Bios: Politica e filosofia* (Einaudi, 2004), translated as *Bíos: Biopolitics and Philosophy* (University of Minnesota, 2008), *Terza Persona: Politica della vita e filosofia dell'impersonale* (Einaudi, 2007) and *Termini della politica: Comunità, immunità, biopolitica* (Mimesis, 2009).

Simon Gikandi is Robert Schirmer Professor of English at Princeton University. His many books include *Reading the African Novel* (Portsmouth, 1987, rep. 1994), *Reading Chinua Achebe,* (Portsmouth, 1991, rep. 1996), *Writing in Limbo: Modernism and Caribbean Literature* (Cornell Univeristy Press, 1992), *Maps of Englishness: Writing Identity in the Culture of Colonialism* (Columbia University Press, 1992) and *Ngugi wa Thiong'o* (Cambridge University Press, 2000). He is the general editor of *The Encyclopedia of African Literature* (Routledge, 2003) and co-editor of *The Cambridge History of African and Caribbean Literature* (Cambridge University Press, 2004). He is currently completing a book on the relation between slavery and the culture of taste.

Martin Hägglund is a Junior Fellow in the Harvard Society of Fellows and a Distinguished International Fellow of the London Graduate School. He is the author of *Kronofobi: Essäer om tid och ändlighet* (Symposion, 2002) and *Radical Atheism: Derrida and the Time of Life* (Stanford University Press, 2008). He is currently completing his next book, *Chronolibidinal Reading: Proust, Woolf, Nabokov.* He is also working on a sequel to *Radical Atheism,* which turns from a critique of transcendence to a critique of immanence, by engaging Bergson and Deleuze on fundamental questions of time, life and desire.

Peter Hallward teaches at the Centre for Research in Modern European Philosophy at Kingston University London and is the author of *Damming the Flood: Haiti and the Politics of Containment* (Verso, 2007), *Out of this World: Deleuze and the Philosophy of Creation* (Verso, 2006), *Badiou: A Subject to Truth* (University of Minnesota Press, 2003) and *Absolutely Postcolonial: Writing Between the Singular and the Specific* (Manchester University Press, 2001). He is currently working on a book-length project entitled *The Will of the People.*

Brian Massumi specializes in the philosophy of experience, art and media theory, and political philosophy. He is the author of *Parables for the Virtual: Movement, Affect, Sensation* (Duke University Press, 2002), *A User's Guide to Capitalism and Schizophrenia: Deviations from Deleuze and Guattari* (MIT Press, 1992) and *First and Last Emperors: The Absolute State and the Body of the Despot* (with Kenneth Dean; Autonomedia, 1993). He is an editor of *The Politics of Everyday Fear* (University of Minnesota Press, 1993) and *A Shock to Thought: Expression After Deleuze and Guattari* (Routledge, 2002). His translations from the French include Gilles Deleuze and Félix Guattari's *A Thousand Plateaus.*

Peter Osborne is Professor of Modern European Philosophy and Director of the Centre for Research in Modern European Philosophy at Kingston University London. He is an editor of the journal *Radical Philosophy.* His books include *The Politics of Time: Modernity and Avant-Garde* (Verso, 1995; 2nd ed., forthcoming), *Philosophy in Cultural Theory* (Routledge, 2000), *Conceptual Art* (Phaidon, 2002), *Marx* (Grant, 2005), *Walter Benjamin: Critical Evaluations in Cultural Theory* (ed.,

Routledge, 3 Volumes, 2005) and *El arte más allá de la estética: Ensayos filosóficos sobre el arte contemporáneo* (CENDEAC, Murcia, 2010). He is currently completing a book on philosophical aspects of contemporary art.

Elizabeth A. Povinelli is Professor of Anthropology and Gender Studies at Columbia University, where she has also served as the Director of the Institute for Research on Women and Gender and Co-Director of the Center for the Study of Law and Culture. Her research focuses on developing a critical theory of late liberalism. This critical task is grounded in theories of the translation, transfiguration and the circulation of values, materialities and socialities within settler liberalisms. She is the author of three books: *Labor's Lot* (University of Chicago Press, 1994), *The Cunning of Recognition* (Duke University Press, 2002) and *The Empire of Love* (Duke University Press, 2006). She was the editor of *Public Culture* and sits on the editorial committees/boards of *Cultural Anthropology*, *American Anthropology* and *Social Analysis*.

William Rasch is Professor of German Studies and Director of the Center for Theoretical Inquiry in the Humanities at the Indiana University. He is the author of *Niklas Luhmann's Modernity* (Stanford University Press, 2000) and *Sovereignty and Its Discontents* (Birkbeck Law Press, 2004), editor of a collection of essays by Luhmann called *Theories of Distinction* (Stanford University Press, 2002) as well as editor or co-editor of numerous volumes and special issues on Luhmann, Carl Schmitt, German film and the bombing war during the Second World War. His current research centres on political and legal theory.

Henry Staten is Lockwood Professor in the Humanities and Adjunct Professor of Philosophy at the University of Washington. He is the author of *Wittgenstein and Derrida* (University of Nebraska Press, 1984), *Nietzsche's Voice* (Cornell University Press, 1990) and *Eros in Mourning: Homer to Lacan* (Johns Hopkins University Press, 1984).

Bernard Stiegler is the Director of the Department of Cultural Development at the Centre Georges-Pompidou in Paris and the founder of the political group Ars Industrialis. He has published more than 25 books in French, his best-known work being the three-volume project *La technique et le temps* published in English translation as *Technics and Time, vol. 1: The Fault of Epimetheus* (Stanford University Press, 1998), *Technics and Time, vol 2: Disorientation* (Stanford University Press, 2009), and *Technics and Time, vol. 3: Cinematic Time and the Question of Malaise* (Stanford University Press, 2011). He also published, with Jacques Derrida, *Echographies of Television* (Polity, 2002). Other books in translation include *Acting Out* (Stanford University Press, 2009) and *For a New Critique of Political Economy* (Polity, 2010).

Eugene Thacker is associate professor in the Media Studies programme at the New School in New York. He is the author of *After Life* (University of Chicago Press, forthcoming) as well as *Horror of Philosophy* (Zero Books, forthcoming).

Cary Wolfe is Bruce and Elizabeth Dunlevie Professor of English at Rice University and founding editor of the *Posthumanities* series at the University of Minnesota Press. His books and edited collections include *Animal Rites: American Culture, the Discourse of Species, and Posthumanist Theory* (University of Chicago Press, 2003), *Zoontologies: The Question of the Animal* (University of Minnesota Press, 2003), *What Is Posthumanism?* (University of Minnesota Press, 2003) and *The Other Emerson* (ed. with Branka Arsic, University of Minnesota Press, 2010).

Linda M. G. Zerilli is Charles E. Merriam Distinguished Professor of Political Science and the College and Professor of Gender Studies at the University of Chicago. She has published in the areas of feminist theory, democratic theory and Continental philosophy. Her most recent book is *Feminism and the Abyss of Freedom* (University of Chicago Press, 2005).

ACKNOWLEDGEMENTS

From the original one-day symposium in 2006 that sparked this collection to its completion, we have been very fortunate in the support and assistance we have received. The symposium was sponsored and hosted by the Department of English and Related Literature at the University of York, and we thank its speakers (Howard Caygill, Claire Colebrook, Miriam Fraser, Chris Fynsk, Peter Hallward and Peter Osborne) for their rich presentations, some of which appear in new forms here. Michelle Kelly, our conference assistant, did a marvellous job ensuring all went smoothly that day. The transition from small symposium to hefty volume was enabled by grants from the F. R. Leavis Fund at the University of York, in support of editorial assistance and translation. Peter Fifield, our editorial assistant, provided excellent copyediting under tight deadlines, and we thank him for his unflagging efforts.

If *Theory after 'Theory'* inevitably reflects our own particular (and often divergent) interests in the realm of theory, we have also been committed to making the volume as wide ranging and representative as possible, and consultations with our contributors and other scholars were invaluable in helping us to identify important new work and areas of theoretical development outside our immediate fields of expertise. In addition to our contributors, we would like to thank Jo Applin, Geoffrey Bennington, Timothy Campbell, Ziad Elmarsafy, Elizabeth Grosz, Brian Price, John David Rhodes, Nikolas Rose, Katherine Sugg, Richard Taws, Alberto Toscano, Elizabeth Weed and Elizabeth Wilson for their recommendations. Our anonymous referees at Routledge also offered excellent advice regarding both contributors to and organization of the volume, and we are grateful for their suggestions. Diana Garvin and Thomas Kelso, who translated Roberto Esposito's essay, and Daniel Ross, who translated Bernard Stiegler's, deserve special thanks for generously undertaking the arduous task of translating theory for us, with brilliant results. As well as being a supportive Head of Department, David Attwell also proved to be a highly efficient postman in the case of one hard-to-reach scholar. Our thanks also go to John David Rhodes and Katherine Sugg for their incisive comments on a draft of the introduction. Routledge has provided enthusiastic support for *Theory after 'Theory'* from its inception, and we are particularly grateful to Polly Dodson, our editor, and Emma Nugent, our editorial assistant, for their keen interest in and commitment to the project.

INTRODUCTION

Theory's nine lives

Jane Elliott and Derek Attridge

Whether the news is met with celebration or lamentation, there seems to be little disagreement that the era of theory's dominance has passed – whatever 'theory' might mean or have meant. The story of theory, as it is usually told, has thus solidified into a recognizable narrative of declension shared even by theory's adherents. According to this narrative, the heyday of 'Theory' is associated with a moment of energy and excitement fuelled in the English-speaking world by the production and translation of works by the seminal figures of postwar French philosophy, particularly Gilles Deleuze, Jacques Derrida, Michel Foucault and Jean-François Lyotard. For some, 'Theory' was already passing with the end of the 1970s, whereas for others, the 1980s and early 1990s represent the height of 'Theory', in which feminist, postcolonial, queer and critical race theorists made their most significant contributions. Since the mid-1990s, the story goes, theory has continued to diversify, drawing on the work of a range of new figures and examining a host of new archives and arenas, but its newer incarnations offer at most a kind of afterlife of the once vital object that was 'Theory', a diluted form lacking in both intellectual substance and institutional prominence. As a result, conversations regarding the status of theory have become akin to an ongoing wake, in which participants debate the merits of the deceased and consider the possibilities for a resurrection desired by some and feared by others.[1]

This funereal narrative regarding theory's fall thus propagates a view, shared by mourners and celebrants alike, that the major difference between theory today and in the period from the 1970s through the mid-1990s is that it no longer possesses the same significance it once did. From this perspective, theory may be perceived as less intellectually rigorous, less politically radical or less epistemologically coherent than when it was at its height; however, it is still seen as retaining its commitment to an array of intellectual and political positions that allowed it to be distinguished as a bounded realm of enquiry in the first place. According to this narrative, theory may have fallen from grace, but, even in its fallen state, it is still located within the same intellectual boundaries.

This volume suggests instead that, where theory continues to thrive, it increasingly adopts positions that challenge some of the fundamental intellectual stances that once defined 'Theory'. The essays collected here indicate that theory is undergoing transformations far more radical than the movement to new thinkers and topics usually referenced in accounts of contemporary theory: when an expert in contemporary continental philosophy makes an argument for the Rousseauist political will, when the English translator of *A Thousand Plateaus* suggests that the temporality of the event has been operationalized in the 'War on Terror', when a postmodernist feminist political theorist insists that freedom is not tied to epistemology, when the newest wave of 'French theory' demands what amounts to a form of scientific realism, it seems abundantly evident that at least some contemporary strands of theory have broken decisively with what were once its defining problematics and stances.[2] If theory today no longer registers an allegiance to these defining problematics and stances, then it is not only subsequent to but also distinct from the body of work once known as 'Theory'.

Of course, even 'Theory' was never a single, self-identical object and, in fact, one of its signature reflexes was the resistance to such 'totalizing' groupings, which were usually seen to commit the epistemological violence of reducing the rich heterogeneity of a complex field to a single homogeneous concept. Yet it was also more or less defined by such recurring gestures – for example, the foregrounding of culture over nature or the conviction that epistemological closure is necessarily a form of domination. It was common throughout the reign of 'Theory' for thinkers on the Right and the Left to express dissent from such signature gestures – but to do so was in effect to exit from the intellectual arena defined by the concept of theory, to place oneself on the other side of the barricades that demarcated what were often called the 'theory wars'. In the current theoretical landscape, by contrast, new work is being produced that mounts such challenges from within theory's now much wider institutional and discursive boundaries.

Bringing together new essays by a large number of important thinkers from across the humanities, this collection is designed to provide readers with a comprehensive view of the most important of these challenges, as well as an array of evaluations of and responses to theory's transformations from key participants in the field. The essays collected here range from spirited defences of crucial poststructuralist insights against what might be considered new theoretical heresies (e.g. the contributions by Eva Cherniavsky, Claire Colebrook, Martin Hägglund and Cary Wolfe) to pointed arguments that theory must now become something distinctly other than it has been before (including the essays by Ray Brassier, Rey Chow, Peter Hallward and Linda Zerilli). What unites our contributors is thus not a shared view of the state of the field, but rather the originality, importance and vigour of their interventions into that field – as well as their manifest, ongoing intellectual commitment to the project of theory, no matter what form each author argues it can or should take in the future.

To the extent that some elements of this ongoing metamorphosis have been noted elsewhere, theory's evolution has been more associated with transformations in content than in position – for example, shifts from one battery of thinkers (among them Adorno, Derrida, Deleuze, Foucault and Lacan) to another (notably Giorgio Agamben, Alain Badiou and Jacques Rancière). Although these last three names appear scattered across this volume, the essays collected here suggest that theory's current transformations have in a sense already outstripped this turn to new defining figures.[3] These newly prominent theorists do not provide the motivating or organizing principle for any of our contributors' interventions, and, when the work of individual thinkers is made central in essays here, the ones chosen are frequently rather less well known than Rancière or Agamben – as in Brassier's engagement with the 'speculative realism' of Quentin Meillassoux or William Rasch's turn to Niklas Luhmann to reconsider the role of critical theory. When our contributors do find fruitful theoretical resources in the work of renowned thinkers, they are far from new – for example, Hannah Arendt (Adriana Cavarero and Zerilli), Bertolt Brecht (Chow), Lionel Trilling (Amanda Anderson), Rousseau (Hallward) and Simone Weil (Roberto Esposito). To the extent that 'Theory' was associated with a tendency to draw obsessively on the work of certain oracular figures, theory as it is manifested in this volume suggests not so much a movement from one set of figures to another as a movement away from the perception that such figures are a necessary or consensual feature of the project of theory in the first place.

While recent work in theory has also been associated with shifts from one type of content (linguistic, discursive and cultural) to another (material, biological and expressly political), such transformations in archive do not necessarily coincide with the more radical alterations in theory expressed and examined in this volume. For instance, as Wolfe notes, much of the work associated with the scientific turn in theory has focused on demonstrating the way in which technoscientific or biological fact can be understood to underwrite and legitimize insights that theory had already achieved (60). Thus, while the scientific turn directs our attention to new archives, it still tends to focus on the threshold, vanishingly perceptible states long favoured in theoretical arguments; it shifts their location from the operations of language to physical experiences such as auto-affection, but such states remain the prime object of interest. Similarly, although it might be argued that some of Agamben's recent work manifests a turn to what Fredric Jameson has called 'a genuinely theoretical political theory', Agamben's approach also tends to demonstrate more of a shift in archive than in methodology or position (Jameson 2004: 406). For example, the location of resistance in the indivisible and unclassifiable experience of life, or what Agamben terms 'whatever being', indicates his perpetuation, in another field of enquiry, of theory's longstanding understanding of conceptual mapping as a mode of political control (Agamben 1993: 1). Thus, despite their different areas of enquiry, both recent work on affect and new forms of political theory frequently continue the defining investments of 'Theory' in temporal disruption, epistemological uncertainty and logical paradox; the groundbreaking nature of such work is thus more apparent than real.

Although *Theory after 'Theory'* provides ample documentation of theory's turn to the material, biological and overtly political – from the engagement with physics in the work of Brassier to the analysis of life in essays by Esposito and Eugene Thacker to the examination of specific political concepts and practices in the work of Massumi, Elizabeth Povinelli and Zerilli – the essays collected here also manifest rather more dramatic shifts at work in current theoretical conversations than those of content or archive. These new positions challenge poststructuralist truisms and cut across disciplinary and content-based groupings, drawing together scholars with radically different concerns and methodologies. Significantly, several of our contributors (including Chow, Simon Gikandi, Hallward, Massumi and Povinelli) continue to examine established poststructuralist tropes such as the event, self-reflexivity and the rejection of mimesis, but they do so to suggest that these familiar operations and positions may no longer have the same necessary relationship to resistance that they once seemed to possess. Whether these authors indicate that the current historical moment requires new approaches or raise questions regarding the utility of such strategies even during theory's heyday, this group of essays offers a startling glimpse of a theoretical landscape no longer united by the perception of a definitive link between epistemological indeterminacy and political freedom. Taking the opposite view, others of our contributors, including Cherniavsky, Colebrook and Wolfe, read some recent incarnations of theoretical endeavour as themselves reaction-formations, suggesting that new forms of theory may serve more as symptoms of current intellectual and political limitations than as tools for overcoming such limitations. Yet, whether they feel theory has changed too much or too little, our contributors read theory's current transformations in relation to its inevitably complex historical relations: born in response to one set of historical circumstances, persisting in the midst of another, and in both cases, required to be in some fashion untimely – to exceed the given terms of the present in a way that allows us to comprehend something hitherto unthinkable.

In the sections that follow, this volume traces theory's current ways of being untimely, suggesting connections between work from across disciplines in six key areas. Our sense that some of the most crucial and original developments in contemporary theory are linked in ways that exceed groupings by methodology, archive or thinker, means we have dispensed with essay groupings based on theory 'schools', the work of particular theorists or the association of the authors in question with theorization of various identity categories. Although we invited contributors who represented a range of fields and specializations, we placed no strictures on them regarding topic, and the results underscore the inability of the identity categories of politics or theory to provide an easy means of grouping contemporary theoretical production – for example, an essay by a feminist political theorist that does not mention gender and by a founding scholar in animal studies that does not mention posthumanity. Our organizational structure thus places Deleuzians cheek-by-jowl with Arendtians, and locates key themes such as the current understanding of postcolonial politics and the theoretical turn to life in various sections across the volume. By foregrounding more implicit connections between essays, this approach offers an opportunity to shift attention away from what might be considered the marketing categories of theory and towards other, potentially more fruitful means of mapping and documenting the vitality of theory after 'Theory'.

Assessing the field

Our first set of essays provides a variety of ways of conceptualizing and evaluating theory's recent transformations. Offering an overview of theory's disparate French and German trajectories during the last 50 years, Peter Osborne argues that it is crucial to understand these developments in the light of theory's relationship to philosophy as a discipline. Having forgotten the specificities of its original motivating critique of philosophy, he suggests, theory after 'Theory' has paid for this amnesia with a return of the disciplinary and particularist forms of philosophy that Theory once contested. Calling instead for a philosophically informed yet transdisciplinary theoretical discourse, Osborne proposes that such a mode would require reopening crucial questions regarding theory's imbrication in temporal categories of modernity, specifically the relationship between the affirmation of the new and the negation of the old, and the tendency to privilege an unreflective sense of contemporaneity. While also placing the German tradition of critical theory in his sights, William Rasch offers a map of the intellectual transformations associated with theory read through the work of Niklas Luhmann. For Rasch, Luhmann's ontological perspectivism makes it possible to discern a distinction between first order, normative observation, to which critical theory would belong, and a more experimental mode of theoretical enquiry, reflected in the work of Luhmann. While 'to critique is to fight the good fight', as Rasch puts it, we misunderstand the perspectivism of modernity if we assume this normative project invalidates other modes of theoretical enquiry, which provide a means of analyzing the norms that animate both critique and its objects (60).

Both Cary Wolfe and Claire Colebrook consider recent turns to biology and 'life' in their accounts of theory today, offering equally critical assessments from different vantage points. For Wolfe, the issue is specifically the boom in appeals to new developments in cognitive science and neuroscience as a way of rethinking the phenomenology of affect, perception and consciousness. Despite the differences among such approaches, Wolfe argues that they are united in their attempt to back a theoretical turn to 'materialism' with the 'the cash value of scientific discovery' (60). Drawing on the work of Derrida and Richard Rorty, Wolfe reads this attempt both in terms of the abandonment of scientific description and explanation, and in terms of the growth of the corporate university, which creates global hierarchies of knowledge production that the scientific turn in theory embodies and propagates. Whereas for Wolfe a return to the insights of classical 'Theory' would require reading scientific knowledge production as functioning within a certain context of human activity,

Colebrook argues that 'Theory' was invested in that which is *not* produced through human agency – a strand associated with Lacan's commitment to the fact of a non-human system and Derrida's view of genesis as 'anarchic'. Colebrook argues that the abandonment of theory's interest in the inhuman in favour of the current 'joyous affirmation of the living, of the multitude, of productivity, of the other, or of pure potentiality and futurity' constitutes a wishful insistence on the priority of human life at the precise moment when its extinction has become a matter of pressing ecological concern (66). In contrast to those who read the turn to 'speculative realism' in French philosophy (to which we return below) as simply a rejection of 'Theory', Colebrook thus posits that theory's own, currently overlooked investments in the inhuman may have found a continuation in the speculative realist view that 'it is possible to think beyond human knowledge' (67).

Between theory and practice: potentiality, will and judgement

In the 1980s and early 1990s, the relationship between theory and political practice was a matter of continual struggle. Not only did the achievement of self-determination or freedom seem an absurdly naive goal in light of the Foucauldian understanding of power – not to mention the Derridean view of language and the Lacanian model of subjectivity – but such ideals of Liberal selfhood were also usually seen to require the production of Others who were necessarily designated incapable of achieving these ideals of rationality and self-determination. Yet common Left alternatives to Enlightenment models of political subjectivity, from Marxism to identity politics, came to many to seem compromised by their tendency to reproduce the same totalizing and teleological operations that Theory aimed to resist. Thinkers working at the intersection of theory and politics, particularly in the late 1980s and early 1990s, thus found themselves caught between the perception that Enlightenment modes of freedom and individuality were both impossible and unethical and the concern that the Left theorization of resistance would fail to deviate sufficiently from the logics that structured the realm of domination it hoped to displace. The most widely circulated concepts of poststructuralism, from *différance* to the event to the virtual, can be read as shaped by an investment in negotiating such concerns, particularly the attempt to locate a form of thought or experience that might escape current systems without immediately becoming a system itself. Despite the divergent intellectual projects marked out by terms such as *différance* and the virtual, for example, they both attempt to register some process or principle that cannot be fixed and pinned down within existing structures of thought without ceasing to be worthy of its name. While such entities thus suggest a fleeting escape from structures that map and delimit the world, their ungraspable status was also taken to mean that they could not be put in the service of totalizing or teleological programmes of political transformation – thus ensuring that resistance would not simply end in the reproduction of modes of domination from another political vantage point.

If this emphasis on the transitory and ineffable was the answer that 'Theory' provided to the question of resistance, the essays gathered here suggest that contemporary theory is actively rethinking the viability of this response from a number of directions. In Brian Massumi's examination of the current theories and practices adopted by the United States in the 'war on terror', not only are Deleuzian figures such as potentiality and the event revealed to be instrumentalized in the campaign, but, more sweepingly, the very logics of epistemological and temporal indeterminacy associated with so much poststructuralist thought become a mode of military aggression. To act on potential in the fashion it desires, Massumi argues, the military aims to affect the indiscernable 'off-beat of time, a missed step in the cadence of actions and reactions, an elided present between one moment and the next' (81). It seems that the sorts of fissures in temporal progression and epistemological coherence in which poststructuralism invested so much utopian energy have now become the precise leverage points targeted in new US military practices. Writing from a perspective that might also be described as 'post-Deleuzian', Elizabeth Povinelli offers a related interrogation of the political value of potentiality that draws on her anthropological work in Australia. Examining transformations wrought by neoliberalism and late liberalism in one set of indigenous communities in particular, Povinelli documents the ways in which existing in potentiality becomes a mode of suffering for those trapped in a 'spiralling order of virtuality' in which 'they themselves and their social projects neither are nor are not' (113; 114). Pointing to the crucial role that immanent critique grants to such spaces of virtuality, Povinelli suggests that if these spaces both reduce being and yet at the same time allow for the possibility of being otherwise, critical theory may need to consider what it means to invest political value in forms of embodied living that others endure at great cost.

While Massumi's and Povinelli's readings imply that favoured Deleuzian categories may need to be revalued for a different historical moment, Peter Hallward offers a more sweeping indictment of the conception of the political offered by 'Theory' in its most prominent guises. Hallward suggests that the hostility to the idea of the will, and more particularly the general will, characteristic of recent philosophy and cultural theory has led theorists to focus on the political status of either indetermination, including 'the interstitial, the hybrid, [and] the ambivalent', or 'hyper-determination', including '"infinite' ethical obligation, divine transcendence, [and] unconscious drive' (93). In a radical break with this longstanding tendency to see collective political determination as simultaneously precluded and perilous, Hallward argues for a form of 'dialectical voluntarism' that privileges the purposeful will of the people over the forms of knowledge and authority that govern behaviour.

Although arguing from a very different direction, Linda Zerilli raises similar concerns regarding accounts of the political realm that obscure the capacity for human action through a focus on objective determination. Taking particular issue with the assumption that democratic politics must function according to rational, rule-following procedures, Zerilli suggests that such an approach conceives of the political realm as inherently unfree, since such logical, determinate judgements compel rather than solicit agreement. Zerilli draws on the work of Arendt to argue instead that political judgements should be considered more akin to Kantian aesthetic judgements, which make claims on universal validity but must rely on persuasion rather than indisputable logic to produce agreement. In contrast to communitarian thinkers who argue that community norms are required to facilitate judgement, Zerilli suggests that it is judgements that create our sense of community and the common space in which objects and meanings come into being. Judging is the capacity proper to the political realm precisely because it functions through the positing of a common world that has nothing logically necessary or compulsory about it, that only comes into being through the act of judging itself, and its implicit appeal – always contestable – to what Zerilli, after Wittgenstein, calls 'our mutual attunement in language' (129).

Rethinking the politics of representation

It is perhaps no surprise that two of the essays in this section are specifically concerned with representation and postcoloniality. From Edward Said's *Orientalism* to Spivak's infamous query, 'Can the subaltern speak?', to Chandra T. Mohanty's interrogation of Western feminism in 'Under Western Eyes: Feminist Scholarship and Colonial Discourses', questions of postcoloniality, race and ethnicity became, under the auspices of theory, inextricable from questions of representation. While identity-politics models of scholarship usually highlighted exclusions and called for full and equal representation of racial and ethnic minorities in both the political and cultural realms, 'Theory' tended instead to focus on the inevitably fraught and compromised status of representations of those marked out as racialized others. In the years that followed Said's foundational argument regarding the relationship between knowledge of the colonial other and the exercise of colonial power, much of this work came to focus specifically on the way in which putatively liberatory efforts to represent colonized and racialized subjects fell into much same traps as overtly colonial representations—as, for example, in Mohanty's critique of the way in which Western feminist writing on the 'third world woman' tended to reproduce rather than resist colonizing gestures. In what is arguably the most radical of these arguments, Spivak suggests that, given the necessary and categorical distance of the subaltern from the politicized scholarship that purported to represent her, there was no way for the subaltern either to be audible within the realm of academic discourse or to act legibly within existing configurations of the political sphere.

Given the iconicity of Spivak's critique, it is striking that Eva Cherniavsky finds that key postcolonial theorists, including Spivak herself, have increasingly abandoned what Cherniavsky considers the most salient aspects of this intervention. Examining recent arguments by Spivak and Dipesh Chakrabarty in particular, Cherniavsky suggests that they manifest a shift towards an attempt to learn from the subaltern that overlooks, without resolving, the problem Spivak originally pointed out: our inability to learn anything from the subaltern that we have not

first imputed to her. In contrast, Cherniavsky suggests that contemporary retrench-
ments of public reason may indeed have created a shift in subaltern status, but this
movement still does not render subaltern agency legible within the spaces of the
political. If Cherniavksy attempts to redirect our attention to theoretical insights
that she suggests we forget at our political and intellectual peril, Simon Gikandi
argues instead that the representational stances of postcolonial theory, in particular
its rejection of mimesis, had unfortunate effects on the construction of both the
archive and the methodology of postcolonial literary theory. Not only did 'the
relentless critique of the referential function of language' tend to direct attention
to certain novels – 'as if postcolonial literature began with Salman Rushdie' – but
it also produced readings invested in demonstrating that postcolonial fiction
thwarts referentiality through a textualized production of difference (167; 164).
Turning such a reading practice on its head, Gikandi argues that difference and
metonymy in anti-colonial novels function not so much to thwart mimesis as to
register as a 'reality effect' a colonial condition marked by a gap between representation and experience. If we look beyond the representational obsessions of postcolonial theory, Gikanki suggests, we will be able to discern in these novels a form
of what he terms 'postcolonial mimesis', an aesthetic mode characterized by irony,
empty time and the consciousness of absence (176).

In an essay that returns to what might be considered the theoretical ground zero
of the political rejection of mimesis – Bertolt Brecht's epic theatre – Rey Chow
examines the continuity between poststructuralist theory and a modernist form of
artistic practice whose goal is 'defamiliarizing and making conscious conventions
(literary, historical, or social) that have become so conventionalized as to be unrecognized' (137). For Brecht and other modernist thinkers, Chow posits, this goal is
pursued through what she terms the 'mediatization of reflexivity', a spatialized
process in which one form of media interrupts another in order (142). Arguing that
poststructuralist theory draws on similar strategies in its attempts to create a space
for critical thought, Chow turns to the films of Michael Haneke to demonstrate
that this form of politicized aesthetic reflexivity has entered a crisis in relation to
contemporary cultural and technological forms, which themselves rely on proliferating frames, screens and other modes of interruption. In the work of Haneke,
Chow suggests, the mediatized objectification of reflexivity has become so vexed
that it makes manifest a pornographic drive for absolute revelation that was previously latent in modernist staging practices – thereby raising pressing questions
regarding the continued viability of staging as a form of critical thought.

Biopolitics and ethics

In essays throughout this volume, our contributors raise questions about 'life' as
a central category for theory after 'Theory'. In addition to the arguments offered
by Colebrook and Wolfe, Chow and Massumi both interrogate the utility of
Agamben's conception of 'bare life' as a descriptor in the contemporary theoretical
landscape. For Chow, 'bare life' becomes another example of the pornographic

drive to uncover a primary, unadulterated mode of being, whereas, for Massumi, the operationalization of life pursued by the US military must be understood more as an intensification of life – what he terms 'life primed' – than as a denuding of it. In this section, our contributors provide instead a range of theoretical arguments that suggest the power of the categories currently shaping conversations in biopolitics, biophilosophy and ethics. For example, Eugene Thacker examines the contradictions between living and life in the abstract, arguing that, while life can be imagined in its concrete instances, Life as an abstract entity cannot be thought, though it is precisely this void that enables instances of the living to proliferate. Exploring what he terms the 'vitalist antinomy' in texts ranging from RAND research on swarming to Dante's *Inferno* to the works of H. P. Lovecraft, Thacker argues that while life is a problem of philosophy, it is also a problem *for* philosophy, since every '"philosophy of life" presupposes a non-philosophical vantage point from which "life" as such can continue to be thought' (192).

Roberto Esposito offers a different means of conceptualizing the contemporary theoretical emphasis on life by reading the history of biopolitics through the category of the 'person'. Tracing the development of the category from its Roman precursors to its centrality in the UN Declaration of Human Rights, Esposito suggests that, while the philosophy of the person evolved in response to the reduction of human life to mere biological being, it ends by merely reifying from another direction the division between the biological and the rational–spiritual. As it relies on a paradoxical combination of unification and division, in which the personal exists in reference to an impersonal zone, personalism does not so much resolve the problems of the biologization of life as offer another ground on which such a reduction might take place. Turning to the work of Maurice Blanchot, Freud and Weil, Esposito suggests an alternative to the philosophy of the personal in which rights adhere not to persons but to bodies which offer their own normativity, one that is immanent to life and its infinite multiplicity. Although she focuses more specifically on intersubjectivity, ethics and ontology, Adriana Cavarero also places certain bodily experiences at the centre of her explorations. Outlining debates in which a 'vertical' notion of autonomous subjectivity is contrasted with a 'horizontal' reorientation of the subject that replaces the ideology of individualism with a focus on relationality and dependence, Cavarero develops a theory of the intersubjective based on Arendt's understanding of natality, in which the mother inclines over the child and both verticality and horizontality cease to be operative. Through a focus on this inclined subject, Cavarero argues, we shift the terrain from ethics to ontology and obtain a means of imagining the subject outside the twinned models of autonomy and dependence.

Renewing the aesthetic

The following titles, with their dates, tell a story: *The Anti-Aesthetic* (1983), *The Ideology of the Aesthetic* (1990), *The Radical Aesthetic* (2000), *The New Aestheticism* (2003), *The Politics of Aesthetics* (2003 and 2004), *Return to Aesthetics* (2005), *Aesthetics and Its Discontents* (2009), *The Aesthetic Unconscious* (2009) and *Politics and Aesthetics in the Arts* (2010).[4] The history of the theorization of the aesthetic over the past three decades is, of course, much more complex than the simple narrative implied by this sequence of titles, but they serve to outline its main features: a suspicion of the category of the aesthetic during the 1980s and 1990s, amounting at times to hostility, followed, in the last 10 years, by a more positive re-engagement with aesthetic questions. The various intellectual movements that went under the banner of 'Theory' all participated in one way or other in the critique of the aesthetic, exposing the manner in which it made illegitimate claims to objectivity, transcendence and universality while in fact endorsing particular, historically-determined, structures of dominance. Disenchantment with the aesthetic did not necessarily mean a dismissal of art, even of 'high art', however: there was a strong positive valuation of the arts in some rooms of the house of 'Theory'. Derrida, Blanchot, Adorno, Kristeva, Lacan, Lyotard and Barthes – to go no further – all made powerful claims for the value of artistic practices, and did so while sharing the widespread scepticism regarding the pretensions to objectivity and universalism of the traditional notion of the aesthetic. But with the rise of New Historicism and cultural studies in the 1990s, the distinction between art (especially elite art) and other cultural practices increasingly became the target of critique, and even a deconstructive privileging of the work of art became suspect.[5]

It is against this background that a revaluation of the aesthetic has begun to take place.[6] No single school of aesthetic theory has arisen to replace the discredited view of the world of art as autonomous, transcendent, detached from the messy business of social and political life and susceptible of disinterested, objective judgement. One line of argument has been to challenge the reading of Kant that underlies the prevailing notion of the aesthetic, finding in Kant's Third Critique an understanding of aesthetic judgement much more in tune with contemporary thought, noteworthy examples being Rodolphe Gasché's *The Idea of Form* (2003; subtitled *Rethinking Kant's Aesthetics*) and Jonathan Loesberg's *A Return to Aesthetics* (2005). (Zerilli's essay in this volume is another example of this re-evaluation of Kant's aesthetic theory, albeit in the service of an argument about politics.) Another tack has been to introduce into the discussion a different kind of universal, one more amenable to a left-leaning viewpoint: thus Isobel Armstrong, in *The Radical Aesthetic*, appeals to 'the components of aesthetic life [. . .] already embedded in the processes and practices of consciousness – playing and dreaming, thinking and feeling' (2). The relation between affect and the aesthetic has been explored in several works; see, for example, Sianne Ngai (2005) and Marco Abel (2008). The original link between the aesthetic and the senses – a link Eagleton had stressed in 1990 – has been restored by some theorists: Osborne's collection *From an Aesthetic Point of View* (2000) is subtitled *Philosophy, Art and the Senses*, and Derrida's late work on touch (see Derrida 2005) has contributed to a new interest in the haptic dimension of artistic practices. Translations of a series of works by Rancière on the inseparability of the aesthetic and politics (2004, 2009a, 2009b, 2009c, 2010) have further served to dispel, or at least reduce, the suspicion of the discourse of aesthetics on the left.

The term 'aesthetic' may be avoided altogether in discussions of art's distinctiveness, as too compromised to admit of recuperation; thus, one of the editors of this collection draws on a vocabulary of alterity, singularity and inventiveness to offer a theory of the artwork as an event that introduces the previously unthought and unfelt into a culture (Attridge 2004).

The three essays in this volume that we have grouped under the title 'Renewing the Aesthetic' offer quite distinct approaches. Henry Staten argues for a rehabilitation of the notion of *techne*, the shared know-how that constitutes the cultural material from which the artwork is created. The loss of this notion as central to the understanding of both the production and the reception of art, he contends, has resulted in the mystification of art and the fetishization of the art object – a process that the post-Duchamp emphasis on the centrality of the conceptual in art has done nothing to halt. Art is neither something that has its being beyond culture, in some realm of the ineffable, but nor is it merely a derivative cultural product; rather, it is the outcome of the artist's manipulation of the available resources of a specific techne-history, and needs to be analysed as such. Laurent Dubreuil, challenging the increasing emphasis on the 'real', puts forward a strong claim for the role of literature – as the place where limits of language are explored – in today's theoretical enterprise. For Dubreuil, the most influential thinkers in the aesthetic field today, including Deleuze, Badiou, Agamben and Rancière, are still operating in terms of philosophical protocols. Arguing for a relation between theory and philosophy very different from that proposed by Osborne in this volume, Dubreuil calls for an elaboration of the work of 'Theory' into a fuller analysis of the necessary failure of language, an analysis that would challenge the claims of philosophy. A reading of one of D. H. Lawrence's poems serves as an example of literature's role in this programme. In her contribution, Amanda Anderson invites us to reconsider the relation between aesthetics and liberalism, arguing that the liberal tradition is more complex and open to formal and conceptual energies than its critics assume, and could play a vital part in the revitalization of the aesthetic. Admitting that there is a 'temperamental aversion' in literary and cultural studies to some of the key values of liberalism, notably its emphasis on argument, proceduralism, transparency and explicitness, she argues that the liberal tradition, properly understood, nevertheless embraces energies, aspirations and 'threshold experiences' that are much closer to the values endorsed in contemporary revaluations of the aesthetic. All three of these essays, from different perspectives, see a significant role for a version of the aesthetic, clearly distinct from the aesthetic of old, in the contemporary work of theoretical thought.

Philosophy after theory

Quantitatively speaking, most philosophy in the English-speaking countries today shows very few traces of the upheavals created over the past 40 years in neighbouring disciplines by the explosion of 'Theory'. This is because it was continental philosophy from which theoretical work took its bearings, and continental philosophy remains a minority enterprise in the Anglophone arena, dominated as this arena is by the analytic tradition. Indeed, no clear line can be drawn between continental philosophy and theory, or what we have tried to capture by means of the label 'theory after "Theory"'; the issues that continue to be central to this tradition of philosophy are also those that animate much discussion in studies of literary and visual culture from a theoretical perspective. One version of this complex history is traced by Peter Osborne in the first essay in the volume, and the final section, 'Philosophy after Theory', takes up some of the questions raised by Osborne in that essay.

The fundamental Kantian question of the relation between the world as it is and the world as we know it has recently been revisited in a philosophical movement that has come to be called 'speculative realism': Quentin Meillassoux, Alberto Toscano and Ray Brassier, among others, have mounted a critique of 'correlationism'—the claim that we cannot know what is real independently of our mode of knowing—and argued that we *can* achieve a knowledge of the real that does not depend upon our conceptual resources. In his contribution, Brassier sets out the logic of this claim, asserting the validity of the scientific model in which it is the reality of the object that determines the meaning of its conception, rather than the reverse. Athough he builds on Meillassoux's critique of correlationism, he takes Meillassoux to task for failing to appreciate the flaws in Fichte's 'strong correlationism', which radicalizes Kant's argument by abolishing the thing-in-itself. For Brassier, *that* an object is is a quite different matter from *what* it is. Working at a similarly funda-mental level, Martin Hägglund mounts a challenge to the speculative realists, and Meillassoux in particular. In contrast to Meillassoux's conception of time as imply-ing absolute contingency, he draws on Derrida's account of the trace-structure of time to argue that the material support of temporality necessarily places conditions on what is possible. For Derrida and Meillassoux, nothing is ever wholly in itself, but is always already subject to the processes of ceasing-to-be. Where Meillassoux offers a vitalist account of the emergence of life from non-living matter, Hägglund's 'arche-materialism' supports a Darwinian explanation of the route from one state to another. The living, on his reading, differs from the non-living by virtue of its care for survival – a property, Hägglund points out, that is completely contingent and destructible. Finally, Bernard Stiegler, in an essay that forms part of a longer work on what Stiegler terms 'the pharmacology of spirit', also develops one of Derrida's key notions, in this case the ambiguous nature of the *pharmakon*. In 'Plato's Pharmacy' Derrida demonstrated how the double meaning of this word – as both dangerous poison and health-giving drug – operates in Plato's *Phaedrus* to complicate the relation between speech and writing. Without any indication that he is conscious of doing so, Plato simultaneously condemns writing as under-mining the delivery of true meaning in speech and acknowledges that speech depends on just those properties for which writing is denounced. Stiegler's essay extends the notion of a double-edged *pharmakon* into an account of the workings of our contemporary consumerist industrial system and its psychic dimension, to ask finally how life is made worth living.

★★★

To read the essays in this volume is to be made aware of just how varied the workings of theory are in the humanities today, and to register a series of possible new beginnings that may in future grow into much larger enterprises. Nevertheless, this collection can only gesture towards the full range of discourses and practices, initiatives and projects that may be seen to descend from the 'Theory' of the 1970s. Interesting and important work is being done in many other areas, including disability studies, ethics (including animal ethics), ecocriticism, book history, genetic studies and globalization, as well as, of course, new subfields opening up in older areas such as queer theory, feminism, material culture, race and ethnicity studies, narratology and psychoanalysis. In all these fields there is a lively sense of a continuing debate about fundamental issues such as life, representation, contingency, subjectivity and freedom and at the same time a vigorous conversation about wholly practical questions relating to political change, living conditions, institutional practices and so on. The present theoretical inheritance from the later decades of the twentieth century does not look like anything that could have been predicted at the time, but it is powerful testimony to the rich possibilities inherent in the intellectual ferment of that period. 'Theory' is dead; long live theory.

Notes

1   For a sampling of such accounts, see the *Critical Inquiry* symposium on 'The Future of Criticism' (Mitchell 2004), Grossberg (2006), Latour (2004), Eagleton (2003) and Patai and Corral (2005).
2   See Hallward, Massumi, Zerilli and Brassier in this volume, respectively. See also Zerilli (2005) and Meillassoux (2007, 2008).
3   The 2010 second edition of the widely used *Norton Anthology of Theory and Criticism* is doubly belated, not including work by Badiou, Agamben and Rancière (or, for that matter, Levinas), let alone any of the contributors to this volume.
4   The works referred to are Foster (1983), Eagleton (1990), Armstrong (2000), Joughin and Malpas (2003), Redfield (2003), Rancière (2004), Loesberg (2005), Rancière (2009a, 2009b) and Kemal and Gaskell (2010).
5   It should be noted that within the parallel tradition of analytic philosophy, there has never been a downgrading of the aesthetic as a subject for enquiry; one only has to look at such substantial volumes as *The Routledge Companion to Aesthetics* or *The Oxford Handbook of Aesthetics* to be aware of the continuity and productivity of this field.
6   This is not to say that there were no significant contributions to the discussion of the aesthetic during the period of 'Theory'; for a representative collection, see Levine (1994). Bernstein (1992) presents an important reconsideration of the relation between the discourses of aesthetics and of truth. The new translation of Adorno's *Aesthetic Theory* (1997) had a powerful impact and was no doubt partly responsible for the awakened interest in the aesthetic in the following decade.

Bibliography

Abel, M. (2008) *Violent Affect: Literature, Cinema and Critique after Representation*, Lincoln, NE: University of Nebraska Press.
Adorno, T. (1997) *Aesthetic Theory* (1969), trans. R. Hullot-Kentor, Minneapolis, MN: University of Minnesota.

Agamben, G. (1993) *The Coming Community*, Minneapolis, MN: University of Minnesota Press.

Armstrong, I. (2000) *The Radical Aesthetic*, Oxford: Blackwell.

Attridge, D. (2004) *The Singularity of Literature*, London: Routledge.

Bernstein, J. M. (1992) *The Fate of Art: Aesthetic Alienation from Kant to Derrida and Adorno*, University Park, PA: State University of Pennsylvania Press.

Derrida, J. (2005) *On Touching – Jean-Luc Nancy* (2000), Stanford, CA: Stanford University Press.

Eagleton, T. (1990) *The Ideology of the Aesthetic*, Oxford: Blackwell.

Eagleton, T. (2003) *After Theory*, London: Penguin.

Foster, H., ed. (1983) *The Anti-Aesthetic: Essays on Postmodern Culture*, Port Townsend, WA: Bay Press.

Gasché, R. (2003) *The Idea of Form: Rethinking Kant's Aesthetics*, Stanford, CA: Stanford University Press.

Gaut, B. and Lopes, D. M. (2001) *The Routledge Companion to Aesthetics*, London: Routledge.

Grossberg, L. (2006) 'Does Cultural Studies Have Futures? Should it? (or What's the Matter with New York?)', *Cultural Studies*, 20.1: 1–32.

Jameson, F. (2004) 'Symptoms of Theory or Symptoms for Theory?', *Critical Inquiry*, 30.2: 403–8.

Joughin, J. J. and Malpas, S., eds. (2003) *The New Aestheticism*, Manchester: Manchester University Press.

Kemal, S. and Gaskell, I. (2010) *Politics and Aesthetics in the Arts*, Cambridge: Cambridge University Press.

Latour, B. (2004) 'Why Has Critique Run Out of Steam? From Matters of Fact to Matters of Concern', *Critical Inquiry*, 30.2: 225–48.

Levine, G., ed. (1994) *Aesthetics and Ideology*, New Brunswick, NJ: Rutgers University Press.

Levinson, J., ed. (2005) *The Oxford Handbook of Aesthetics*, Oxford: Oxford University Press.

Loesberg, J. (2005) *A Return to Aesthetics: Autonomy, Indifference and Postmodernism*, Stanford, CA: Stanford University Press.

Meillassoux, Q. (2007) 'Speculative Realism', in *Collapse: Philosophical Research and Development*, Vol. III: 408–35.

Meillassoux, Q. (2008) *After Finitude: An Essay on the Necessity of Contingency*, trans. R. Brassier, London: Continuum.

Mitchell, W.J.T., ed. (2004) 'The Future of Criticism: A *Critical Inquiry* Symposium', *Critical Inquiry* 30.2: 324–479.

Ngai, S. (2005) *Ugly Feelings*, Cambridge, MA: Harvard University Press.

Osborne, P., ed. (2000) *From an Aesthetic Point of View: Philosophy, Art and the Senses*, London: Serpent's Tail.

Patai, D. and Corral, W. H., eds. (2005) *Theory's Empire: An Anthology of Dissent*, New York: Columbia University Press.

Rancière, J. (2004) *The Politics of Aesthetics: The Distribution of the Sensible* (2000), trans. G. Rockhill, London: Continuum.

Rancière, J. (2009a) *Aesthetics and Its Discontents* (2004), trans. S. Corcoran, Cambridge: Polity.

Rancière, J. (2009b) *The Aesthetic Unconscious* (2001), trans. D. Keates and J. Swenson, Cambridge: Polity.

Rancière, J. (2009c) *The Emancipated Spectator*, trans. G. Elliott, London: Verso.

Rancière, J. (2010) *Dissensus: On Politics and Aesthetics*, trans. S. Corcoran, London: Continuum.

Redfield, M. (2003) *The Politics of Aesthetics: Nationalism, Gender, Romanticism*, Stanford, CA: Stanford University Press.

Zerilli, L. M. G. (2005) *Feminism and the Abyss of Freedom*, Chicago: University of Chicago Press.

PART I

Assessing the field

1

PHILOSOPHY AFTER THEORY

Transdisciplinarity and the new

Peter Osborne

In what sense is something called 'theory' over? And in what way might the manner of its passing have opened up a space for its renewal? At first sight, these questions appear parochial and outmoded. 'Theory' did not end, it lost a brief and extraordinary institutional hegemony; a hegemony that was restricted to particular disciplinary sites within the Anglophone humanities during its heroic 'French' period (1975–1995): primarily, literary studies of various sorts (Cussett 2008). Yet, to confine this episode to the past would itself be to fall prey to fashion. For there are deep-seated issues at stake in the struggles around 'theory', going as far back as German philosophy in the last decade of the eighteenth century, which not only retain their relevance today, but have acquired new pertinences – and not merely for reasons of expediency, associated with the global expansion of the English-language academic publishing industry. ('Theory' is also a marketing category, of course.)[1] These issues concern, among other things, the possibilities and manner of knowing the whole – the totality of conditions that pertain to experience – a question which has been given a new lease of life by the tendentially global dominance of a single economic system. It appears today, in part, as a question about the possibility and modes of knowing oneself (Socrates's old question) as a subject of capitalistic social relations, social relations into which is inscribed a relentless production of both novelty and crisis (Osborne 2010a). To see how this might be connected to the fate and prospects of 'theory' in the Anglophone humanities, it will be useful to start with a sketch of the two main traditions of theory at issue in these debates.

The kind of theory whose moment is supposedly past is that which became known colloquially in the 1970s as 'high theory', 'theory with a capital T' or, more polemically but also in various ways more neutrally, 'critical theory'. *High* theory by association with uses of the term 'high' in the Anglican Church and art criticism (that is, a particular combination of ritual, universalism and exclusivity); theory *with a capital T*, by dint of a passing use of capitalization by Louis Althusser; *critical* theory, more variously, but largely via its occupation of the institutional space of literary criticism, in conjunction with an aspiration to social criticism. The plurality of connotations indicates something of the multiplicity of investments at stake in the field. 'High theory' cross-codes a hierarchical ecclesiastical designation with the metaphorical height of abstraction to invest such abstraction with social and intellectual *gravitas*. 'Theory with a capital T' extends the theological metaphor (from God to Theory), drawing on the philosophical heritage of German idealism via the archaic practice in English and French of citing the nouns translating its central concepts in upper case, reifying concepts by treating them as proper names: *Spirit*, *Notion*, *Idea*, etc. By dint of its capitalization, *Theory* posits itself as the successor to these categories. More ambiguously, the institutional convenience 'critical theory' suggests a transition from theory to practice within theory itself, and hence within the educational practices of the academy. This was the ground on which the so-called 'culture wars' were fought in the wake of the heyday of theory in the United States; not just between Left and Right, but within the Left itself. (In the first case, the issue was the political content of educational practices; in the second, it was the political relevance of cultural issues.)

The phrase 'critical theory' carries more content than its popular synonyms. However, this is more often than not seriously misleading, since much of the French work it is now habitually used to describe operates with a notion of 'science' in tension with, if not direct opposition to, the philosophical notion of critique. This applies to structuralism, in particular, including its Marxist variants.[2] Moreover, another significant portion of this work, part of the Heideggerian legacy – deconstruction, in particular – was constituted in explicit opposition to the claims of theory, in its classical sense (Gasché 2007). In this respect, at least, 'critical theory' really did function within the Anglo-American academy of the 1980s as a mere name for a heterogeneous assemblage of French, or French-inspired, theoretical writings – a label for a list of thinkers responding to a common situation with often diametrically opposed intellectual projects.

At the same time, however, 'critical theory' was also the long-established designation for a quite different, German tradition that first achieved self-consciousness in the mid-1930s and continued to identify itself as such into the 1990s: the Frankfurt School of critical theory associated with the Institute for Social Research (Wiggershaus 1994). This often-confusing coincidence, nonetheless, has its productive side insofar as it hints at the possibility of features common to the two traditions, deriving from deeper sources. It thus allows us to ask the question of what precisely has been surpassed in a situation defined as being 'after theory' from a slightly broader standpoint than is usual. The main thing the two traditions have in common is the thought that they have surpassed, or at least displaced, 'philosophy' in its modern disciplinary sense.

Theory after philosophy: two traditions

In France, 'theory' was an effect of, on the one hand, conceptual developments in the human sciences (structuralism/poststructuralism) and, on the other, the Marxist critique of philosophy. Althusser famously briefly used the term *Théorie* with a capital 'T' to designate what he had previously referred to as 'Marxist philosophy' (namely, 'the theory of theoretical practice'), in order to 'reserve the term *philosophy* for *ideological* philosophies', in line with Marx and Engels's diagnosis of the ideological character of philosophy per se ('self-sufficient philosophy') in *The German Ideology* (Althusser 1977: 162; Marx and Engels 1976: 37). This inconsistent combination of the idea of historical materialism as a general theory of practices (derived from Marx's sixth fragment of 'On Feuerbach') with a neo-Kantian conception of philosophy as second reflection on science ('theoretical practices') was, by and large, representative of an effective practice of theory more generally deriving from certain privileged disciplinary objects: linguistics (Saussure), anthropology (Levi-Strauss), psychoanalysis (Lacan), history of thought (Foucault) and literature (*Tel Quel*), in particular. It is the singularity of the term 'theory' here that registers its internal relation to the traditional aspirations of philosophy. However, it aspired to a general scientificity of a non-'philosophical' (and in particular, decisively non-Hegelian) kind associated with the rationalism of French studies in the history of science (Lecourt 1975).

If French thinkers have dominated theoretical developments in the Anglophone humanities since the mid 1970s, it is primarily because of the powerfully 'post-philosophical' coding of the philosophical aspects of their work – post-philosophical, that is, in a delicately dialectical sense, whereby everything intellectually productive about the European philosophical tradition is maintained outside the disciplinary setting of philosophy. There are a number of conditions of possibility of this situation, not the least being the irrelevance of the domestic analytical philosophical tradition to the rest of the humanities and the internal, philosophical problematicity of the disciplinary autonomy of philosophy itself. Indeed, recognition of this problematic character (the contradiction between an inherited aspiration to absolute universality and a disciplinary particularity) is more or less a condition of philosophical modernity itself. It thus comes in a variety of forms. However, because 'Theory' with a capital 'T' was generally adopted in a *non*-Marxist form in the Anglo–American reception of French thought in the 1970s, it tended to sidestep (rather than to specify, as was its desired role in Althusser's writings) that thought's complex relationship to European philosophy. This allowed for the uninhibited investment of broad transdisciplinary fields by general-theoretical categories, the ultimate status of which was unclear: be it the 'textuality' of a general semiotics, the 'discourses' of a Foucauldian historicism or the 'topography' of Lacanian metapyschology.

As a result, in its Anglo–American guise 'theory' became largely either pragmatic or deconstructive – that is, either over-determined by specific (often political) uses, or marked by a reflective distance from the metaphysical claims acknowledged to be implicit in its concepts – or both. That is to say, 'theory' became in a certain sense *anti*-theoretical, insofar as 'theory' had previously been associated, within philosophy, with metaphysics or doctrine (*Lehre*) more generally. 'Theory' rejected the doctrinal; hence its ironic dialectical identity with that which turned 'against' it in the US academy in the mid-1980s. As the prevailing philosophical mode of Anglo–American intellectual life, pragmatism became the philosophical unconscious of post-Marxist literary and cultural studies (Osborne 2000, 2006). By the early 1990s, however, as the left political cultures orienting the academic intellectuals of the 1970s and 1980s collapsed, theory's pragmatic orientation became, on the one hand, increasingly symbolic (the 'culture wars') and, on the other, increasingly individualistic and wishful (Dollimore 2000). And as theory became increasingly commodified (branded by author's names), its reception began to succumb to the reification and repetitions of commodification. At the same time, the disavowal of philosophy involved in the forgetting of a critique that had largely constituted theory in the French context became increasingly problematic, especially once the far less equivocally philosophical writings of thinkers like Emmanuel Levinas and Gilles Deleuze were subjected to the same discursive conditions. Under these conditions they were (and continue to be) frequently travestied by the pragmatic uses to which they are put. One reaction to this situation was a rejection of 'T/theory' (both with and without a capital T) and a return to disciplinarity (and with it, both 'old' historicism and aesthetics) within the humanities. At the same time, pressure began to build up within the discursive space of Theory for a re-evaluation of the virtues of philosophy. From the standpoint of the Anglo-American reception of the tradition of French theory, the current empirical answer to the question 'What is theory (in the Anglophone humanities) after "Theory"?' is most definitely 'Philosophy'.

This turn to explicitly philosophical references in theoretical work across the humanities (often a turn to the *citation* of philosophical writings as a substitute for theoretical work) is broadly a turn to what Marx called 'self-sufficient philosophy', philosophy in its classical modern sense. It has taken two main antagonistic forms: quasi-Levinasian and other post-Derridean forms of 'ethics' – a convergence of topic with the post-analytical mainstream of liberal political philosophy – on the one hand (Butler 2004 and Critchley 2007, for example), and the full-blown metaphysics of Deleuze and Alain Badiou, on the other (Osborne 2007).[3] This is the ironic endpoint of the main Anglo-Saxon trajectory of 'French theory' today. It represents a more-or-less wholesale renunciation of the epistemo-critical concerns of the 1960s and 1970s.[4] This tradition of 'theory' has been paid for its disavowal of philosophy (the forgetting of the specificities of its critique) with a belated philosophical vengeance.[5] What of its German cousin?

French 'critical theory' was the product of the reception of a philosophically heterogeneous body of theoretical writings from France into the literary departments of the Anglo-American academy, where criticism was an established literary pursuit. The critical theory of the Frankfurt School, on the other hand, was both self-designating and the object of explicit and ongoing theoretical reflection. Consequently, while the emphasis in the former was on theory, in general – the main opposition being between theoretical and atheoretical or anti-theoretical (everyday or aesthetic) interpretative practices – the emphasis within the latter was more decisively on criticism or critique (*Kritik*), the main opposition being between 'traditional' and 'critical' theory.

The Frankfurt notion of critical theory derives from the critical turn that took place in the self-conception of the work of the Institute for Social Research in Frankfurt in 1937, in Max Horkheimer's famous essay 'Traditional and Critical Theory' – an essay that sets out from the question 'What is theory?' (Horkheimer 1972). Horkheimer used the term 'critical theory' to denote what we might call the 'negative' turn in his conception of historical materialism as an interdisciplinary social theory. This was the consequence for his Hegelian methodology (dialectically totalizing the results of the positive sciences) of his inability to identify a representative of the future within the present (as a result of the degeneration of communism in the Soviet Union), from the standpoint of which the totality might be unified. It involved the transformation of 'critical activity' itself into the 'subject' of a theory that consequently related to totality only negatively, as a purely speculative methodological standpoint for a critique of the present. This theory is 'German' in that it represents the philosophical heritage of the strong programme of German idealism within a dialectically interdisciplinary social theory, first evoked by Engels in his 1888 *Ludwig Feuerbach and the Exit from Classical German Philosophy*. (The standard English translation of *Ausgang* – 'exit' or 'way out' – as 'end' in the title of this book has led to a century of philosophical confusion.) The model of 'critique' here was Marx's critique of political economy: a coincidence of philosophical universality and the historical projection of practice, via the critical relation to a specialized science, albeit here in a form in which critical activity ('theoretical reflection') stands in as the place-holder for the current absence of emancipatory politics on a world-historical scale.

In the history of the Frankfurt School, 'critical theory', in Horkheimer's technical sense, lasted only for about 3 years, 1937–1940, after which it was replaced by the critique of instrumental reason, which became the basis for the Ur-historical narrative of *Dialectic of Enlightenment* (Dubiel 1985; Horkheimer 2004; Horkheimer and Adorno 2002). Critique of instrumental reason is not 'critical theory' in the sense of 'theory' in which the phrase derives its meaning from its opposition to 'traditional theory'. Rather, it has more affinities with the Kantian sense of 'critique', which is precisely *not* theory as such, although here it occupies the discursive space of the theoretical, by other means: the literary-philosophical constructivism of the Romantic fragment, for example; hence *Dialectic of Enlightenment*'s subtitle, *Philosophical Fragments*, which also evokes Kierkegaard, of course. In the early 1960s, in reaction against this Romantic and at times almost Schopenhauerian negativism, Horkheimer's early 1930s Institute programme of interdisciplinary materialism (the prequel to Critical Theory) was revived by the young Habermas. It briefly represented a methodological model for overcoming the perceived impasse of a philosophy conscious only of its own critique, represented by the purely negative restoration of philosophy in Adorno's work, summed up in his 1966 *Negative Dialectics*. Habermas's 'Between Philosophy and Science: Marxism as Critique' was published in 1963 – the same year as Althusser's 'On the Materialist Dialectic'. If there is a year in which 'theory' in its recent sense was born, 1963 was that year. This early Habermasian revival of 'Marxism as critique' was subsequently developed into a model of critique as 'the unity of knowledge and interest' in Habermas's quasi-transcendental, 1968 *Knowledge and Human Interests*. However, it was a hermeneutically reduced conception of psychoanalysis that provided the model of a critical theory there (rather than the critique of political economy), in which the individual subject was related to political collectivity only by weak analogy or via the transcendentally ideal conditions of a discourse ethics. In this respect, the break in the Frankfurt critical tradition in 1968 anticipated (in a different form) the psychoanalytical reorientation of political thinking to which part of the Anglophone version of the French tradition has more recently increasingly had recourse, through Butler and Žižek in particular. 'After 1968' and his famous declaration of the 'fascism' of elements of German student radicalism, Habermas departed from the trajectory of critical theory as previously conceived, towards the restoration of liberal Kantian political and legal philosophy, via the transcendentalization of American pragmatism into a theory of 'communicative action' (Habermas 1991, 1987b, 1996). The subsequent generation (Honneth 1995; Wellmer 1998) has remained within the broad parameters demarcating this conjoint theoretical and political retreat.

Meanwhile, Adorno's paradoxically entitled *Aesthetic Theory*, published posthumously in 1970 – suspended between philosophical criticism of art and the construction of a historical art theory – has gradually acquired the status of the most important philosophical work in German in the second half of the twentieth century. If there is a *model* of theory in the Frankfurt tradition that remains intellectually alive today, it lies embedded in this resolutely singular and thematically restricted text. At the same time, the philosophical and general-theoretical significance of Walter Benjamin's writings has come to the fore, in the wake of the belated, 1982 publication of the mass of notes and materials making up his 1927–1939 *Arcades Project* (Benjamin 1999). Benjamin's work increasingly appears as the richest, most complex and also the most 'living' source of critical-theoretical insight in the twentieth-century German tradition. Yet it resists easy assimilation into the Anglophone context of 'theory' and its aftermath: in part because of its sophisticated but understated philosophical character. The Derridean appropriation, mainly via a deconstructive reading of the 'messianic' (Derrida 1992, Part 2; Weber 2008) is highly partial and, crucially, cuts off the speculative aspect of Benjamin's thought from the critical relation to the multiplicity of knowledges which gives it concrete historical and political meaning. *Aesthetic Theory* aside, the Frankfurt tradition has paid for its failure to maintain an active relationship with the 'positive' disciplines in the humanities and social sciences with a vengeance of philosophy not dissimilar from in the French tradition: albeit, in this case, one that is wholeheartedly liberal and post-analytical (that is, focused almost exclusively on problems of normativity), rather than being residually, generically radical and fundamentally ontological.

Broadly speaking, the main French and German trajectories of critical theory thus have a common point of departure (Marxism) and a common point of arrival

(Philosophy), although the paths they traverse are radically divergent and the philosophies at which they arrive are correspondingly different. The Frankfurt variant (and its imaginary continuation) is self-consciously post-Hegelian and anti-Heideggerian, while the French theory in question is insistently anti-Hegelian and generically post-Heideggerian, even in its Marxist variants (theoretical anti-humanism). As Jean-Luc Nancy puts it at the end of the 1980s: '"French" thought today proceeds in part from a "German" rupture with a certain philosophical "France" (which is also a rupture with a certain "Germanity")' (Nancy 1991: 3). It was this displaced Germanicism of late twentieth-century French thought, associated with Nietzsche and Heidegger, that was the main object of attack of Habermas's notorious 1985 *Philosophical Discourse of Modernity* (which also attacked *Dialectic of Enlightenment*, as itself a Nietzschean text), in the context of the extraordinary success in Germany of the quasi-*French* Nietzscheanism of Peter Sloterdijk's 1983 *Critique of Cynical Reason* – a book that in certain respects inadvertently prepared the ground for the reception of Deleuze in Germany.

Nonetheless, for all these polemics, the coordinates shared by these two traditions of 'theory' define a field characterized by a number of common features: (1) suspicion of the self-sufficiency of philosophy, derived from the thought of Marx, Nietzsche and Freud (Paul Ricoeur's three 'masters of suspicion'), along with the desire to continue the classical philosophical project by other means; (2) a consequent orientation towards anti-, inter- and trans-disciplinary objects, although not necessarily explicitly conceived as such; (3) an openness to the general text of writing, associated with a reception of literary modernism conscious of its sources in philosophical Romanticism; (4) a critical attitude towards the established forms of Western capitalist societies; (5) a certain underlying, transformed rationalism. At a certain level of abstraction, this is sufficient to define a common problematic.

Furthermore, from the standpoint of the concepts of theory at issue, the moral of the two tales is broadly similar: namely, the imperative to sustain the critique of philosophy out of which both types of theory emerged, if theoretical practices are not merely to return to previously established, particularistic modes. This implies the need to develop an *anti*-disciplinary and *trans*-disciplinary conception of philosophy as a dual practice of *criticism* and *construction*, within which theoretical reflection on non-philosophical materials is paramount. Or to put it another way: *there is no adequate 'theory'* (in the sense of general theory) – just as there is no adequate philosophy – *without reflection on its relations to both the history of philosophy and the critique of self-sufficient philosophy*. Theory cannot be viably practised merely as scholarly reflection upon – let alone mere citation of – philosophical texts, which is the form into which it has to a great extent deteriorated, in the wake of the passage in the English-language publishing industry from the sale of theory to the sale of theorists; a passage corresponding to that from readers as producers to readers as consumers.

If 'theory after Theory' is to be philosophy, or rather, one aspect of philosophizing (not the philosophy before Theory, but a philosophizing 'after' the critiques of self-sufficient philosophy and Theory alike), a philosophizing *of* 'Theory', one might say, then theory after Theory will be the element of conceptual construction in a transdisciplinary philosophizing – a philosophizing without *disciplinary* limits, but precisely *not*, thereby, without limits, since this opens philosophy up to the test of experience. What would a philosophically self-conscious theorizing of this kind be like? One way to think about this is to reflect upon the developmental dynamic that is at stake in the issue at hand, when the intellectual present is posited as 'the after' of some purportedly concluded period, open to a yet-to-be-determined future: the logic of the 'post' in its more positive, forward-looking guise as the *logic of the new*.

Philosophy after Theory: the problem of 'the new'

As a critique of self-sufficient philosophy and (in Foucault's case, in particular) of the cultural dominance of the history of philosophy within the history of ideas, 'theory' posited itself as the intellectual form of the new: not merely the modern of its day, but its vanguard (Ffrench 1995). The very idea of 'theory after "theory"' represents a reprise of the now-classical avant-garde logic of temporal negation. What theory after 'theory' is to be will be determined in large part, but by no means exclusively, by the character of this negation. Furthermore, if such theory – or better, theorizing – is to live up to the structure of dialectical appropriation and transcendence implicit in the historical logic posited by this 'after', it will need to incorporate an account of its own development, an account of the new. 'The new' is in many ways paradigmatic of a transdisciplinary philosophical concept. As a time-determination, the new is at once a philosophical and a historical concept. It is at work in (one might say that it over-determines) the theoretical domains of art, culture, economics and politics. Yet it is pre-eminently, by virtue of its unification of the relations between such fields, a category of the philosophy of history. Indeed, it is in fact *the* central category of the philosophy of history of modernity. The temporality of the new defines modernity as an historical epoch. Competing conceptions of the new thus both serve to situate philosophies within the field of the philosophy of history, and thereby indicate different ways of positioning that field within broader parameters, such as, for example, its relationship to nature, or to the more basic ontological categories of being and becoming.

Thus, for post-Hegelian modernists such as Benjamin and Adorno, the concept of the new problematizes and transforms the concept of history – rendering it messianic or aporetic, respectively (Adorno 1973: 320; Benjamin 2003: 389–97). In contrast, for an anti-Hegelian such as Deleuze, arguably, 'the question of the new ... takes the place of the question of history' (Marrati 2008: 21, emphasis removed). This is a crucial marker of the ontological monism – one might call it a kind of naturalism – of Deleuze's thinking of time. For Deleuze, 'difference', 'life', 'event' and 'the new' ultimately refer to a single, ontologically undifferentiated process. Competing conceptions of the new thus stand at the crossroads of the philosophy of history and the philosophy of time, struggling over the very possibility of 'history' as a philosophical concept. This junction is also that of the most politically crucial of issues, the theorization of the future. For in philosophical-political terms, there is a future to the extent to which there is qualitative historical novelty, not merely in the sense of new occurrences or new 'events' (whatever 'events' may turn out to be – which is a significant and contested issue here), but in the sense of changes in the dynamics of historical temporalization that effect the existential-ontological character of the human itself. It is fundamental political changes of this kind that the concept of history is ultimately called upon to think. In Negri's words, time is the 'material from which communism is constructed' (Negri 2003: 47), although quite what 'time as material' means here remains to be explicated. At this level of abstraction, then, just as one can identify a common problematic determining the character of the differences between the traditions of 'French' and 'German' theory, so within that problematic there is a more particular problematic of the new, motivating certain of the decisive philosophical differences between, for example, Deleuze and Adorno. Each forges a distinctively post-Romantic philosophical form, in part via reflection on disjunctive conjunctions of Marx, Nietzsche and modernism (Osborne 2010b).[6]

One important result of this subjection of history to the temporality of the new (however precisely conceived) is a transformation in the concept of tradition, and hence the sense in which one may still speak of philosophical, or theoretical, traditions in modernity: ('German') post-Hegelian versus ('French') anti-Hegelian, in this particular case. Philosophical traditions cease to be best understood as forms of intellectual continuity forged by the intergenerational transmission of authoritative texts, principles and procedures, and become self-consciously retrospective constructions of continuity over-determined by the perceived needs of a philosophical present – the products of paradoxical 'choices' of philosophical authority, willing different philosophical (and social) futures. That is, 'traditions' become genealogical, in a strong Nietzschean-Foucauldian sense: subjected to, as well as providing the means of articulation for, what Foucault famously called critical ontologies of the present. This is the temporal-ontological truth underlying what often appears as a more superficial, merely politically conjunctural 'pragmatism'. In Nietzsche's words, 'If you are to venture to interpret the past you can do so only out of the fullest exertion of the vigour of the present' (Nietzsche 1997: 94, emphasis removed). It is the claim on the future here that distinguishes this Nietzschean pragmatism from more narrowly conceived and reductively 'presentist' pragmatisms (Osborne 2006: 43–4): claims on the future require totalizations of the past. Genealogy is modernist historiography. Heidegger, Benjamin and Deleuze are all prime examples of polemically genealogical historians of philosophy, who undertook the enormous hermeneutical labour of constructing new 'traditions' out of which to produce their own work; although Heidegger's history of philosophy, and phenomenology more generally (which was Heidegger's own 'philosophical modernity'), also furnishes the exemplar of regression to received authority within philosophical modernity, via certain proto-Catholic institutional forms.

When I speak of post-Hegelian versus anti-Hegelian philosophical traditions, then, I refer to two highly constructed competing philosophical lineages (provisionally, we might say, dialectical and anti-dialectical), which, in the form currently received in the Anglophone literature, were largely the retrospective 'invention' of the French philosophical imaginary of the 1960s – produced in the light of philosophy in Europe since the 1920s, with their antipathies projected back to the period of the mid-nineteenth century (1830–1870s). Furthermore, since 1968, it has increasingly been in the name of 'the new' that this division has been made and legitimated, on both sides. Thus, from the standpoint of the anti-Hegelian vanguards, not only was Hegelianism/dialectics/orthodox Marxism (sutured here into a single subject) 'antiquated', in its relations to both the philosophical and the political present, it was its conception of the new as the product of a dialectical negation that was the primary marker of this antiquation: source of an alleged structural inability to think the so-called 'radically', 'rupturally' or 'creatively' new. Philosophies of difference, broadly speaking, figure dialectical thought in terms of *identity*, *sameness*, *totality* (all actually dialectically relative terms) in order to credit anti-dialectical philosophies with *difference*, *otherness*, *singularity* and *incompletion*. Alternatively, from the standpoint of the post-Hegelian position, the anti-dialectical embrace of the new as pure difference or pure event appears as a flight from history – a structuralist or post-structuralist negation of history (Schmidt 1983: 108) – leading, philosophically, only backwards, towards various forms and combinations of 'the old': namely, post-Kantian positivisms and onto-theologies of the event. Separating itself out from the Hegelian dialectics that forms the object of the anti-Hegelian antipathy, through the dialectical negation constitutive of its own particular afterwardness, the post-Hegelian position identifies itself with 'new', open or unresolved dialectical forms of experience: be they proto-Romantic (Benjamin), negative (Adorno), or 'concrete' (Kosik). Yet from the standpoint of anti-Hegelianism, such post-Hegelian forms fail to differentiate themselves sufficiently from the conceptuality of Hegelian dialectics. And so the debate continues....

This genealogical subjection of history to the present, as the new, is at the same time, necessarily, its subjection to the problematic of the subject. For the primary determination of the philosophy of the subject lies not (as might be thought) in its relations to 'consciousness' and 'reason' but in its relations to time – ultimately, this is true even of Kant himself (Heidegger 1990). And the subject of modernity is a collective one. As Ricoeur put it: the 'full and precise formulation' of the concept of modernity is achieved only 'when one says and writes "our" modernity' (Ricoeur 2004: 305). And one can say and write 'our' modernity, philosophically, only by positing Hegel's '"I" that is "We" and "We" that is "I"' as its speculative subject (Hegel 1977: 110). 'Modernity' became a philosophical concept at the point at which it came to denote the temporal structure of experience of this subject: 'history' in the collective singular. However, it became the central category of the philosophy of history – transformed into a philosophy of historical time – only *after* the critique of Hegel's absolute, within which, its critics have always insisted, time is ultimately abolished (Feuerbach 1972: 53–96). In the end, Ricoeur himself actually favours this annulment of time over modernity, making the options in the philosophy of history quite clear: after Hegel, there is modernity *or* the philosophy of religion. There is no third way. Schematically, we may say: modernity becomes the central category of the philosophy of history via *the extraction of the formal structure of temporal negation from the totalized narrative of necessary development* in Hegel's philosophy of history. This formal structure of temporal negation, extracted from teleological narratives of necessary development, *is* the new. Modernisms – as isms – are collective affirmations of this formal temporal structure of the new, under the conditions of particular negations. Avant-gardes collectively affirm this formal temporal structure of the new, and its attendant negations, from the standpoint of particular politically defined futures. In this respect, in the move from 'Theory' to the theoretical practices that currently dominate an increasingly transnational English-language market in humanities, we see a dual retreat, first, from 'theory' as avant-garde to a general modernism of theory (an emphasis on the present as a negation of the past); and second, from a modernism of theory, to the illusory present of the space of 'the contemporary'. Much of what passes for theory today, especially in the degraded form of the circulation of 'marketable names', aspires to be contemporary – to join together the times of the spaces it addresses, discursively, via its mode of address, rather than merely via the exchange relations that give such contemporaneity its actuality. Yet it rarely pauses to reflect upon the philosophical structure of the idea of the contemporary, the transcendental illusion of co-presence that it carries (Osborne 2011), or its relationship to the idea of the new. A philosophically informed transdisciplinary theoretical discourse alone is adequate to that task. It calls for a new kind of reckoning between post-Hegelian and anti-Hegelian positions; a reckoning that would return to the most basic philosophical stakes at issue between them in thinking the new – negation, affirmation and the relationship between them – in the context of concrete forms, instances and connotations of the new.

The problem of the new, motivating its construction as a general-theoretical category of a transdisciplinary philosophizing, is simple: 'How to think the "newness" of the new?' That is, how to think the new's transcendence of its conditions, as 'novelty', without reducing it to either (1) a relation of negation to those conditions (i.e. a form of dependence), or (2) the pure transcendence of a quasi-theological 'creation'? In other words, wherein lies the immanent, rather than purely relational, intelligibility of the newness of the new? Part of the answer clearly lies in 'affirmation': the new is an *affirmative mode of negation*, otherwise called (by Nietzsche, Heidegger, Benjamin and Deleuze alike) 'destruction'. This is a crucial part of the affirmation of the new, but only a part, for while destruction clears the space for the new, the positivity of its specific newness still needs to be accounted for. How then, precisely, does the affirmation of the new stand in relation to its negation of the old? This is the temporal-ontological problem that no reflection on the future of theory itself can avoid. Conceptually, it requires a renewed investigation of the underlying affinities between Hegel's and Nietzsche's thought, at their deepest levels, at the very moment at which they appear most opposed;[7] in its historical dimension, it requires philosophizing about, and out of, non-philosophical experience. It is here that Benjamin's later work stands out as exemplary in its theoretical-political intent; and it is here also that, in his collaboration with Guattari in the two-volume *Capitalism and Schizophrenia*, Deleuze's writing distances itself from the classically metaphysical problematic that it otherwise appears to share with Badiou, and to which Badiou would have us reduce Deleuze's thought (Badiou 2000).

In *What is Philosophy?*, it is argued that 'The history of philosophy means that we evaluate not only the historical novelty of the concepts created by a philosopher but also the power of their becoming when they pass into one another' (Deleuze and Guattari 1994: 32). The example given there is the conjoined production in Kant's writings of new concepts of time, space and the cogito. Transformations in the concepts of space and time produced a new concept of the cogito. Here, my suggestion is that in critically reflecting on the received oppositions between negation and affirmation, in the context of the history of the new, we can look towards the conjoined production of new concepts of negation, affirmation and the new. Or to put it another way: perhaps the new might be made to *work on* and *transform* the concepts of negation and affirmation, from its ambiguous location somewhere between the ontological and socio-historical 'realms'. Such a position refuses any straightforwardly resolved sense of the historically ontological, not least because of its radicalization of the problem of the future, which problematizes even retroactive ontologizations of the historical. It categorically refuses the internality to a conventionally constructed philosophical field characteristic of the Kantian series cited in *What is Philosophy?*, affirming instead the openness of a philosophically informed theoretical discourse to the present as a whole. This is a trajectory for which Benjamin's *Arcades Project* and Deleuze-Guattari's *Capitalism and Schizophrenia* offer us flawed but living models, models that retain the aspiration of theoretical work to both truth and the transformation of experience.

Notes

1 As part of this market, 'French theory' is even being sold back to France, in an ironic 'modernizing' importation of self as other (Alizart *et al.* 2005, 2006; Alizart 2007). A philosopher in France must now circulate through English-language academic networks in order to become a 'French philosopher' even in non-English-speaking zones such as South America and South-East Asia.

2 See Dosse and Glassman (1997).

3 The reception of these thinkers is too pervasive to merit singling out any particular texts. It is worth noting, however, that this provides the context for the promotion of Žižek's work via the manner in which he has inserted into it his own brand of Hegelian Lacanianism, in the polemical form of a new 'Cartesianism' (Žižek 1999, 2004). Žižek alternates tactically across the theory/philosophy divide: playing 'philosophy' (Hegel) against 'theory', and 'theory' (Lacan) against 'philosophy'. This constant tactical manoeuvring, characteristic of his writings, places them performatively within the more narrowly pragmatic band of the pragmatist mainstream.

   With regard to Deleuze, it is important to distinguish his more classically philosophical work (be it interpretative or constructive), from the more complicated, experimental status of his two main books with Félix Guattari (Deleuze and Guattari 1983,1987) – for which, see below. However, the nominally co-authored *What is Philosophy?* (Deleuze and Guattari

1994) reinstates the classically modern disciplinary divisions between 'philosophy', 'art' and 'science'.

The theoretical side of feminism ('French feminism' as a part of 'French theory') presents a more complicated trajectory; in part because of the reception of its founding mothers – Kristeva, Cixous, Irigaray – through the category of writing (*écriture féminine*). Nonetheless, one can still discern a movement in the history of reception from psycho-analytically influenced forms of theory (Kristeva, in particular) to more metaphysical versions of sexual difference (Irigaray) and 'woman' (Braidotti's and others' Deleuzean 'becoming woman').

4 The partial exception to this rule is Jacques Rancière, who remains in many ways a politicized post-Foucauldian historian of 'systems of thought'. However, the English-language reception of his work has to a large extent focused on his 'aesthetics', in strict distinction from the successor discipline of 'art theory'. As such, it represents something of a mediated return to the classical modern philosophical field. His political thought similarly draws heavily on classical philosophical sources (Rancière 1995), but it distinguishes itself from them, nonetheless, by deploying them in the context of a theory of subjectivation. In this respect, it is resistant to the dominant US tendency to situate Foucault and his legacy within an expanded field of liberal political philosophy. Whether this resistant quality extends to his aesthetics is more doubtful.

5 Quentin Meillassoux and the so-called 'speculative realists' provide a comic footnote to this history – the return as farce. They are the Louis Bonapartes of metaphysics.

6 This problematic extends well beyond the Franco-German theoretical axis, providing one of the unifying forms of the increasingly transnational domain of 'theory', within which Italian work plays a growing role (see Chiesa and Toscano 2009).

7 Cf. 'The philosophy of Nietzsche takes its distance from dialectical philosophy less in contesting it than in repeating it'; specifically,

> in repeating the principle concepts or moments that it deflects . . . the idea of contradiction, the idea of going beyond, the idea of transvaluation, the idea of totality, and above all the idea of circularity, of truth or of affirmation as circular.
>
> (Blanchot 1993: 159)

Bibliography

Adorno, T.W. (1973) *Negative Dialectics*, trans. E.B. Ashton, London: Routledge.

Adorno, T.W. (1997) *Aesthetic Theory*, trans. R. Hullot-Kentor, Minneapolis: Minnesota University Press.

Alizart, M. (ed.) (2007) *Fresh Théorie III: Manifestations*, Paris: Editions Leo Scheer.

Alizart, M., Kihm, C. and Collectif (2005) *Fresh Théorie*, Paris: Editions Leo Scheer.

Alizart, M., Nicolin, P., Zaoui, P., Ronell, A. and Collectif (2006) *Fresh Théorie II: Black Album*, Paris: Editions Leo Scheer.

Althusser, L. (1977) 'Remarks on the Terminology Adopted' – 1965 Preface to the 1963 essay 'On the Materialist Dialectic: On the Unevenness of Origins', in *For Marx*, trans. B. Brewster, London: New Left Books. 162.

Badiou, A. (2000) *Deleuze: The Clamour of Being*, trans. L. Burchill, Minneapolis: Minnesota University Press.

Benjamin, W. (1999) *The Arcades Project*, trans. H. Eiland and K. McLaughlin, Cambridge, MA: Harvard University Press.

Benjamin, W. (2003) 'On the Concept of History', *Selected Writings. Volume 4, 1938–1940*, Cambridge, MA: Harvard University Press. 390–400.

Blanchot, M. (1993) *The Infinite Conversation*, trans. S. Hanson, Minneapolis: Minnesota University Press.

Butler, J. (2004) *Precarious Life: The Powers of Mourning and Violence*, London: Verso.

Chiesa, L. and Toscano, A. (eds) (2009) *The Italian Difference: Between Nihilism and Biopolitics*, Melbourne: re.press.

Critchley, S. (2007) *Infinitely Demanding: Ethics of Commitment, Politics of Resistance*, London: Verso.

Cussett, F. (2008) *French Theory: How Foucault, Derrida, Deleuze, & Co Transformed the Intellectual Life of the United States*, trans. J. Fort, Minneapolis: University of Minnesota Press.

Deleuze, G. and Guattari, F. (1983) *Anti-Oedipus: Capitalism and Schizophrenia*, trans. R. Hurley, M. Seem and H. Lane, Minneapolis: Minnesota University Press.

Deleuze, G. and Guattari, F. (1987) *A Thousand Plateaus: Capitalism and Schizophrenia*, trans. B. Massumi, Minneapolis: Minnesota University Press.

Deleuze, G. and Guattari, F. (1994) *What is Philosophy?*, trans. G. Burchell and H. Tomlinson, London: Verso.

Derrida, J. (1992) 'Force of Law: The "Mystical Foundations of Authority"', in D. Cornell, M. Rosenfeld and D.G. Carlson (eds), *Deconstruction and the Possibility of Justice*, London: Routledge. 3–67.

Dollimore, J. (2000) 'Wishful Theory and Sexual Politics', *Radical Philosophy* 103: 18–24.

Dosse, F. and Glassman, D. (1997a) *History of Structuralism. Volume 1: The Rising Sign, 1945–1966*, Minneapolis: University of Minnesota Press.

Dosse, F. and Glassman, D. (1997b) *History of Structuralism, Volume 2: The Sign Sets, 1967–Present*, Minneapolis, MN: University of Minnesota Press.

Dubiel, H. (1985) *Theory and Politics: Studies in the Development of Critical Theory*, trans. B. Gregg, Cambridge, MA: MIT Press.

Feuerbach, L. (1972) 'Towards a Critique of Hegel's Philosophy', in *The Fiery Brook: Selected Writings of Ludwig Feuerbach*, ed. and trans. Z. Hanfi, New York: Anchor Books. 53–96.

Ffrench, P. (1995) *The Time of Theory: A History of* Tel Quel *(1960–1983)*, Oxford: Clarendon Press.

Gasché, R. (2007) *The Honor of Thinking: Theory, Philosophy, Criticism*, Stanford, CA: Stanford University Press.

Habermas, J. (1974) 'Between Philosophy and Science: Marxism as Critique' (1963), in *Theory and Practice*, trans. J. Viertel, London: Heinemann. 195–252.

Habermas, J. (1978) *Knowledge and Human Interests* (1968), trans. J.J. Shapiro, 2nd edn, London: Heinemann.

Habermas, J. (1987a) *The Philosophical Discourse of Modernity: Twelve Lectures*, trans. F. Lawrence, Cambridge, MA: MIT Press.

Habermas, J. (1987b) *The Theory of Communicative Action, Volume 2: The Critique of Functionalist Reason* (1981), trans. T. McCarthy, Cambridge: Polity Press.

Habermas, J. (1991) *The Theory of Communicative Action, Volume 1: Reason and the Rationalization of Society* (1981), trans. T. McCarthy, Cambridge: Polity Press.

Habermas, J. (1996) *Between Facts and Norms: Contributions to a Discourse Theory of Law and Democracy*, trans. W. Rehg, Cambridge, MA: MIT Press.

Hegel, G.W.F. (1977) *Phenomenology of Spirit*, trans. A.V. Miller, Oxford: Oxford University Press.

Heidegger, M. (1990) *Kant and the Problem of Metaphysics*, trans. R. Taft, Bloomington: Indiana University Press.

Honneth, A. (1995) *The Struggle for Recognition: The Moral Grammar of Social Conflicts*, trans. J. Anderson, Cambridge: Polity Press.

Horkheimer, M. (1972) 'Traditional and Critical Theory', in *Critical Theory: Selected Essays*, New York: Continuum. 188–252.

Horkheimer, M. (2004) *Eclipse of Reason*, London: Continuum.

Horkheimer, M. and Adorno, T.W. (2002) *Dialectic of Enlightenment: Philosophical Fragments*, trans. E. Jephcott, Stanford, CA: Stanford University Press.

Kosik, K. (1976) *Dialectics of the Concrete: A Study of Problems on Man and World*, trans. K. Kovanda and J. Schmidt, Dordrecht: Reidel.

Lecourt, D. (1975) *Marxism and Epistemology: Bachelard, Canguilhem and Foucault*, London: New Left Books.

Marrati, P. (2008) 'Life and Event: Deleuze on Newness', in J.J. Bono, T. Dean and E.P. Ziarek (eds), *A Time for the Humanities: Futurity and the Limits of Autonomy*, New York: Fordham University Press. 17–28.

Marx, K. and Engels, F. (1976) 'The German Ideology', in *Collected Works, Volume 5, 1845–1847*, London: Lawrence & Wishart.

Nancy, J-L. (1991) 'Introduction', in Nancy, J-L. *et al.* (eds), *Who Comes After the Subject?*, New York: Routledge. 1–8.

Negri, A. (2003) 'Constitution of Time', in *Time for Revolution*, trans. M. Mandarini, London: Continuum. 19–128.

Nietzsche, F. (1997) 'On the Uses and Disadvantages of History for Life', in *Untimely Meditations*, trans. R.J. Hollingdale, Cambridge: Cambridge University Press. 57–123.

Osborne, P. (2000) 'Philosophy in Cultural Theory', in *Philosophy in Cultural Theory*, London: Routledge. 1–19.

Osborne, P. (2006) '"Whoever Speaks of Culture Speaks of Administration as Well": Disputing Pragmatism in Cultural Studies', *Cultural Studies* 60 (1): 33–47.

Osborne, P. (2007) 'Neo-Classic: Alain Badiou's *Being and Event*', *Radical Philosophy* 142: 19–29.

Osborne, P. (2010a) 'A Sudden Topicality: Marx, Nietzsche and the Politics of Crisis', *Radical Philosophy* 160: 19–26.

Osborne, P. (2010b) 'Modernism and Philosophy', in P. Brooker, A. Gasiorek, D. Longworth and A. Thacker (eds), *The Oxford Handbook of Modernisms*, Oxford: Oxford University Press. 388–409.

Osborne, P. (2011) 'The Fiction of the Contemporary: Speculative Collectivity and Transnationality in The Atlas Group', in A. Avanessian and L. Skrebowski, eds, *Aesthetics and Contemporary Art*, Berlin: Sternberg Press.

Rancière, J. (1995) *On the Shores of Politics*, trans. L. Heron, London: Verso.

Ricoeur, P. (2004) *Memory, History, Forgetting*, trans. K. Blamey and D. Pellauer, Chicago: Chicago University Press.

Schmitt, A. (1983) *History and Structure: An Essay on Hegelian–Marxist and Structuralist Theories of History*, trans. J. Herf, Cambridge, MA: MIT Press.

Sloterdijk, P. (1988) *Critique of Cynical Reason*, trans. M. Eldred, London: Verso.

Weber, S. (2008) *Benjamin's -abilities*, Cambridge, MA: Harvard University Press.

Wellmer, A. (1998) *Endgames: The Irreconcilable Nature of Modernity*, trans. D. Midgley, Cambridge, MA: MIT Press.

Wiggershaus, R. (1994) *The Frankfurt School: Its History, Theories and Politics*, Cambridge: Polity Press.

Žižek, S. (1999) *The Ticklish Subject: The Absent Centre of Political Ontology*, London: Verso.

Žižek, S. (2004) *Organs Without Bodies: On Deleuze and Consequences*, New York: Routledge.

2

THEORY AS A RESEARCH PROGRAMME – THE VERY IDEA

Cary Wolfe

Any discussion of the role and future of theory today has to begin, I think, with contextualizing the question. 'Theory' today – and I will drop the quotation marks from here on out – is not what it was in, say, 1985, when (to take a notorious example) Walter Benn Michaels and Steven Knapp, in their *Against Theory* polemic, called it 'a special project in literary criticism' (a characterization that Fredric Jameson – shrewd and politically attuned reader that he is – at the time called 'reassuringly restricted') (Jameson 1990: 181–2; Knapp and Michaels 1985: 30). Twenty-five years later it seems even more restricted, as theory has simultaneously become more varied, more widely disseminated and more interdisciplinary than ever. (Think of the impact, in the intervening years, of thinkers like Giorgio Agamben, Antonio Negri or Slavoj Žižek, to name only three high-profile examples.) For that very reason, perhaps, theory has become more and more invisible even as it has become more pervasive. This dissemination allows those who want no truck with theory to make premature announcements of its demise (to borrow from Mark Twain), but even a cursory glance at any major university press catalogue will readily testify to the fact that theory has never been more alive and well.

This dissemination, however, has also been a kind of domestication (perhaps inevitable), as anyone who lived through the heady days of the late 1970s and the 1980s of line-in-the-sand warring factions – Marxists versus poststructuralists, feminists versus Marxists, psychoanalytic theorists versus all three – will readily testify. Arguably, this domestication of theory is thanks in no small part to the phenomenon known as 'cultural studies' which has, if we believe Tilottama Rajan, evolved over the past couple of decades from a site of 'decentering innovation' into 'a symbiosis with globalization' and the New World Order. In her view, the 'inclusiveness' for which cultural studies is famous – an inclusiveness made possible in no small part, of course, by the assimilation of theory – masks the fact that it has also become subtly, and predictably, selective, carrying out the work of what used to be called 'identity politics' by other means (Rajan 2001: 69, 71).

I will return to Rajan later in this essay, but what I want to stress at the outset is that theory is not now and never was a question of 'the latest thing', as if what makes it theory is its more or less automatically avant-garde nature. Rather, it is a question of thinking a genealogy of theory in Foucault's sense of the term in his famous essay 'Nietzsche, Genealogy, History', one that involves not just an intellectual constellation or conceptual trajectory but also their conjuncture with forces that are disciplinary, institutional and even (to use the good old Marxist term that Foucault disliked) 'ideological' (Foucault 1984: 60, 77, 81). In that light, I think, we have to ask after the current role and future of theory in the context of hegemonic disciplinary norms and the changing nature of the university as an institution. (And I hasten to add that my remarks on both counts will thus be based on the situation as I see it in the United States and, to a lesser extent, Canada. The extent to which they can be generalized beyond that I will leave to readers in the United Kingdom, Australia and elsewhere.) Crucial to such a genealogy, I think, is the emergence of the 'corporate' university, its protocols and values and how they over-determine particular knowledge practices in the humanities.

I will pursue that question in more detail in a moment, but for now, I would like to consider briefly an increasingly visible movement in the humanities that, implicitly or explicitly, sets itself against both cultural studies and identity politics as glossed by Rajan – a movement that is quite conspicuously informed by a commitment to theory. I refer to the growing body of work that attempts to retool the phenomenology of perception, affect and consciousness in areas such as media studies by integrating new developments in cognitive science and neuroscience. I should say at the outset that my aim here is not to engage in a detailed critique of any of the work I will be mentioning, but rather simply to tease out some of its underlying assumptions and reflect upon what we might call (to borrow Kenneth Burke's phrase) its 'unintended by-products'. In doing so, I hope to provide at least a partial sketch of a contemporary landscape within which the specific role of theory as I see it may become clearer, and offer a plausible picture of how and why theory can intervene in productive ways at this particular moment, ways that turn out to be political in an important but far from straightforward sense.

As for this new work in cognitive science and phenomenology and its importation into the humanities, the beginnings of a very long list of players might look something like this: at one end of the spectrum, it includes scholars in the sciences carrying out actual research in neurophysiology, perception and the like. Such a group would include figures such as psychologist Russell Gray at the University of Auckland, a key figure in Developmental Systems Theory (DST); V.S. Ramachandran, Director of the Center for Brain and Cognition at the University of California-San Diego and, perhaps most conspicuous of all, Antonio Damasio, Director of the Brain and Creativity Institute at the University of Southern California. In the middle, as it were, are scholars whose training and research are not in the sciences per se, but in the philosophy of science in the analytic tradition: Russell's collaborator, philosopher of science Paul Griffiths at the University of Sydney; Andy Clarke, Chair of Logic and Metaphysics at the University of Edinburgh; and philosopher Evan Thompson at the University of Toronto, who collaborated with biologist Francisco Varela earlier in his career, would be representative examples.

Closest to home of all (at least for me) are those scholars working in a range of disciplines in the humanities whose orientation towards these problems is shaped by training in, and sometimes a deep commitment to, one form or another of contemporary continental philosophy: Mark Hansen in New Media Studies and N. Katherine Hayles in narrative and electronic textuality, both in Duke University's Literature Program; Barbara Stafford in Art History at the University of Chicago; New Media and Art History theorist Anna Munster at the University of New South Wales; Brian Massumi, who co-organizes the SenseLab at the Université de Montréal; philosopher Manuel DeLanda, who has held a variety of posts in a variety of disciplines and departments; and John Protevi at Louisiana State University, who co-edits the series 'New Directions in Philosophy and Cognitive Science' at Palgrave Macmillan.

My main concern here, as you might guess, is with the last grouping in this list, in which we find scholars who have taken it upon themselves to develop a very serious (if non-specialist) acquaintance with the work being carried out by figures who would belong in the first grouping. But even here, the range of sensibilities, intellectual commitments and projects, and philosophical and epistemological orientations is quite extensive. I have no intention, therefore, of even attempting an overview that would do justice to that range or the remarkable accomplishment of the individual contributions, but only want to linger over a tendency common to them all: the tendency to see the project of theory as one that models itself on the sciences. Common to them all, that is to say, is an attempt to further articulate what is variously characterized as 'materialism', 'realism' or 'empiricism' by backing it with the cash value of scientific discovery, and, in some cases, an ongoing search for something like a common underlying language between philosophical concepts (taken mainly from continental philosophy) and scientific models.

John Protevi, for instance, in his recent book *Political Affect*, calls for a 'Deleuzean neo-materialism that does not begin with consciousness (even a fragmented and internally hollowed-out consciousness), but which accounts for consciousness and for signification on the basis of a non-mechanistic and non-deterministic materialism underlying historically variable subjectification and signification practices', one that 'allows for a productive engagement with contemporary scientific findings' such as dynamical systems modelling, autopoiesis theory in biology, DST and the 'situated cognition' school of cognitive science (Protevi 2009: 2, 5).

And Barbara Stafford, working on a theory of images rather than political affect, argues that 'the huge and conjoined problem of interiority and the life of forms . . . is ripe for reassessment from the neurological perspective' (Stafford 2004: 346). She argues that 'integrating a cognitive perspective into humanistic inquiry allows us both to imagine and to construct an alternative framework for representation-as-presentation – that is, for the creation of a public object-event that existentially expresses a private inward performance', by means of which we can formulate a 'soma-poetics of human interiority', or what Thomas Metzinger has dubbed 'a truly internalist state space semantics' (quoted in ibid.: 316).

This is not to say that these scholars accept lock, stock and barrel the scientific materials with which they work. Protevi is surely right that 'affective neuroscience' and the 'embodied-embedded mind' schools both 'tend to presuppose an adult subject that is supposedly not marked in its development by social practices, such as gendering, that influence affective cognition' (Protevi 2009: 1–2). And Stafford offers a similar corrective in her call to 'deepen the presentist focus of much current research on the connection of the human senses to the image world by invoking the historical', thereby 'inserting evidence from past states-of-mind into contemporary cognitive research' (Stafford: 319; 317). At the same time, however, we often find formulations such as the following from Stafford left largely unquestioned:

> [T]he autonomic nervous system is a primal theater modeling the body to itself. We have limited control over its flitting set-changes. The behind-the-scenes actors are those steady-state, coordinated, and emotionally colored physiological reactions that permit the living organism to represent its internal states to itself.
>
> (Ibid.: 319)

Similarly – taking for granted, for the moment, the terms of his characterization – Mark Hansen is surely right to reject 'the thoroughgoing hostility to anything biological that literally permeated the ethos of theory'. And he observes that even theories that have attempted to move beyond the 'antibiological imperative of cultural constructivism' have 'to date hardly succeeded in producing a viable – not to mention widely palatable – account of the role played by biological embodiment in cultural experience, identity, and community' (Hansen 2006: 7). I will leave aside the assumption that frames this charge – namely, the ascription of 'failure' to theories that might not, in fact, think of this as their charge or measure of success at all – and instead note the extremely problematic assumption underlying the critique of constructivist theory that Hansen cites as exemplary: Eve Sedgwick and Adam Frank's argument that the distinction '"discursively constructed" rather than "natural"', as Hansen puts it, 'is *precisely what constitutes theory*'; that 'theory', in the words of Sedgwick and Frank, 'has become almost simply coextensive with the claim (you can't say it often enough), *it's not natural*' (Hansen 2006: 7). At least two problems can be noted here. The first, of course, is the ham-fisted dichotomy of 'discursive' versus 'natural' – a dichotomy for which Hansen's own commitment to a fundamentally, indeed constitutively, prosthetic relationship of technogenesis in the human between the two domains (following primarily the work of Bernard Stiegler and André Leroi-Gourhan) would presumably have little tolerance (ibid.: 9). The problem, to put it in a shorthand we will unpack later, is a thoroughgoing philosophical representationalism (and the either/or-ism that goes with it), of which such a dichotomy is both symptom and offspring. Second, what is missing here, in a rather straightforward philosophy-of-science sort of way, is a sufficiently sceptical engagement with scientific realism and empiricism. The assumption, to varying degrees, seems to be that scientific findings can be taken more or less at face value and then can be supplemented by a second-order operation of philosophical, historical or cultural reflection and refinement. What is missing, in other words, is an adequate account of scientific description and explanation itself.

On this point, we might in fact cite two scientists who are themselves often invoked in the body of work I have been sketching – Humberto Maturana and Francisco Varela – who write that:

> the domain of discourse is a closed domain, and it is not possible to step outside of it through discourse. Because the domain of discourse is a closed domain it is possible to make the following ontological statement: *the logic of the description is the logic of the describing (living) system (and his cognitive domain).*

> This logic demands a substratum for the occurrence of the discourse. We cannot talk about this substratum in absolute terms, however, because we would have to describe it. . . . Thus, although this substratum is required for epistemological reasons, nothing can be said about it other than what is meant in the ontological statement above.
>
> (Maturana and Varela 1980: 39)

This 'ontological statement' does not mean, of course, that that substratum cannot be manipulated and predicted in various ways with high degrees of pragmatic success and experimental repeatability. Nor does it mean that that substratum does not have powerful influences on human action, communication and so on. It is simply to draw attention to the precise nature of the claims being made. What this means, Maturana argues, is that scientific explanations 'do not and cannot operate as phenomenic reductions or give rise to them'; scientific description, the phenomenon described and the processes that generate the phenomenon 'intrinsically take place', as he puts it, 'in independent and nonintersecting phenomenal domains'. In this way, he concludes, 'science and the understanding of science lead us away from transcendental dualism', such as the dichotomy between 'nature' and 'discourse' invoked by Hansen above (Maturana 1991: 34).

Here – to take a rather different theoretical discourse from Maturana's – I would recommend as especially lucid and incisive on these issues the work of Richard Rorty and Barbara Herrnstein Smith (but others, such as Paul Feyerabend or Bruno Latour, could also be cited). I turn to this work – Rorty's, primarily from the late 1980s/early 1990s, Smith's, from roughly a decade later – because of its powerfully de-ontologizing impulse, its refusal to see theory's role as providing more accurate or authentic access to an ontological substrate upon which various projects – be they interpretive or political – might then be grounded. And yet – in no small part, I think, because of the 'against theory' backlash that took hold from the mid to late 1980s and into the 1990s (and its side effect of driving a wedge

between continental and North American thought) – this work was often associated with a broader brand of 'neo-pragmatism' of the sort found in Stanley Fish
(or, for that matter, in Walter Benn Michaels). That neo-pragmatism was in turn
often taken to be either apolitical or even, by its more strident critics, an apology
for liberalism's status quo (a charge abetted, no doubt, by certain ethnocentric
strains in Rorty's writings, as I have noted elsewhere).[1] But as I hope to show, we
can make use of this view of theory as what Rorty calls anti-essentialist contextualization – the idea that the 'desire to know the truth' is better 'construed as the
desire to recontextualize rather than (with Aristotle) as the desire to know essence'
(Rorty 1991: 110) – to contextualize and locate the politics of the desire called
'science' in current theory more precisely. Such an approach is not at all, in my
view, apolitical; indeed, it is, as Rorty puts it, 'to modulate philosophical debate
from a methodologico-ontological key into an ethico-political key' (ibid.).

As for the 'methodologico-ontological' orientation, the lynchpin for 'scientific
realism', as Rorty notes, is the view that scientific knowledge is 'guided' to agreement, convergence and the like 'by the way the world is in itself' (Rorty 1991: 49).
The realist, Rorty writes, 'must explain something called "science" on the basis of
something called "the relation of scientific inquiry to reality" – a relation not possessed by all other human activities' (ibid.: 54). It should be stressed here that it is
not enough to explain experimental predictability, repeatability and the like; the
pragmatist (or the 'whiggish' Baconian, as Rorty puts it) can do that by being willing to 'call a cultural achievement "science" only if they can trace some technological advance, some increase in our ability to predict and control, back to that
development' (ibid.: 47). 'Once one sees', as Rorty writes elsewhere,

> that 'Science can predict insofar as it gets reality right' is an incantation
> rather than an explanation (because we have no test for the explanans dis-
> tinct from our test for the explanandum), it seems enough simply to define
> scientific progress as an increased ability to make predictions.
>
> (Rorty 1998: 5)

This 'trivializes', as he puts it, both the term 'true' and science's privileged
relationship to it. 'The only criterion we have for applying the word "true"', Rorty
writes,

> is justification, and justification is always relative to an audience. So it is also
> relative to an audience's lights – the purposes that such an audience wants
> served and the situation in which it finds itself. This means that the ques-
> tion 'Do our practices of justification lead to truth?' is as unanswerable as
> it is unpragmatic.
>
> (Ibid.: 4)

Two points should be stressed here. First, this does not mean that we are in denial
of 'facts', only that facts are similarly resituated, as is 'truth', *vis-à-vis* the knowledge

claims of science. As Smith lucidly summarizes it, choosing the label 'constructivist' rather than 'pragmatist',

> In contrast to referentialist views of language, constructivist accounts of *truth* conceive it not as a matter of a match between, on the one hand, statements or beliefs and, on the other, the autonomously determinate features of an altogether external world (Nature or Reality), but, rather, as a situation of relatively stable and effective mutual coordination among statements, beliefs, experiences and practical activities.
>
> (Smith 2006: 4)

Moreover, she continues, with regard to specifically *scientific* truth and knowledge claims, it sees these not 'as duly epistemically privileged products of intrinsically orthotropic methods of reasoning or investigation', but rather as 'the more or less stable products of an especially tight mutual shaping of perceptual, conceptual and behavioural (manipulative, discursive, inscriptional and other) practices' (ibid.).

As Rorty notes, once you have accepted all of this you have also disposed of the problem of 'relativism' because

> relativism (either in the form of 'many truths' or 'many worlds') could only enter the mind of someone who . . . was antecedently convinced that some of our true beliefs are related to the world in a way in which others are not.
>
> (Rorty 1991: 51)

That is to say, the charge of relativism only makes sense if you think a 'God's-eye-view' is possible (ibid.: 202) – a non-contingent point of view from which all descriptions and beliefs could be seen and declared equally relative. Similarly, Smith refuses to play the game demanded by the realist's charge of 'relativism' – a game Rorty calls trying 'to put a metanarrative in the postmodernist's mouth' (ibid.: 202). Smith thus rejects Ian Hacking's criticism of those who deny 'realism's affirmation, that Nature is inherently structured in certain ways' (Smith's words, not Hacking's). The constructivists and/or pragmatists, she writes,

> do not characteristically 'deny' *metaphysically* what realists evidently metaphysically maintain: namely, first, that Nature *is* structured in certain ways inherently (meaning independently of our perceptions, conceptions, and descriptions) and, second, that we properly assume (Hacking says 'hope') that those ways are largely in accord with our perceptions, conceptions and descriptions of them. Rather, constructivists typically decline, in their historical, sociological or psychological accounts of science and cognition, to presume either any particular way the world inherently is *or* such an accord. This professional ontological agnosticism is not, as realists may see it, a perverse refusal of common sense but an effort at due methodological modesty and theoretical economy.
>
> (Smith 2006: 6)

Smith's position offers a point of possible *rapprochement* with the work of Protevi, Stafford, Hansen and others of similar ilk, but we need Rorty's articulation of what he, following Donald Davidson, calls 'non-reductive physicalism' to show how. That view holds that the inability 'to pair off brain-states with sentences which are believed to be true by the possessor of the brain, should be no impediment to a materialist outlook' (Rorty 1991: 114); one need not

> raise the question . . . of whether there are things in the world which make algebraic and moral truths, or aesthetic judgments, true. For although there are causes of the acquisitions of beliefs, and reasons for the retention or change of beliefs, there are no causes for the *truth* of beliefs.
>
> (Ibid.: 121)

Rorty draws two important conclusions from the Davidsonian view. First, it is 'to grant the materialist everything he should want – to gratify all his legitimate needs, to permit him to pay compliments to the physical sciences which they deserve. *But it will not permit him to gratify his metaphysical, reductionist needs*' (ibid.: 116–17, emphasis added). And second, it is to abandon the idea of a 'True Self' (ibid.: 123) that has plagued Western philosophy seemingly forever, and think instead of subjectivity as embedded and embodied in multiple ways, in 'causes that include both micro-structural and macro-structural, and both mental and physical, items: among them are hormones, positrons, neural synapses, beliefs, desires, moods, diseases, and multiple personalities' (ibid.: 121). 'There is no more of a center to the self than there is to the brain', Rorty writes,

> Just as the neural synapses are in continual interaction with one another, constantly weaving a different configuration of electrical charges, so our beliefs and desires are in continual interaction, redistributing truth-values among statements. Just as the brain is not something that 'has' such synapses, but is simply the agglomeration of them, so the self is not something which 'has' beliefs and desires, but is simply the network of such beliefs and desires.
>
> (Ibid.: 123)

I want to emphasize this last set of points because they are particularly pertinent to a project such as Protevi's, which is surely right to insist not only on the importance of affect in political behaviour, but also on a critique of the atomistic rational subject as the constitutive unit of political behaviour, a subject who needs to be newly thought as physically, psychologically and socially embedded and distributed in multiple ways. But having said that, it is not clear why we need to introduce, either tacitly or explicitly, distinctions between reality and appearance, biology and discourse, materialism and idealism, and so on, to make such claims. Rather, I share Rorty's aim 'to find a position which is beyond realism and antirealism', and also beyond the larger 'representationalist' frame that gets resuscitated, either through the front or back door, in the mobilization of such terms (ibid.: 49).

Let me be clear about this: there is no question in my mind that pursuing inter-
changes, and increased mutual literacies, between the sciences and the humanities
is a good thing – a project called for in Stafford's search for 'finding ways to reinsert
the biological into the investigation of cultural practices' (Stafford 2004: 317).
Indeed, in my own work, I have drawn upon life sciences such as zoology and
cognitive ethology, and have insisted that we largely have the sciences to thank for
bringing to our attention the evolutionary and biological bases of the complexity
and fullness of the mental, emotional and social lives of non-human animals – a
fact that the humanities otherwise surely would have been even slower to register.[2]
But what I *am* saying is that such claims need to be mounted within a fully elaborated and carefully articulated context of inquiry in which the status of scientific
truth claims is not treated as essentially unproblematic – a project in which theory
has a key role to play. Such a project is short circuited, unfortunately, by moves such
as Stafford's reductive characterization of 'the poststructuralist claim that the self is
a linguistic construct' (ibid.: 347–8) as the straw man against which the more
'materialist' or 'realist' accounts of science assert themselves.

To put it another way, Rorty's Davidsonian 'non-reductive physicalism' gives us
a way to do everything Protevi wants to do *politically* without taking on the extra
baggage of assuming that such claims, to have political efficacy, have to be
'grounded', either 'ontologically' or 'materially'. And it also would open up a space
of cross-talk between the position I am sketching here and the philosopher most
important to Protevi: Deleuze, but Deleuze the philosophical pragmatist (the
Deleuze, most pronouncedly, of *What Is Philosophy?*), not Deleuze the ontologist.
The sense of Deleuze's pragmatism is captured well by Martin Joughin in his translator's preface to Deleuze's *Expressionism in Philosophy: Spinoza*, where he writes
that in Deleuze's studies

> the development of a 'philosophy' is traced from some version of an initial
> situation where some term in our experience diverges from its apparent
> relations with some other terms, breaking out of that 'space' of relations
> and provoking a reflection in which we consider reorientations or rein-
> scriptions of this and other terms with a 'virtual' matrix of possible unfold-
> ings of these terms and their relations in time. . . . Such a 'philosophy'
> comes full-circle when the 'subject' . . . 'orients' its own practical activity
> of interpretation, evaluation or orientation of the terms of experience
> within this universal matrix it has itself unfolded.
>
> (Deleuze 1990: 9)

The echoes of Rorty's position as sketched above are clear enough here, I think.
But such a reading of Deleuze would also seem to run counter to the impulse of
projects such as Protevi's or Hansen's, in which the point of stitching together new
work in the neurophysiology of perception and consciousness with, say, the work
of Deleuze or Simondon or Bergson, seems less to challenge prevailing scientific
models of knowledge than it is to use scientific discoveries to show how the work

of these philosophers is even more 'ontologically correct', you might say, than we previously thought.

I mention this shift in context – from ontology to pragmatics and politics – because it leads me to the last set of questions I want to explore around the issue of theory as a research programme modelled on and, as it were, legitimized by scientific knowledge claims. The issues in the context I want to open here are not so much epistemological (or anti-epistemological) as they are institutional, for, as Rorty notes, the sort of change in 'intellectual habits' he encourages – getting rid of the notions of 'objectivity' and 'truth' in any seriously epistemological sense, moving beyond realism and anti-realism –

> would put an end to attempts to set up a pecking order among cultural activities and among parts of our lives. . . . [I]t would stop the 'hard' sciences from looking down on the soft, stop both from looking down on the arts, and end attempts to put philosophy on the secure path of a science. It would stop people from worrying about the 'scientific' or 'cognitive' status of a discipline or of a social practice.
>
> (Rorty 1998: 6–7)

– a process many of us have lived through at least once with the attempts of various varieties of structuralism to do just that.

The irony here is that it is precisely this worry about such 'softness' – and the attendant attempts to make thought 'scientific' – that spawned the very forms of *analytic* philosophy with which Protevi and Hansen, to be sure, would have little patience. For as Rorty observes, one of the main benefits of jettisoning the idea of 'the intrinsic nature of reality' is that it

> helps you reject the suggestion that natural science should serve as a paradigm for the rest of culture, and in particular that philosophical progress consists in philosophers getting more scientific. These latter bad ideas played a part in the genesis of the intellectual tradition now known as 'analytic philosophy'.
>
> (Ibid.: 8)

Some of the fallout of these 'latter bad ideas' may be observed in John Searle's dismissal of what he calls 'the general air of vaguely literary frivolity that pervades the Nietzscheanized Left', a phrase that,

> like his reference (quoted later) to 'the more scientific portions of our civilization', is characteristic of the traditional alliance of analytic philosophy with the natural sciences against the humanities . . . But this apparent weakness [of the humanities] is a product of the mistaken idea that consensus among inquirers . . . is the goal of any responsible intellectual activity.
>
> (Ibid.: 80–1 n.21)

I would like to put an even finer point on Rorty's observation, however – two points, actually. First, the broader context in which Rorty's observation about the unequal split between the 'two cultures' – serious/scientific/objective versus non-serious/literary/subjective – may be understood as fully political is what Smith calls 'the increasingly "production"-centered ethos' of the 'corporate university' (Smith 2006: 122).The growing pressure here is 'to identify intellectual activity and achievement with the production of palpable, visible, measurable and more less imme-diately applicable knowledge' – a view of knowledge whose very paradigm, both in and out of the academy, is, of course, the natural sciences (ibid.: 122).

Much has been written about this topic, but one of the more insightful treat-ments is Gregg Lambert's *Report to the Academy*, which examines the gradual shift, beginning in the 1960s, away from the university's traditional 'critical' function in society and towards a different logic governed by efficiency, 'excellence' (to use a favourite euphemism highlighted by Bill Readings in *The University in Ruins*), the utility of knowledge and social 'relevance'. In this context, Lambert notes, the bal-ance of power has shifted decisively to the sciences. 'Current universities are gradually being re-configured (or re-tooled) by a new set of social objectives', he writes, that are 'more economic in nature' (Lambert 2003: viii).To this shift in the governing models of knowledge in the university we must also add the fact, as Smith notes, that 'the intellectual authority of the natural scientist is rarely in doubt for a general public audience. . . . When authorities clash across the two-culture divide, the benefit of the doubt is likely to be given to the scientist' (Smith 2006: 120–1).

In this broader context (both institutional and social), as Lambert notes, some observations made by Derrida at the very dawn of the Reagan era on the university and the changing forms of knowledge privileged by it are revealed to be more politically pointed than they might seem at first glance. Derrida's remarks, published under the title 'The Principle of Reason: The University in the Eyes of Its Pupils', must be taken, Lambert writes, in an institutional context of 'the rise and the domi-nance of the hard sciences during the post-World War II years and the concentration in the study and invention of new technologies in the university that resulted from direct state or federal sponsorship' (Lambert 2003: 28). In this context – which has only inten-sified, clearly, in the intervening years – 'many humanities' faculties themselves aban-doned an earlier liberal arts agenda and re-cast their knowledge as more scientific in form and methodology in order to compete with the "hard sciences"' (ibid.: 28).

Against this background, Derrida asks, 'what is the *raison d'etre* of the university?' – a question that has never been less rhetorical, it seems, than at present (Derrida 1983: 129). But here, he notes, we find more than one kind of 'reason': there is the reason of 'oriented' research, 'research that is programmed, focused, organized in an authoritarian fashion *in view of its* utilization' (ibid.: 11), and the 'unconditional' reason which 'demands and ought to be granted in principle, besides what is called academic freedom, an *unconditional* freedom to question and to assert . . . all that is required by research, knowledge, and thought concerning the *truth*'. And this is where the university finds its reason for being: 'The university *professes* the truth, and that is its profession' (Derrida 2002: 202).

But then we must ask, what exactly does it mean to *profess*? First of all, when one professes – rather than merely applying a formula of technical or scientific knowledge, a calculation – one professes *faith*: in this case, faith in the freedom of thought, wherever it may lead. Faith, that is to say, in the future or the 'to come' of thought. Or to put it in the more homespun idiom of Rorty – and I call on Rorty here to forestall the predictable objection that Derrida's view of these matters is, if you like, excessively Heideggerian – 'philosophy makes progress not by becoming more rigorous but by becoming more imaginative' (Rorty 1998: 8). 'Philosophical achievements' in his view are 'the ones that let us see everything from a new angle, that induce a Gestalt-switch', and this 'cannot be encouraged by sedulously follow- ing a "method"' (ibid.: 10) or by 'the painstaking carrying-out of research pro- grams' (ibid.: 11). By 'imaginative' here Rorty does not mean merely 'playful' or 'fanciful', however, because for him such an undertaking is a matter of ethical, even social and political, responsibility. 'As I see it', he writes, 'philosophical progress occurs to the extent that we find a way of integrating the worldviews and the moral intuitions we inherited from our ancestors with new scientific theories or new sociopolitical institutions and theories or other novelties' (ibid.: 5–6). This 'imaginative' or forward-looking function of philosophy then enables us to

> drop the question of how to get in touch with 'mind-independent and language-independent reality'. One will replace it with questions like 'What are the limits of our community? Are our encounters sufficiently free and open?' . . . These are political questions rather than metaphysical or epistemological questions.
>
> (Rorty 1991: 13)

Here, however, it is worth remembering a point made by Smith that perhaps receives insufficient emphasis in Rorty's work: that the asymmetries between the humanities and the natural sciences

> are commonly joined and amplified by the more general public partiality toward *traditional* views. That is why terms such as 'fashionable' or 'trendy' do so much work so cheaply. Like political incumbents, intellectual incum- bents have a strong advantage over newcomers, and for many of the same reasons – greater name familiarity, more visible marks of authority, readier access to public platforms, more control over the procedures of institutional certification (degrees, titles, awards) and so on.
>
> (Smith 2006: 122)

In this light, the task of theory is made doubly formidable when the corporate ethos of the university is wedded to the intellectual traditionalism that furthers it, you might say, by other means. It is precisely for these reasons that the humanities must, in Derrida's view, dedicate themselves to the principle of *unconditional* discus- sion, *unconditional* freedom of thought (Derrida 2002: 202, 203), even though this unconditionality is never entirely possible. For Derrida, if that unconditional freedom is the *raison d'etre* of the university (versus, say, technical training and the development of applied knowledge), the humanities are its 'originary and privileged place of *presentation*, of manifestation, of safekeeping' (ibid.: 207). In the context of the humanities so understood, then, theory serves as 'a place of irredentist resistance or even, analogically, as a sort of principle of civil disobedience, even of dissidence in the name of a superior law and a justice of thought' (ibid.: 208).

This last passage helps underscore the fact that what might seem 'apolitical' or 'uncommitted' to some in Derrida's approach to such questions is, in fact, a product of his taking quite seriously his responsibility to the humanities and to the university *as a philosopher* or, if you like, a theorist (leaving aside for the moment how we might want to precisely conjugate those terms). In fact, as he points out in 'The Principle of Reason', many ostensibly more 'committed' forms of 'political thought' in the contemporary university are quite easily recontained as part of its standard operating machinery of *dissensus* – a shopping mall pluralism, if you like, serving a fundamentally neoliberal project of incorporation. Here, we would do well to remember Rajan's contextualization of the changing role of cultural studies – not in terms of the ostensibly political projects it announces and embraces for itself, but in terms of the hegemonic norms of the contemporary university and its disciplinary protocols: a situation in which 'the social is now the unquestioned ground of the humanities', and the humanities refuse to 'claim a way of thinking the social from the outside' (Rajan 2001: 74).

Regarding 'sociology or politology', Derrida writes that 'I would be the last to want to disqualify them. But whatever conceptual apparatus they may have', he continues,

> they never question scientific normativity, beginning with the value of objectivity or objectification, which governs and authorizes their discourse ... These sociologies of the institution remain in this sense internal to the university, intra-institutional, controlled by the deepseated standards, even the programs, of the space that they claim to analyze.
>
> (Derrida 1983: 149)

In this light, to model knowledge in the humanities on the sciences is to remain 'homogeneous with the discourse that dominates the university in the last analysis'. And to use such a project to create an 'objective' basis for politics, no matter how 'revolutionary', as Derrida puts it, is therefore to leave unquestioned 'the most conservative forces of the university' (ibid.: 149). This is not to say that such work is a waste of time; it is simply to say that it is *situated* in multiple ways – conceptually, institutionally and ideologically. And here, it seems to me, theory finds a crucial role at the present moment in asserting itself against the representationalism (to use Rorty's term) that links what at first might look like strange bedfellows: a cultural studies that thinks the social 'as the unquestioned ground of the humanities' (Rajan 2001: 74) and a 'scientific' orientation that grounds the humanities on a 'methodologico-ontological' basis. Moreover, to remember that Derrida pens his critique in the early 1980s, at the dawn of the Reagan era, is to recall those pressures of corporatization and federal divestment (well glossed by Lambert, among others) that will in the years that follow exert increasing pressure on the humanities to justify themselves in terms of a 'relevance' whose ground lay elsewhere, in 'society' or 'nature'.

And it is here that we may bring into sharper focus, an additional context for the political work of 'professing' theory that I mentioned earlier: the context of globalization (or '*mondialisation*', to use the French term Derrida prefers). If the effect of current cultural studies in this context is, according to Rajan, 'to simulate the preservation of civil society after the permutation of the classical public sphere' into an essentially market and consumerist logic of 'representation' (ibid.: 69–70), then the attempt to meet *that* shortcoming by deploying 'scientific' or ontological models of theory (which would, precisely, *not* depend on the continuation of identity politics by other means) runs aground on a different set of problems. In Derrida's view, globalization is driven by (indeed would be impossible without) the kind of 'calculation' of reason that anchors the production-centred ethos of the corporate university: namely, the standardization and commodification of knowledge via information technologies (Derrida 1983: 14). So if (to put it very schematically) in the corporate university, theory-qua-cultural studies serves globalization by helping along the neoliberal project of ideological incorporation, then theory-qua-scientific-research-programme serves globalization not so much by its direct subordination to utility, but rather by extending a picture of what counts as 'real' knowledge – 'realist', 'scientific', 'materialist', 'empiricist' and 'hard' – that underwrites a production-centred ethos. Over and against both, theory as 'unconditional' thought may feel 'soft', frivolous or even risky, but 'to claim to eliminate that risk', Derrida writes, 'by an institutional program is quite simply to erect a barricade against a future' – not *the* future, crucially, but *a* future (Derrida 1983: 18–19). It is to duck theory's challenge to 'define new responsibilities in the face of the university's total subjection to the technologies of informatization' (Derrida 1983: 14).

And it is on this point that we may most clearly distinguish Derrida's view from Rorty's. For Derrida, theory is indeed crucial to democratic society, and to the place of institutions of higher learning within it. But he does not exactly subordinate theory to politics (as in Rorty's declaration of 'the priority of democracy to philosophy'), much less to any specific politics (such as Rorty's liberalism) (Rorty 1991: 175). For Derrida, the commitment to theory as unconditional thought means that 'the university should thus also be the place in which nothing is beyond question, not even the current and determined figure of democracy, not even the traditional idea of critique' (Derrida 2002: 205). But neither does Derrida's view subordinate politics to theory, since theory is always situated within a historical, ideological and institutional conjuncture of the sort we have been tracing here, the sort that enframes the corporate university and its hegemonic forms of disciplinarity. Or – to put it in a shorthand that sharpens his distance from Rorty's liberal pragmatism – for Derrida, it is not possible to talk about the 'unconditional' duty of theory without also talking about the 'conditional' contexts of capitalism, globalization and the corporate university that over-determine theory's role *at this present moment*. And in that light – at that nexus of institutional power, economic pressure and disciplinary hegemony – a final irony of the idea of theory as a research programme is that one might well wonder why the 'science' that it aspires to would ever take it seriously.

Notes

1 See Wolfe (1998), in particular, Chapter 1.
2 See, for example, Wolfe (2003: 78–94).

Bibliography

Deleuze, G. (1990) *Expressionism in Philosophy: Spinoza*, trans. M. Joughin, New York: Zone Books.

Derrida, J. (1983) 'The Principle of Reason: The University in the Eyes of Its Pupils', *Diacritics*, 13.3 (Fall): 3–20.

Derrida, J. (2002) 'The University Without Condition', in J. Derrida, *Without Alibi*, ed., trans. and intro. P. Kamuf, Stanford, CA: Stanford University Press.

Foucault, M. (1984) *The Foucault Reader*, ed. P. Rabinow, New York: Pantheon.

Hansen, M.B.N. (2006) *Bodies in Code: Interfaces with Digital Media*, New York: Routledge.

Jameson, F. (1990) *Postmodernism, or, The Cultural Logic of Late Capitalism*, Durham, NC: Duke University Press.

Knapp, S. and Michaels, W.B. (1985) *Against Theory: Literary Studies and the New Pragmatism*, Chicago: University of Chicago Press.

Lambert, G. (2003) *Report to the Academy*, Aurora, CO: Davies Group Publishers.

Maturana, H. (1991) 'Science and Daily Life: The Ontology of Scientific Explanations', in F. Steier (ed.) *Research and Reflexivity*, London: Sage.

Maturana, H. and Varela, F. (1980) *Autopoiesis and Cognition: The Realization of the Living*, Dordrecht: Reidel.

Protevi, J. (2009) *Political Affect: Connecting the Social and the Somatic*, Minneapolis, MN: University of Minnesota Press.

Rajan, T. (2001) 'In the Wake of Cultural Studies: Globalization, Theory, and the University', *Diacritics*, 31.3: 67–88.

Readings, B. (1997) *The University in Ruins*, Cambridge, MA: Harvard University Press.

Rorty. R. (1991) *Objectivity, Relativism, and Truth: Philosophical Papers, Volume One*, Cambridge: Cambridge University Press.

Rorty. R. (1998) *Philosophical Papers, Volume Three*, Cambridge: Cambridge University Press.

Smith, B.H. (2006) *Scandalous Knowledge: Science, Truth and the Human*, Durham, NC: Duke University Press.

Stafford, B. (2004) 'Romantic Systematics and the Genealogy of Thought: The Formal Roots of a Cognitive History of Images', *Configurations* 12.3 (Fall): 315–48.

Wolfe. C. (1998) *Critical Environments: Postmodern Theory and the Pragmatics of the 'Outside'*, Minneapolis, MN: University of Minnesota Press.

3

THEORY AFTER CRITICAL THEORY

William Rasch

In his justly famous lecture of 1917, 'Science as a Vocation', Max Weber attempts to save the honour of 'science' (*Wissenschaft*), namely sober, coherently and purposively reasoned argument with reference to specific perspectives ('values') by way of which one may marshal, logically or empirically, relevant evidence. In Kantian fashion – the only way available to him that would not require a 'sacrific[e] of intellect' (Weber 2004: 29) – he retains the vitality of reason by limiting its scope. No longer seriously able to consider the cosmos a meaningful whole accessible to human reason or the experimental procedures of natural science, indeed, no longer able to deny that reason and science are the very culprits that have forced into eternal exile all theological and metaphysical assurances of a cosmic order to which the human is essentially linked, we are left, according to Weber, with the challenge of Tolstoy's telling condemnation: 'Science is meaningless because it has no answer to the only questions that matter to us: What should we do? How shall we live?' (ibid. 17). Tolstoy's despair stems from Kant's radical separation of theoretical and practical reason, knowledge and morality, the 'is' and the 'ought'. Weber's response is to throw Kant, or at least the first half of Kant, back in his face. *Wissenschaft* is nothing more – but also, and more importantly, nothing less – than a tool to aid us in our daily round. Modern rationality can provide us with clarity about the alternatives we face, can say that *if* one chooses to pursue this and not that particular end, then these means would most likely be the most efficacious; but can then also point out that these particular consequences – perhaps desirable and perhaps undesirable – would most likely attend one's actions. Modern reason, now 'instrumentalized', as critics say, cannot dictate the choice of ends but can only advise us in the pursuit of deliberatively but a-rationally chosen ends by evaluating the various means available. After Europe's great experimentation with – one is tempted to say – 'monotheistic' reason, born of Plato's attempt to leave the cave of illusory shadows, we have returned to the world of myth in which, famously, the 'numerous gods of yore, divested of their magic and hence assuming the shape of impersonal forces, arise from their graves, strive for power over our lives, and resume their eternal struggle among themselves' (ibid. 24). We are left with the 'incompatibility of ultimate possible attitudes', the 'inability ever to resolve the conflicts between them' and thus the 'necessity of deciding between them' (ibid. 27).

Tolstoy would not have been pleased. Neither have been a century of hand-wringers since. Weber's 'reduction' of reason to a mere advisory capacity was of course not new. In the wake of Idealism's (Fichte, Schelling, Hegel) apparent failure to reconcile Kant's stubborn dualisms, in the wake of Marx's diagnosis that the illness of dualism had material, social causes, and in the wake of Nietzsche's more radical critique of the pretensions of *Wissenschaft* and the will to truth that lay behind it, Weber's novum was not to declare that imperial reason had no clothes, but that it never again would have, because, lamentation aside, the social-structural reasons for the modern predicament were incorrigible. Even the overcoming of 'capitalism', could it ever be achieved, would not, despite fervent desire, necessarily alter the fundamental form of modern society – which is not to say that with capitalism we have reached the end of history, but only that capitalism is not the Antichrist making his appearance on the eve of the *parousia*. The famed 'rationalization' of society with its resultant 'disenchantment' of the world and 'polytheism' of incommensurable 'value spheres' (which have found subsequent cousins german in 'language games', 'social systems', etc.) remain with us today, no matter the industry of discontent that is contemporary critical thought. That discontent usually goes under the name of 'nihilism', an epithet that originally emerged at the end of the eighteenth century to describe what was perceived by some as both the instrumental-rationalist, deterministic fatalism of modern philosophy and the overweening pride directing human self-assurance, and has since become the favoured term for all that ails us. The charge's two-pronged attack aims at, on the one hand, the polytheism or relativism of 'values' with its resultant loss of (metaphysical) truth and (moral) meaning and, on the other hand, the radical subjectivity (and therefore, again, relativism) of decision, which is to say, ungrounded, 'irrational' human assertion. Depending on whom one reads one can trace fascism, communism, liberalism, godless secular humanism, slippery-slope-anything-goes-ism and a host of other terrors to these roots. Conversely, if one's gaze were removed from the Nothingness that is feared, one might see in Weber's warring gods the condition of possibility of the world as we have it; and the world as we have it is a world that gives us the means to navigate the uncharted waters we find ourselves on as well as to voice our concern and discontent. This is not to say that we must complacently accept all we suffer – discontent, after all, is undeniably not only the ineluctable by-product of critique but also its cause – but is to say that our very critique, our very ability to observe from a distance the world we inhabit is made possible by, not in spite of, the jealousy of Weber's warring gods. It is only because they quarrel that we can. The shadows on Plato's cave are all we have. Our task is not to escape but to read better the patterns these shadows make to improve our navigational skills and for the pleasure such 'reading' gives us. We will find that the light that is the source of those shadows is the light of our own eyes.

What I would like to do, then, is to sketch, in bare outline, some of the consequences for social theory of our fall from monotheistic grace. I propose to view this 'fall' as a lateral shift from ontological realism to perspectivism, one that parallels the shift from pre-modern, stratified to modern, functionally differentiated society. My guide will be Niklas Luhmann. I presuppose no prior knowledge of Luhmann's thought, but neither do I intend to go into it in any great detail. The aim of this essay is to suggest possibilities and wonder about the task of social theory.

Using the skills but cutting against the grain of their analytic training, philosophers Steven D. Hales and Rex Welshon have made a rigorous case for treating Nietzsche's famous perspectivism as a serious and consistent philosophical position. Their claim is *not* that Nietzsche championed a mere epistemological or linguistic perspectivism, which, they write, 'is nothing more than the claim that human languages or concepts carve the world up according to human interests or that knowledge is no more than the successful imposition of concepts on segments of reality' (Hales and Welshon 2000: 76); rather, they assert that Nietzsche's is a perspectivism across the board, encompassing truth-claims, logic, causality, epistemology, consciousness and the self. This pervasive perspectivism is of necessity, then, ontological. Nietzsche, they claim, posited that the world 'is perspectivist all the way down' to the 'most fundamental levels of ontology', that 'there are no things except those composed entirely of quanta of power that have perspectives' and are relational and that '[s]ince each quantum of will to power is a perspective and perspectives are loci of interpretation, there exists nothing but loci of interpretation, and hence it is not possible that there be an interpretation-independent world' (ibid. 77, 202). That is, our knowledge of the world is perspectival not because of the limits of knowledge on the basis of our finitude but because 'there are no facts in the world to which ideas and propositions could possibly correspond, even if, counterfactually, epistemic capacities were not perspectival' (ibid. 202).

A similar claim can be made for Niklas Luhmann's social theory, namely that it is pervasively pespectival in a Nietzschean sense; that his perspectivism is not merely epistemological – that is, not only tied to the question of what we can know or what we can say – but rather, and contrary to his explicit protestations, thoroughly ontological; and finally that this perspectivist ontology is itself only a perspective, namely the perspective of something commonly referred to as modernity. In place of 'quanta of power', posited by Nietzsche (in Hales' and Welshon's account), Luhmann posits, as it were, 'quanta' of observation, composed of operative distinctions that construct the visible world about which we communicate. These constructs, these 'observables', are by their very nature partial worlds in competition with the partial worlds that other observations, using other distinctions, create. These perspectives are not perspectives on a pre-given world, but are the world. In short, a case can be made that Luhmann developed the possibility of a consistent perspectivist ontology of modernity, even if he was not always consistent in his own articulations. The phrase 'perspectivist ontology of modernity' may strike us as oxymoronic in more than one way. Even if one could be convinced that a coherent perspectivism is a possibility, either epistemologically or ontologically, and not self-refuting, one might, nevertheless, stumble over the notion that ontology can be subject to historical periodization. I cannot thoroughly demonstrate the claim I make here, only hope to make it plausible and outline some of the consequences such a view entails for social theory.

Semantics and social structure

There is no denying that we live in a world in which plural perspectives are available, each vying for our attention, none commanding it exclusively. Luhmann explains this pluralism as a consequence of functional differentiation, the non-hierarchical ordering of social systems that serve as the necessary points of reference for our actions and communication. Rather than bemoan the lack of transparency, the lack of a single, unifying perspective from which all could be surveyed, Luhmann sees in functional differentiation the condition of possibility for something he calls second order observation or the observation of observation (Luhmann 1997: 1123–24). Modernity, in other words, is defined structurally by its form of differentiation ('functional') and discursively or 'ideologically' by a peculiar notion of observation, to which we will turn later. First we need to understand how functional differentiation might serve as the condition of possibility of a 'modern', perspectival ontology.

To ease us into this understanding, I cite the following opening gambit of an essay devoted to the idea of modernity:

> I would like to start my analysis of the modernity of modern society by making a distinction between social structure and semantics. My preference for such a beginning, a preference that cannot be justified at the outset, is based on a confusing characteristic of this distinction, namely that it includes itself. It is itself a semantic distinction, just as the distinction between operation and observation, from which it comes, is itself a distinction made by an observer. I must leave it with the simple statement that this logical form is the foundation of productive analyses that can resolve their own paradoxes. In addition, this point of departure already contains at its core the entire theory of modernity.
>
> (Luhmann 1998: 1)

I wish to highlight three features of this passage. First, Luhmann showcases the contingency of beginnings. His is not the geometric method. There are no axioms from which an argument is built, no *ur*-distinction from which others could be deduced. Instead, we are given a distinction that broadcasts itself as one of many that could have been chosen. Indeed, in his career, Luhmann has more often than not opted for the system/environment couplet to begin his tale of modern systems theory; but here he relies on a more conventionally sociological terminology.

Admittedly, 'semantics' seems an odd choice (it refers to the mammoth project headed by Reinhard Koselleck to chart the 'semantic' changes of traditional concepts in or around the eighteenth century [Brunner *et al.* 1972–1997]), but we recognize the rose of 'superstructure' in this other name. Arguably, relating the content of our discursive self-understanding to shifts in social structure is a fundamental sociological task, at least within the sociology of knowledge. Though Luhmann evades the issue of linear or dialectical causality by assuming the correlation of evolutionary development on both the semantic and structural levels, his 'point of departure', and this is the second point, will lead us to an account of the relationship of structural change and narratives of self-description. Finally, Luhmann's real point of departure is not this particular, contingently chosen distinction, but the form of the distinction itself. It is self-referential– a semantic distinction between semantics and structure – and thus potentially paradoxical. Herein lies 'the entire theory of modernity'. Since, for Luhmann, the basic element of society is communication (not actions and not persons to whom actions can be attributed), any description (any communicated observation) of modern society will share the same feature; it will be a social description of society, a modern description of modernity, a communicated description of communication and thus a description of what it is a part – a partial description. Luhmann's narrative of modernity, then, must also partake of this form of distinction.

Differentiation is a venerable sociological/anthropological notion that describes the form social organization takes at any one time or place. Luhmann focuses primarily on two forms of differentiation in his descriptions of the European tradition and the emergence of the modern world: stratification and functional differentiation. In depicting modernity as distinct from what came before, Luhmann contrasts modern functional differentiation of autonomous social systems (e.g. law, politics, education, economy, religion, art, etc.) with social stratification, Marx's famous 'feudal' society. Luhmann's is not a teleological tale of historical progress, but one would be extremely hard pressed to find a hint of nostalgia for a by-gone era in his writings, nor does he look to the future as if its outlines could be even faintly discerned. He starts from the assumption that functionally differentiated social systems exist, labels the society thus organized as modern, and uses 'modernity' as one side, the side he occupies, of the basic distinction with which he operates. Stratification serves as the other side of the distinguishing mark from functional differentiation. As of yet, there is no *other* other side. There is no postmodernity that one could contrast with modernity (Luhmann 1997: 1143–9; Luhmann 2000).

The condensed historical narratives that Luhmann produces to characterize a given period's social structure and correlated self-description can, at their best, be a delight to read because of their nonchalant demystifications of cherished traditions, though experts who work in the specialized areas he breezes through are seldom charmed. Luhmann's flyover account of pre-modern, stratified Europe goes something like this: stratified (Greco-Roman-Christian) society is defined by naturalized hierarchies and, therefore, develops a realist ontology to serve as its self-description. The unity and order of society as a function of the unity and order of the world is presumed. Belief in the eternal verities, guaranteed by reason or revelation, requires a society in which privileged centres – Luhmann habitually refers to aristocratic courts and urban centres – become the nodes of decision that are able to distinguish true from false descriptions of the cosmos. And for its part, a stratified society requires a metaphysical notion of cosmic order to serve as its source of legitimacy. Hierarchies can be non-arbitrary only in a non-arbitrarily ordered universe. One might invoke here Horkheimer's and Adorno's famous image of Odysseus surveying the campfires of his loyal and subordinate shepherds from his castle walls (Horkheimer and Adorno 1972: 14). It is as if this noble land-lord saw in the visual pattern of the campfires a reflection of the divine order of the spheres in the night-time sky. The ontological distinction that protects this order, according to Luhmann, contrasts being with nonbeing, using logic, with the law of the excluded middle as its weapon of choice, to serve as the gatekeeper that regulates traffic between meaningful statements on the one side, which can be either true or false, and nonsense or meaningless statements on the other side. The role of description, then, is simply to distinguish between the true and the false and, in its most stringent form, compile the finite set of true statements about the world. There are, after all, only so many campfires, and one can calculate the distances between their respective flames. By definition, then, true statements are non-perspectival, because the true perspective, 'structurally' located on the castle wall, is 'semantically' ordained as the view from nowhere.

With modern functional differentiation – 'caused' by a variety of factors that are bundled together under an ever-evolving sense of evolution – the 'rationality con-tinuum' (Luhmann 1998: 23–9) is broken and the view of the social and the cosmic world becomes a good deal more complicated. If, as Luhmann asserts, the primary distinction for pre-modern, stratified society was the one between being and non-being, then for functionally differentiated modernity this distinction becomes a relic of tradition and observation takes centre stage, with the crucial distinction now between observer and observed (Luhmann 1997: 902). To be sure, observation was of importance for pre-modern self-description, but it was secondary. In the terms we have been using we would have to say that both being itself and the observations of being were subject to observation; but the aim was control, the mode of operation was representational, and observation seemed to be executed from a position outside the distinction itself. The task was to match description with what was being described to check for accuracy. With modernity, however, observation is all we have. There is nothing to compare except observations and no single observation can serve as the standard for all the others. We must remember that there is nothing ocular in Luhmann's notion of observation except the meta-phor. It is an operation in which distinctions are manipulated to make aspects of a world appear. The distinction observer/observed is already the result of observa-tion and becomes the tool for further observations. To go back to Luhmann's 'point of departure', the distinction semantics/social structure entails a series of related observations that we can participate in by observing. For instance, we can focus our attention on social structures – institutions, say – and thereby 'construct,' through statistical methods of empirical research or participant–observer ethnographic studies, the reality of modern society. We may notice that others construct different social realities – by observing systems, say, or networks, instead of institutions or kinship structures – and we can move from one to the other without necessarily making judgements of correctness. We could attempt to correlate those who make differing claims about the nature of society with various segments of the society from which they come and even this we could do in differing ways. Some may invoke 'identities', such as those putatively provided by class, race and gender. Others may invoke 'systems' and their theorized codes of operation or 'networks' and their 'flows'. In noting these differences we do not necessarily judge them to be inherently correct and mistaken versions of reality, even when we beg to differ with specific methodologies or analyses. And, were we to pay attention to what we were doing, were we to observe ourselves observing, we might now also notice that our attention has strayed from 'social structure' and drifted to 'semantics', that is, from the social order to its various descriptions. In doing so, we have landed in the realm of what Luhmann refers to as second order observation.

There are no clear borders between first order and second order observation. Observation is observation; it operates the same no matter what world it cracks open. However, once we observe that descriptions differ because of differing operative distinctions that serve as different systemic references, and decide that no system and thus no code of operation has hierarchical priority over the others – no religious or moral supervision, no totalitarian political surveillance, no ultimate economic control, not even under capitalism – then we might want to say that the horizontal differentiation of function systems (whether we like it or not) brings with it a functioning relativism of values or value-spheres (Weber) or, with Nietzsche, unavoidable plurality of perspectives. If we do not hark back to tradition and wish to clamp down on this plurality of standards of right and wrong and declare the world to be in the grips of nihilism, then we are faced with the task of trying to account for the way the world appears to us now.

This has been a rather breathless race through some of the basic features of the Luhmannian landscape. We should take a few snapshots of some of the central points.

As an operation, all observation (all production of descriptions by way of distinctions) is blind to itself. One may use Wittgenstein's image of the eye that remains outside (behind, so to speak) the field of vision it opens up (Wittgenstein 1981: §5.633–5.6331). This eye can be observed by another, which of course also operates blind. There is no self-seeing eye that can view all eyes, including itself, and thereby produce a complete single-perspective portrait of society or the cosmos. Instead, what emerges is a kind of multi-perspectival cubist painting that itself must be in competition with other such visual depictions. To paste them together in some kind of postcard panorama would still not give us a 'world picture' according to classical outlines.

This network of blindness and insight correlates with a social form of organization that similarly lacks a central command post – no universal church that would provide an all-seeing god in whom we could see our order perfectly reflected.

Social systems function like observers, blind to the impossible unity of its own operations. Weber already gave examples in 1917. The legal system, for one, views the world through a lens ground by the legal/illegal distinction. Whatever comes up before the law must be judged either legal or illegal. The one judgment the law cannot make is whether the law itself is legal. For the law not to stumble over this blind spot – one clearly visible to others – the system engages in a type of self-reflection that produces legal theory. We have natural law theories that seek the ground for its operation in god, reason or (divinely or rationally ordered) nature. We have positive law theories that see in the state, in historically sanctioned procedures, or in transcendental presuppositions the legitimacy that is sought for. However, all this comes from the outside (as a kind of Derridean supplement, as Luhmann was fond of saying) and can be seen from the outside as necessary fig leaves covering nakedness. *This*, the legal/illegal distinction itself cannot see.

Experimental and critical theory

Niklas Luhmann started his (belated) academic career with a debate with Jürgen Habermas and his running argument with the Frankfurt school and all forms of critical theory continued until the end. This acrimonious passage, devoid of his usual irony and cool wit, will give a taste.

> First, it is simply necessary to contest that they [the Frankfurt School] represent the philosophical discourse of modernity at all. This contestation does not rely on the absurd thesis of a postmodern age . . . What has to be concluded appears instead to be a transitional semantics that had to leave behind the old world of aristocratic societies but could not yet observe and describe modern society; rather, out of this inability, it had to create a project of the future. I mean the semantics of the Enlightenment, the ideas of the French Revolution, as well as the technical-economic optimism of progress of the nineteenth century. This transitory semantics is obviously exhausted . . . The distinction, above all, between affirmative and critical, a distinction so beloved in Frankfurt, misses the connection to what offers itself to observation . . . for it excludes the possibility that what has become realized as society gives cause for the worst fears, but cannot be rejected . . . Finally, one will be allowed to inquire as to the foundations of the emphasis that, if no longer subject-theoretical, is at least humanist. Apparently one requires this engagement in order to make normative claims plausible. The theory sides with the human to join the latter in battle against enemy forces . . . . These are very rough arguments whose details certainly need fine-tuning. But a rough survey of the possible positions suffices if one is interested in the question of whether, and how, modern society at the end of this century can achieve a representation of itself in itself (where else?). And, all things considered, my verdict is: not in Frankfurt.
>
> (Luhmann 2002: 192–3)

Now, one could go through this passage with the fine comb of ideology critique and come up with familiar ticks – the dismissal of the 'ideas of the French Revolution' being the fattest – the taxonomy of which would be 'Counter-Enlightenment'. Luhmann responds by rejecting the notion of ideology altogether, for though the world may give rise to our 'worst fears', there need be neither ideological affirmation nor heroic rejection. There is observation and, by way of observation, involvement. We recognize in this rejection of critique the linkage Luhmann makes between what he habitually calls Old European semantics – here marked as aristocratic – and the putatively progressive semantics coming out of the Enlightenment. Critical theory, on this view, is simply not a *theory* of modernity, but a symptom of a transition stage, an attempt to deal with a changed world in a language not yet adapted to the change. The distinctions it uses, its reliance on classically metaphysical assumptions and its infinite, temporal deferral of impossibly utopian demands all mark critical theory as inadequate to the modernity it claims to describe.

We do not have to agree that his assessment does justice to a rich tradition that has had an enormous impact on the modernity it putatively cannot understand. This impact can be, and has been, evaluated in various diverging ways and it need not be our concern to add more varieties to the pile. However, the key not only to understand Luhmann but also to make use of his analysis is the term 'normative'. Normative discourse, directly or indirectly, deals with values – justice, human dignity, sanctity of life and what have you. It is with such virtues that first order observation operates (Luhmann 1997: 1123). Keeping one's nose close to the grindstone, the first-order observer champions various values in competition with others. We do not want fascism, military dictatorship, oligarchy, we want democracy, more democracy, radical democracy, liberal democracy, deliberative democracy, participatory democracy and we will fight to get what we want. Then, having achieved what we have fought for, we find the goal elusively gliding away from us. The various values do not cohere, the diverse 'hegemonized' interests break apart and re-articulate unmet demands, and norms once harmoniously united now 'tragically' conflict. We come up again face to face with Weber's warring gods. We must choose and on choosing we stumble into the land of unintended consequences, while the hunt for the resolution of newly resurrected problems continues. Put another way: social order justifies itself by explicitly articulated and, more often than not, implicitly assumed norms. If flexibly defined, these norms can remain relatively uncontested. Again, we all want peace, freedom, social justice; we all hate war, poverty and cruelty. Yet, in the name of those norms, we also find ourselves supporting war to achieve justice, tolerating poverty in the name of liberty or abridging liberty to eliminate poverty. The norms themselves are seldom directly challenged, but nevertheless silently denied when choices must be made between them. Do security and civil peace trump the liberal rights that are guaranteed to the individual? Are there states of emergency in which it is right to suspend basic rights? Does one argue against torture because it is ineffective or impermissible? If the latter, is no price too high to uphold the prohibition? Such disputes may be contingently resolved, remain principally open, and then erupt again as new circumstances dictate. At this level of argumentation, norms – values – are the points of departure and reference; and the disputes can intensify to life and death struggles. And it is precisely on this level that Luhmann locates critical theory (ibid. 1115–16). With reference to (at times vaguely defined) norms – to name a few more: solidarity, consensus, tolerance, emancipation, absence of coercion or authoritarian rule – the critic offers a double description of society, a description of existing social order as the negative picture of the order that should come into being if only the obstacles were recognized correctly and proper measures to remove them were taken. When, however, the populace remains unmoved by the theorist's arguments – when they are perceived to side with the enemies of progress and against their own interests – then, Luhmann writes, critical theory sets as its task the ideological-critical examination of ignorance and obstinacy. What are questioned are not the norms and not the picture of society these norms paint, but the false consciousness of individuals and the groups to which they belong. Accordingly, in the mode of perpetual crisis, the demand is raised: more critique, more education, more enlightenment.

I make no plea for the accuracy of Luhmann's Nietzschean enlightenment of enlightenment in all its details. Nor has it escaped me that the reader might be justified in rehearsing variations of the performative paradox or *tu quoque* charge. Luhmann too, it seems, offers a description of modernity and then explains why critical theorists resist the allure – reliance on an outdated, transitory semantics, for example. Yet, I do not find these perceived contradictions debilitating, otherwise, I would not have got this far in my argument. Therefore, I wish to hang onto two of his central insights to formulate a possible relationship between what I will call Luhmann's experimental mode of pitching theory and traditionally normative critical theory (of not just the Frankfurt variety). First, critical theory is unabashedly normative and thus, in Luhmann's terms, operates as first order observation. No matter how reflectively or philosophically sophisticated, it is never far from the battlefield. Indeed, engagement (however intricately mediated) is its self-described virtue and the fact that the barricades have become by and large virtual does not alter the ethos. Secondly, I posit that it makes sense to accept the structural features of the modern world as they are (perceived to be by Luhmann) and not as correctable aberrations. To accept them is not to celebrate but to study them. Accordingly, if one assumes that what we call modernity represents a fundamental structural shift in the way society is organized, accompanied by a change in the way we attempt to make 'semantic' sense of the world in which we find ourselves, a perceptual shift, so to speak, that views the cosmos in a similarly differentiated – perspectivist – manner, then one ought also to differentiate among the various functions of theoretical reflection itself. One need not, in other words, operate exclusively morally-politically by way of the traditional affirmative/critical distinction (in all its many versions) or exclusively experimentally. Each mode may have its place and time.

At the risk of further prejudicing the reader against what I propose, let me introduce a figure adapted from the work of Leo Strauss. I have little sympathy with Strauss's political philosophy – his archaic insistence that only revelation or natural reason could be a viable basis for society, his nihilism-mongering, his eso-teric/exoteric distinction or his contempt for the non-philosopher – but his depic-tion of the relationship of philosophy to law might give us a useful model for understanding the functions of the two types of theorizing I propose. For Strauss, law is the condition of possibility for the philosopher. For a society guided by revealed religion, the law, founded by the prophet, is the truth; for a secular society guided by a belief in the sufficiency of natural reason, the law, founded by the legislator, is a project. Thus the task of the philosopher is different within the two social orders. According to Strauss, this difference is best understood as Hermann Cohen's posited

> opposition between Platonic (Socratic) and Aristotelian philosophizing as the opposition between the primacy of inquiry about the good, about the right life, about the true state, and the primacy of interest in the contem-plation of that which is and in knowledge of being.
>
> (Strauss 1995: 130)

Released from searching for the truth by the prophet, who has given to them 'the binding and absolutely perfect regimen of human life,' medieval Jewish and Arab philosophers 'stand in fact under the law' and 'no longer need, like Plato, to seek the law, the state, to inquire into it . . . Hence they are, as authorized by the law, free to philosophize in Aristotelian fashion: they can therefore aristotelize' (ibid. 132–33). The philosopher, whose activity is founded on the law given solely by the lawmaker who is guided exclusively by natural reason, is, on the other hand, obli-gated to address the law directly. Counter-intuitively, under revealed religion, the philosopher, who owes his existence to the law that he obeys as the truth, is free to speculate unfettered by moral concerns. The philosopher in secular society, whose existence is also legitimated by the law, is obligated to investigate the nature of the law because of the law's inherent imperfection, understood as incompletion. According to Cohen's and Strauss's typology, the religious philosopher may aristo-telize (contemplate the nature of being) that the rational one must platonize (engage in moral-political analyses). By analogy, then, according to the typology I have suggested, the former is free to 'luhmannize', the latter to critique.

Now, according to Strauss, these two opposed social orders cannot or should not co-exist. Each claims access to absolute truth. Belief in the revealed truth of a transcendent, omnipotent and omniscient god is based on faith and requires obedi-ence. The prophets establish the possibility of the law and it is to the prophets that revelation points for evidence of the existence of the transcendent origin of the truth. Reason replies that the human being needs only to obey its own powers and the evidence of clear and rational demonstration to know the truth. Strauss, however, cannot abide an impasse. He requires a resolution of the argument, one or the other of the two contestants must acknowledge defeat and leave the field of combat to the undisputed victor. Either reason must irrefutably refute revelation – something, he claims, that the Bible criticism of modern rationality, beginning with Spinoza, has failed to do – or revelation must produce clear and irrefutable evidence of the incapacity of reason to understand the transcendent ground of truth and obedience – something, again according to Strauss, that uncorrupted Greek reason, if we could only understand it correctly, makes impossible. To a third party who wishes to choose between the two, revelation can only obey its own truth, but cannot produce irrefutable evidence that its obedience is to a transcendent command. Reason, in turn, cannot demonstrate by way of reason that the truth it produces is the truth. Thus neither can display its own necessity. The issue for Strauss is of the utmost importance, for if neither claim can succeed beyond doubt, we fall back into 'myth', into the 'polytheism' Weber described, into modern 'nihilism'.

It is on this hook of 'myth' that we now hang our hats. Neither mode of theorizing compels, yet each remains available. The 'religious' mode of philosophizing assumes the world is as it is and, therefore, allows speculation freed from the moral imperative to affirm or contest social norms – that is, freed from fixating on norms as the only 'object' of inquiry. Yet, seeing the modern, non-revealed and a-rational world as it is has become a far more difficult task. A radically perspectival natural and social world without central focus is hard, if not impossible, to visualize, much like nineteenth-century non-Euclidean geometries and early twentieth-century physics. What mathematics shows us is not for the eye to see. We require new tools, or new uses of old ones. During the last decade of his life, Luhmann began all his theoretical experiments where others only found dead ends, namely with the figure of logical paradox. Within philosophy, paradoxes have conventionally been seen as markers for conceptual confusions that can, in principle, be clarified. For Luhmann, however, paradoxes are the productive origins of social systems, whose communicative operations and self-description are charged with unfolding, by covering up, their own impossible beginnings. To recall the example of the legal system mentioned before, the logical inability to apply the legal/illegal distinction to itself leads to the variety of ways with which legal scholars justify the legitimacy of the law. Observing how social, discursive paradoxes appear (as 'crises') and then are made to disappear, asking of their functions, tracing their diverse historical paths and examining the ways all this can be described as belonging to something we find meaningful to call 'modern' becomes the way observational, experimental theory does its business.

If 'aristotelian' contemplation becomes experimental observation, critique dons the 'Platonizing' mantle of moral scrutiny. The 'rational', critical mode of theorizing, observing a flawed but perfectible world, demands moral-political commitment. Working in a necessarily partisan manner, it recognizes that the world is as it is and sets as its task the project of making the world different – better – than it is. The link between 'experimentation' and critique exists in the fact of the norm. Norms are the devices that are used to hide impossibilities and posit foundations. To 'luhmannize' is to observe how norms function, how the conflicts of norms are resolved and then re-ignite, and how those who fight the good fight describe their battles. To critique is to fight the good fight.

Would it be too much to ask that each mode of observing the social world also observe each other in the spirit of curiosity without mutual recrimination? Perhaps! However, because neither of the two options can irrefutably refute the other, each continues to exist. I say we take advantage of their co-existence.

Bibliography

Brunner, O., Conze, W. and Koselleck, R. (Eds.) (1972–1997) *Geschichtliche Grundbegriffe: Historisches Lexikon zur politisch-sozialenSprache in Deutschland*, 8 vols, Stuttgart: Klett-Cotta.

Hales, S.D. and Welshon, R. (2000) *Nietzsche's Perspectivism*, Urbana, IL: University of Illinois Press.

Horkheimer, M. and Adorno, T.W. (1972) *Dialectic of Enlightenment*, trans. E. B. Ashton, New York: Seabury.

Luhmann, N. (1997) *Die Gesellschaft der Gesellschaft*, Frankfurt: Suhrkamp.

Luhmann, N. (1998) *Observations on Modernity*, trans. William Whobrey, Stanford, CA: Stanford University Press.

Luhmann, N. (2000) 'Why Does Society Describe Itself as Postmodern?', in W. Rasch and C. Wolfe (eds) *Observing Complexity: Systems Theory and Postmodernity*, Minneapolis, MN: University of Minnesota Press. 35–50.

Luhmann, N. (2002) *Theories of Distinction: Redescribing the Descriptions of Modernity*, trans. E. Schreiber, K. Behnke and J. O'Neil, ed. W. Rasch, Stanford, CA: Stanford University Press.

Strauss, L. (1995) *Philosophy and Law: Contributions to the Understanding of Maimonides and His Predecessors*, trans. Eve Adler, Albany, NY: State University of New York Press.

Weber, M. (2004) *The Vocation Lectures*, trans. R. Livingstone, ed. D. Owen and T.B. Strong, Indianapolis, IN: Hackett.

Wittgenstein, L. (1981) *Tractatus Logico-Philosophicus*, trans. C.K. Ogden, London: Routledge and Kegan Paul.

4

EXTINCT THEORY

Claire Colebrook

Of the Earth, the present subject of our scenarios, we can presuppose a single thing: it doesn't care about the questions we ask about it. What we call a catastrophe will be, for it, a contingency. Microbes will survive, as well as insects, whatever we let loose. In other words, it is only because of the global ecological transformations we can provoke, which are potentially capable of putting in question the regimes of terrestrial existence we depend on, that we can invoke the Earth as having been put in play by our histories. From the viewpoint of the long history of the Earth itself, this will be one more 'contingent event' in a long series.

(Stengers 2000: 144)

To the shame of philosophy, it is not uncommonly alleged of such theory that whatever may be correct in it is in fact invalid in practice. We usually hear this said in an arrogant, disdainful tone, which comes of presuming to use experience to reform reason itself in the very attributes which do it most credit. Such illusory wisdom imagines it can see further and more clearly with its mole-like gaze fixed on experience than with the eyes which were bestowed on a being designed to stand upright to scan the heavens.

(Kant 1991: 62–63)

If we were serious about considering what theory *after* theory might mean, then perhaps we should push this notion to its limit: not simply theory after the 1980s indulgence or heyday of high theory – those days when we could afford to think of texts as such with (some say) little concern for real political conditions – and not simply theory today when no one could be said to be anti-theory – both because theory has been thoroughly assimilated, and because what is left remains a toothless tiger, legitimating all sorts of positivisms and moralisms. (Evidence for assimilation is everywhere: no monograph in literary studies appears without some cursory footnote to a theoretical concept; no undergraduate education proceeds without some basic overview of 'feminism', 'post-colonialism' and 'post-structuralism'; and no graduate student would be advised to avoid theory altogether.) More often than not, being 'after theory' signals nothing more than that one is aware of some textual mediating condition – there is no sex in itself, race in itself, history in itself. This contemporary theoretical astuteness, consisting of acknowledging the provisional status of one's position, then allows for local attention to minute particulars without any consideration of the problems, possibilities and impossibilities of reading as such. The new historicism that supposedly emerged after theory allows for a mode of positivism justified by an avoidance of grand narratives (Gallagher and Greenblatt 2001: 6). Other modes of theory – queer theory, race studies, gender studies, disability studies, digital media studies – seem to be theoretical not so much by a distinct mode of reading but because of a choice of a marginal object. If anything, 'theory' as it is now practised – with its emphasis on the lived, bodies, multitudes, emotions, affects, the political, the ethical turn – is indeed *practised*; it avoids the problem of theory – what we can say there is, or the limits of existence – by grounding itself in what one ought to do.

Theory, if it is *critical* in the Kantian sense, would need to begin from Kant's distinction between theoretical knowledge, concerning objects about which we can speak because they are given *to us*, and practice, which follows from the absence of knowledge about ourselves. Lacking anything objective or experienced that might give us a moral law we are left without foundation; that is, practical. Theory follows from being exposed to a world that is *not* ourselves; theoretical knowledge is directed to something that is only given mediately. Theory is at once necessary and impossible, just as its 'relation' to practice is necessary and impossible. Theory, or distance from the real, is necessary: 'we' are faced with an existing world that, precisely because it *exists*, is not ourselves; without that 'outside' world there could be no inner subject, no 'we', no agent of practice. But this existing world to which we are definitively bound is therefore impossible: the given world is given *to* us, never known absolutely. To avoid theory and pass directly to practice would require forgetting that the self of practice is only a self insofar as it is placed in a position of necessary not-knowing. Recent forms of Kantianism that conclude from this separation that there is an inevitable ideal of humanity and human normativity (Korsgaard 2009; Korsgaard and Cohen 1996) focus all too easily on the practical side of reasoning – whereby the absence of knowledge forces us to be self-governing – and forget too happily the theoretical problem. This self that gives the law to itself is necessarily exposed to a domain which it must theorise but can never grasp as such. There would be two senses in which theory would fail. The first sense of failure is necessary and critical: one must at one and the same time be placed in relation to an existence that is never given as such, and it is this world of necessarily given but distanced existence within which we act. (In an era of encroaching extinction this failing theoretical condition becomes a forceful practical problem precisely because we are obliged, practically, to think not only about the unknowable but also the unimaginable. The world we inhabit is becoming increasingly impossible to know and imagine.) The second sense in which theory fails occurs with its seeming triumph; here, theory feels no qualms about the limits of imagination. Indeed, theory *as* imagination allows 'us' to affirm humanity, the lived, meaning, community, the future and life – precisely when the incoherence of these terms should block any easy praxis.

Symptomatic of this failure of theory is theory's complete success, and this can be gauged by considering what is now no longer possible: anti-theory. In 1982, Stephen Knapp and Walter Benn Michaels published 'Against Theory' in *Critical Inquiry,* and posed the following thought experiment. Imagine encountering the marks 'a slumber did my spirit steal' drawn in the sand on the beach; the marks appear to be drawn but then a subsequent wave flows and recedes and leaves the rest of Wordsworth's poem. This, the authors argue, at first seems to present intention-less meaning, but this is not so. Once we *read* we attribute intention; any of those supposedly detached, non-referential objects of theory – texts without context, readers or authors – are proven (supposedly) to be impossible. Michaels felt that this point still had relevance in 2001 in his 'The Shape of the Signifier' which was, again symptomatically, an appeal to *the political.* Reading and texts go together to yield intentions and contexts; there are not just signs as such, mere markers of ostensive identity, but historically sedimented and meaningful intentions. In a recent review in *The London Review of Books,* Michaels insists again that identity itself cannot bear significance, for 'class' is always a marker of social and economic groupings which, in turn, presuppose some understanding of a common humanity that is unfairly differentiated (Michaels 2009). Whereas Knapp and Michaels could articulate this insistence on the necessarily contextual and political production of meaning as an argument 'against' theory, Michaels's position is now exemplary of what counts *as theory.* That is, theory is just this attention to the human, intentional and interested ground of the emergence of texts. This is what theory is and ought to be. What was once anti-theory – a reaction against the detachment of texts from any supposition of humanity or meaning – is now so mainstream that the same argument can be rehearsed and become central to a defence of theory 'after theory'.

Theory 'today' is not an acceptance that we do not know the political or the practical and that what we are given as objects of theory are inhuman – despite all our projections and imaginations to the contrary. Even so, theory, I would argue, can be considered rigorously only with something like an extinction hypothesis. Let us not fall too readily into assuming the human, assuming its intentional presence behind texts, its continuing readability of itself in the context of texts *and* its reflexive mode of judgement whereby it sees marks drawn in the sand and immediately recognizes its own presence.

Theory *after* theory might take a more robust form whereby we consider what it might be to think in the absence of theoria. What would be left without the distanced gaze the thinking human animal directs towards the world? This absence of the look or point of view of theory could take two forms, one of which (I would suggest) is dominant in whatever remains of theory today, and another that represses theory. The first mode was articulated by Hannah Arendt in *The Promise of Politics*. Politics – being in common, speaking in common, living as a multitude – has always been repressed, since Plato at least, by the ideal of *bios theoritikos* (Arendt 2005: 85). The contempt for labour and for the multitude has meant that political philosophy has always been oriented towards contemplation rather than action, a privileging of theoria over praxis:

> [S]ince Socrates, no man of action, that is, nobody whose original experience was political, as for instance Cicero's was, could ever hope to be taken seriously by the philosophers . . . Political philosophy never recovered from this blow dealt by philosophy to politics at the very beginning of our tradition. The contempt for politics, the conviction that political activity is a necessary evil, due partly to the necessities of life that force men to live as labourers or rule over slaves who provide for them, and partly to the evils that come from living together itself, that is, to the fact that the multitude, which the Greeks called *hoi polloi*, threatens the security and even the existence of every individual person, runs like a thread throughout the centuries that separate Plato from the modern age.
>
> (Ibid.: 83–84)

Since Arendt that targeting of theoria has intensified, particularly in the work of those whose redemptive *political* theory has seemed to save theory from the cartoon characterizations that consigned the supposedly irresponsibly formalist and textualist modes of 'French' thought to a past that was not yet properly attuned to the politics of life. I will consider this retrieval or saving of theory later. For now, I want to suggest that there might be another, opposed, sense of theory *after* theory. This would not be a return of theory to life, and certainly not a return of theory to the body, to affects, to living systems, living labour or praxis. One could create an exhaustive and exhausting list of all the ways in which theory has been reterritorialized back onto the lived, all the ways in which a radical consideration of force without centre, without life, without intention or sense is continually relocated in practical life, in *doing*. One diagnostic point, for example, would concern the migration of certain terms, such as 'performativity' or 'difference' (which harbour the potential to think an act without an actor). Although Judith Butler insists on a Nietzschean 'doer without the deed' in her theory of performativity (Butler 1990: 142), one might observe that performance was nevertheless for Butler that which, ex post facto, produced a body who would recognize itself as human (Butler 2005). This aspect of human recognition, with a specific focus on the face, comes to the fore in her later work (Butler 2006).

Whereas theory might be approached beginning from estrangement and distance, considering a world that is not ourselves and a force that cannot be returned to the human, theory is moving precisely in the opposite direction to being nothing more than the expression of praxis, nothing more than relations of recognition. Antonio Negri with Michael Hardt insisted that 'living labour' and the self-producing body of 'homo homo humanity squared' allowed for a world that would be liberated both from the centralizing exploitation of capitalism *and* freed from any position of knowledge and cognition outside the collective body (Hardt and Negri 2000). This, in turn, led Negri to go on and create a thoroughly practical and human plane of theory. How, we might ask, is it that a Lacan whose corpus was devoted to the necessarily alien and inhuman fact *that there is system*, and a Derrida who began by considering genesis as 'anarchic', are read as modes of vital living expression?:

> [T]he living expressions of our culture are not born in the form of synthetic figures but, on the contrary, in the form of events; they are untimely. Their becoming is within a genealogy of vital elements that constitute a radical innovation and the very form of the lack of measure. Some contemporary philosophers have set off in pursuit of this new expressive force of postmodernity, and they have attempted to characterize it. Already Lacan had pointed to the absence of measure in the new; for Derrida, the productivity of the margins seeks new orders as it disseminates; as for Nancy and Agamben, we find them picking the flowers that grow in these fields of extreme limit.
>
> (Negri 2008: 66–67)

This joyous affirmation of the living, of the multitude, of productivity, of the other or of pure potentiality and futurity is but one way of reading theory. But is this the best mode of thinking and reading when we are at a moment when there is no shortage of information about life and its temporality – no shortage of data bombarding us daily with the inevitable end of the human organism – while we are all the more insistent that whatever else they are thinking and theory are primarily organic? Does not one of theory's earliest gestures towards a force without production, or a potentiality without actuality or presence, at least suggest that one might consider relations beyond life and creation? How would theory confront the absence of theoria: 'life' without the human look? Life without praxis, life without meaningful action, life without production or labour: such would be theory *after* theory, or theory that opened itself to the thought of extinction. Hints of such a theory were articulated at theory's very genesis: not only explicitly in texts such as Derrida's 'No Apocalypse, Not Now: Seven Missiles, Seven Missives' (1984) or Gilles Deleuze and Félix Guattari's suggestion that one might need to think of the world beyond or before the gaze of the organism ('becoming-imperceptible'), but also in theory's most scandalously 'apolitical' moments, such as Paul de Man's suggestion that theory begins when one reads a text as if there were no readers, no contextual life that would be its site of emergence, and no living horizon that might maintain or animate its sense (de Man 1972). More recently, hints of a surviving or nascent theory occur in extensions of Alain Badiou's promising 'theoretical antihumanism' that push theory beyond Badiou's own decision of the subject (Badiou 2001: 5). Ray Brassier (2008) takes up Badiou's antihumanism, along with Quentin Meillassoux's insistence that it is possible to think beyond human knowledge (Meillassoux 2008), to move further into a world without cognition. Graham Harman has also taken up phenomenology, *not* to insist that the world as given is always given *to* some subject or body, but to demand that we think of relations of givenness beyond self-present thinking (Harman 2005). Despite the fact that Kantian philosophy defines theory as that which is given to a necessarily presupposed subject, we might say that these gestures are theoretical insofar as they begin from what is not immediately present to a subject of action.

One might want to go further than these suggestions from within philosophy to consider what *literary* theory might offer to a present that is dominated by information calculating the end of time, alongside a range of cultural productions striving to witness such an end – however paradoxical such an end might be. That is, how would theory approach the influx of data regarding irreversible threats to the human species – an onslaught of evidence that is met at one and the same time by increasing climate change denial, a resurgence in 'theories' of human praxis and a widespread cultural production that intimates the end of human life? How would a theory that was *literary* – or that considered the remnants of the letter – 'read' the spate of films of the last decade or more witnessing the possible end of all human life? Such films include, especially, redemption narratives where the potential extinction of the species is averted by a popular or ecological victory over techno-science: James Cameron's *Avatar* (2009) would be the most recent example. Such a literary theory would not, as Derrida suggested concerning literature, be an opening to democracy insofar as literature is a right to 'say anything' (Derrida 1992: 36). Rather the 'text' would operate as an 'anarchic genesis' or 'mal d'archive': a force or disturbance not felt by the organism but witnessed after the event in its having always already occurred.

Leaving those suggestions aside for now, I want to begin by addressing the question of why such a strong sense of theory after theory ought to be entertained. First, one might consider the current terrain of theory as a reaction formation. In response to a world in which 'the political' is increasingly divorced from meaningful practice (whatever that would be) theory has insisted in ever more shrill tones on the grounding of theoria in meaningful, practical, productive and human-organic life. Second, our context or life is one in which a radical sense of '*after theory*' – the non-existence of thinking beings – is all too obvious, despite the fact that the one area theory has failed to address is what it might mean in this sense to be 'after theory'. That is, one might ask why it is just as the world faces its annihilation, or at least the annihilation of something like the organic life that was capable of *bios theoretikos*, that 'theory' turns back towards productive embodied and affective life? Third, if popular culture is dominated by a genuinely post-theoretical meditation – by a constant, obsessive and fraught imagination of a life or non-life beyond the gaze of the organism, and by the literal image of extinction – why is this the one mode of post-theory that 'theory' has failed to consider?

The twentieth century witnessed several waves of extinction threat coming in various modes with various temporal intensities: the sudden nuclear annihilation of the cold war was perhaps the only potential extinction threat that has abated (and is perhaps the only event that would produce apocalyptic annihilation; all other possible annihilations would be gradual, allowing for a minimal 'human' presence to witness the slow and violent departure of the human. Cormac McCarthy's *The Road* is counter-apocalyptic in just this sense, for it figures the remainder of human bodies and not a sudden annihilation). Indeed, this is what an ethics of extinction requires: not an apocalyptic thought of the 'beyond the human' as a radical break or dissolution, but a slow, dim, barely discerned and yet violently effective destruction. Since the cold war, other threats to human species survival have succeeded each other, with the public imagination being turned now to one human extermination menace, now to another. One might note that although the threat of AIDS – the initial figuration of which was highly apocalyptic – has hardly gone away, little mention was made of viral disaster once other concerns such as climate change began to attract attention. After 9/11 and the shift from a war on drugs to a war on terror, various viral disasters have deflected 'attention' from bio-weapons, nuclear arsenals and suicide bombers, 'focusing' instead on SARS, bird flu and the H1N1 virus. Interspersed among those surges of panic have been waves of other threats (including the threat of panic itself, for it may be the case that it is the fear and chaos of terrorism and viral pandemic that pushes the system into annihilating disorder). Before the financial meltdown of late 2008 the 'era of cheap food' came to an end (due partly to the shift in production towards bio-fuels), with food riots in Haiti presaging intense global aggression from the hungry. This was eclipsed by waves of lawlessness and violence that followed the stringencies caused by economic chaos, which in turn would lead to a fear of disorder that would be both precipitated by diminishing resources while also exacerbating the increasing fragility and incompetence of systems of social order that would suffer from widespread uncertainty and confusion.

These terrors – viral, political, economic, climatic and affective – have not failed to dent the cultural imaginary. In addition to quite explicit texts about viral disaster, from *Outbreak* (1995) to the more recent *The Invasion* (2007), *28 Days Later* (2002) and *28 Weeks Later* (2007), other disaster epics have focused on spectacular catastrophes prompted by global warming (including Danny Boyle's *Sunshine*, in which a space mission to reignite the dying sun is thwarted when the space travellers fail to resist the desire to stare directly at the source of the light that would have saved the earth, so drawn are they to its destroying intensity). Like *The Invasion*, in which humans are infected by a virus that robs them of all affect and thus annuls their capacity for violence and emotion, fiction and documentary culture has asked the question theory has failed to ask: why should the human species wish for or justify its prolongation, and what would be worth saving? How might it imagine its non-existence, and how would we adopt a relation to those whose miserable future will be 'our' legacy? (In *The Day After Tomorrow* [2004], survivors taking refuge in the over-frozen New York Public Library decide not to burn the works of Nietzsche, choosing an economics text book for some final warmth.) Other texts have passed judgement on a self-extinguishing humanity, with the recent remake of *The Day the Earth Stood Still* (2008) featuring a dead-pan Keanu Reeves informing humanity that it has no right to live given the waste and violence of its history. Such worlds are *after theory* in a quite banal and literal sense. There are no theorists.

This site of theory after theory has been considered by 'theory', if at all, either in the mode of mournful despair (by an Agamben who wishes to retrieve the political in the face of the hedonism of spectacle) or re-humanizing emancipation (by a Hardt and Negri who regard liberation from any external point of judgement as the consequence of living labour no longer subjected to spatial fragmentation or material production). These new trends in theory are accompanied by a series of returns or relocations of the previous generation of thinkers to their less threatening philosophical fathers. Derrida is returned to Husserl to avoid the radically disembodied and inhuman forces of writing; Deleuze and Guattari are returned to Bergson to re-affirm the boundaries of the organism; the machinic potentials of digital media are located in the bodies of meaning-generating audiences. A Merleau-Ponty whose concept of 'flesh' bore the possibility of taking the body and even 'life' beyond the sense of the lived has, for theorists of biopolitics, become a way of positing vital norms (Esposito 2008).

More specifically still: if theory after theory has any meaning, should it not refer to a hyperbolic *and* minimal theoretical condition in which we consider not simply the formal absence of a population but an actual disappearance? Theory is constitutively distinct from practice precisely because theory relates to that which is not ourselves; theory is the consideration of that which is given to us (while practice is the law one gives to oneself in the absence of knowledge). Hyperbolically, then, theory ought to relate to cultural production *not* in terms of bodies, affects, multitudes and identities, unless these too were also considered not as self-evidently familiar and living as but strangely dead to us. This would also give us a minimal approach to an ethics of extinction, which would have to be a counter-ethics. We would not assume an ethos, a proper way of being, community, 'we' or humanity that would be the ground and value of literary or other objects. Just as Foucault's counter-memory sought to consider all those forces that had some power in the present but were not present to living history, a counter-ethics would be theoretical in beginning from the condition of the present – looming extinction – without assuming the ethos of the present. That is, one would – as the world after theory ought to compel us to do – consider what is worthy of concern or survival, what of the human, the multitude, the living would enable an ethos that was not the ethos of the present.

We can return again to the question of theory after theory, today, and ask why it has so focused on an empty tomorrow – a future of open creativity and unbounded possibility – that it has not considered the tomorrow of its own non-existence. Given even the minimal assumption that reading theoretically requires some necessary distance from any actual audience, and given the now literal threat of the absence of the human species, why has theory survived, after theory, in a mode of increasing humanization and organicism? Why, when events and timelines would seem to demand just the contrary, does theory take its current self-englobing form? As an example of the ways in which theory has, just as Arendt suggested it ought to do, retrieved a political of living in common (a polity of the multitude with no outside), we might consider three dominants. First, a deconstruction that now mourns Derrida does so precisely by insisting on a dimension of deconstruction oriented towards hospitality and towards a future whose radical openness defies all calculation (saving justice and democracy to come). Such a mode of deconstruction would survive at the expense of a Derrida who suggested an 'untamed genesis' that would be neither living nor dead, neither before nor after the human but nevertheless disruptive of any mode of good conscience. Second, a turn to life or naturalism insists that the world is always the world for this or that living system, always embedded in a milieu given as a range of affordances: this ranges from the retrieval of phenomenology and the embedding of mind in life (Petito *et al.* 1999) *against* an anti-organicism or textualism that would draw attention to forces beyond the lived, to the celebration of biopolitical production and the multitude against a bio-power that is seen as extrinsic and opposed to life (Hardt and Negri 2000). Finally, one might cite a return to the aesthetic, whether that be an aesthetics of language that separates man as a speaking being who gives himself his world from animality (Agamben 2004), to a re-affirmation of literature (Attridge 2004; Joughin and Malpas 2003), or art in general as grounded in the human organism's sense-making capacities of its world. It would be far too obvious to add to this list the affirmations of identity politics or, worse, subjectivity, that would posit a self that is nothing more than the negation of a world in itself (knowable, measurable and presentable) precisely because the subject is that which gives a world, law and norm to itself.

Theory might have both interest and worth – if we accept the thorough contingency of such worth – only if it is as destructive of the imagination as our milieu of possible extinction allows. There is no shortage of data regarding the possible or inevitable absence of humans: terror threats are calculated meticulously by government think tanks; climate change protocols and negotiations require detailed prediction and scenario plotting, and popular news is dominated by economic, climatic, viral and political 'updates' regarding a range of intruding violences. Such information, far from indicating the location of texts in a polity, suggests just the sort of approach deemed to be horrifically absurd in Knapp and Michaels's miserable summation of theory. Let us imagine texts as lines drawn without any preceding or ideal community. Let us also, more importantly, be aware (insofar as we can) that the text of the current multitude includes information regarding climate change, terror, destruction and extinction expressed in a vocabulary of mitigation, adaptation, viability policy and sustainability, none of which can figure the non-existence of the human. If theory were to operate as it ought then it would be destructive of such an imaginary; it would be theory after theory.

Bibliography

Agamben, G. (2004) *The Open: Man and Animal*, Stanford, CA: Stanford University Press.
Arendt, H. (2005) *The Promise of Politics*, ed. J. Kohn, New York: Schocken.

Attridge, D. (2004) *The Singularity of Literature*, London: Routledge.

Badiou, A. (2001) *Ethics: An Essay on the Understanding of Evil*, trans. P. Hallward, London: Verso.

Brassier, R. (2008) *Nihil Unbound: Naturalism and Anti-phenomenological Realism*, New York: Palgrave Macmillan.

Butler, J. (1990) *Gender Trouble: Feminism and the Subversion of Identity*, New York: Routledge.

Butler, J. (2005) *Giving an Account of Oneself*, New York: Fordham University Press.

Butler, J. (2006) *Precarious Life: The Powers of Mourning and Violence*, London: Verso.

Deleuze, G. and Guattari, F. (1986) *Kafka: Toward a Minor Literature*, trans. R. Bensmaïa, Minneapolis, MN: University of Minnesota Press.

de Man, P. (1972) 'Genesis and Genealogy in Nietzsche's *The Birth of Tragedy*', *Diacritics*, 2.4: 44–53.

Derrida, J. (1984) 'No Apocalypse, Not Now (Full Speed Ahead, Seven Missiles, Seven Missives)', trans. C. Porter, P. Lewis, *Diacritics*, 14.2, Nuclear Criticism: 20–31.

Derrida, J. (1992) 'This Strange Institution Called Literature', in D. Attridge (ed.) *Acts of Literature*, London: Routledge. 33–75.

Derrida, J. (2002) 'Force of Law: "The Mystical Foundation of Authority"', in G. Anidjar (ed.) *Acts of Religion*, London: Routledge. 228–98.

Esposito, R. (2008) *Bíos: Biopolitics and Philosophy*, trans. T. Campbell, Minneapolis, MN: University of Minnesota Press.

Gallagher, C. and Greenblatt, S. (2001) *Practicing New Historicism*, Chicago, IL: University of Chicago Press.

Hardt, M. and Negri, A. (2000) *Empire*, Cambridge, MA: Harvard University Press.

Harman, G. (2005) *Guerrilla Metaphysics: Phenomenology and the Carpentry of Things*, Chicago, IL: Open Court.

Joughin, J. and Malpas, S. (eds.) (2003) *The New Aestheticism*, Manchester: Manchester University Press.

Kant, I. (1991) *Political Writings*, ed. H.S. Reiss, Cambridge: Cambridge University Press.

Knapp, S. and Michaels, W. Benn (1982) 'Against Theory', *Critical Inquiry*, 8.4: 723–42.

Korsgaard, C.M. (2009) *Self-constitution: Agency, Identity, and Integrity*, Oxford: Oxford University Press.

Korsgaard, C.M. and Cohen, G.A. (1996) *The Sources of Normativity*, ed. O. O'Neill, Cambridge: Cambridge University Press.

Meillassoux, Q. (2008) *After Finitude: An Essay on the Necessity of Contingency*, trans. R. Brassier, London: Continuum.

Michaels, W. Benn. (2001) 'The Shape of the Signifier', *Critical Inquiry*, 27.2: 266–83.

Michaels, W. Benn. (2009) 'What Matters', *London Review of Books*, 31.16: 11–13. Negri, A. (2008) *Empire and Beyond*, trans. E. Emery, Cambridge: Polity.

Petito, J., Varela, F.J., Pachoud, B. and Roy, J-M. (1999) *Naturalizing Phenomenology: Issues in Contemporary Phenomenology and Cognitive Science*, Stanford, CA: Stanford University Press.

Stengers, I. (2000) *The Invention of Modern Science*, trans. D. Smith, Minneapolis, MN: University of Minnesota Press.

PART II

Between theory and practice: judgement, will, potentiality

5

PERCEPTION ATTACK

The force to own time

Brian Massumi

Syncopating politics

'We remember what we do not see'. This is how Governor George Pataki of New York, pious before unseen towers, inaugurated the 2004 Republican Party Convention that was to carry George W. Bush to a second term in office, riding the surf of 9/11 and the 'war on terror' one last time before the swell subsided (Associated Press 29 August 2004). Standing in the ebb, years later, far from Ground Zero, a reminder may be in order that the swell was more like a tidal wave. It burst levees, eroded embankments and laid down sediment, leaving the political land-forms over which it swept reshaped. The Governor's dictum might capture some-thing more of the altered landscape than it might first appear from its proffering as a rhetorical flourish. It locates the flourishing of the political between memory and perception. This would be familiar ground, were the relation between the two presented as one of continuity: we remember now what once we saw (the towers); or, now we see what we shall henceforth remember (the towers' reduction to ruins). Pataki, however, telescopes the moments of memory and perception into a single present tense. Memory and perception share the moment, entering into immediate proximity, while remaining strangers. Their disjointed immediacy syn-copates the instant from within. We do not see now what we can never have seen, even as we watched: the enormity of the *event*. The present tense where memory and perception come disjunctively together is the time of the event that is like a lost between of the towers and their ruins, an interval in which life was suspended for an instantaneous duration that was more like a stilled eternity than a passing present, comprehending reflection gone AWOL. In this time of the event, percep-tion and memory fall out of step together, jointly retaining the syncopated power to affect. The off-beat time of the event disallows any one-to-one correlation between perception and memory. This makes the ground fall out from under the notion of representation, as applied to politics. It also makes time a directly political issue: the present's relation to the past – or for that matter, to itself – is politically operationalized.

Kierkegaard distinguished two regimes of memory. 'What is recollected has been, is repeated backward, whereas repetition is recollected forward' (Kierkegaard 1983: 131). Whereas memory is normally understood as a recollection of what has been, repetition is a recollection of what has not yet come – a memory of the future. This is not so hard to grasp if we think of repetition as self-contracting, on the model of habit. Habit moves us to the other pole of the event: from the enormity of the once in lifetime macro-event to the micro-events that are the stuff of everyday life. We say we have a habit, but we all know that it is really the habit that has us. It is an automatism that has taken hold and *in*habits us. It is of its nature as an automatism to pass under the radar of awareness. We are only ever aware of an habitual action *having* occurred. What we consciously perceive are its next effects. Otherwise we would catch it in the act and decide whether to execute the action or not, in which case it will not have acted as a habit. A habit is self-deciding. It is a self-effecting force from the past that acts in a present which appears only in a next-effect. The present of the force's actual operation is elided. This is a kind of syncopation of time itself, where the skipped beat is the operative present, the present of the operation. This active present is expressed only in the nextness that comes of it. It actively disappears into its forward expression. We normally think of habit as bare repetition, and of repetition as barren by nature. In Kierkegaard, as in Nietzsche and Deleuze, repetition is a positive force carrying the past forward into the next expression. It is a positively organizing, even creative, force of time. This implies that it may be captured and put to use. The elision of the operative moment may be operationalized.

The US military knows this, judging by the currents in war theory on which it has nourished itself since the fall of the Soviet Union and the sustained priorities of its research wing, the Defense Advanced Research Projects Agency (DARPA). In its future repetition of war, the military has been an off-step or two ahead of Governor Pataki. Like him, it knows that we habitually remember what we do not see. It also knows that this is a political-time issue critical to the 'war on terror' so loudly trumpeted by the Bush administration, with which the policies of the Obama administration have quietly remained in continuity despite its abnegation of the phrase. But it goes further, to the philosophical realization that there is a positive power to repetition which means that it is not barren and that even so humdrum a species of it as habit partakes of the creative force of time.

We need only to think of attention. Attention is the base-state habit of perception. Every awareness begins in a shift. We think of ourselves as directing the shifts in our attention. But if you pay attention to paying attention, you quickly sense that rather than you directing your attention, your attention is directing you. It pulls you into your coming perception, which dawns on you as attention's next-effect. Attention is the perceptual automatism that consists in tagging a change in the perceptual field as new and potentially important and building awareness on that change, for the very good reason that it may signal the necessity of a response or an opportunity for action. The next perception into which you are pulled is already a convocation to action–reaction. According to contemporary perception studies, in a confirmation of attention's habitual nature, this happens in the elided present of repetition.[1]

The possibility, evoked by Pataki's statement, of operationalizing the elided present of attention at political ground zero must be understood against the backdrop of the realignment of military doctrine over the past 20 years on 'full-spectrum' force.[2] This is the extension of military affairs to 'grey areas involving non-traditional Operations Other Than War (OOTW)' (Ullman and Wade 1996: 18), in the words of Ullman and Wade, the authors of *Shock and Awe*, one of the classic statements of the doctrine. This expansion of the compass of military operation beyond the classical battlefield to areas formerly considered the exclusive purview of civil institutions is a response to the blurring of boundaries characterizing contemporary war, in which the archetype of the enemy is no longer the uniformed soldier but the 'terrorist'. The assumed organization of the adversary, as another contemporary classic drives home (Arquilla and Ronfeldt 2001), is then no longer the identifiable regular army and its centralized State scaffolding but the diffuseness of the network.

The network is recessive. It melts into the population. It is pervasive, 'unbounded and expanding' (ibid.: 10). It insinuates itself across the technological and communicational nerve paths of society. The attacks it enables irrupt without warning. They rise up from within an unbounded field, rather than striking out in a determinable direction from a locatable base. Netwar's infiltrating reach is potentially coextensive with social and cultural space. This irrevocably blurs the boundaries between the civil and military spheres. Other boundaries blur as a consequence, for example that between offence and defence (ibid.: 13).

When the civil is no longer clearly demarcated from the military, nor offence from defence, it becomes impossible to say where the exercise of force begins and ends. Military affairs bleed across the spectrum. They span a continuum stretched between two poles or extremes. At one end lies the traditional application of 'force on force' (Ullman and Wade 1996: xiii, 21–22). This is the pole of traditional engagement on the model of the battle, siege or occupation. At the other pole lies what some call 'soft power' (Arquilla and Ronfeldt 2001: 2). As a first approximation, soft power can be understood as the military use of information and disinformation, and of 'psy ops' or what used to be called psychological warfare. Arquilla and Ronfeldt characterize soft power as 'epistemological' warfare because its business is what people know or think they know.

Of course, epistemological warfare is nothing new. But the paradigm has significantly shifted. Traditionally, what is now called soft power was a helper to hard power. It was secondary to force-on-force, whose effectiveness it was meant to boost. It was an additive, like leavening. Now, on the other hand, according to Arquilla and Ronfeldt, *all* conflict is *by nature* epistemological. Soft power, rather than an additive or booster, is a baseline state. This is a necessary consequence of the full-spectrum situation. War is no longer punctual, like a battle. It's on low boil all the time. It is no longer localized, like an occupation. The heat is everywhere. The definition of action underpinning the force-on-force of hard power is fundamentally that of friction: matter on matter, metal on metal, projectile against shielding, metal in flesh, flesh splayed, splashed on hard surfaces. Force of attack against opposing force of resistance. The overall aim of force-against-force is attrition (Ullman and Wade 1996: xxiii, xxviii). It meets the enemy head-on and wears down his capabilities across an extensive series of frictional engagements. Its aims and means are painfully tangible.

In the current field of conflict, this kind of punctual engagement has lost its centrality. It has been replaced by waiting. Being in the thick of war has been watered down and drawn out into an endless waiting, both sides poised for action. The base-line state is now this always-on of low-boil poising for action. One is always in the thin of it. When a strike of force-against-force comes, it stands out against the background continuity of this thin condition, which Paul Virilio presciently called the 'non-battle' years before it became the obsessive concern of leaders both military and civilian (Virilio 1975). When it comes, the irruption of action is an ebullition, a momentary boiling-over in this low-intensity broth of the always-on conflict of the non-battle. In the non-battle, the relation between action and waiting has been inverted. Waiting no longer stretches between actions. Action breaks into waiting.

Soft power is how you act militarily in waiting, when you are not yet tangibly acting. It is a way of preventing the wait itself from being an attrition, or even a way of turning it to advantage. In the condition of non-battle, when you have nothing on which to act tangibly, there is still one thing you can do: act on that *condition*. Act to change the conditions in which you wait. After all, it is from these same conditions that any action to come will have emerged. By acting on the wait-time conditions in the intervals between boilings-over, you may well be able to reduce the potential of an eventual attack, moderate its powers of attrition if it comes, or even better induce it to take tangible shape when and where you are ready for it. That way you have a chance of disabling it before it reaches its full magnitude, or even in the case where it bursts forth at full strength, you can be reasonably confident that you will be able to respond to it with rapid and over-whelming counter-force.

Thus you take as your military field of operation the environmental conditions in which both combatants and the non-combatant population lives: what Ullman and Wade call the 'total situation' (Ullman and Wade 1996: 9). The only way to act on the total situation is to act on the conditions of emergence of the battle, prior to its occurrence. These conditions concern threats which in the parlance of the doctrine of pre-emption, which has come to define the present era of conflict as integrally as deterrence did the Cold War, are 'not yet fully formed'.[3] What is not yet fully formed is still in potential. It may already be on the horizon, brewing like a recipe for disaster, or ominously looming like an unclear, almost-present threat.

It carries an irreducible degree of indeterminacy. That measure of indeterminacy makes it as intangible as it is ominous. It is a tall order: you must act 'totally' on the intangibles of the situation. The ultimate boundary blurred is between the tangible and the intangible, the corporeal and the incorporeal. Because to act on the former you have to act on the latter.

There are two ways to act totally and intangibly on a situation. The first is by transposing your action from the spatial axis of the battle, siege or occupation to come, onto a time axis. You operate in and on the *interval* in which what is not yet fully formed is already imperceptibly brewing. You can act on that *almost-present* to influence the active form of its next-awaited emergence. Pre-emption is proaction: action on the conditions of action, prior to its actually taking shape. The second way to act totally and intangibly on a situation is to act on perception. It is perception that prepares a body for action and reaction. By modulating perception, you can *already* modulate subsequent action–reaction. This in fact makes perception a royal road to the almost-present. The two ways of acting intangibly with a view to the total situation are convergent.

It was perception's powers of proaction that motivated Arquilla and Ronfeldt's characterization of contemporary war as epistemological. But it is a mistake to take too cognitive of an approach. The move into perception is accompanied in the contemporary theatre of war with a correlative move towards the 'capabilities-centred' approach much touted by Donald Rumsfeld and his fellow neocons (Rumsfeld 2002). In this approach, you move into perception in order to operate not at the level at which actions are decided, but at the level at which the very capacity for action is forming. Operating on the level at which decisions *have been made* focuses on the properly cognitive aspect of knowledge: its informational contents, their availability, reliability and manipulability, their actual usability. Operating on the level at which the capacity for action is *in the making* is a very different proposition. It focuses on a pre-decision process occurring in an interval of emergence antecedent to both informed knowing and deliberative action. This is a point before know-ability and action-ability have differentiated from one another. At that point, a modulation of perception is directly and immediately a change in the parameters of what a body can do, both in terms of how it can act and what it will know. This antecedent level of capacitation or potentialization is *proto*-epistemological – and already ontological, in that it concerns changes in the body's degree and mode of enablement in and towards its total situation or life environment. Any application of force at this level is an *ontopower*: a power through which being becomes. An ontopower is not a force against life, as any force-against-force must inevitably be at its point of application. It is a positive force. It is positively productive of the particular form a life will take next. It conditions life's nextness. It is a force *of* life.

The force to own time

Ullman and Wade are unambiguous about the fact that operating on this level is indeed an exercise of force, even though its object is intangible. It is not a lesser force, even though it is exerted in the thinness of non-battle. It is, they say, '*more than an application of force*' (Ullman and Wade 1996: xxvii) – a surplus of force. It exceeds the parameters of tangible applications of battle-force and of the known contents of life upon which those applications bear and to which they add a hard permutation through their action of attrition. The productive force of the non-battle returns to the level of conditioning at which the parameters for attritional force are set. There is always a follow-up action–reaction to an exercise of force-against-force. There is a second-next enveloped in the next, and a third in that. What is conditioned is a forward series of potential repetitions. There is a power of potential continuation, a power of a continuum, wrapped up in each exercise of force-against-force. The power of the continuum is an *excess* over any next, immanent in each one. Non-battle force or the force-to-own-time takes this excess as its field. This is what makes it a surplus of force – or a *surplus-value* of force. The relation of non-battle force to the force-against–force is analogous to the relation discovered by Marx between money as a means of payment and money as capital.

Capital is the driving force of the series of payment exchanges: money in the making; money beyond money. At each payment, a punctual return is made to capital. Profit is fed back into investment, replenishing the forward-driving force of capital. Money loops from its punctual exercise as means of payment into a feeding of the conditions of its own continuing. This excess of forward-driving force over any given payment-engagement is surplus-value, as distinguished from profit. Surplus-value is not the amount fed back. That is profit. Surplus value is different from profit. It is not quantitative. It is processual. It is the processual quality from which quantities of money are generated in forward-driving fashion. It is the ever-nextness of proliferating quantities of economic value. Surplus value is realized punctually in the explicit act of exchange, in such a way as to cyclically exceed any such exchange. Value beyond value, immeasurably on the make (on the immeasurability of surplus value, see Negri 1996: 151–4).

Nations make war the same way they make wealth. (Cebrowski and Garstka 1998: unpaginated)

Like capital, non-battle force is at the same time forward-driving and cyclic. At each frictional engagement, it feeds back into itself towards the conditioning of what will come next. It is the ever-nextness of actual military value as realized punctually in explicit acts of war. *Force beyond force*, intangibly on the make. The force-beyond-force is the processual quality of conflict from which tangible military outcomes are generated.

Ulmann and Wade do not hesitate to link the force-beyond-force, as processual quality of war, to time. This is not, they say, a force to overcome resistance. Rather, it is the force 'to own time' (Ullman and Wade 1996: xxvii, 53). Recent military thinking has revolved around the concept of rapid dominance. '"Rapid" means the ability to move quickly before an adversary can react' (ibid.: xxv). The *force-to-own-time* operates in an interval smaller than the smallest perceivable. 'The target is perception' (ibid.: 28) always and at every band along the full spectrum. Even in the thick of things, when conflict boils over and force-against-force is to be engaged, the force-to-own-time must still operate. It must squeeze into an interval smaller than the smallest perceivable between actions, so as to condition the enemy's reaction. This is the 'shock' of shock and awe. The exercise of force-against-force is qualitatively different from the force-to-own-time, but, if its exercise is separated from the force-to-own-time, it rapidly loses its effectiveness. The force-to-own-time is infra-level force. It is infra-active because it occurs in a smaller than smallest interval between actions. It is infra-perceptual because this same interval is also smaller than the smallest perceivable. And it is infra-temporal because, being imperceptible, the interval of its exercise is an off-beat of time, a missed step in the cadence of actions and reactions, an elided present between one moment and the next.

In the thin of things, at the non-battle end of the spectrum, the force-to-own-time still operates to infra-condition action by 'controlling the enemy's perception' (ibid.: 9, 54) in the interests of total-situation control. In the absence of dramatic action spiking punctually from the baseline of the non-battle, the conditioning of the environment by the force-to-own-time appears continuous. But this is only so because we are not paying attention to paying attention. The off-beat is still there. The baseline habit of perception has not ceased contracting itself in us. It still inhabits us. The pull of attention has not ceased to take hold of us. It still directs us to a next perception, and through it to next action–reaction. The baseline of war has accordioned into the baseline of perception. At the infra-level where the two baselines converge, war at the macro-scale of the battle, siege and occupation falls into absolute processual proximity with war at the micro-scale of everyday civilian life.

The life bare active

The infra-interval is where perception itself is in absolute processual proximity with the body. The automatism that attention possesses by virtue of its sharing a nature with habit means that its operation rejoins the reflex workings of body matter. It is our bodies that contract habits, which are acquired reflexes. The operation of attention occurs at a point of indistinction between emergent perceptual experience and the autonomic mechanisms of the brain and nervous system. To a certain degree you can bypass the shielding or immunizing effects of pre-operative cultural conditioning as well as of personal histories, dispositions and allegiances, by plugging into the nervous system and approaching attention from that autonomic angle. It is possible to find tangible handles to leverage the intangible dimensions of the life of the body. It is possible, within limits, to machine experience.

The limits are due to the fact that the system of perception, like capital, essentially involves feedback and is thus, like an economy, non-linear. By definition, in a non-linear system you cannot guarantee a one-to-one correspondence between a given punctual input and an outcome. You do not *cause* an effect. You effect a *modulation*. You can create resonance and interference effects at the emergent level. The smaller-than-smallest interval of the force-to-own-time vibrates with infra-level agitation. The innervated body poises, in vital commotion. It reacts:

habits are *primed*. It proacts: its reacting is already a tensing and a tending to the future. The body is attending in the instant to the immediacy of life's unfolding. Everything hangs in the balance. Except, far from equilibrium, the balance is off. Everything hangs in the off-balance of the instant. The nature and duration of the agitation formatively filling the instant inflects what follows.

The object of full-spectrum power's force-to-own-time is not 'bare life'. It is not human life re-animalized, stripped of its human content, its vitality reduced to the physical minimum, in absolute proximity with death. It is *bare activity*. This is human life in the instant's off-beat. In that instant, a life is *barely* there, recoiled, bodily consumed in its infra-relation to itself. It is a life without determinate content. In that imperceptible instant, what its content will be next is in the making. A life is *formatively* barely there, tensely poised for what comes next. In that measureless instant, a life is intensely barely there, regathering in the immediacy of its capabilities. This is not vitality reduced to the minimum, this is *life primed*. This is also war. The life primed may indeed be in proximity to death. Yet the body is already arcing towards a next vital exercise of its capacity to act. Not re-animalization: re-*animation*: a stoking for the next step. This is a far cry from a life reduced to brute matter. It is the embodied event of a life regathering in recoil. This is life self-enfolding in *affective* vitality.

The object of full-spectrum power is the affective body regathering in its capacities across a stepped interval of change. Which is to say that full-spectrum power does not actually have an object. Rather than having an object, it finds a fulcrum – if a fulcrum can be said to leverage time. It leverages the future, in the bare activity of action dawning.

Shock, in the next instant, spills over into action. Infra-agitation amplifies, issuing in a macro-move. The actual resulting action does not exhaust the commotion of bare activity preceding it. That infra-activity coincides with a recapacitation of the body poising it for any number of potential outcomes, only one of which eventuates. The unacted remainder of capacitation constitutes a background modulation of the operational parameters of the field of potential action. It is by virtue of this reconditioning of the pragmatic field that the outcome is always in some degree non-linear. The conditioning interval of shock does not simply issue an ensuing action. It sets that next actual action against an unexhausted background of potential actions, many of which are in actuality mutually exclusive. The outcome overall is a changed *relation* between the action that has actually resulted and the newly modulated experiential field from which it emerged. It is 'ecological'.[4] The field of potential action vibrates with the resonances and interferences of poisings unperformed, unsatisfied in action. This ecological remainder of actionability accompanies the ensuing action, retensing it even as it happens.

This poses a problem – and an opportunity – for the military exercise of force-beyond-force. As a force-to-own-time, its avocation is to leverage futurity by altering action's conditions of emergence. The fact that the outcome of shock it administers towards this end is complex – a dynamic relation between a punctual action and its continuously modulated background conditioning – means that the future it inflects retains a significant degree of uncertainty. Force-beyond-force must concern itself with managing uncertainty, not only that associated with pre-existing field conditions into which it intervenes, but with its own future success. Strategies must be put in place to manage the arc of the action line to prevent it from drifting too far afield or reaching a sudden turning point where it bifurcates unexpectedly. A kind of shock therapy becomes necessary. Military strategy cru-cially assumes the task of shock management as a central feature of its ontopower-ful conduct of proto-epistemological warfare.[5]

Thought (as we barely know it)

The point of departure for the contemporary theory and practice of war can be summed up in a phrase: the world is an increasingly complex place full of unpre-dictable and proliferating dangers. The military must be reorganized along the full-spectrum to bring it up to the task of responding to these threats whatever form they take, whenever they arise, and wherever they fall. The reason regularly cited for the increase in complexity is the globalization of the deregulated econ-omy and the accelerated circulation of goods, information and people upon which it is predicated. These premises are shared by all of the major texts. They all take this uncertain ground as a given.[6]

In a way, the appeal to globalization may understate the problem, if it is taken to imply that complexity sets in at the global level due to the sheer number of interactions its system subsumes. This assumes that the local components are simple and that their definition poses no problem when they are taken separately on their own level. A global field of complexity, however, is not composed of simple units, the complexity added by the quantity of their higher level interactions. The local components are complex sub-systems in their own right. The local miring of glo-bal US strategy in Iraq (not to mention Afghanistan and Pakistan, each in its own way) is evidence enough that complexity, and the uncertainty accompanying it, 'goes all the way down' (Stengers 1997). How much more complex and funda-mentally uncertain the situation when it is acknowledged that the ground is groundless, that even when you go 'all the way down' there is always more to go, or worse, while on the way down you may suddenly find yourself back at the top, as through an Alice in Wonderland rabbit-hole in reverse. Feedback between levels, including between the highest and the lowest, is a defining characteristic of a complex system. A complex system, grounded in groundlessness, bootstraps itself on the non-linear playing-out of its own complexity.

In classical war theory, it is true, uncertainty was already acknowledged as a constant. 'The great uncertainty of all data in war is a peculiar difficulty', Clausewitz wrote in his classic nineteenth-century text *On War*, 'because all action must, to a certain extent, be planned in a mere twilight' or as in a 'fog'. The 'fog of war' has since become a household term. The difference is that for Clausewitz it came in the middle as a caveat (Clausewitz 1874: vol. 1, bk. 2, ch. 2, sec 24). It now comes in the preface as mantra.

For Clausewitz, war was by nature intelligible. It can be fully comprehended if one 'consider[s] first the single elements' then 'advance[s] from the simple to the complex' (ibid.: vol. 1, bk. 1, ch. 1, Introduction). For him, the fog of war was but a 'peculiarity' of perception. It could be dissipated by the personal battle experience and 'extraordinary mental power' of the general. 'If *we have seen* War, all becomes intelligible ... Everything is very simple in War, but the simplest thing is difficult.' The difficulty is due to the 'friction' of 'petty circumstance' (ibid: vol. 1, bk. 1, ch. 7; emphasis added). At bottom circumstantial, the friction can be overcome by the well-oiled will and honed intelligence of the general.

In today's war, we always have not seen. Not only is perception syncopated, its ground is indeterminate. These two conditions are intrinsically linked: it is the ground of indeterminacy's heaving rhythmically into view that suspends perception mid-making. We remember what we do not see. But this is not the memory of conscious reflection. It is not the kind that nourishes a character-building accumulation of personal wisdom and a strengthening of rational will for well-considered control. The crux of the matter, in the words of a recent war theorist, is that 'we must appreciate that we cannot hope to control what we cannot see, hear or understand' (Szafranski 1994: 52). Even if under certain circumstances it is possible to reduce the fog of war, under no circumstances can it be eliminated (Alberts *et al.* 1999: 11, 71–72). The fog of war no longer appears circumstantial, but essential and undissipatable. It is not only of the very nature of war, but of human perception itself. The field of war cannot be fully comprehended even by the experienced general, so much less so the first-tour trooper on the fog-befuddled ground. Not to mention the 'first responder' on crisis-ridden civil soil. Personal intelligence and individual will never suffice. In war and security, there is an ineradicable margin of unknowability. It follows that there is an equally unavoidable a degree of strategic undecidability in any operation wherever it may lie on the spectrum. What is to be done?

Returning to military preparedness in the narrower sense as attuned towards battle, complexity must be 'appreciated' in the strategy itself. A way to begin is to build enhanced operational responsiveness into the machinery of war. Tactics on the ground must be fluidly adaptable. There must be channels for the adaptions to feed up the chain of strategic command in order to make it self-correcting, giving it a built-in capacity to evolve. The evolutionary adaptions must then be able feed back down to the lowest level 'battlespace entity' (as the terminology goes), each and every one wherever they are stationed. Considering that time is now of the essence of war, the evolutionary feedback must operate in as close to real-time as possible. This means instant information sharing. Instant information sharing means enhanced networking using the latest in communication technology. Hence the obsessive concern in recent war theory, particularly in shadow of the failure in Iraq, for the deployment of new information and communicational technologies designed to revolutionize command and control. The slogan is 'augmented intelligence'.

It would be seriously to miss the operational point of this renewed focus on intelligence to interpret it as a simple return to an information processing model within the traditional horizon of mediated human communication. It is difficult to communicate what one does not 'hear, see or understand'. Augmenting intelligence is not about making space in war for informed reflection based on complete information. If the fog of war is not merely circumstantial, information is and will remain lacunary. Improved networking cannot change that fact of complexity. The stubborn epistemological fact of asymmetrical warfare is that there will be gaps in intelligence, essentially and necessarily.

This epistemological incompleteness theorem is an expression of an ontological condition: the 'real time' of war is now the formative infra-instant of suspended perception. What are normally taken to be cognitive functions must telescope into that non-conscious interval. What would otherwise be cognition must zoom into the blink between consciously registered perceptions. It must coincide with the 'attentional blink' contemporary perception studies has shown to stagger consciously registered perceptions. This is the 'human terrain' of war. This is the embodied terrain of priming, or the modulation of readiness potential effecting what comes next. Increasingly, it is the site of decision itself. In the bare-active blink, thought enters a new alliance with action, and action with perception in-the-making, each of the terms fusing with the others such that all become something else together, and together overspill the terrain of the human as we think we have known it, returning, militarily, to what has always lain emergently, evolutionarily, at the heart of it.

Key military texts of the early 2000s call for a far-reaching reorganization of the military around augmented network intelligence revolving around the infra-instant.[7] The texts pay lip-service to an easily digestible image of this strategic agenda, articulated in terms of enhancing the military's ability to fight across the spectrum and prevail by enriching its ability to gather and effectively process high-quality information. But under pressure from the infra-instant, they in fact push further. It does not take much scratching under the 'info-structure' surface to see that that the operative logic represents a radical departure from the conventional model of optimizing intelligence by enhancing the quantity and quality of information. If information is understood as conveying factually precise and semantically rich content, information is not what is fundamentally at stake.

The larger goal of improved networking is not to augment human intelligence by better *informing* it. It is to integrally *transform* the machinery of war – and the place of the human actor in relation to it. It is to create a military machinery capable of dipping into the infra-conscious action potentials of bare activity in order to extract from it a surplus value of force expressing itself emergently as a self-deciding military *will* performing itself in real-time, distributed across a self-adapting network of functions fused into operational solidarity through complex relations of mutual feedback. The networking is for distributing not so much information, as this self-deciding of action potential. The complexity is not so much cognized without, in the military system's environment, as it is *enacted* within, full-spectrum, immanently constitutive of the system itself. The reorganization of the military that the strategists advocate is not just aimed at transforming it, but at making it self-transforming. Self-constituting and self-transforming: integrally, infra-lly ontopowerful.

What is at stake for network centric warfare, in the words of one strategy text, is the '*topology of power*' (Alberts and Hayes 2003: 165, 203). 'Battle space', conventionally centred and hierarchically organized, must disseminate into a radical topology of the 'edge'. This transposes it onto another dimension, for the edge is not simply located in space. More shockingly, it is the edge of time (the just-in-time of infra real-time). It is where intelligence gets integrally distributed, for cognition to go infra-lly bare-active. What is produced is not knowledge but, directly and self-augmentingly, power, ontopower, the playing-out of the force-to-own-time, as a militarized force-of-life. Where once was the peak of human cognition – the 'extraordinary mental power' of the steely-willed general – is now the everywhere cutting edge of a self-enacting will-to-power, one with the machinery of war, on a full-spectrum continuum with the 'non-battle' field of peace.[8] What is at stake is the place of human perception, cognition and intention in the evolving and expanding onto-topology of war-power.

What forms does or will this onto-topology of power take on the 'civil' end of the continuum of power, now full-spectrum fogged into a zone of indistinction with war? By what self-emergent network may the intangible dimensions of the life of the body be machined on the 'human terrain' of everyday life? What mechanisms infra-modulate the everyday at the proto-epistemological level of life primed, for its affective vitality? Can human-centred cognition and its action potential be brought back from the edge? Is it enough to reclaim a decisive power for it? Or must decision be alter-machined, in an onto-battle *for* the edge? Where could or should the next beat fall? These are pressing questions not only for cultural theory and philosophy but for the syncopated future of politics.[9]

Notes

1 The gap between consciously registered shifts in attention is called *attentional blink* in the experimental psychology literature. It refers to a fraction-of-a-second blanking out of conscious awareness that occurs between successive changes in the perceptual field. The gap in awareness corresponds to a latency period in perceptual processing during which the coming perception is undergoing '*potentiation*'. The gap in awareness during the potentiation of emerging perception was first brought to general attention by Benjamin Libet in the 1970s. The term attentional blink was introduced in 1992 (Raymond *et al.* 1992) and has since become a major field of specialization in experimental psychology. For a regularly updated summary of the research, see Shapiro *et al.* (2009).

  Much of the research has been dedicated to studying non-conscious perceptual processes occurring in the attentional gap in awareness during which a next conscious perception is pre-forming in potential. It has been found, for example, that conscious shifts in attention are pre-rehearsed on the non-conscious level in the form of emergent patterns forming amid the largely random autonomic micro eye movements (or saccades) that coincide with the blink in attention. Another major area of research has been the phenomenon of '*priming*'. This refers to the capacity of micro-events occurring in the attentional gap to modulate the coming perception. The modulations involve what would be considered 'higher' cognitive functions were they occurring consciously (face, object and word recognition; situational understanding of images that pass by too fast to enter conscious awareness; generalizations concerning for example cultural difference, gender and race; and even decisional cost-benefit analysis). What distinguishes priming from the outmoded concept of subliminal influence is that priming does not imply a linear causality of stimulus–response. Priming *conditions* emergent awareness (creatively modulates its formation) rather that *causing* a response (reproducing a pre-existing model by reflex). It implies complex thought-like processes occurring as a non-conscious dimension of emergent perception, too rapidly for thought actually to have been performed.

The DARPA programme concerned with attention and related perceptual issues is the Augmented Cognition Program. The programme's purpose is to develop wearable technology enabling real-time brain and physiological monitoring of states of awareness, lapses in attention and the non-conscious perceptual processes occurring in the gaps. The monitoring technology is designed to be networkable in such a way as to enable tactical coordination aimed at diagnosing and overcoming limitations in battlefield performance related to deficits in attention, reaction time and memory-formation capacity. The technology is meant to be used in soldiers who develop perceptual techniques to increase their 'cognitive load' capacities beyond average parameters. These techniques include ways of increasing vigilance by diffusing attentiveness across the perceptual field ('continuous partial attention') or by intensifying focused attention ('multitasking'). The strategy of increasing vigilance by diffusing attention is particularly relevant here, in that it amounts to an operationalization of what is discussed below in terms of the 'in-bracing' of 'bare activity' understood as incipient actionability. For an overview of the 'AugCog', see St. John *et al.* (2004). For a popular account of attentional blink in the context of DARPA, see Motluk (2007). The military theory texts cited below share a central interest in operationalizing the 'blink' in perception and cognition through techniques of attention and priming integrated systemically into informational networks.

2 For an analysis of the processual tendencies continuing across the Bush and Obama administrations as they relate to the concept of full-spectrum war and strategies of pre-emption, see Massumi (2009a). For a long (but by no means complete) inventory of particular military and security policy decisions of the early Obama administration that aligned it with Bush-era policies, see footnote 19 of that work.

3 On the centrality of pre-emption and its difference from deterrence, see Massumi (2007).

4 Cebrowski and Garstka (1998) speak of an integrated 'warfighting ecosytem'. Ullman and Wade (1996: xvii) speak of the need to 'control the environment' rather than win punctual engagements.

5 It is here that the homology between war and economics signalled in the brief discussion of surplus value above becomes dramatic. See Klein (2008).

6 It is a constant of full-spectrum force military doctrine to motivate the need for new strategies by evoking the 'dynamic and unstable' nature of the new economy as a complex system. War and the economy, it is then argued, are isomorphic. Both require what amounts to an ecological approach to find ways of managing the uncertainty inherent to complex systems. Arquilla and Ronfeldt (2001), Ullman and Wade (1996) and Cebrowski and Garstka (1998), all contextualize themselves in this manner, as does the Revolution in Military Affairs current embraced by Donald Rumsfeld as US Secretary of Defense during George W. Bush's first term (Rumsfeld 2002). For a technical study of complexity theory and recent military strategy, see Moffat (2003).

7 The key texts most palpably concerned with the infra-instant are Alberts *et al.* (1999) and Alberts and Hayes (2003). The concept of network centric warfare became official US military doctrine in 2001.
8 For an analysis of full-spectrum power as a self-driving dynamism or 'operative logic' powered by the paradoxical time-structure of pre-emption, see Massumi (2007).
9 For some preliminary considerations on civil sphere affective modulation of political potential, see Massumi (2005) and on the potential of politically re-inhabiting the interval of bare activity, see Massumi (2009b).

Bibliography

Alberts, D.S. and Hayes, R.E. (2003) *Power to the Edge: Command and Control in the Information Age*, Washington, DC: Department of Defense Command and Control Research Program, 3rd printing 2005. Online. Available HTTP: http://www.dodccrp.org/files/Alberts_Power.pdf (accessed 26 May 2010).

Alberts, D.S., Garstka, J.J. and Stein, F.P. (1999) *Network Centric Warfare: Developing and Leveraging Information Superiority,* Washington, DC: Department of Defense C4ISR Cooperative Research Program, 2nd revised edition 2000. Online. Available HTTP: http://www.dodccrp.org/html4/research_ncw.html (accessed 26 May 2010).

Arquilla, J. and Ronfeldt, D. (2001) *Networks and Netwars: The Future of Terror, Crime, and Militancy*, Santa Monica, CA: RAND.

Associated Press (2004) 'Cheney Arrives in N.Y. via Ellis Island', August 29, 2004. Online. Available HTTP: http://www.msnbc.msn.com/id/5859896/ (accessed 26 May 2010).

Cebrowski, A. and Garstka, J. (1998) 'Network-centric Warfare – Its Origin and Future', *Proceedings of the United States Naval Institute*, 124.1 (January): 28–35.

von Clausewitz, C. (1874) *On War*, trans. J.J. Graham, London: N. Trübner. Online. Gutenberg Galaxy e-text. Available HTTP: http://www.gutenberg.org/etext/1946 (accessed 26 May 2010).

Kierkegaard, S. (1983) *Fear and Trembling, and Repetition*, trans. H.V. Hong and E.H. Hong, Princeton, NJ: Princeton University Press.

Klein, N. (2008) *The Shock Doctrine: The Rise of Disaster Capitalism*, New York: Picador.

Massumi, B. (2005) 'Fear (the Spectrum Said)', *Positions: East Asia Cultures Critique*, Special issue 'Against Preemptive War', 113.1 (Spring): 31–48.

Massumi, B. (2007) 'Potential Politics and the Primacy of Preemption', *Theory and Event*, 10.2. Online. Available HTTP: http://muse.jhu.edu/journals/theory_and_event/v010/10.2 massumi.html (accessed 26 May 2010).

Massumi, B. (2009a) 'National Enterprise Emergency: Steps Toward an Ecology of Powers', *Theory, Culture & Society* 26.6: 153–85.

Massumi, B. (2009b) 'Of Microperception and Micropolitics', *Inflexions: A Journal for Research-Creation*, 3. Online. Available HTTP: http://www.senselab.ca/inflexions/volume_3/node_i3/PDF/Massumi%20Of%20Micropolitics.pdf (accessed 26 May 2010).

Moffat, J. (2003) *Complexity Theory and Network Centric Warfare*, Washington, DC: US Department of Defense, Command and Control Reseach Program Publications. Online. Available HTTP: http://www.dodccrp.org/html4/research_ncw.html (accessed 26 May 2010).

Motluk, A. (2007) 'How Many Things Can You Do at Once?', *New Scientist,* 2598.7 (April): 28–31.

Negri, A. (1996) 'Twenty Theses on Marx', in *Marxism Beyond Marxism*, ed. S. Makdisi, C. Casarino and R.E. Karl, London: Routledge. 149–80.

Raymond, J.E., Shapiro, K.L. and Arnell, K.M. (1992) 'Temporary Suppression of Visual Processing in an RSVP Task: An Attentional Blink?', *Journal of Experimental Psychology: Human Perception and Performance*, 18: 849–60. doi: 10.1037/0096-1523.18.3.849.

Rumsfeld, D. (2002) 'Transforming the Military', *Foreign Affairs*, 81.3 (May–June, 2002): 20–32.

Shapiro, K.L., Raymond, J. and Arnell, K. (2009) 'Attentional Blink', *Scholarpedia*, 4.6: 3320.

St. John, M., Kobus, D.A., Morrison, J.G. and Schmorrow, D. (2004) 'Overview of the DARPA Augmented Cognition Technical Integration Experiment', *International Journal of Human–Computer Interaction*, 17.2: 131–49.

Stengers, I. (1997) 'Turtles All the Way Down', in I. Stengers, *Power and Invention*, Minneapolis, MN: University of Minnesota Press. 61–75.

Szafranski, R. (1994) 'Neocortical Warfare?', *Military Review* (November): 41–55.

Ullman, H.K. and Wade, J.P. (1996) *Shock and Awe: Achieving Rapid Dominance*, Washington, DC: National Defense University Press. Online. Available HTTP: http://www.dodccrp. org/files/Ullman_Shock.pdf (accessed 26 May 2010).

Virilio, P. (1975) *L'insécurité du territoire*, Paris: Stock.

6

THE WILL OF THE PEOPLE

Dialectical voluntarism and the subject of politics

Peter Hallward

> However great the military and economic potential of your adversary, it
> will never be great enough to defeat a people united in the struggle for
> their fundamental rights.
>
> (Giap 1998)

From the Jacobin constitution of 1793 through the ANC's Freedom Charter of
1955 to the new Bolivian constitution of 2009, a long and versatile emancipatory
tradition has affirmed the militant will of the people as the basis of political action
and legitimacy. The ANC's Charter, for instance, before it denounces apartheid,
racism and social inequality, opens with the assertion that 'no government can
justly claim authority unless it is based on the will of all the people', and insists as
its first demand: 'The People shall govern!' (African National Congress 1955). In
what follows I will identify the key features of this popular-voluntarist tradition, and
try to explain why I think that it retains much of its revolutionary force to this day.

In keeping with a neo-Jacobin logic first anticipated by Rousseau, by 'will of
the people' I mean a deliberate and inclusive process of collective self-determination. Like any kind of will, its exercise is voluntary, emancipatory and autonomous,
a matter of practical freedom; like any form of collective action, it involves assembly and organization. Recent examples of the sort of popular will that I have in
mind include the determination, assembled by South Africa's United Democratic
Front, to overthrow an apartheid based on culture and race, or the mobilization of
Haiti's Lavalas to confront an apartheid based on privilege and class. Conditioned
by the specific strategic constraints that structure a particular situation, such mobilizations test the truth expressed in the old cliché, 'where there's a will there's a
way'. Or to adapt Antonio Machado's less prosaic phrase, taken up as a motto by
Paulo Freire: the partisans of such mobilizations assume that 'there is no way, we
make the way by walking it' (Machado 1978).

To say that we make the way by walking it is to resist the power of the historical, cultural or socio-economic terrain to determine our way. It is to insist that, in an emancipatory political sequence, what is 'determinant in the first instance' is the will of the people to prescribe, through the terrain that confronts them, the course of their own history. It is to privilege, over the complexity of the terrain and the forms of knowledge and authority that govern behaviour 'adapted' to it, the purposeful will of the people to take and retain their place as the 'authors and actors of their own drama' (Marx 1966: 109). We will not come to understand the 'social life-process' as a deliberate process of our own making, Marx reminds us, 'until it becomes production by freely associated people, and stands under their conscious and planned control' (Marx 1976: 173).

To say that we make our way by walking it is not to pretend, however, that we invent the ground we traverse. It is not to suppose that a will creates itself and the conditions of its exercise abruptly or ex nihilo. It is not to assume that the 'real movement which abolishes the existing state of things' (Marx and Engels 1975: 49) proceeds through empty or indeterminate space. It is not to disregard the obstacles or opportunities that characterize a particular terrain, or to deny their ability to influence the forging of a way. Instead it is to remember, after Sartre, that obstacles appear as such in the light of a project to climb past them. It is to remember, after Marx, that we make our own history, without choosing the conditions of its making. It is to conceive of terrain and a way through a dialectic which, connecting both objective and subjective forms of determination, is oriented by the primacy of the latter.

Affirmation of such relational primacy informs what might be called a 'dialectical voluntarism'. A dialectical voluntarist assumes that collective self-determination – more than an assessment of what seems feasible or appropriate – is the animating principle of political action. Dialectical voluntarists have confidence in the will of the people to the degree that they think each term through the other: 'will' in terms of assembly, deliberation and determination and 'people' in terms of an exercise of collective volition.

I

The arrival of the 'will of the people' as an actor on the political stage was itself a revolutionary development, and it was experienced as such by the people themselves. In the run-up to the great revolutions of the late eighteenth century, to assert the deliberate, rational and collective will of the people as the source of political legitimacy and the mainspring of political action was to reject alternative conceptions of politics premised on either the mutual exclusion of society and will (a politics determined by natural, historical or economic necessity), or on the primacy of another sort of will (the will of God, of God's representative on earth, or of his semi-secular equivalent: the will of an elite entitled to govern on account of their accumulated privileges and qualifications).

If the French and Haitian revolutions of the late eighteenth century remain two of the most decisive political events of modern times, it is not because they affirmed the liberal freedoms that are so easily (because unevenly) commemorated today. What was and remains revolutionary about France 1789–94 and Haiti 1791–1803 is the direct mobilization of the people to assert these universal rights and freedoms in direct confrontation with the most powerful vested interests of the day.[1] The taking of the Bastille, the march upon Versailles, the invasion of the Tuileries, the September Massacres, the expulsion of the Girondins and the innumerable confrontations with 'enemies of the people' up and down the country: these are the deliberate interventions that defined both the course of the French revolution, and the immense, unending counter-revolution that it provoked. The Haitian revolutionaries went one step further and forced, for the first time, immediate and unconditional application of the principle that inspired the whole of the radical enlightenment: affirmation of the natural, inalienable rights of all human beings.

The campaign to re-pacify the people has been running, in different ways in different places, ever since. Today, preservation of popular deference and passivity remains the first priority of our single-party democracies at home and their various 'stabilization' missions abroad. People in those places still too stubborn to accommodate themselves to such priorities – most obviously in Gaza and Haiti – find themselves criminalized, quarantined or crushed.

The decisive events of 1792–93, and the popular mobilization that enabled them, have defined the basic political spectrum ever since: the most fundamental modern political choice is between empowerment or disempowerment of the will of the people.

Different versions of this choice have come to the fore every time there is an opportunity to go to the roots of the system of domination that structures a specific situation. Haiti, Palestine, Venezuela and Bolivia are some of the places where in recent years the people have managed, in the face of extraordinary levels of opposition and intimidation, to formulate and to some extent impose their will to transform the situation that oppresses them. Responses to such imposition have tended to follow the Thermidorian model. The mix of old and new counter-revolutionary strategies for dividing, disarming and then dissolving the will of the people – for restoring the people to their 'normal' condition as a dispersed and passive 'flock' – are likely to define the terrain of emancipatory struggle for the foreseeable future.

II

In a European context, philosophical expression of a confidence in the will of the people dates back to Rousseau, and develops in different directions via Kant, Fichte, Hegel and Marx. The optimism that characterizes such an approach is still emphatic in Gramsci (who seeks 'to put the "will", which in the last analysis equals practical or political activity, at the base of philosophy', Gramsci 1971: 345; cf. 125–33, 171–2) and in the early writings of Lukács (for whom 'decision', 'subjective will' and 'free action' have strategic precedence over the apparent 'facts' of a situation, Lukács 1972: 26–7; cf. Lukács 1971: 23, 145, 181). Comparable priorities also orient the political writings of a few more recent philosophers, such as Sartre, Beauvoir and Badiou. Obvious differences aside, what these thinkers have in common is an emphasis on the practical primacy of self-determination and self-emancipation. The older Sartre stopped short of repeating Hegel's insistence that 'even if I am born a slave ..., still I am free in the moment that I will it' (cited in Buck-Morss 2009: 61); nevertheless, however constrained your situation, you remain free voluntarily 'to make something of what is made of you' (Sartre, 1969: 45).

Overall, however, it is difficult to think of a canonical notion more roundly condemned, in recent 'Western' philosophy, than the notion of will, to say nothing of that general will so widely condemned as a precursor of tyranny and totalitarian terror. In philosophical circles voluntarism has become little more than a term of abuse, and an impressively versatile one at that: depending on the context, it can evoke idealism, obscurantism, vitalism, infantile leftism, fascism, petty bourgeois narcissism, neocon aggression, folk-psychological delusion.... Of all the faculties or capacities of that human subject who was displaced from the centre of post-Sartrean concerns, none was more firmly proscribed than its conscious volition. Structuralist and poststructuralist thinkers, by and large, relegated volition and intention to the domain of deluded, imaginary or humanist-ideological miscognition. Rather than explore the ways in which political determination might depend on a collective subject's self-determination, recent philosophy and cultural theory has tended to privilege various forms of either indetermination (the interstitial, the hybrid, the ambivalent, the simulated, the undecidable, the chaotic...) or hyper-determination ('infinite' ethical obligation, divine transcendence, unconscious drive, traumatic repression, machinic automation...). The allegedly obsolete notion of a *pueblo unido* has been displaced by a more differentiated and more deferential plurality of actors – flexible identities, negotiable histories, improvised organizations, dispersed networks, 'vital' multitudes, polyvalent assemblages and so on.

Even the most cursory overview of recent European philosophy is enough to evoke its general tendency to distrust, suspend or overcome the will – a tendency anticipated, in an extreme form, by Schopenhauer. Consider a few names from a list that could be easily expanded. Nietzsche's whole project presumes that 'there is no such thing as will' (Nietzsche 1968: §488) in the usual (voluntary, deliberate, purposeful ...) sense of the word. Heidegger, over the course of his own lectures on Nietzsche, comes to condemn the will as a force of subjective domination and nihilist closure, before urging his readers 'willingly to renounce willing' (Heidegger 1969: 59). Arendt finds, in the affirmation of a popular political will ('the most dangerous of modern concepts and misconceptions' [Arendt 1990: 225]) the temptation that turns modern revolutionaries into tyrants. For Adorno, rational will is an aspect of that enlightenment pursuit of mastery and control which has left the earth 'radiant with triumphant calamity' (Horkheimer and Adorno 2002: 1). Althusser devalues the will as an aspect of ideology in favour of the scientific analysis of historical processes that proceed without a subject. Rancière is one of the few philosophers of his generation to emphasize the category of 'the people', but does so in terms that privilege disruption and dis-location, terms geared towards the aesthetic criteria ('free play of appearance', suspension of 'the opposition of activity and passivity, will and resistance' etc. [Rancière 2002: 136]) that have come to dominate his recent work (see Hallward 2006). Negri and Virno associate a will of the people with authoritarian state power. After Nietzsche, Deleuze privileges transformative sequences that require the suspension, shattering or paralysis of voluntary action. After Heidegger, Derrida associates the will with self-presence and self-coincidence, a forever futile effort to appropriate the inappropriable (the unpresentable, the equivocal, the undecidable, the differential, the deferred, the discordant, the transcendent, the other…). After these and several other philosophers, Agamben summarizes much recent European thinking on political will when he effectively equates it with fascism pure and simple.

Even those thinkers who, against the grain of the times, have insisted on the primacy of self-determination and self-emancipation have tended to do so in ways that devalue political will *per se*. Take Foucault, Sartre and Badiou. Much of Foucault's work might be read as an extended analysis, after Canguilhem, of the ways in which people are 'de-voluntarised' by the 'permanent coercions' at work in disciplinary power, coercions designed to establish 'not the general will but automatic docility' (Foucault 1977: 169). Foucault never compromised on his affirmation of 'voluntary insubordination' in the face of newly stifling forms of government and power, and in crucial lectures from the early 1970s he demonstrated how the development of modern psychiatric and carceral power, in the immediate wake of the French revolution, was designed first and foremost to 'over-power' and break the will of people who had the folly literally to 'take themselves for a king' (Foucault 1997: 32; cf. Foucault 2006: 11, 27–8, 339); nevertheless, in his published work Foucault tends to see the will as complicit in forms of self-supervision, self-regulation and self-subjection. Sartre probably did more than any other philosopher of his generation to emphasize the ways in which an emancipatory project or group depends upon the determination of a 'concrete will', but his philosophy offers a problematic basis for any sort of voluntarism. He accepts as 'irreducible' the 'intention' and 'goals' which orient an individual's fundamental project, but makes a sharp distinction between such intention and merely 'voluntary deliberation' or motivation: since for Sartre the latter is always secondary and 'deceptive', the result is to render the primary intention opaque and beyond 'interpretation' (Sartre 2003: 585–6, 472, 479). Sartre's later work subsequently fails to conceive of a collective will in other than exceptionalist and ephemeral terms. Badiou's powerful revival of a militant theory of the subject is more easily reconciled with a voluntarist agenda (or at least with what Badiou calls a *volonté impure* [Badiou 2003; cf. Badiou 2005: meditation 32]), but suffers from some similar limitations. It is no accident that, like Agamben and Žižek, when Badiou looks to the Christian tradition for a point of anticipation, he turns not to Matthew (with his prescriptions of how to act in the world: spurn the rich, affirm the poor, 'sell all thou hast'…) but to Paul (with his contempt for the weakness of human will and his valorization of the abrupt and infinite transcendence of grace).

Pending a more robust philosophical defence, contemporary critical theorists tend to dismiss the notion of will as a matter of delusion or deviation. But since it amounts to little more than a perverse appropriation of more fundamental forms of revolutionary determination, there is no reason to accept fascist exaltation of an 'awakening' or 'triumph of the will' as the last word on the subject. The true innovators in the modern development of a voluntarist philosophy are Rousseau, Kant and Hegel, and the general principles of such a philosophy are most easily recognized in the praxis of people like Robespierre, John Brown, Fanon, Che Guevara, Vo Nguyen Giap. . . . It is to such people that we need to turn in order to remember or reconceive the true meaning of popular political will.

III

On this basis we might enumerate, along broadly neo-Jacobin lines, some of the characteristic features of a will of the people, understood as the self-determining and self-emancipating subject of politics:

1

Political *will* commands, by definition, voluntary and autonomous action. Unlike involuntary or reflex-like responses, if it exists then will initiates action through free, rational deliberation. As Rousseau puts it, the fundamental 'principle of any action lies in the will of a free being; there is no higher or deeper source . . . . Without will there is no freedom, no self-determination, no "moral causality"' (Rousseau 1962: 499; see also Rousseau 1762: §1008). Robespierre soon drew the most basic political implication of Rousseau's approach when he realized that when people will or 'want to be free they will be' (Robespierre 1910–67: IX, 310). Sieyès anticipated the point on the eve of 1789: '[E]very man has an inherent right to deliberate and will for himself', and 'either one wills freely or one is forced to will, there cannot be any middle position'. Outside voluntary self-legislation 'there cannot be anything other than the empire of the strong over the weak and its odious consequences' (Sieyès 2003: 10).

An intentional freedom is not reducible to the mere faculty of free choice or *liberum arbitrium* (see Arendt 1978: 6–7). If we are to speak of the will of the people we cannot restrict it (as Machiavelli and his successors do) to the passive expression of approval or consent (see Machiavelli 1983: 2:24, 3:5; cf. 1:16, 1:32; Machiavelli 2004: ch. 9). It is the process of actively willing or choosing that renders a particular course of action preferable to another. 'Always engaged', argues Sartre, freedom never 'pre-exists its choice: we shall never apprehend ourselves except as a choice in the making' (Sartre 2003: 501). Augustine and then Duns Scotus already understood that 'our will would not be will unless it were in our power' (Augustine 1993: 76–7; see Duns Scotus 1987: 54–6). Descartes likewise recognized that 'voluntary and free are the same thing' (Descartes 1984b: 246), and finds in the 'indivisible' and immeasurable freedom of the will, our most fundamental resemblance to divinity (see Descartes 1984a: 39–40; Descartes 1985: 204–5). Kant (followed by Fichte) then radicalizes this voluntarist approach when he defines the activity of willing as 'causality through reason' (Kant 1996: 4:461) or 'causality through freedom' (Kant 1996: 4:446).[2] For Kant, will achieves the practical liberation of reason from the constraints of experience and objective knowledge, and it is the active willing that determines what is possible and what is right, and makes it so. As the French revolution will confirm, it is as willing or practical beings that 'people have the quality or power of being the *cause* and . . . *author* of their own improvement' (Kant 1970: 181). Those sceptical of political will, by contrast, assume that apparently voluntary commitments mask a more profound ignorance or devaluation of appetite (Hobbes), causality (Spinoza), context (Montesquieu), habit (Hume), tradition (Burke), history (Tocqueville), power (Nietzsche), the unconscious (Freud), convention (Wittgenstein), writing (Derrida), desire (Deleuze), drive (Žižek)....

2

Political will, of course, involves collective action and direct participation. A democratic political will depends on the power and practice of inclusive assembly, the power to sustain a common commitment. The assertion of what Rousseau calls a general will is a matter of collective volition at every stage of its development. The inaugural 'association is the most voluntary act in the world', and to remain an active participant of the association 'is to will what is in the common or general interest'. Insofar (and only insofar) as they pursue this interest, each person 'puts his person and all his power in common under the supreme control of the general will' (Rousseau 1988a: 4:2, 1:6). Defined in this way, 'the general will is always on the side most favourable to the public interest, that is to say, the most equitable, so that it is necessary merely to be just to be assured of following the general will' (Rousseau 1988b: 66; see also Rousseau 1988a: 2:4).

A general interest exists only if the will to pursue it is stronger than the distraction of particular interests. To say that a general will is 'strong' does not mean that it stifles dissent or imposes uniformity. It means that in the process of negotiating differences between particular wills, the willing of the general interest eventually finds a way to prevail. There is an inclusive general will insofar as those who initially oppose it correct their mistake and realize that 'if my private opinion had prevailed I would have done something other than what I had willed' (Rousseau 1962: 4:2), that is, something inconsistent with my ongoing participation in the general will (see Saint-Just 2004: 482). So long as it lasts, participation in a general will, be it that of a national movement, a political organization, a social or economic association, a trade union, etc., always involves a resolve to abide by its eventual judgement, not as an immediate arbiter of right and wrong but as the process of collectively deliberating and *willing* what is right. Participation in a general will involves acceptance of the risk of finding yourself being, at any given moment, 'wrong with the people rather than right without them', as Jean-Bertrand Aristide put it (Slavin 1991: 6, citing Jean-Bertrand Aristide). By the same token, it is precisely insofar as it remains actively capable of seeking and willing the collective right that we can agree with Rousseau and Sieyès when they insist that, in the long run, a general will can neither err nor betray.

After Robespierre, Saint-Just summarizes the whole Jacobin political project when he rejects 'purely speculative' or 'intellectual' conceptions of justice, as if 'laws were the expression of taste rather than of the general will'. The only legitimate basis of political action is 'the material will of the people, its simultaneous will; its goal is to consecrate the active and not the passive interest of the greatest number of people' (Saint-Just 2004: 547). There are good reasons why Bolivia's current vice-president sees himself as 'one of the last Jacobins of the French Revolution' (García Linera 2006) and his president Evo Morales as a contemporary version of Robespierre (see García Linera 2008: 9).

Mobilization of the general will of the people must not be confused, then, with a merely putschist vanguardism. An abrupt appropriation of the instruments of government by a few 'alchemists of revolution' is no substitute for the deployment of popular power (see Marx and Engels 1978). In spite of obvious strategic differences, Lenin is no more tempted than Luxemburg to substitute a Blanquist conspiracy for 'the people's struggle for power', via mobilization of the 'vast masses of the proletariat' (Lenin 2004; cf. Draper 1990). It is not a matter of imposing an external will or awareness upon an inert people, but of people working to clarify, concentrate and organize their own will. Fanon makes much the same point, when he equates a national liberation movement with the inclusive and deliberate work of 'the whole of the people' (Fanon 1968: 155–6).

Such work likewise serves to distinguish political will from any merely passive opinion or preference, however preponderant. The actively general will distinguishes itself from the mere 'will of all' (which is 'nothing but a sum of particular wills' [Rousseau 1962 2:3]) on account of its mediation through the collective mobilization of the people.[3] The people who sustain the 'will of the people' are not defined by a particular social status or place, but by their active identification of and with an emergent general interest. Sovereignty is an attribute of such action. Conceived in these terms as a general *willing*, the power of the people transcends the power of privilege or government, and entitles the people to overpower the powers that oppose or neglect them. If such powers resist, the Jacobins argue, the only solution is to 'arm the people' in whatever way is required to overcome, with a minimum of violence, this resistance.

3

The will of the people is thus a matter of material power and active empowerment, before it is a matter of representation, authority or legitimacy. What divides society is its response to popular self-empowerment. This is as much a Marxist as it is a Jacobin insight. Any social 'transformation can only come about as the product of the – free – action of the proletariat', notes Lukács, and 'only the practical class consciousness of the proletariat possesses this ability to transform things' (Lukács

1971: 205). Such a praxis-oriented philosophy did not die out after the political setbacks of the 1920s. Sartre took up the same theme in the early 1950s (before Badiou in the 1970s): as far as politics is concerned a 'class is never separable from the concrete will which animates it nor from the ends it pursues. The proletariat forms itself by its day-to-day action. It exists only by action. It *is* action. If it ceases to act, it decomposes' (Sartre 1968: 89).

Will commands the initiation of action, not representation. An exercise in political will involves taking power, not receiving it, on the assumption that (as a matter of 'reason' or 'natural right') the people are always already entitled to take it. 'The oppressed cannot enter the struggle as objects', Freire notes, 'in order *later* to become human beings' (Freire 1996: 50). It makes no sense, as John Brown argued during his trial in 1859, to treat the imperatives of justice merely as recommendations that must bide their time: 'I am yet too young', Brown said on the eve of his execution, 'to understand that God is any respecter of persons' (Jordan 1960). A similar impatience informs the strategic voluntarism of Che Guevara, who knew that it is pointless to wait 'with folded arms' for objective conditions to mature. Whoever waits for 'power to fall into the people's hands like a ripe fruit' will never stop waiting (Guevara 1969:104, 106; see Zikode 2008). Whoever waits for history to do the work that only popular determination can achieve will share the same fate, since '*history* does *nothing*' and

> wages *no* battles. It is *man*, real, living man who does all that …: 'history' is not, as it were, a person apart, using man as a means to achieve *its own* aims; history is *nothing but* the activity of man pursuing his aims.
>
> (Marx 1997)

Between confidence in the people and confidence in historical progress, as Rousseau anticipated, there is a stark choice.

4

Like any form of free or voluntary action, the will of the people is grounded in the practical sufficiency of its exercise. Will is no more a 'substance' or object of knowledge than the cogito variously reworked and affirmed by Kant, Fichte and Sartre. A 'fundamental freedom' or 'practical exercise of reason' proves itself through what it does and makes, rather than through what it is, has or knows. Reading Hegel's *Logic* in 1914, Lenin rediscovers the strategic significance of the equation 'freedom = subjectivity ("or") goal, consciousness, endeavour' (Lenin 1976:164; see Dunayevskaya 2003: 100–1). Freedom demonstrates and justifies itself through willing and acting, or else not at all. 'True human freedom', Kojève insists, can only be 'actively acquired by struggle or work: people are free only when they make themselves free' (Kojève 1980: 220, translation modified). We *are* free, repeats Beauvoir, but freedom '*is* only by making itself be' (de Beauvoir 1976: 25). We are free insofar as 'we will ourselves free' (de Beauvoir 1976: 24), and we will ourselves free by crossing the threshold that separates passivity and 'minority' from volition and activity. We will ourselves free across the distance that our freedom puts between itself and a previous unfreedom. We are free as self-freeing, or as Freire puts it, 'freedom is acquired by conquest, not by gift' (Freire 1996: 29).

5

If it is to persist, a voluntary political association must be disciplined and 'indivisible' as a matter of course.[4] Internal difference and debate within an organized association is one thing, debilitating factional divisions or schisms are another. Popular freedom persists as long as the people assert it. 'In order that the social pact may not be an empty formula', as Rousseau's notorious argument runs,

> it tacitly includes the commitment, which alone can give force to the others, that anyone who refuses to obey the general will shall be compelled to do so by the entire body; this means nothing else than that he will be forced to be free.
>
> (Rousseau 1988a, 1:7)

Preservation of public freedom, in Robespierre's arresting phrase, requires acknowledgement of the 'despotism of truth' (Robespierre 1910–67: IX, 83–4). Collective freedom will endure, in short, only so long as the people can defend themselves against division and deception.

'Virtue' is the name that Rousseau and the Jacobins gave to the practices required to defend a general will against deception and division. To practice virtue is to privilege collective over particular interests, and to ensure that society is governed 'solely on the basis of the common interest. … Each person is virtuous when his private will conforms totally to the general will' (Rousseau 1988a: 2:1). If then 'we wish the general will to be accomplished' we need simply to 'make all the private wills agree with it, or in other words . . .: make virtue reign' (Rousseau 1988b: 69, 67, translation modified).

6

The practical exercise of will only proceeds, as a matter of course, in the face of resistance. To will is always to continue to will, in the face of difficulty or constraint. To continue or not to continue – this is the essential choice at stake in any militant ethics (see Beauvoir 1976: 27–8; Badiou 2001: 52, 91). Either you will and do something, or you do not. Even as it discovers the variety of ways of doing or not-doing, these are the alternatives a political will must confront: yes or no, for or against, continue or stop, where 'to stop before the end is to perish' (Robespierre 1910–67: X, 572).

If for the Jacobins of 1793 'terror' comes to figure as the complement to 'virtue', it is above all as a consequence of their determination to overcome the resistance of the privileged and their political protectors. Terror in the Jacobin (as opposed to Thermidorian) sense is the deployment of whatever force is required to overcome those particular interests that seek to undermine or disempower the collective interest. The reasons why the Jacobin terror (in both France and Haiti) continues to terrify our political establishment, in a way that the far more bloody repression of the 1871 Commune does not, has nothing to do with the actual amount of violence involved. From the perspective of what is already established, notes Saint-Just, 'that which produces the general good is always terrible' (Saint-Just 2004: 1141). The Jacobin terror was more defensive than aggressive, more a matter of restraining than of unleashing popular violence. 'Let us be terrible', Danton said on 10 March 1793, 'so that the people need not be' (Wahnich 2003: 62).

7

By the same token, the practical exercise of will distinguishes itself from mere wish or fantasy through its capacity to initiate a process of genuine 'realization' (see cf. Sartre 2003: 505; Gramsci 1971: 175 n.75). After Fichte, Hegel complements the voluntarist trajectory initiated by Rousseau and Kant, and opens the door to Marx, when he identifies a free collective will − a will that wills and realizes its own emancipation − as the animating principle of a concrete political association. Thus conceived, the will is nothing other than

> thinking translating itself into existence. . . . The activity of the will consists in cancelling and overcoming [*aufzuheben*] the contradiction between sub-jectivity and objectivity and in translating its ends from their subjective determination into an objective one.
> (Hegel 1991: §§4A, 28, translation modified; cf.
> Kojève 1980: 135–6)

After Hegel, Marx will expand the material dimension of such concrete determina-tion, without ever abandoning the idea that what is ultimately determinant are not given economic or historical constraints but free human action − the ability of 'each single individual' to prescribe their own ends and make their own history (Marx and Engels 1975: 1A; cf. Marx 1976: 739).

8

Realization of the will of (the) people is oriented towards the universalization of its consequences. As Beauvoir understood better than Sartre, I can only will my own freedom by willing the freedom of all; the only subject that can sustain the work of unending self-emancipation is *the* people as such, humanity as a whole. Kant, Hegel and Marx take some of the steps required to move from Rousseau's parochial conception of a people to its universal affirmation, but the outcome was again anticipated by Jacobin practice: '[T]he country of a free people is open to all the people on earth' (Saint-Just 2004: 551), and the only 'legitimate sovereign of the earth is the human race .... The interest, the will of the people, is that of humanity' (Robespierre 1910–67: IX, 469; VII, 268).

9

A final consequence follows from this insistence on the primacy of political will: voluntary servitude, from this perspective, is more damaging than external domination. If the will is 'determinant in the first instance' then the most far-reaching forms of oppression involve the collusion of the oppressed. This is the point anticipated by Etienne La Boétie, and then radicalized in different ways by Du Bois, Fanon and Aristide, among many others: in the end, it is the people who empower their oppressors, who can harm them 'only to the extent to which they are willing to put up with them' (La Boétie 2002, translation modified).

★ ★ ★

It would not be hard to write a history of the twentieth century, of course, in such a way as to illustrate the apparent futility of political will. The failure of German communism in the 1920s, the failure of 'Soviet man' in the 1930s, the failure of anti-colonial liberation movements in the 1950s and 60s, the failure of Maoism, the failure of 1968, the failure of anti-war and anti-globalization protests – all these seeming failures might seem to demonstrate one and the same basic point: the diffuse, systemic and hence insurmountable nature of contemporary capitalism, and of the forms of state and disciplinary power that accompany it.

Such a distorted history, in my opinion, would amount to little more than a rationalization of the defeats suffered in the last quarter of the twentieth century. In the late 1940s, Beauvoir already bemoaned our tendency to 'think that we are not the master of our destiny; we no longer hope to help make history, we are resigned to submitting to it' (de Beauvoir 1976: 139). By the late 1970s, such complaint, revalorized as celebration, had become the stuff of a growing consensus. This consensus has now been dominant, in both radical politics and philosophy, for more than 30 disastrous years. It is time to leave it behind.

Notes

Most of this chapter is a revised abbreviation of a longer article that first appeared under the title 'The Will of the People: Notes Towards a Dialectical Voluntarism'.

1 See, in particular, Wahnich (2003), Wahnich (2008), Gauthier (2007) and Nesbitt (2008).
2 In his 1930 lectures on Kant's practical philosophy, Heidegger emphasizes this point – 'to give this priority in everything, to will the ought of pure willing' (Heidegger 2002: 201).
3 Here is the crux of the difference, often noted, between Rousseau's *volonté général* and Montesquieu's *esprit général*. Occasions for the self-determination of the former arise when the collapse or exhaustion of existing social relations give the people an opportunity to assert a new and deliberate beginning. The latter, in contrast, emerges through the combination of the 'many things that govern people: climate, religion, the laws, the maxims of the government, examples of past things, mores, and manners' (Montesquieu 1989: 19:4). As a

general spirit is largely the product of its environment and the 'organically' established order of things, Montesquieu's philosophy recommends, in anticipation of Burke and de Maistre, that 'we should accommodate ourselves to this life and not try to force it into patterns of our own devising' (Montesquieu 1989: 1:2; see Hampson 1983: 9).

4 'For the same reason that sovereignty is inalienable, it is indivisible, for the will is general, or it is not' (Rousseau 1988a: 2:2; cf. Robespierre 1910–67: VII, 268).

Bibliography

African National Congress (1955) *The Freedom Charter*, adopted at the Congress of the People, 26 June 1955 Online. Available HTTP: http://www.anc.org.za/docs/misc/1955/charter.html (accessed 6 June 2010).

Arendt, H. (1978) *The Life of the Mind* vol. 2: *Willing*, New York: Harcourt.

Arendt, H. (1990) *On Revolution*, London: Penguin.

Augustine, Saint (1993) *On Free Choice of the Will*, trans. T. Williams, Indianapolis, IN: Hackett.

Badiou, A. (2001) *Ethics*, trans. P. Hallward, London: Verso.

Badiou, A. (2003) 'La Volonté: Cours d'agrégation', notes taken by F. Nicolas. Online. Available HTTP: http://www.entretemps.asso.fr/Badiou/02-03.2.htm (accessed 6 June 2010).

Badiou, A. (2005) *Being and Event*, trans. O. Feltham, London: Continuum.

de Beauvoir, S. (1976) *Ethics of Ambiguity*, trans. B. Frechtman, New York: Citadel Press.

Buck-Morss, S. (2009) *Hegel, Haiti, and Universal History*, Pittsburgh: University of Pittsburgh Press.

Descartes, R. (1984a) *Meditations on First Philosophy*, in *Philosophical Writings of Descartes* vol. 2, ed. J. Cottingham, R. Stoothoff and D. Murdoch, Cambridge: Cambridge University Press. 37–43.

Descartes, R. (1984b) Letter to Père Mesland, 9 February 1645, in *Philosophical Writings of Descartes* vol. 3, ed. J. Cottingham, R. Stoothoff and D. Murdoch, Cambridge: Cambridge University Press.

Descartes, R. (1985) *Principles of Philosophy*, in *Philosophical Writings of Descartes* vol. 1, ed. J. Cottingham, R. Stoothoff and D. Murdoch, Cambridge: Cambridge University Press. 177–291.

Draper, H. (1990) 'The Myth of Lenin's "Concept of The Party"'. Online. Available HTTP: http://www.marxists.org/archive/draper/1990/myth/myth.htm (accessed 6 June 2010).

Dunayevskaya, R. (2003) *Philosophy and Revolution*, Lanham, MD: Lexington Books.

Duns Scotus, J. (1987) 'The Existence of God', in *Philosophical Writings*, trans. A. Wolter, Indianapolis, IN: Hackett. 34–81.

Fanon, F. (1968) *The Wretched of the Earth*, trans. C. Farrington, New York: Grove Weidenfeld.

Foucault, M. (1977) *Discipline and Punish*, trans. A. Sheridan, New York: Pantheon Books.

Foucault, M. (1997) 'What is Critique?', in M. Foucault, *The Politics of Truth*, ed. S. Lotringer, New York: Semiotext(e). 41–82.

Foucault, M. (2006) *Psychiatric Power*, trans. G. Burchell, New York: Palgrave.

Freire, P. (1996) *Pedagogy of the Oppressed* (1968), trans. M. Ramos, London: Penguin.

García Linera, A. (2006) 'Que Bolivia tenga la mayoría de acciones de Repsol garantiza su seguridad jurídica', *La Fogata*, 21 March. Online. Available HTTP: http://www.lafogata.org/06latino/latino3/bol_26-3.htm (accessed 6 June 2010).

García Linera, A. (2008) *La Potencia plebeya*, Buenos Aires: CLACSO – Prometeo Libros.

Gauthier, F. (2007) 'The French Revolution: Revolution and the Rights of Man and the Citizen', in M. Haynes and J. Wolfreys (eds), *History and Revolution: Refuting Revisionism*, London: Verso. 71–92

Giap, V.N. (1998) Interview with *People's Century*, PBS. Online. Available HTTP: http://www.pbs.org/wgbh/peoplescentury/episodes/guerrillawars/giaptranscript.html (accessed 6 June 2010)

Giap, V.N. (2008) *La Potencia plebeya*, Buenos Aires: CLACSO – Prometeo Libros.

Gramsci, A. (1971) *Selections from the Prison Notebooks*, ed. and trans. Q. Hoare and G. Nowell Smith, London: Lawrence & Wishart.

Guevara, E. (1969) 'The Marxist–Leninist Party', in *Che: Selected Works of Ernesto Guevara*, ed. R.E. Bonachea and N.P. Valdes, Cambridge, MA: MIT Press. 104–6.

Hallward, P. (2006) 'Staging Equality: Rancière's Theatrocracy', *New Left Review*, 37 (February): 109–29.

Hallward, P. (2009) 'The Will of the People: Notes Towards a Dialectical Voluntarism', *Radical Philosophy*, 155 (May/June): 17–29.

Hampson, N. (1983) *Will and Circumstance: Montesquieu, Rousseau, and the French Revolution*, London: Duckworth.

Hegel, F. (1991) *Elements of the Philosophy of Philosophy of Right*, trans. H.B. Nisbet, Cambridge: Cambridge University Press.

Heidegger, M. (1969) *Discourse on Thinking*, New York: Harper & Row.

Heidegger, M. (2002) *Essence of Human Freedom*, trans. T. Sadler, London: Continuum.

Horkheimer, M. and Adorno, T.W. (2002) *Dialectic of Enlightenment* (1944), trans. E. Jephcott, Stanford, CA: Stanford University Press.

Jordan, A. (1960) 'John Brown's Raid on Harper's Ferry', *International Socialist Review*, 21:1. Online. Available HTTP: http://www.marxists.org/history/etol/newspape/isr/vol21/no01/jordan.htm (accessed 6 June 2010).

Kant, I. (1970) 'The Contest of Faculties', in *Kant's Political Writings*, ed. H. Reiss, Cambridge: Cambridge University Press. 176–90.

Kant, I. (1996) *Groundwork of the Metaphysics of Morals*, in *Practical Philosophy*, ed. and trans. M. McGregor, Cambridge: Cambridge University Press. 37–108.

Kojève, A. (1980) *Introduction to the Reading of Hegel*, ed. A. Bloom, trans. J. Nichols Jr, Ithaca, NY: Cornell University Press.

La Boétie, E. (2002) *The Discourse of Voluntary Servitude* (1548), trans. H. Kurz, New York: Columbia University Press. Online. Available HTTP: http://www.constitution.org/la_boetie/serv_vol.htm (accessed 6 June 2010).

Lenin, V.I. (1976) 'Conspectus of Hegel's Book *The Science of Logic*', in *Collected Works* vol. 38, Moscow: Progress Publishers.

Lenin, V.I. (2004) 'The Conference Summed Up' (7 May 1906). Online. Available HTTP: http://www.marxists.org/archive/lenin/works/1906/may/07.htm (accessed 6 June 2010).

Lukács, G. (1971) *History and Class Consciousness*, trans. R. Livingstone, London: Merlin Press.

Lukács, G. (1972) 'What is Orthodox Marxism?', *Political Writings 1919–1929*, ed. R. Livingstone, trans. M. McColgan, London: NLB.

Machado, A. (1978) 'Proverbios y Cantares – XXIX', in *Selected Poems of Antonio Machado*, trans. B.J. Craige, Baton Rouge, LA: Louisiana State University Press.

Machiavelli, N. (1983) *Discourses*, trans. H.C. Mansfield and N. Tarcov, London: Penguin.

Machiavelli, N. (2004). *The Prince*, trans. G. Bull, London: Penguin.

Marx, K. (1966) *The Poverty of Philosophy*, Beijing: Foreign Languages Press.

Marx, K. (1976) *Capital I*, trans. B. Fowkes, London: Penguin.

Marx, K. (1978) 'Meeting of the Central Authority, September 15, 1850', in *Marx/Engels Collected Works* vol. 10, New York: International Publishers.

Marx, K. (1997) *The Holy Family*, chapter 6. Online. Available HTTP: http://www.marxists.org/archive/marx/works/1845/holy-family/ch06.htm (accessed 6 June 2010).

Marx, K. and Engels, F. (1975) *The German Ideology*, in *Marx/Engels Collected Works* vol. 5, New York: International Publishers.

Marx, K. and Engels, F. (1978) '*Les Conspirateurs*, par A. Chenu' (1850). Online. Available HTTP: http://www.marxists.org/archive/marx/works/1850/03/chenu.htm (accessed 6 June 2010).

Montesquieu, C. de (1989) *The Spirit of The Laws* (1748), ed. A.M. Cohler, B.C. Miller and H.S. Stone, Cambridge: Cambridge University Press.

Nesbitt, N. (2008) *Universal Emancipation: The Haitian Revolution and the Radical Enlightenment*, Charlottesville, VA: University of Virginia Press.

Nietzsche, F. (1968) *The Will to Power*, ed. Walter Kaufmann, New York: Vintage.

Rancière, J. (2002) 'The Aesthetic Revolution and Its Outcomes', *New Left Review*, 14 (March/April): 134–51.

Robespierre, M. (1910–67) *Oeuvres complètes*, ed. Eugène Déprez *et al.*, Paris: Société des Études Robespierristes.

Rousseau, J-J. (1762) *Emile, ou de l'éducation*, Institute for Learning Technologies online edition. Available HTTP: http://www.ilt.columbia.edu/pedagogies/rousseau/em_eng_bk4.html (accessed 9 July, 2010).

Rousseau, J-J. (1962) *Contrat social*, first version, in *Political Writings* vol. 1, ed. C. Vaughan, New York: Wiley. 434–511.

Rousseau, J-J. (1988a) *The Social Contract*, in *Rousseau's Political Writings*, ed. Alan Ritter and Julia Conaway Bondanella, New York: Norton.

Rousseau, J-J. (1988b) 'Discourse on Political Economy', in *Rousseau's Political Writings*, ed. Alan Ritter and Julia Conaway Bondanella, New York: Norton.

Saint-Just, L.A. de (2004) *Oeuvres complètes*, ed. A. Kupiec and M. Abensour, Paris: Gallimard 'Folio'.

Sartre, J-P. (1968) *The Communists and Peace*, trans. M. Fletcher, New York: Braziller.

Sartre, J-P. (1969) 'Itinerary of a Thought', *New Left Review*, 58 (November/December): 43–66.

Sartre, J-P. (2003) *Being and Nothingness*, trans. H. Barnes, London: Routledge.

Sieyès, E.J. (2003) *Views of the Executive Means Available to the Representatives of France in 1789*, in *Political Writings*, ed. and trans. M. Sonenscher, Indianapolis, IN: Hackett.

Slavin, J.P. (1991) 'Haiti: The Elite's Revenge', *NACLA Report on the Americas*, 25:3 (December): 57–61.

Wahnich, S. (2003) *La Liberté ou la mort: Essai sur la terreur et le terrorisme*, Paris: La Fabrique.

Wahnich, S. (2008) *La Longue Patience du peuple: 1792, la naissance de la République*, Paris: Payot.

Zikode, S. (2008) 'The Burning Issue of Land and Housing', 28 August. Online. Available HTTP: http://www.diakonia.org.za/index.php?option=com_content&task=view&id=129&Itemid=54 (accessed 6 June 2010).

7

THE PERSISTENCE OF HOPE

Critical theory and enduring in late liberalism

Elizabeth A. Povinelli

Striving

Since the mid 1960s, immanent critique has sought to conceptualize the source and space of 'new possibilities of life' (Deleuze 1983: 101) independent of philosophical notions of transcendental consciousness. In his Vincennes lectures on Spinoza, for instance, Gilles Deleuze slowly differentiated between a mode of thought defined by its representational character (ideas) and a mode of thought that is not defined representationally (affects) (Deleuze 2007: unpaginated). Deleuze concedes that affects can have an ideational form ('there is an idea of the loved thing, to be sure, there is an idea of something hoped for') and that ideas have a chronological and logical primacy in relation to the affects ([i]n order to will, it's necessary to have an idea, however confused or indeterminate it may be, of what is willed'). But he insisted that affects like hope and love 'represent nothing, strictly nothing' (ibid.). Affects may be ultimately determined by the given system of ideas that one has, but they are not 'reducible to the ideas one has' whether one considers these ideas in their objective extrinsic reality or in their formal intrinsic reality.[1] Ideas and affects are 'two kinds of modes of thought' that differ 'in nature'. An idea represents something whereas an affect does not. An affect is not nothing, but it is also not something in the same way as an extrinsic or intrinsic idea. An affect is a force of existing (*vis existendi*) that is neither the realized thing (an idea), nor the accomplishment of a thing (an act, *potentia agendi*). This perspective on the force of existing is clearly engaging Spinoza's claim that things, finite and determinate kinds of existence, strive (*conatus*) to persevere in their being. For Deleuze, the perpetual variation between *vis existendi* and *potentia agendi* – between striving to persevere and any actual idea or action that emerges from this striving – provides a space of potentiality where new forms of life can emerge. But it is exactly in this onto theoretical spacing that a different, sociological question emerges: How do new forms of social life maintain this force of existing in specific social spacings of life? How do they endure the effort it takes to strive to persevere? And how in answering these questions do new, if not ontotheoretical, then political and ethical concerns emerge?

The question of how new possibilities of life are able to maintain their force of existence in specific organizations of social space becomes especially acute in the wake of Giorgio Agamben's reflections on Deleuze's immanent philosophy and his own work on the biopolitical. In his reflections on Deleuze's *Immanence: A Life...*, Agamben calls for the development of a coherent ontology of potentiality (*dynamis*) that would upend the primacy of actuality (*energeia*). For Agamben, potentiality has a dual nature: while the actual can only be, the potential can be or not be.[2] And it is exactly within this ontological duality of the potential that new possibilities of life are sheltered. But for Agamben, not all potentialities have the same potential when it comes to the kinds and degrees of difference necessary to disturb current biopolitical formations. In the difficult last few sections of *Homo Sacer*, Agamben turns to a series of 'uncertain and nameless terrains' where life and death, *bios* and *zoē*, enter 'zones of indistinction' (Agamben 1998: 187). The American comatose patient, Karen Quinlan, exemplifies such spaces:

> Karen Quinlan's body – which wavers between life and death according to the progress of medicine and the changes in legal decisions – is a legal being as much as it is a biological being. A law that seeks to decide on life is embodied in a life that coincides with death.
>
> (Ibid.: 186)

The concept of death 'far from having become more exact, now oscillates from one pole to other with the greatest indeterminacy' (ibid.: 162). Unable to rest on a 'decisive criterion,' the line between death and life becomes pure potential. It might be or not be here or there. And it is in these maximally intensified zones of oscillation and indeterminacy that new forms of life and worlds will emerge and the 'ways and the forms of a new politics must be thought' (ibid.: 187). But rather than answering our question of how new forms of social life can survive the perpetual variation of being, Agamben's examples intensify it. How can new forms of life, let alone the political thought they might foster, persevere in such spaces? How can new social worlds endure the 'wavering of death' (ibid.: 163) that defines these spaces? Indeed, so unlikely are the possibilities of new life surviving in these spaces that, cribbing off Brian Massumi, we might describe instances of survival as moments of 'miraculization' (Massumi 1993: 25).

Attempting to address the question of the endurance, let alone the survival, of alternative forms of life in the gale force of curtailing social winds opens a set of new ethical and political questions. If the possibilities of new forms of life dwell and are sheltered within the variation between the force of existing and the power of acting within these intensified zones of being and not being, then what does immanent critique demand of those who live in these zones? This problem becomes particularly clear if we think of potentiality as the ethical substance of immanent critique. If, as Michel Foucault defined it, ethical substance is the prime material (*matière*) of moral reflection, conduct and evaluation, then the ethical substance of immanent critique would be intensified potentiality, insofar as intensified potentiality is the material on which ethical work (*travail éthique*) is carried out. But this work is distributed across different social groups. Thus it is important to note, again following Foucault's reading of the use of pleasure among the Greeks and the practice of critique more generally, that pleasure and critique are generally available materials and practices, irrespective of the fact that only some people make use of them. But the general availability of intensified potential does not seem to be equally available in the same way. Certainly all subjects exist in the variation between *vis existendi* and *potentia agendi* and between modes of being and not being. But, the intensity of this variation and its zoning are neither uniform nor uniformly distributed. As a result, a gap seems to open between those who reflect on and evaluate ethical substance and those who are this ethical substance.

In some ways, the gap between those who reflect on and evaluate ethical substance and those who are ethical substance mirrors a much older gap in critical theory. We can think here of the ways that Louis Althusser struggled to differentiate how intellectuals and the proletariat were situated in and represented class struggle.[3] But, rather than dwell on the question of critical theory's proper stance towards the subject it posits as the engine of history, in this essay I want to examine a slightly different set of concerns. First, I should note that I am myself aligned with the general project of immanent critique to find a source of a social otherwise outside a gesture of transcendental consciousness. My alignment with immanent critique is no doubt due to a certain aesthetic and theoretical predisposition to this framework. But it also emerges out of a longstanding commitment to a set of local Indigenous Australian understandings of the immanent geontological (the being of geology) source of life and its possibilities. Second, given these commitments, I want to turn from an ontology of potentiality to a sociology of potentiality. Rather than the question of the variation of being and not being or affects and ideas in general, I want to understand this variation in specific historical contexts. But I am making a general claim; namely, that potentiality and its perpetual variations never occur in a general way, but always, as Deleuze himself noted, in specific *agencements* – arrangements of connecting concepts, materials and forces that make a common compositional unity. Finally, when I say that I am interested in the sociology of potentiality I am gesturing to specific arrangements that extend far beyond simple human sociality. The will to persevere is linked to the endurance of things, and these things might be human or might be determinate arrangements that include humans and a host of other modes of existence being composed and decomposed.

The following turns to a social seam in contemporary Australia where the variation between affect, idea and act and between potentiality and actuality are foregrounded: a digital archive project that I am working on with Indigenous friends and colleagues in northern Australia. This seam of social life is hardly as horrific as those that interested Agamben at the end of *Homo Sacer*. But it is exactly for this reason that I turn away from zones of indistinction as witnessed in the cases of Quinlan and the Muselmann and towards zones of endurance as witnessed in the social seams of contemporary Indigenous Australia. How can we assess the possibilities of enduring striving in zones where life has yet to be absorbed into the extreme wavering of death? How do these possibilities help us to assess the hope that immanent critique places in the ethical work of intensified potentiality?

Enduring

On 10 July 2009, I was driving along a back highway that connects the Darwin suburbs in the Northern Territory of Australia to the Palmerston suburbs, a distance of about 25 kilometres. In the small rented truck with me were several Indigenous friends and colleagues of mine, some of whom I have known since they were teens: Gigi Lewis, then 35; her partner, Rex Edmunds, then 46, and three young teenage boys in their care. We were moving some household items, including a washing machine tied down in the back of the truck, from Gigi's mother's house in Darwin to Gigi and Rex's new house in Palmerston. Rex was drinking in the backseat, relaxing after a long week of laying a water pipe in a small rural community, Bulgul, located about 300 kilometres south of Darwin. The water pipe was part of the infrastructure of an augmented reality project that we and another set of families had been working on for the previous two years, in collaboration with various Northern Territory government agencies and libraries and the local university. The idea of the project is easy enough to convey. Imagine a tourist preparing for a trip to far north Australia. While researching the area online, she discovers our website that highlights various points of interest. She then downloads a version of a GPS-activated tour into her smartphone for a fee much the same way a person downloads a song from iTunes. Now imagine this same person in a boat, floating off the shore of a pristine beach off the coast of Bulgul. She activates her GPS and video camera and holds up her smartphone. As she moves the phone around, she sees various hypertext and video options available to her – a story of the Indigenous Dreaming site where she finds herself; archival photos of traditional uses of that area; et cetera. Along with this tourist portal would be two others: one for environmentalists and one for Indigenous participants. The Indigenous members of the project would have control over all the portals, the information available through them, and its distribution. My colleagues hoped that this augmented reality project would provide a means of training themselves and their children in the new communication technologies, provide a source of income and support their belief that knowledge about places should be learned in places so as to build an obligation to places.

However, between the idea of the project and the effects we hoped the project would produce and the actual project lay a material and discursive world. And, although it should be common sense at this point, it is still necessary to note that, while the actual world stood between all of us and the idea we had of the project, the actual world does not address all of us in the same way. We are and are not the same thing in the sense that we may be an aggregation vis-à-vis our intentions to build this augmented reality project, but we are constantly disaggregated by the world around us. Take for instance our efforts to lay the pipeline. To lay the pipeline, we decided to rent a small trench-digging machine, which meant driving into Darwin to rent it, dig the ditch the same day and then drive it back. The other option was to dig the 100-metre trench by hand through sun-baked hardened soil with crow bars and pickaxes. But to rent the trench digger we needed a credit card and the ability to pay. Of the ten adults working on the project, and their extended family, no one had a credit card or the ability to pay, so we used mine. On the long drive down to Bulgul, on one of the many dirt roads, several attachments on the trench digger flew off, which meant several of us had to drive back along the road to find them. When we finally got the trench digger off the truck, Rex learned to use it by using it. The piping was donated. We collaboratively consulted on how to attach various parts of the piping and how to bury it as we attached the parts and buried the pipe. After finishing there was a little leakage at the tap. More than we'd like to have seen, but not so much that we were willing to dig up the entire pipeline after an exhausting day.

What is at stake here then is the materiality of our idea as it encounters different *agencements*. These arrangements shape and direct actions such as our decision to move large household appliances a day after returning from Bulgul, no matter that we were all exhausted, because my truck was still available (I was leaving in a couple of days for the United States). But these arrangements are also continually and slowly decomposed by the material conditions that support and run through them. When we reached our destination, we were chagrined to discover that the lid of the washing machine had flown off. Or, maybe, we hoped, we had never put it on the truck and so we would find it at Gigi's mother's house. But when we drove back to Darwin, carefully following our tracks, there it was on the side of the road, crumpled and flattened from having been repeatedly run over in rush hour traffic. The next morning I got up from a flat at the university where I stayed when in town, and drove to their house where they were still lamenting the lid. Without it the machine would not run. How would they afford a new washing machine? Why hadn't someone tied down the washing machine more carefully and securely? 'Don't blame me', I said, guilty because I had been among those securing the washing machine to the back of the truck. 'I am blaming Rex', Gigi said, 'He was drunk'. 'Not really', said Rex, and besides, 'We are getting somewhere'. One of Gigi's daughters laughed and asked, 'Where's that?' 'We're still alive', Rex said. 'We're still trying', Gigi agreed conciliatorily.

When Gigi and Rex said that they were still alive and trying, their words foreground the differential value of the pure force of existing (*vis existendi*) across social groups. For people like their family, the phrases 'still trying', 'still going', 'still alive' are condensed statements about the miracle of persevering against the play of social forces that address them and maintaining or elaborating another mode of being in the face of those forces. So what are the summary characteristics of this play of forces? Let me just note two broad formations, neoliberalism and late liberalism, and their specific Australian expressions.

Neoliberalism is a notoriously inexact concept. Depending on who is using this term, it may be referring to: a formation of the market; an ideology about human value; or an organization of life and death and their cognates, care and abandonment. Thus on one hand, neoliberalism refers to the transformation of state politics and market relations between the postwar Bretton Woods agreement (loosely the Keynesian period) to its collapse in the 1970s. With the collapse of Bretton Woods, neoliberals argued for the privatization and deregulation of state assets, the territorial dispersion of production through subcontracting and a shift in tax policies that favoured the rich. But, as everyone from Amartya Sen to Tony Judt to Michel Foucault has noted, neoliberalism also marks a very different philosophy about the proper relationship among market, state and social values than both classical laissez-faire liberalism and Keynesian liberalism.[4] Neoliberals do not merely wish to free the economy from the Keynesian regulatory state, they wish to free the truth games of capitalism from the market itself – market value should be the general measure of all social activities and values (Judt 2009; Sen 2009).[5] Once freed, new powers of life and death emerge, breaking the older liberal duality of making life and letting die and instigating a new triangular formation of power in relation to life. Neoliberal governance makes die, makes live and lets die; indeed, making die is proposed as a form of caring for others.

By late liberalism, as distinct from the varieties and specificities of capital and state relations, I mean the shape that the liberal governance of social and cultural difference took as it responded to a series of legitimacy crises in the wake of anti-colonial and new social movements. Late liberalism is not independent of the ideological struggles between market and state relations as articulated by laissez-faire liberalism, Keynesian liberalism and neoliberalism, but neither is it purely and simply a projection of these struggles. From the 1950s onwards, and culminating in the dramatic world events of 1968, anti-colonial and new social movements transfigured the prior way in which liberalism governed alternative forms of life by putting extreme pressure on the legitimating frameworks of paternalistic civilizational uplift or moral rectitude. Activists and their theorists claimed that the Western arts of caring for the colonized and the subaltern were not rectifying human inequalities but creating and entrenching them. In short, these movements created a crisis of legitimacy for the governing. But this legitimacy crisis was, over time, turned into a crisis of culture for the governed as state after state instituted formal or informal policies of cultural recognition (or cognate policies such as multiculturalism) as a strategy for addressing the challenge of internal and external difference. Soon to care for difference was construed as making a space for culture to care for difference. And to assess care in late liberalism was to assess the capacity of culture to act as an agent of care.

We can see what is at stake in the distinction between neoliberalism and late liberalism by returning to Gigi and Rex's claim that their family was getting somewhere on the basis of nothing more than the fact that they are still alive and trying. Their statements condense a set of tacit references to shared background. For nearly two years prior to moving into their new home in Palmerston, they and the other Indigenous members of the augmented reality project had been homeless. Prior to that they had spent their lives, as had their parents and grandparents, in a small rural Indigenous community across the Darwin harbour. They had grown up in the shadow of the land rights movement and the celebration of Indigenous cultural difference more generally. Land rights and cultural recognition in Australia was exemplary of the logic of care in late liberalism. By making a space for traditional Indigenous culture, the state argued it was making a space for this traditional culture to care for Indigenous people. But land rights legislation, and public discourse on Indigenous culture more generally, differentiated among Indigenous people on the basis of the tradition–effect – the assessment of different Indigenous people on the basis of their correspondence to a modernist anthropological understanding of the clan and its territory (Kogacioglu 2004). In caring for Indigenous people in this way, land rights placed a division into Indigenous social worlds that then internally divided Indigenous communities.

However imperfect, this way of life started to unravel in 2007. As reported in the local Darwin newspaper, on 15 March 2007, Gigi and her family, and five other families, were threatened with chainsaws and pipes, watched their cars and houses being torched and their dogs beaten to death. Four families lost rare, well-paying jobs in education, housing and water works. Why they were driven out – what caused this explosion of violence – cannot be answered, except in the most narrow sense (so-and-so hit so-and-so and then their friends got involved), without immediately being drawn into discourses of care and harm in late liberalism and neoliberalism. For instance, the newspaper did not report that Gigi's grandparents, and most of the senior and now deceased members of the community, had continually petitioned the government to recognize all community members as traditional owners irrespective of their clan affiliations in order to avoid creating internal divisions and the violence they feared would flow from them. Instead, follow-up news stories insinuated that traditional land struggles were to blame for the riot: the violence was caused by ancient clan conflicts rather than by the modern creation of clans as a way of managing the critique of colonialism. Public meetings were held, attended by the leaders of Department of Family, Housing, Community Services and Indigenous Affairs in the Northern Territory Labor government, in which the displaced people were held up as examples of the failures of land rights policies to protect Indigenous people living in communities outside their traditional country. The families driven out were promised new housing, schooling and jobs at Bulgul, a site closer to their traditional countries. Fifty people promptly moved to Bulgul and set up a tent settlement.

But then, on 21 June 2007, the then Prime Minister of Australia, John Howard, declared a 'national emergency' in relation to the abuse of children in Indigenous communities in the Northern Territory. Howard's declaration came in the wake of the *Little Children Are Sacred* report of the Northern Territory Board of Inquiry into the Protection of Aboriginal Children from Sexual Abuse. In the name of this national emergency, Howard's government assumed broad and unprecedented powers over Indigenous affairs in the Northern Territory, including Indigenous welfare, education, land tenure and health. Howard's announcement came with a carrot and stick. As a carrot, Howard promised millions of dollars for Indigenous health, housing, education and employment training. As a stick, the federal government assumed control over 73 Indigenous townships through the forcible acquisition of five-year leases over townships on Aboriginal-owned land, community living areas and other designated Indigenous areas, and sent, under the cover of military police, medical personnel to conduct compulsory sexual health exams for all children under the age of 16. Indigenous people living in remote communities, or those who, like my friends, were promised housing in or nearer to their traditional country, were told to move closer to the cities where infrastructural and service delivery costs were lower, even if doing so would endanger their lives. The people who made the promises to the displaced persons confronted the budgetary consequences of these promises and suddenly became difficult to reach. In the year that followed the income of two of the six families driven off went from roughly 28,000 to 12,000 Australian dollars per year (£16,800 and £7,200, respectively) after they lost their permanent jobs and were moved onto the Community Development Employment Program (CDEP, a work and training programme within a social welfare framework, loosely called 'work for the dole').

The Intervention was widely proclaimed as part of a neoliberal ('enterprise') approach to Indigenous affairs – and the end of the failed policy of cultural recognition. Whereas in the regime of recognition, the recognition of culture was presented as the solution to care for Indigenous people, now it was claimed to be the condition of their harm. Sexual abuse was portrayed as caused by traditional culture even though the authors of the *Little Children Are Sacred* carefully argued that contemporary sexual abuse should never be thought of as caused by traditional culture (Anderson and Wild 2007). 'Business managers' with powers to control and direct all Indigenous programs and their assets, including the monitoring of all community communication and video equipment, were also sent to take control of all Commonwealth programs in Indigenous town camps and rural communities.[6] One of the first actions of these business managers was to shift Indigenous workers from the CDEP to welfare. A shift from work to welfare was necessary because the federal government wished to control the wealth and spending of Indigenous people in remote communities and town camps. For legal reasons, persons on the CDEP could not have their wages managed. Once all Indigenous people were placed on welfare, payments could be tied to school attendance and other behavioural indices; furthermore, 50 per cent of payments were given in the form of debit cards that restricted purchasing choices of Indigenous men and women to selected stores and selected items and prohibited them from purchasing alcohol and pornography. But shifting from CDEP to welfare came with a dramatic lowering of incomes. And the government announced that the CDEP would itself be slowly phased out, an event that would reduce the income of members of our augmented reality project by half again.

But it was exactly within this play of historically specific forces that our augmented reality project emerged, supporting immanent critique's claim that these spaces of indeterminacy provide the conditions for new forms of life. Before the riot and the Intervention, I had been working with these same families and others on a digital archive whose initial content would come from material I had accumulated over the previous 25 years working with the project member parents and grandparents. The digital archive was going to be part of the Northern Territory Libraries' innovative Library Knowledge Centers. The Northern Territory Library had already established 10 Library Knowledge Centers in remote communities. We were petitioning to become the eleventh. These digital archives were anchored to a 'brick and mortar' model of the library meaning that they were located on a dedicated computer in a building on a community. But after March 2007, this computer, this building and this community were suddenly not available to the project members. And after November 2007, it was becoming clear that no other building would be built at Bulgul. But rather than emptying the space absolutely, these new formations of neoliberalism and late liberalism opened up the possibility of designing something that more tightly connected the digital archive with a local epistemology in which knowledge's end was not truth, though truth was a critical anchor of knowledge, but embodied obligation.

But before we simply start the celebration, we must ask, if this kind of potentiality is where new forms of life emerge, can the forms of life that emerge in these zones endure the material nature of these spaces of potentiality? Can our bodies or our things endure the conditions in which they must exist as they wait for the virtual to become actual? On the day we were moving the washing machine, as we paused for a red traffic light, Gigi showed me two large staph infections growing on her leg under her skin and I showed her the staph infections I had on my forehead. As I have discussed elsewhere, these sores are ubiquitous in Indigenous communities where bodies lack the resources to clearly differentiate human and certain bacterial life (Povinelli 2006a). And the inability to separate these forms of life is located within such things as the washing machine, now broken, that might not endure the way Gigi and Rex must live their lives. So Gigi and Rex's statement that they are alive and trying must be read within these material conditions of *agencement*. Rex and Gigi's insistence that they had the right to say they were getting somewhere insofar as they remained 'alive' and were still 'trying' is understandable given how they experience the world addressing them – a world in which endurance is for some written in the progressive mood. This point is only intensified when we acknowledge that Gigi and Rex are right. Right next door to them is a vast world of close and distant kin who are not enduring, who are dying on average 20 years sooner than non-Indigenous Australians, who have the disease profile of Third-World spaces within a state with widely accessible public health care.

Decomposing

Part of the struggle Gigi and Rex face is the spiralling order of virtuality that characterizes how the state cares for them and the kinds of events that confront them. Gigi and Rex, and their kin, face an exponential form of the virtual: they themselves and their social projects neither are nor are not; the disciplines of care that address them neither exist nor do not; and the kinds of events that decompose their lives neither occur nor do not occur. It is in these escalating conditions of virtual being, in which being and not being unfolds in a spiral structure, that the striving to endure, to persevere, must be situated.

Take for example the disciplines of care that address Indigenous people like Gigi and Rex. Even if we believe that cultural recognition indexed some significant transformation of the liberal governance of difference, we might ask how completely this change of heart was institutionalized. After all, social programs were underfunded, unfunded and sporadically funded. Certain groups had access to power-laden spaces of Indigenous bureaucracies, others did not. Different programmes enshrined cognate but incommensurate forms of 'culture' (Povinelli 2006b). These incommensurate and partial political fields of cultural recognition provided significant room for Indigenous people to manoeuvre within the manoeuvres of late liberalism (sometimes for the benefit of broad groups, sometimes to the benefit of small groups). But these incommensurate and partial fields also continually disrupted the socialities of Indigenous lives, sorting and resorting people into different kinds of piles: traditional, historical, too cultural or not cultural enough. And these techniques of sorting populations created new lines of tension within Indigenous communities. In this sense, cultural recognition never happened; not because nothing happened but because some things happened, some things did not happen and some things happened too much. And the same thing can be said about the Intervention. Intervention programmes are also underfunded, unfunded and sporadically funded. The majority of the AUS$672 million set aside by the Strategic Indigenous Housing and Infrastructure Program for new housing has been spent on administrative costs rather than on the houses promised. And older forms of cultural recognition remain on the books, making the field of manoeuvre ever more complex and hazardous for Indigenous actors. Not surprisingly, two years after the riot, two of the families driven out of their old community had been given public housing in Darwin and Palmerston, half of the families were still homeless and two families had moved back to their original community, crowding into already overcrowded houses. Everyone struggles to maintain a position on the CDEP without being sure how long the CDEP itself will last.

If the formations of care that address people like Gigi and Rex are incommensurate, indefinite and virtual, the kinds of events that continually decompose their lives are equally difficult to pinpoint or mobilize for ethical or political projects. The *quasi-events* that saturate their worlds and social projects are kinds of events that neither happen nor not happen. As quasi-events, they are difficult to aggregate and thus apprehend, evaluate and grasp as ethical and political demands in specific markets, publics and states. This is especially so when these quasi-events are opposed to crises and catastrophes which seem to necessitate ethical reflection and political and civic engagement. The ethical and political stakes of such quasi-events face-off with spectacularly reported catastrophes like riots and sexual abuse. Not surprisingly, then, these kinds of catastrophic events become what inform the social science of suffering and thriving, the politics of assembly and dispersal and the socially constituted senses of the extraordinary and everyday.[7]

Take for example the washing machine. As we drove past the crumpled washing machine lid, orphaned on the side of the highway, unable to endure the actualities of the human lives to which it was attached, something like an event was felt and commented upon. Gigi sighed and half-heartedly asked whether we could pull off the road, pick it up and try to repair it. One of the young adults in the car, frustrated by the tedious trips back and forth between Darwin and Palmerston, snapped at her, 'old lady, it's really busted' ('*wulgow, im butedup properly*'). Exhausted, I agreed, 'it's ruined' ('*im wedjiyirr*'), and kept driving. My daughter's partner leaned out the back window, squinted at the smashed metal and suggested we throw out the entire washing machine. But on AUS$12,000 a year (£7,300) – if they never miss a day of work on the CDEP – they could not afford a new washing machine and a used one would be no more reliable. Rex said he could figure out a way to jerry-rig the machine to run without a top. Gigi said he could jerry-rig it, but wouldn't. And later in the day, Gigi's daughter remarked that this tug of war between Gigi and Rex would go on and on and on with everyone left doing the laundry by hand (*finger finger job*).

But what form of support can this kind of event provide to Rex and Gigi? Surely the moment that the lid flew off the washing machine, a moment none of us witnessed and so cannot describe – Did it strain at its joints? Did it snap? Was it hinged to the bed of the truck in the first place? – a new kind of individuation and differentiation emerged; a *thisness* could be discerned. What once fit together no longer did. And this fitting together was not merely between lid and machine but between how we fit in the machine's world and it fit in ours. What was barely considered, lifting and lowering a lid, became a matter of exertion, mental and physical. And yet, really, this *thisness* is hardly anything. If an event, it was a very small event. The lid itself was standard size, maybe a little less than a half a metre square. It was made out of light metal. To be sure, we were lucky that it didn't hit the windscreen of the cars behind us when it flew off; the truck I was driving was rented in my name and so they would not have been liable, but even my budget strains if at a higher order of income. Moreover, nothing, except the snippets of local Indigenous English and Emiyenggal that I quoted above, would distinguish Rex and Gigi in the sea of class-based disadvantage – or from the ordinary life of things in any class location. I have had little things break in the process of moving too many times to remember. What makes class matter, of course, is the difficulty of replacing material objects, even those without explicit sentimental value. But class can ramify quite slowly, little events heap up, one after another, and yet never become anything large enough to divide being decisively – to make local headlines. Thus, as Gigi's and Rex's lives moved away from the explosion of violence to the erosion of their lives, they went from being poster children for why the Intervention was needed to just another anonymous statistic in the discursive war on the success and failure of the Intervention.

In other words, the issue of potentiality meets the problems of support and threshold. Speaking about the way that mass media reduces eventfulness, rather than the problem of eventfulness per se, Brian Massumi discusses how an event's specific content is short-circuited into an endless series of 'like' events' (Massumi 1993: 25). The weakness of the will is coextensive with the wobbly order of the everyday. Our flying lid was just the latest in a series of flying objects – for instance, just a week before, a second hand Esky lid flew off, making the Esky unusable as an Esky but functional as a bush bathtub. So why don't we tie things down? Or tie them down more securely? Why don't we – they – put more effort into our – their – striving? If the washing machine lid's adventure in flight was just the latest in a series of errant take-offs, then why didn't we double check that all the ropes were secure, the appliances turned in the right direction (so the wind ran over the washing machine in such a way that it held the lid down), the right cords with the right machines, etc? One answer is that they are not a separate thing from the world in which they live. And there is nowhere in which something like ease of coping is experienced. Everything is jerry-rigged in a landscape of hindrance. And yet all of this *everywhere* and *everything* is usually nothing. It's usually a lid. It is always someone saying, 'maybe', 'wait' or 'be patient'. Spinoza may have thought that things that do not strive to preserve in being are not things, but we might understand that in some places such things are miracles of being.

The reduction of the event by 'like events' is further reduced by the spectacular violence that envelopes Indigenous worlds such as the public narrative surrounding the release of the *Little Children Are Sacred* report. The horrific stories of rape circulated throughout the press drowned out every aspect of Indigenous life operating on a lower frequency. These lower-level frequencies could not break through the threshold of the spectre of spectacular violence. Side by side with these violent narratives, and further reducing events such as flying lids, circulated other kinds of spectacular events. As if caught in a millennial fantasy, the state and press publicized how enormous amounts of money would be channelled into remote communities in order to transform their living conditions. But the promised funds never arrived. And just months after their promise the financial markets collapsed. So, if enterprise culture (neoliberalism) was going to save us, who was going to save enterprise capital? How is a AUS$20 washing machine lid going to make headway in the wake of these shifts of national imaginaries and capital markets?

Hoping

If immanent critique is right and it is within these spaces of intensified potentiality where nothing is nor is not and where affect, idea and act are continually disturbed, then critical theory faces a critical question. If the potentiality of new forms of life is located in the differential capture and distribution of embodied and exposed life in late liberalism, then what qualities of embodied living are we as critical theorists hoping to impose on others in the concrete spaces of neoliberalism and late liberalism?

In other words, if it is true that *to be* in these spaces radically reduces *being* and yet it is *being in* these spaces that provides the possibility of *being otherwise*, then what stance should an ethically and politically informed version of critical theory take? Should a political movement work to make these spaces less lethal and enervating? But what if it is exactly this enervating lethality that is the condition of this particular kind of world-making activity? And what about the fact that Gigi, Rex and other members of the augmented reality project may not want to be potentiality, or mere potentiality or potentiality like this? They want to strive to persist in the being they find proper to the world, but not in the mode of striving they find themselves in. In other words, they do not merely wish to strive to preserve in being; they want to modify the given order so that they can endure; they want their striving to be less exhausting.

At the beginning of this essay I proposed that when viewed from the perspective of ethical substance, a gap opened between those who hope and reflect on ethical substance and those who are ethical substance. But clearly my colleagues and I also hope and reflect. We continue to push the project no matter hostile relatives in the region, the refusal of government agencies to help lay a water pipe, the biggest financial collapse since the Great Depression and everyday obstacles of poverty and racism. As Gigi said, we were getting somewhere simply because they have a house and we have a project. Grants are still outstanding. And even if this idea does not ever get the funding it needs, the will to persist does, at least for now. They continue to get on and remain in any car or boat going anywhere.

If Gigi, Rex and their children are not terrified of falling into the vast, more intensified zone of the living dead – the spacings of wavering death – they are not ignorant of these zones or their intimate proximity to them. Since being run out of their community their income had been slashed in half. And so the used cars they can afford break down at a faster rate than they can afford to fix them. Their second-hand boats are stranded offshore without petrol. Neighbours call the police for quality of life infractions. Other relatives with nowhere to spend the night sleep in makeshift tents on nearby beaches or in overcrowded flats. And still other relatives, involved in assaults and petty thefts, must be bailed out of jail. But that my friends have hope in the mere fact that they continue to persevere in being does not mean that immanent critique can singularly focus on them and others like them. The vast shadow army of the merely dead and the living dead should terrify immanent critique – should force it, us, to confront what account we can give not merely of the space of intensified potentiality but the force of enduring in the strivings that occur there.

Notes

1 The idea may have an objective (extrinsic) reality in so far as it represents a thing. It also has a formal (intrinsic) reality in so far as it is a thing independent of what it represents. See Deleuze (2007).
2 See Agamben (1999, 1998).

3 In an interview, Althusser noted, 'Proletarians have a "class instinct" which helps them on the way to proletarian "class positions." Intellectuals, on the contrary, have a petty-bourgeois class instinct which fiercely resists this transition.' But this instinct is the 'consciousness and practice which conform with the *objective* reality of the proletarian class struggle'. Thus, the proletariat need only be *educated*. Not so the intellectual. '[T]he class instinct of the petty bourgeoisie, and hence of intellectuals, has, on the contrary, to be *revolutionized*' (Althusser 1971: 12–13).

4 In 1944, the leaders of Allied forces met at Bretton Woods Hotel in New Hampshire to plan for a joint postwar economic policy. For a general discussion of neoliberalism, see Foucault (2008), Wallerstein (2001), Harvey (2007) and Palley (2005).

5 See also Brown (2006).

6 Under pressure from human rights activists, the federal government made the programme voluntary.

7 A point that Veena Das has also made. See Das (2006).

Bibliography

Agamben, G. (1998) Homo Sacer: *Sovereign Power and Bare Life*, Stanford, CA: Stanford University Press. 44.

Agamben, G. (1999) 'Absolute Immannence', in D. Heller-Roazen (ed. and trans.) *Potentialities: Collected Essays in Philosophy*, Stanford, CA: Stanford University Press. 220–39.

Althusser, L. (1971) 'Philosophy as a Revolutionary Weapon, Interview conducted by M.A. Macciocchi', in *Lenin and Philosophy and Other Essays*, New York: Monthly Review. 11–22.

Anderson, P. and Wild, R. for the Northern Territories Government (2007) *Ampe Akelyernemane Meke Mekarle 'Little Children Are Sacred'*, Report of the Northern Territory Board of Inquiry into the Protection of Aboriginal Children from Sexual Abuse. Government Printer: Canberra.

Brown, W. (2006) 'American Nightmare: Neoliberalism, Neoconservatism, and De-Democratization', *Political Theory*, 34: 690–714.

Das, V. (2006) *Life and Worlds: Violence and the Descent into the Ordinary*, Los Angeles: University of California Press.

Deleuze, G. (1983) *Nietzsche and Philosophy*, trans. H. Tomlinson, New York: Columbia University Press.

Deleuze, G. (2007) 'On Spinoza'. Online. Available HTTP: http://deleuzelectures.blogspot. com/2007/02/on-spinoza.html (accessed 16 January 2010).

Donald, P. (2010) 'Indigenous child abuse a "national emergency": PM', ABC-PM, Thursday, 21 June 2007. Online. Available HTTP: http://www.abc.net.au/pm/content/2007/ s1958368.htm (accessed 5 May 2010).

Foucault, M. (2008) *The Birth of Biopolitics: Lectures at the College de France, 1978–1979*, London: Palgrave Macmillan.

Harvey, D. (2007) *A Brief History of Neoliberalism*, Oxford: Oxford University Press.

Judt, T. (2009) 'What Is Living and What Is Dead in Social Democracy', *The New York Review of Books*, 56.20. Online. Available HTTP: http://www.nybooks.com/articles/ 23519 (accessed 16 January 2010).

Kogacioglu, D. (2004) 'The Tradition Effect: Framing Honor Crimes in Turkey', *differences: A Journal of Feminist Cultural Studies*, 15.2: 119–51.

Massumi, B. (1993) *The Politics of Everyday Fear*, Minneapolis: University of Minnesota Press.

Palley, T. (2005) 'From Keynesianism to Neoliberalism: Shifting Paradigms in Economics', in D. Johnston and A. Saad-Filho (eds) *Neoliberalism: A Critical Reader*, London: Pluto Press. 20–9.

Povinelli, E.A. (2006a) *The Empire of Love: Toward a Theory of Intimacy, Genealogy and Carnality*, Durham, NC: Duke University Press.

Povinelli, E.A. (2006b) 'Finding Bwudjut: Common Land, Private Profit, Divergent Objects', in T. Lea, E. Kowal and G. Cowlishaw (eds) *Moving Anthropology: Critical Indigenous Studies*, Darwin: Charles Darwin University Press. 147–66.

Sen, A. (2009) 'Capitalism beyond the crisis', *The New York Review of Books*, 56.5. Online. Available HTTP: http://www.nybooks.com/articles/22490 (accessed 16 January 2010).

Wallerstein, I. (2001) *The End of the Worlds as We Know It: Social Science for the Twenty-First Century*, Minneapolis: University of Minnesota Press.

8

THE PRACTICE OF JUDGEMENT

Hannah Arendt's 'Copernican revolution'

Linda M. G. Zerilli

I

For those of us seeking new directions in political theory, Hannah Arendt's unfinished work on judgement continues to be a rich resource. Arendt herself was deeply critical of the tendency of theory to foreclose the power of judgement insofar as it pre-empts the need to make sense of what is novel in any given event. Drawing a strong distinction between theories and events, Arendt insists, for example, that before Galileo's telescope there was Nicholas of Cusa and Giordano Bruno, Copernicus and Kepler. We are tempted, she says, to think it was not Galileo but the philosophers and scientific theoreticians who abolished the geocentric world-view. When we look back – and reflecting on what is past is a central feature of judging – we are tempted to conclude that no event was needed to abolish that worldview. This confusion of theories with events, she suggests, is inherent in our tendency to deny what is new, refiguring it as the reappearance of what is old, for example, already there in the form of a potentiality. The discovery of the telescope and the astronomical discoveries it enabled become, on this reading, a mere realization of that which already existed in theory.[1] The notion of a potentiality that pre-exists any actuality was, in Arendt's view, a denial of freedom, a denial, that is, of the radical contingency of human action that inheres in an event qua event.

Rejecting Kant's two-world solution to the problem of freedom (i.e. his effort to save freedom by housing it in the noumenal realm), Arendt underscores the experience of freedom, its worldly character. And yet Arendt insists that our ability to affirm human action as contingent, hence free, is not simply a matter of 'knowing' that acts are caused contingently (Scotus) or that any act that was done could just as well have been left undone. For freedom as it relates to politics is not a matter of what one knows, or does not know. Like Kant, Arendt sees that whenever we reflect on an act, it seems to come under the sway of causality in such a way that we seem unable to recall its 'original randomness' (Arendt 1978: 138). She does not treat the tendency to think strictly in terms of causality as a failure on our part, which could be corrected by better knowledge of what has come to be. When treated as an epistemological question, freedom appears to require that we step outside the condition of our own existence, take up the external standpoint, jump over our own shadow, as it were. Hence freedom is affirmed, but at the price of scepticism and worldlessness. Indeed freedom, when posed as a philosophical question that concerns *the* subject or 'Man in the singular,' almost always leads to the impasses Arendt describes in *The Life of the Mind*. To avoid these impasses, Arendt suggests that we think about freedom not as the substance or property of the subject; not as something we attain once we leave the world and others behind, but as a practice that begins by affirming plurality and non-sovereignty as the very condition of freedom.

'If men wish to be free, it is sovereignty that they must renounce,' declares Arendt (Arendt 1993a: 165). It is easy to miss the significance of this declaration because we do not see just how beholden we are to the Occidental tradition's notion of Man in the singular; just how tied our political concepts and theories are to the ideal of sovereignty that haunts us as a lost origin: in the beginning there was Man, not men. On Arendt's account, plurality is more than an ontological condition of human differences. As I have argued elsewhere, plurality is no mere state or condition of being human ('men not Man'), which we have a tendency to deny – though we do tend to deny that human condition of finitude, as both Stanley Cavell and Arendt in their different accounts of modern subjectivism and scepticism show (Zerilli 2005: 145). Rather, plurality requires that we *do* something in relation to whatever empirical differences may exist: plurality names not a *passive* state of ontological difference but an *active* and imaginative relation to others in a public space. Plurality, as a political relation, as the condition of action and freedom, I want to suggest, is based in the faculty of presentation (imagination) and not – or not initially – in the faculty of concepts (understanding). I can *know* that empirical differences exist as part of the human condition yet fail to *acknowledge* them, for the latter act involves more than cognition or the application of concepts to particulars (or, more precisely, *where* cognition is involved, acknowledgement requires that I *do* something on the basis of what I know).

II

In the view of critics such as Jürgen Habermas, Arendt's insistence on plurality as the condition of democratic politics is admirable, but it offers no way to adjudicate different points of view. Because she refuses to grant any 'cognitive foundation' for politics and public debate, he holds, Arendt leaves us with 'a yawning abyss between knowledge and opinion that cannot be closed with arguments' (Habermas 1994: 225). Likewise, Ronald Beiner, editor of *Arendt's Kant Lectures*, reiterates the problems associated with 'the all-important contrast between persuasive judgement and compelling truth' in Arendt's thought and wonders why she failed to recognize that '*all* human judgments, including aesthetic (and certainly political) judgments, incorporate a necessary cognitive dimension' (Beiner 1992: 137). (You will be a better judge of art if you know something about the art you are judging.) A

Kantian approach, which excludes knowledge from political judgement, says Beiner, 'renders one incapable of speaking of "uninformed" judgment and of distinguishing differential capacities for knowledge so that some persons may be recognized as more qualified, and some as less qualified, to judge' (ibid.: 136).

Does Arendt sever the link between argument and judgement or even forbid the place of reasoned argument in the practice of judgement? As I have argued elsewhere, the critical charge that she does entirely misses the mark. Arendt's deep suspicion of a cognitively-based practice of political judgement is not disqualified by her reliance on a supposedly naïve concept of logical reasoning.[2] *Her point is not to exclude so-called rational discourse from the practice of aesthetic or political judgement – as if something or someone could stop us from making arguments in public contexts – but to press us to think about what we are doing when we reduce the practice of politics or judgement to the contest of better arguments.* Arendt is struggling with a difficult problem to which her critics, focused as they are on issues of the rational adjudication of political claims, are blind: our misplaced but deep sense of necessity in human affairs. If Arendt brackets the legitimation problematic that dominates the thought of Habermas, it is because she sees in our practices of justification a strong tendency towards compulsion, which, in turn, destroys the particular *qua* particular and, with it, the very space in which political speech (including arguments) can appear.[3] What shapes Arendt's critique of the public realm as a rationally-driven culture of argument is a conception of politics as the space of freedom, singular events, rhetorical speech and plurality. She sees how we tend to run the space of reasons into the space of causes: we risk transforming logical reasoning from a dialogic tool of thought, with which we aim at agreement, into a monologic tool of thought, with which we compel it. What Habermas calls 'the claim to rational validity that is immanent in speech' (Habermas 1994: 213) risks becoming what Wittgenstein once called 'the hardness of the logical *must*' (Wittgenstein 1996: I §121).

For Arendt, political judgements have the structure of aesthetic judgements. What does that mean exactly? And why is this shared structure different from what her critics call rational discourse? We can begin to answer the first question by recalling that, for Arendt, both political claims and aesthetic claims are practices of reflective judgement, that is, a form of judgement according to which, in contrast to what Kant called a determinative judgement, the rule is not given.[4] In the absence of the rule under which to subsume the particular, we are confronted with an event of singularity. As Arendt reminds us in her lectures on Kant, 'If you say, "What a beautiful rose!" you do not arrive at this judgment by first saying, "All roses are beautiful, this flower is a rose, hence this rose is beautiful"' (Arendt 1992: 13–14).

What confronts you in a reflective judgement is not the general category 'rose', but the particular, '*this* rose'. As Beiner puts it,

> [R]eflective judgment means attending to the unique qualities of the particular, to the particular *qua* particular, rather than simply subsuming particulars under some universal formula. Or, as Arendt would put it, judgment involves attending to the particular as an end in itself – that is, as a singular locus of meaning that isn't reducible to universal causes or universal consequences.
>
> (Beiner 2001: 94)

That *this* rose is beautiful is not given in the universal nature of roses. There is nothing necessary about the beauty of *this* rose. The claim about beauty is not grounded in a property of the object, which could be objectively ascertained (as is the case with cognitive judgements); such a claim belongs to the structure of feeling rather than concepts (i.e. *sensus communis*, discussed below).[5] *This* rose *is* beautiful because it is judged to be beautiful.[6]

This Kantian point is also crucial to what we might call Arendt's own 'Copernican Revolution', that is, her claim that political space does not precede political judgement, but rather is constituted by it. 'The public realm is constituted by the spectators and not the actors or the makers', as she puts it (Arendt 1992: 62). That is another way of saying that the public realm is constituted through a practice of judgement; it is constituted by us and what we hold (e.g. 'that these truths are self-evident'). If that is the case, then the public space, as we have constituted it, could be constituted differently: we do not have to hold these truths to be self-evident, nothing compels us. That we do so hold is an expression of our freedom. How, then, can we gain critical purchase on what we hold?

To argue, as Arendt following Kant does, that beauty is not a property of the object but an expression of the subject in the act of contemplating it, raises the problem of what deliberative democrats such as Habermas call intersubjective validity. As Jennifer Nedelsky puts it, Kant

> identified the central problem of judgment: how can a judgment that is genuinely and irreducibly subjective also be valid. What does the claim of validity mean if we do not transmute the subjective into something objective – and thus lose the essence of judgment as distinct from ascertaining a truth that can be demonstrably, and thus compellingly proven?
>
> (Nedelsky 2001: 104)

Does Arendt herself suggest how we might adjudicate competing judgements about particulars? Although Arendt accepts (some version of) Kant's argument that aesthetic judgements must claim universal agreement to be valid (e.g. *this* rose *is* beautiful, not just beautiful *for me* – the latter being a misuse of the word 'beautiful'), she eliminates what Albrecht Wellmer calls 'the context of possible arguments' in which a particular claim could be 'redeemed' (Wellmer 2001: 169). If we follow Arendt, it would seem, every political qua aesthetic claim reduces to subjectivism and raises the spectre of decisionism, for there is no way to judge such judgements: there is no public measure or standard or criteria according to which we might evaluate them. What Arendt's critics fear is that, if all we have is the contention of opinions with no standards to redeem claims as valid, we will have no way of distinguishing between rhetoric and rational argument. This worry is as old as Western philosophy.

III

> Wherever people judge the things of the world that are common to them, there is more implied in their judgments than these things. By his manner

of judging, the person discloses to an extent also himself, what kind of person he is, and this disclosure, which is involuntary, gains in validity to the degree that it has liberated itself from individual idiosyncrasies.

(Arendt 1993a: 221)

What one discovers in the act of judging, says Arendt, is both one's differences with some judging persons and one's commonalities with others.

> We all know very well how quickly people recognize each other, and how unequivocally they can feel that they belong [or do not belong] to each other, when they discover [or fail to discover] a kinship in questions of what pleases and displeases.
>
> (Ibid.: 223)

Based in the activity of taste ('the it-pleases-or-displeases-me'), judging allows differences and commonalities to emerge that are by no means given in advance of the act itself. Arendt refuses to specify what values must already be in place to serve as the ground for community (though she nowhere denies that certain values are already in place). Judging may well call into question my sense of political community with some persons and reveal a new sense of community with others. This discovery of community is not guaranteed by the kind of rule-following Arendt associates with what Kant calls a 'determinative judgment', that is, a judgement in which a particular is subsumed under a universal (Kant 1987: 18). The rule-following associated with determinative (logical) judgements, says Arendt, compels everyone who has the power of reason and could just as well be discovered in solitude.

I said earlier that plurality might be the fragile achievement of democratic politics rather than a permanent threat to such politics or a mere ontological condition of being human. We can now better appreciate what might be at risk in a theory of political judgement that relies on reason and proof. Plurality is irrelevant when I proceed by means of rational arguments and proofs – irrelevant, that is, to whatever judgement I reach. As Salim Kemal observes,

> Proofs begin with generally accepted premises, asserting that certain relations hold between concepts and, from these, on the basis of inferential rules, draw relevant conclusions. If we accept the premises and the validity of the argument, then, unless there is a mistake, we must accept the conclusion. In some sense our agreement is compelled, for a dissenting individual's claim will be dismissed as false – because it does not tally with some part of the premises; or as irrational – because it cannot tally with any proof or procedure. Disagreement is still possible, because premises are questionable and proofs may be inadequate. But such arguments and conclusions are objective and universally valid on the basis of given procedure. Agreement between subjects does not determine the truth of cognitive claims; rather the truth of judgments depends on the nature of objects and their relations in the world.
>
> (Kemal 1997: 76)

Though proofs may well play a role when one speaks politically, speaking politically is not reducible to the ability to give proofs.

Arendt does not dismiss the question of validity but rather asks: what kind of
validity is proper to the realm of politics, where we are concerned with the problem of human freedom – how to affirm rather than deny it – and with sustaining
the condition of such freedom, namely, plurality? Whatever premises we do share
rely on a sense of realness derived from seeing from multiple perspectives.
Objectivity requires not simply that one 'be in agreement with one's own self
[logic's principle of non-contradiction], but ... consist[s] of being able to "think in
the place of everybody else"', she writes (Arendt 1993a: 221). That is what it means
'*to see politically*' (Arendt 1993b: 96). The origins of this political way of seeing lie
in 'Homeric objectivity' (i.e. the ability to see the same thing from *opposite* points
of view: to see the Trojan War from the standpoint of *both* of its greatest protago-
nists, Achilles *and* Hector).[7] This is different from the kind of seeing that ends with
the cognition of an object, which involves not seeing from the viewpoints of others, but the ability to subsume particulars under rules.

In Arendt's reading of Kant's *Critique of Judgment*, aesthetic judgement

> never has the validity of cognitive or scientific propositions, which are not
> judgments, properly speaking. (If one says, 'The sky is blue' or 'Two and
> two are four', one is not 'judging'; one is saying what is, compelled by the
> evidence either of one's senses or one's mind.)
>
> (Arendt 1992: 72)

As the last sentence suggests, the affect at issue in judgement is different from the
first-hand experience of our senses. Arendt's reading of Kant foregrounds judging
as an activity, not judgements as the result of an activity, judgements which, being
universally valid, could be extended beyond the activity of judging subjects and
applied in rule-like fashion by other subjects.[8] It is this emphasis on judging as an
ongoing practice that leads Arendt to eschew tying reflective judgement to rational
argument and claims of truth. The emphasis is on judging rather than judgements
because, according to Arendt, judging comes into its own only once the rules for
judging the objects of the common world are lacking, that is, are not given in
advance of the activity of judging itself. Judging concerns particulars for which the
rule under which to subsume them is missing.

Citing Kant, Arendt emphasizes that judgements of taste, far from being private
and subjective (*de gustibus non disputandum est*), have (what he calls) 'subjective
validity' (Kant 1987: 85–95), which entails, as Arendt puts it, 'an anticipated communication with others with whom I know I must finally come to some agreement' (Arendt 1993a: 220–21). This anticipated agreement relies on *sensus communis*,
'the very opposite of "private feelings"', *sensus privates* (ibid.: 222). What Arendt
calls *sensus communis* is more akin to what Wittgenstein means by our pre-reflective
'agreement in judgments', which underlies our practices of justification, and which
is itself a practice not susceptible to or in need of proof, than it is to Kant's idea of
sensus communis as a transcendental, a priori principle which grounds the universal

validity of judgements of taste (and which, therefore, is in no way the product of some social process, of deliberation or agreement in a particular community).[9] Some readers of Arendt (e.g. Lyotard 1994) accuse her of losing sight of the a priori character of the Kantian *sensus communis*, and of treating judgement as if it entailed reaching actual agreement with others or were based on some form of empirical sociality.[10] Judgement according to Arendt would then entail little more than striving for agreement with a community's norms. Rhetoric, understood in its conventional sense as a sophistic technique of persuasion, would then rear its ugly head, threatening to lure us back into the Platonic cave, where we are unable to distinguish the shadowy shapes of things from the things themselves, opinion from truth.

Clearly, Arendt, for whom totalitarianism raised the whole problem of judgement, cannot be taken to limit judgement or the *sensus communis* in this way. Although Arendt does not accept the transcendental character of the Kantian *sensus communis*, like Kant, she recognizes that empirical communities can be deeply flawed in their judgements. Furthermore, to judge according to the common understanding of a given community is, as Kant himself says, 'to judge not by feeling but always by concepts, even though these concepts are usually only principles conceived obscurely' (Kant 1987: 87). For Kant, however, what makes concepts obscure is itself often connected to feeling: it is none other than rhetoric or 'the arts of speech', which, in the *Critique of Judgment*, he accuses of being a perfect cheat and of 'merit[ing] no respect whatsoever'. Rhetoric stands accused of being 'the art of transacting a serious business of the understanding as if it were a free play of the imagination'. As Robert Dostal observes, 'it is just this play of imagination that Arendt wishes to affirm' (Dostal 2001: 154). In contrast to Kant, for whom the *ars oratoria* 'insofar as this is taken to mean the art of persuasion' deceives us by means of a 'beautiful illusion' and makes our 'judgments unfree,' Arendt affirms that 'the rhetorical arguments of our fellow spectators free us' (ibid.: 154). It is all the more curious that Arendt, though she emphasized imagination over reason and understanding as the primary political faculty, never developed the account of imagination that her ruminations on judgement required, for she never thought about the imagination as anything but reproductive.[11] I will leave aside the question of why in this context and concentrate, by way of concluding, on what a theory of productive imagination might contribute to an account of political judgement based in the Kantian idea of subjective validity.

IV

Imagination is much more than the faculty of re-presentation, that is, the faculty of making present what is absent, which is 'the reproductive imagination' in Kant. On the one hand, Arendt is clearly concerned with imagination as the faculty that gives me objects as representations so that I can be affected by them, but not in the direct way I am when the object is given to me by the senses. Imagination prepares the object so that I can reflect upon it, which is to say, judge it. It also allows me to visit standpoints not my own, creating the conditions for the relations of proximity and distance that are vital to Arendt's understanding of political space (Arendt 1992: 68–9). 'Imagination alone enables us to see things in their proper perspective', she writes,

> to put that which is too close at a certain distance so that we can see and understand it without bias and prejudice, to be generous enough to bridge abysses of remoteness until we can see and understand everything that is too far away from us as though it were our own affair.
>
> (Arendt 1994: 323)

Citing Kant's observation that imagination brings together sensibility and under-standing by 'providing an *image for a concept*', a 'schema' (Arendt 1992: 81) in the absence of which there would be no experience in the Kantian sense, Arendt once again reduces imagination to its reproductive function and subordinates it to the faculty of understanding. Writes Arendt,

> Our sensibility seems to need imagination not only as an aid to knowledge but in order to recognize sameness in the manifold. As such, it is the con-dition of all knowledge: the [in Kant's words] 'synthesis of imagination, prior to apperception, is the ground of the possibility of all knowledge, especially of experience'.
>
> (Ibid.: 83)

She never considers Kant's claim, in the A-edition of the *Critique of Pure Reason*, that this synthesis of the manifold 'is the mere effect of the imagination, of a blind though indispensable function of the soul, without which we should have no cog-nition at all, but of which we are scarcely ever conscious' (Kant 1998: A78). This is Kant's discovery of the 'transcendental imagination' as a productive power, the discovery of an 'unknown root' [*unbekannte Wurzel*] from which, according to Arendt's teacher Heidegger, he 'recoiled' and subsumed under reason (Heidegger 1988: 161).

Put somewhat differently, the generative power of imagination is its capacity to create relationships among otherwise disparate things. We can see it in Kant's idea of the 'example'. Although the example plays a role in both reflective and deter-minant judgements, it is particularly important as the third or mediating term in a reflective judgement, in which there is no rule for thinking the particular. The example, writes Arendt, 'is the particular that contains in itself, or is supposed to contain, a concept or a general rule' (Arendt 1992: 84). She explains,

> I cannot judge one particular by another particular; in order to determine its worth, I need a *tertium quid* or a *tertium comparationis*, something related to the two particulars and yet distinct from both. In Kant we find actually two altogether different solutions to this difficulty.
>
> (Ibid.: 76)

The first solution, 'a real *tertium comparationis*', includes 'the idea of an original compact of mankind as a whole, and derived from this idea is the notion of humanity', and, in *Critique of Judgment*, 'the idea of purposiveness [without a purpose]', that is, the idea that things like aesthetic objects and human beings, which are not defined by their use, please us, but this pleasure 'can never be proved' (ibid.: 76). The second and, in Arendt's view, far more valuable, solution is *exemplary* validity. ('Examples are the go-cart of judgments.')

> Let us see what this is. Every particular object – for instance, a table – has a corresponding concept by which we recognize the table as a table. This can be conceived as a 'Platonic' idea or Kantian schema; that is one has before the eyes of one's mind a schematic or merely *formal table* shape to which every table somehow must conform. Or one proceeds, conversely, from the many tables one has seen in one's life, strips them of all secondary qualities, and the remainder is a table-in-general, containing the minimum properties common to all tables; the *abstract table*. One more possibility is left, and this enters into judgements that are not cognitions: one may encounter or think of some table that one judges to be the best possible table and take this table as the example of how tables actually should be: the *exemplary table* ('example' comes from *eximere*, 'to single out some particular'). This exemplar is and remains a particular that in its very particularity reveals the generality that otherwise could not be defined. Courage is *like* Achilles. Etc.
>
> (Ibid.: 76–7)

As Arendt's other examples (e.g. 'Goodness is like Jesus of Nazareth') of the example make clear, this is but another way of saying that the 'go-cart of judgment', that which enables us to think the particular, is not a principle but a metaphor, and its condition is the *sensus communis*.[12]

But Arendt's account of exemplary validity, far from being a clear alternative to a rule-governed judgement, can start to sound like the application of concepts by other means. The only criterion for the validity of the example, says Arendt, is that it must be 'well chosen'. The example must resonate for others in a particular cultural context. Although this does not mean that the example must repeat or confirm the views of any given community, it seems important to recognize that some examples can do just that; that is, they can function as concepts that effectively preclude the ability to see something new. This risk seems unavoidable when the imagination is reduced to its reproductive function, as it is in Arendt's reading of Kant.

If we see imagination as generative, as the creator of new social forms, however, we can think about the example as having an inventive character that can by no means be reduced to a combination of pre-existing elements. According to Ernesto Grassi, 'this function of establishing relationships [is] the act of *ingenium*', which 'penetrates and binds together *in a common relationship* . . . things that appear . . . uncommonly fragmentary and disparate'. Put slightly differently, '*ingenium* is the ability to reveal similitude as a common element in things which, as such, attains to universality' (Grassi 1976: 561).

The kind of universality at issue in reflective judgement and its vehicle, the example, obtains in the realm of the probable; that is, this form of universality is never eternally valid, as logical judgements claim to be. To cite Grassi again,

> Here the universal, on the basis of which we define and recognize something, is *not* the product of abstracting from previous insights but arises in a concrete comparison with the principle of our own life itself. It is therefore a 'commonness' of 'similarity' that is ascertained concretely from case to case.
>
> (Grassi 1980: 98)

Accordingly, the truth that emerges is different from that attained through the exercise of logical reasoning (truth as consistency) or the adequation of our concepts to their objects (truth as correspondence). As Arendt says of logical truth,

> It is the only reliable 'truth' human beings can fall back upon once they have lost the mutual guarantee, the common sense, men need in order to experience and live and know their way in a common world. But this 'truth' is empty or rather no truth at all, because it does not reveal anything [that is not already given in the premises].
>
> (Arendt 1973: 477)

Notwithstanding Arendt's claim that truth is at odds with political (rhetorical) speech and thus with the practice of judgement, we see that it is possible to speak of truth, only truth is something we reveal rather than prove or deduce. This conception of truth as something revealed is at one with judgement: what they share is the quest for meaning. For Arendt, meaning is what judgement reveals: it is not given in the nature of things, the structure of the world or the objectivity of history, but is a creation of significant relations which generate our sense of the real. 'Reality is different from, and more than, the totality of facts and events, which, anyhow, is unascertainable', she writes. Meaning is what we produce when we judge the objects of the common world apart from their function or utility or necessity.

It is judgement, then, that creates meaning and with it the space in which the objects of the common world can appear, not the other way around. That is Arendt's 'Copernican Revolution' in political thinking. According to Arendt, our very sense of reality – that is, 'a nonsubjective and "objective" world which we have in common and share with others' – depends upon the practice of judgement. Judgement is how we discover community, that is, with whom we are in community. Rather than think about community as the ground of judgement, that is, as that which gives us the grounds for our judgements (as a communitarian view might have it), Arendt suggests that the practice of judgement creates our sense of community. Like our sense of the real, this sense of community is both stable and open to contestation. It is stable because, whenever I judge, I anticipate universal assent: I appeal to the *sensus communis*, not in the Kantian, transcendental sense, but in the Wittgensteinian one of our mutual attunement in language. This sense of community is contestable because I can never compel anyone to agree with my judgements, I can only 'woo' or 'court' the agreement of everyone else. To judge is not only to assume that others share my view of the world, but also to risk discovering that someone does not. I cannot compel another person to see the world as I do; at best I can try to show her or him how I see it, and wait and see what comes from that showing.

Notes

1 See Arendt (1989: ch. 6).
2 See Steinberger (1993: esp. 63).
3 On Arendt's bracketing of the legitimation problematic, see Villa (1996: 72).
4 As Béatrice Longuenesse explains, the peculiar feature of aesthetic and teleological judgements is not that they are reflective judgements *(for every judgement on empirical objects as such is reflective)*; it is rather that they are *merely* reflective judgements, judgements in which reflection can never arrive at conceptual *determination* (Longuenesse 1998: 164).
5 Kant writes,

> If judgments of taste had (as cognitive judgements do) a determinate objective principle, then anyone making them in accordance with that principle would claim that his judgment is unconditionally necessary . . . So they [judgments of taste] must have a subjective principle, which determines only by feeling rather than by concepts, though nonetheless with universal validity, what is liked or disliked. Such a principle, however, could only be regarded as a *common sense*. This common sense is essentially distinct from the common understanding that is also sometimes called common sense *(sensus communis)*; for the latter judges not by feeling but always by concepts, even though these concepts are usually only principles conceived obscurely.
>
> (Kant 1987: 87)

Kant is talking not about empirical opinions of a given community but about an a priori principle.

6 The pleasure obtained in the act of judging is subjective. It is based on a priori principles (ibid.: 396) and entails the agreement or harmony of the faculties (understanding and imagination) in the absence of a concept, for reflective judgement fails to produce any conceptual determination. That is why Kant speaks of aesthetic and teleological judgements as merely reflective judgements *(nur reflektierende, bloß reflektierende)*. See ibid.: 399, 412.
7 Arendt writes,

> This Homeric impartiality is still the highest type of objectivity we know. Not only does it leave behind the common interest in one's side and one's own people which, up to our own days, characterizes almost all national historiography, but it also discards the alternative of victory or defeat, which moderns have felt expresses the 'objective' judgment of history itself.
>
> (Arendt 1993a, 51)

The modern conception of objectivity, in contrast, is premised on the idea that standpoints, intrinsically deceptive, should be eliminated, based as they are on subjective sense experience. 'The "extinction of the self" [...becomes] the condition of "pure vision"', in

Ranke's phrase. Objectivity is a clean relation to the facts; it requires abstention from judgement (ibid.: 49).

8   Judgment is endowed with a certain specific validity, but is never universally valid. Its claims to validity can never extend further than the others in whose place the judging person has put himself for his consideration . . .; it is not valid for those who do not judge or for those who are not members of the public realm where the objects of judgment appear.

(Ibid.: 221)

9   As a work of transcendental philosophy, the *Critique of Judgement* is concerned with the possible validity of our judgements, not with actual judgements. Kant explicitly excludes community standards as the basis for judgement:

Whenever a subject offers a judgment as proof of his taste [concerning some object], we demand that he judge for himself: he should not have to grope about among other people's judgments . . . To make other people's judgments the basis determining of one's own would be heteronomy.

(Kant 1987: 146)

As an a priori principle, *sensus communis* is the condition of what he calls the 'exemplary necessity' of a judgement of taste, that is, the 'necessity of the assent of *everyone* to a judgement that is regarded as an example of a universal rule that we are unable to state' (ibid.: 85). Kant distinguishes exemplary necessity from theoretical and practical necessity, which he elaborates, respectively, in *The Critique of Pure Reason* and *The Critique of Practical Reason*.

10 According to Beiner, Arendt mistakenly reads her favourite concepts from the third *Critique* (common sense, enlarged mentality and so on) as if they were empirical, whereas for Kant they are strictly transcendental (Beiner 2001: 96).

11 See Zerilli 2005: ch. 4.

12 Metaphors, as the go-carts of judgement, do not have universal validity. Arendt writes,

When judging, one says spontaneously, without any derivations from general rules, 'This man has courage'. If one were a Greek, one would have in 'the depths of one's mind' the example of Achilles. Imagination is again necessary . . . If we say of somebody that he is good, we have in the back of our minds the example of Saint Francis or Jesus of Nazareth. The judgement has exemplary validity to the extent that the example is rightly chosen . . . [I] can talk about Napoleon Bonaparte as a particular man; but the moment I speak about Bonapartism I have made an example of him. The validity of this example will be restricted to those who possess the particular experience of Napoleon, either as his contemporaries or as the heirs to this particular historical tradition.

(Arendt 1992: 84)

Bibliography

Arendt, H. (1973) *The Origins of Totalitarianism*, New York: Harcourt Brace.

Arendt, H. (1978) *The Life of the Mind*, ed. Mary McCarthy, 2 vols., New York: Harcourt Brace.

Arendt, H. (1989) *The Human Condition*, Chicago: University of Chicago Press.

Arendt, H. (1992) *Lectures on Kant's Political Philosophy*, ed. R. Beiner, Chicago: University of Chicago Press.

Arendt, H. (1993a) *Between Past and Future: Eight Exercises in Political Thought*, New York: Penguin.

Arendt, H. (1993b) *Was ist Politik?*, ed. U. Ludz, Munich: Piper Verlag.

Arendt, H. (1994) *Essay in Understanding 1930–1954*, ed. J. Kohn, New York: Harcourt Brace.

Beiner, R. (1992) 'Interpretive Essay', in H. Arendt *Lectures on Kant's Political Philosophy*, ed. R. Beiner, Chicago: University of Chicago Press. 89–156.

Beiner, R. (2001) 'Rereading Hannah Arendt's Kant Lectures', in R. Beiner and J. Nedelsky (eds) *Judgment, Imagination, and Politics: Themes from Kant and Arendt*, Boston: Rowman & Littlefield. 91–102.

Dostal, R.J. (2001) 'Judging Human Action', in R. Beiner and J. Nedelsky (eds) *Judgment, Imagination, and Politics: Themes from Kant and Arendt*, Boston: Rowman & Littlefield. 139–64.

Grassi, E. (1976) 'The Priority of Common Sense and Imagination: Vico's Philosophical Relevance Today', *Social Research* 43: 553–80.

Grassi, E. (1980) *Rhetoric as Philosophy: The Humanist Tradition*, Carbondale, IL: Southern Illinois University Press.

Habermas, J. (1994) 'Hannah Arendt's Communications Concept of Power', in L. Hinchman and S. Hinchman (eds) *Hannah Arendt, Critical Essays*, Albany, NY: State University of New York Press. 211–30.

Heidegger, M. (1988) *Kant und das Problem der Metaphysik*, Frankfurt am Main: Klosterman.

Kant, I. (1987) *Critique of Judgment*, trans. W. S. Pluhar, Indianapolis, IN: Hackett.

Kant, I. (1998) *Critique of Pure Reason*, trans. P. Guyer and A. W. Wood, Cambridge: Cambridge University Press.

Kemal, S. (1997) *Kant's Aesthetic Theory*, New York: St. Martin's Press.

Longuenesse, B. (1998) *Kant and the Capacity to Judge: Sensibility and Discursivity in the Transcendental Analytic of the Critique of Pure Reason*, trans. C. T. Wolfe, Princeton, NJ: Princeton University Press.

Lyotard, J-F. (1994) *Lessons on the Analytic of the Sublime (Kant's 'Critique of Judgment', §23–29)*, trans. E. Rottenberg, Stanford, CA: Stanford University Press.

Nedelsky, J. (2001) 'Judgment, Diversity, and Relational Autonomy', in R. Beiner and J. Nedelsky (eds) *Judgment, Imagination, and Politics: Themes from Kant and Arendt*, Boston: Rowman & Littlefield. 103–20.

Steinberger, P. (1993) *The Concept of Political Judgment*, Chicago: University of Chicago Press.

Villa, D. (1996) *Arendt and Heidegger: The Fate of the Political*, Princeton, NJ: Princeton University Press.

Wellmer, A. (2001) 'Hannah Arendt on Judgment: The Unwritten Doctrine of Reason', in R. Beiner and J. Nedelsky (eds) *Judgment, Imagination, and Politics: Themes from Kant and Arendt*, Boston: Rowman & Littlefield. 165–81.

Wittgenstein, L. (1996) *Remarks on the Foundations of Mathematics*, eds G. H. Wright, R. Rhees, and G. E. M. Anscombe, Cambridge, MA: MIT Press.

Zerilli, L. M. G. (2005) *Feminism and the Abyss of Freedom*, Chicago: University of Chicago Press.

PART III

Rethinking the politics of representation

9

WHEN REFLEXIVITY BECOMES PORN

Mutations of a modernist theoretical practice

Rey Chow

It is ... better to shift the vocabulary of reflexivity, and to suggest that all acts are not so much reflexive and self-conscious as they are already proto-dramatic.

(Jameson 1998: 83)

'The Crudest Example'

A striking image appears repeatedly in Walter Benjamin's discussions of Bertolt Brecht's epic theatre.[1] Many of us will remember the cultural politics behind Benjamin's reading, a cultural politics that is in line with Brecht's own radical, non-mimetic investments, and aimed at destroying the Aristotelian aesthetic illusionism from which Western drama has derived its modus operandi for centuries. To begin the present exploration of reflexivity, let me dwell momentarily on Benjamin's image – a family row – to which he returns several times in his various accounts on Brecht:

> The task of the epic theatre, Brecht believes, is not so much to develop actions as to represent conditions. But 'represent' does not here signify 'repro-duce' in the sense used by the theoreticians of Naturalism. Rather, the first point at issue is to *uncover* those conditions. (One could just as well say: to *make them strange* [*verfremden*].) This uncovering (making strange, or alienat-ing) of conditions is brought about by processes being interrupted. Take the crudest example: a family row. Suddenly a stranger comes into the room. The wife is just about to pick up a bronze statuette and throw it at the daughter, the father is opening the window to call a policeman. At this moment the stranger appears at the door. 'Tableau', as they used to say around 1900. That is to say, the stranger is confronted with a certain set of conditions: troubled faces, open window, a devastated interior. There exists another point of view

from which the more usual scenes of bourgeois life do not look so very different from this.[2]

(Benjamin 1998: 18–19)

This remarkable passage was first published in German in 1939, but the picture Benjamin depicts, together with the types of agency involved, exemplifies a modernist mode of theoretical thinking that has remained with us to this day.[3]

A number of words in the passage pinpoint the emphases characteristic of such thinking. First and foremost is the rendering of a familiar situation *strange*: the point of such estrangement is to allow for a rational *uncovering* (*Entdeckung*, usually translated as discovering) of conditions that have become automatized and thus unnoticeable, even as these conditions precipitate a crisis. Second is the presence of a *stranger*, whose appearance on the scene transforms the dynamics involved in the interior. Positioned in the *doorway*, between the inside and the outside, the stranger turns the happenings inside into an astonishing sight, with bits and pieces of visual information caught as though they were frozen in a still or *tableau*. Third, the setting involved is that of a *family*, in a society where *policemen* may be called to restore domestic order. Fourth, the more usual scenes of the middle class can look similarly astonishing to yet another point of view, that of *the epic dramatist*.[4] Whereas the emotional core of Aristotelian drama depends for its effect on the audience's cathartic identification with the spectacle of closely knit *kinship networks in crisis*, the 'crudest example' (*das primitivste Beispiel*) named here to demonstrate how the epic theatre works is also that of kinship in crisis – in the updated version of the *middle class* family in disarray – but kinship now appears for purposes of soliciting *observation and change* rather than empathy and identification.

Even in a small example such as this, Brecht's well-known principle of alienation (*Verfremdung*), a principle he considers as necessary to all understanding (Brecht 1964: 71),[5] is amply evident. If the hallmarks of the dramatic in the Aristotelian tradition are 'the strong centralization of the story, a momentum that [draws] the separate parts into a common relationship', and '[a] particular passion of utterance, a certain emphasis on the clash of forces', in the case of epic theatre 'one can as it were take a pair of scissors and cut it into individual pieces, which remain fully capable of life' (ibid. 70).[6] Accordingly, with the cutting impulse of the epic work, the aim of the alienation effect, produced by artistic means such as acting, is 'to make the spectator adopt an attitude of inquiry and criticism in his approach to the incident' (ibid. 136).

Staging: a mediatized theoretical practice

As has often been noted, Brecht's theory of alienation shares affinities with the notion of art as argued by the Russian Formalist Victor Shklovsky, who in his famous essay of 1917, 'Art as Technique', advocated an art of 'making strange' (*ostranenie*) as the means to disrupt habitualization and refresh perceptibility of the world. As Shklovsky writes, art exists that one may recover the sensation of life; it exists to make one feel things, to make the stone *stony* . . . The technique of art is to make objects 'unfamiliar', to make forms difficult, to increase the difficulty and length of perception because the process of perception is an aesthetic end in itself and must be prolonged.

(Shklovsky 1965: 12)

Although their political orientations were by no means identical, what Shklovsky and Brecht had in common, it is fair to say, was a predilection for estrangement, and in particular for locating in artistic practice a capacity for defamiliarizing and making conscious conventions (literary, historical, or social) that have become so conventionalized as to be unrecognized.[7] As is well-known, Brecht was also inspired by Chinese acting that he saw in a performance by the Beijing opera actor Mei Lan-fang's company in Moscow in 1935. In this non-Western art form, he found affirmation for the rationality of his own theatrical methods, aimed as they were at the non-fusion and non-integration between audience and actor, between actor and fictional character, and between spectacle and emotion.[8] (What might not have been apparent to Brecht, however, was the determinism of hierarchical role classification in traditional Chinese acting: an actor playing a specific type of operatic role is normally expected to perform, for his entire career, only in that role; the role, in other words, typecasts the actor by consigning him to a fixed identity, which defines his social positioning as well as his part on stage.[9])

Rather than being the synonym for social isolation, alienation in Brecht is attributed with a specific kind of agency, namely, the ability to *de-sensationalize* the emotional effects of Aristotelian drama by puncturing its illusionism, an illusionism premised on transcendent unities and coherent relations. As Stanley Mitchell puts it:

> To be anti-bourgeois or proletarian was to show how things worked, while they were being shown; to 'lay bare the device' (in the words of the Russian Formalists). Art should be considered a form of production, not a mystery; the stage should appear like a factory with the machinery fully exposed.
>
> (Benjamin 1998: xv–xvi)

Obviously, the stranger in Benjamin's example of the family row is a personification of this interruptive work. Alienation may thus, logically, be equated with the camera, whose capacity as a relatively new scientific and artistic apparatus still held the promise, as of the late 1930s, of a revolutionary aesthetics. The stranger's foreign body, accordingly, is the artificial device – a prosthesis – by which the procedure of estrangement is formalized; such formalization is technologically commensurable with the possibilities brought about by the then-novel medium of film.

What remains provocative, however, is perhaps less the felicitous fit between alienation effects as such and the medium of film – a point that is, in retrospect, easy enough to make – than the unfolding, within Brecht's method, of an ambitious conceptual experiment, one that takes the form of an aggressive stilling – the tableau. Roland Barthes's description of the tableau may be borrowed here for clarification:

> The tableau (pictorial, theatrical, literary) is a pure cut-out segment with clearly defined edges, irreversible and incorruptible; everything that surrounds it is banished into nothingness, remains unnamed, irreversible and incorruptible; while everything that it admits within its field is promoted into essence, into light, into view . . . [T]he tableau is intellectual, it has something to say (something moral, social) but it also says that it knows how this must be done; it is simultaneously significant and propaedeutical, impressive and reflexive, moving and conscious of the channels of emotion. The epic scene in Brecht, the shot in Eisenstein are so many tableaux.[10]
>
> (Barthes 1997: 70–1)

By the sheer force of its abruptness (to which theorists such as Benjamin would attribute sensations of shock and astonishment), the tableau captures an existing situation at the same time that it renders it fluid and movable, and hence no longer entirely coincident with itself. What makes the tableau in Brecht's method so interesting to consider from today's point of view is not simply that it is cinematic but also, and more importantly, that it works by incorporating the technicality of a newer medium into an older one. The techniques of film – in particular the principle of montage, as Benjamin stresses – are used by Brecht to form a vision of theatrical productivity that is simultaneously a demand for thinking, something that occurs in the interstice between (two) different media. This is how I would define reflexivity in this context: as it appears in Brecht's method, reflexivity is a conscious form of staging, an intermedial event that exceeds the genre of drama.

Although Benjamin is ostensibly discussing the specifics of Brecht's epic theatre, then, he is really exploring a larger, more difficult aesthetic question: how does thought – and more precisely, thought's critical self-consciousness – emerge, and how can such emergence be grasped, in ways that do not simply collapse back into the ruts of idealism? To this extent, it is possible to see epic theatre as a medium (or an inter-medium) designed for the articulation of epistemic thresholds and thus, utopically, for what may be called a mobilization of thought away from mentation's tendency towards transcendence. As the process in which thought becomes aware of its own activity, reflexivity materializes, in Brecht's hands, in concretely mediatized terms – indeed, as an intermediatized staging. Going a bit further, we may argue that the Brechtian imprint, which eventually found its way into studies of literature and art as well as theatre, film, and performance in a broad sense, has to do with turning reflexivity itself into a perceptible object. In such a process of objectification, the abstract operation of thinking, rather than being seamlessly woven into the fabric of the production (as the actant that motivates what happens but remains itself invisible), is made to assume protruding forms, most notably as gestures but also as captions, posters, fables, songs, and other visible bits and pieces.

Thought, in other words, has been made ex-plicit through staging: rather than drawing things into itself by unifying them, it breaks them up, moves them apart, and gives them independence, in a series of sensuous ex-plications (out-foldings).

It is also possible to state all this in the language of space, and argue that the special theoretical/speculative event embedded in Benjamin's description of the epic theatre is that of (re)conceptualization through spatialization. Space is, in this instance, not a matter of an already-existent physical environment but rather an insertion, into a continuum, of an interval, gap, and area of non-coincidence, such as the deliberate implantation of an outsider perspective in a familiar/familial interior. Space is thus a *phenomenon*, an *apprehending* of a doubling-cum-dealignment that, in turn, allows the epistemic limit of an existing set of conditions to become palpably perceptible – and marked off in their historical particularity. Defined in this manner, the epic theatre anticipates much of the way conceptual art continues to work in our contemporary contexts. The practice of installation art is a good case in point. Often the result of an intermixing of spaces and temporalities, an intermixing that pertains to the complexities of origination, disparateness of collected objects, politics of display, and diversity of reception, installation art, it may be said, exhibits none other than the (otherwise imperceptible) slippages that, when apprehended phenomenally, serve as the means to draw attention to reflexivity as an ongoing process. Insofar as space signifies a discursive-relational production/reception of knowledge, the epic theatre also anticipates much of poststructuralism's way of deconstructing epistemic boundaries.[11]

Reflexivity, artistic form, and the senses

If what we call 'theory' is inextricably bound up with the ramifications of reflexivity, then the protrusion/ex-plication of thought in sensuous forms and the practice of reconceptualization through spatialization may well be the predominant moves of theory in our time. To that extent, we can begin to understand Benjamin's statement that

> Brecht has attempted to make the thinking man, or indeed the wise man, into an actual dramatic hero. And it is from this point of view that his theatre may be defined as epic . . . Following Brecht's line of thought, one might even arrive at the proposition that it is the wise man who . . . is the perfect empty stage [*den vollkommenen Schauplatz*] [on which the contradictions of our society are acted out].
>
> (Benjamin 1998: 17)

This conscious attempt to mediatize reflexivity as a thinking that is sensuous but unsensational, and that appears as a rational rather than tragic performance, is one of the most widely adopted, if largely unacknowledged, of Brecht's legacies. For exactly that reason, Brecht's method has not only been influential in the study of drama proper but, arguably, even more so in trans-disciplinary theoretical practice on the left. In his magisterial account of Brecht's continuing relevance, Fredric Jameson offers an invigorating formulation of this method:

> [I]t is tempting to suggest that it is precisely Brecht's well-known slyness that is his method, and even his dialectic: the inversion of the hierarchies of a problem, major premiss passing to minor, absolute to relative, form to content, and vice versa – these are all operations whereby the dilemma in question is turned inside out, and an unexpected unforeseeable line of attack opens up that leads neither into the dead end of the unresolvable nor into the banality of stereotypical doxa on logical non-contradiction.
>
> (Jameson 1998: 25)

Any examination of theory after the heyday of theory must, I believe, take the legacy of this method into account.

Consider, for instance, the trend-setting intervention in ideology made by Louis Althusser in the 1960s and 1970s, in particular the oft-cited essay 'Ideology and Ideological State Apparatuses'. Although his formulation of ideology as the representation of the imaginary relationship of individuals to their real conditions of existence (Althusser 1971: 162) was inspired by Lacan's psychoanalytic writings on subjectivity, his approach to art bears unmistakable marks of a Brechtian tactic of reading. In essays such as 'The "Piccolo Teatro": Bertolazzi and Brecht', 'A Letter on Art in Reply to André Daspre', and 'Cremonini, Painter of the Abstract',[12] Althusser implements the equivalent of the alienation effect when he invokes an internal distance or dissociation that gives art (such as theatre, painting and literature) a privileged relationship to ideology, a relationship that is yet distinct from scientific knowledge.

Whereas Althusser's analysis of ideology underscores how various institutional agencies (such as the church, the school, the police, and so forth) stabilize and perpetuate the functioning of bourgeois society by recruiting (or, for Althusser, interpellating) the individual subject into a conforming and rewarding pattern of behaviour, in his approach to artistic media, he suggests a rather different set of procedures at work. Unlike the situation in which an individual is interpellated by ideological state apparatuses, in the case of art, reflexivity is possible through a space opening from within the artwork: the function of art, Althusser writes, is 'to make visible (*donner à voir*), by establishing a distance from it, the reality of the existing ideology (of any one of its forms)' (Althusser 1977: 241–2). The spectator, in other words, is not solicited by art in the same way the subject is interpellated by ideology. Instead, according to Althusser, *some* art provides a potentiality for something similar to Brecht's alienation, the point of which, he argues, is to demystify the identification model of consciousness, so that the spectator, placed at a distance from the performance, would have to become 'an actor who would complete the unfinished play, but in real life' (Althusser 1971: 146). Just as the stranger's entry (in Benjamin's description of the family row) introduces a break within the bourgeois family's dynamics, so does a painter such as Cremonini remove, in a process that

Althusser calls *determinate deformation*, all the coherent expression of individuality/ subjectivity from human faces that is part of a mystifying, ideological function of humanistic art. Such deformation means that spectators cannot simply recognize themselves in his pictures, and only thus (that is, in a state of non-recognition) come to know themselves (Althusser 1977: 238–40).

In the realm of literature, Pierre Macherey offers a comparable endeavour to articulate reflexivity to the work of literary criticism. Macherey's analysis is marked by his insistence that 'the emergence of thought institutes a certain distance and separation' (Macherey 1978: 6), and that such distance and separation is a way to reconceptualize the utterances of fiction. Thus literary criticism, in which thought about literature emerges, is an autonomous discourse that 'brings out a *difference* within the work by demonstrating that it is *other than it is*' (ibid. 7). In a homologous fashion, the literary text itself provides an internal distance from ideology: rather than being a mimetic reproduction or reflection of a pre-existing, ideological reality, the literary text is where contradictory social relations confront one another, and where ideology is made visible by refraction, as though in a broken mirror (Macherey's major example being the work of Leo Tolstoy).[13] Macherey also invokes 'Brecht's notion of a dialectic of the theatre' (ibid. 129) to elaborate the phenomenon of doubling, slippage and non-coincidence that constitutes the possibility of a politicized reception. In such reception, both the literary text and literary criticism are made part of a process of discursive production, which takes place through the staging of parallel but non-integrated relations.

In British feminist film studies of the 1970s, the work of theorist Laura Mulvey similarly seeks to break up the illusion of the dominant, classical narrative cinema by revealing its ideological – that is, patriarchal – underpinnings (Mulvey 1985: 303–15). Mulvey's influence on subsequent film studies is too well-known to require repeating, but what may be said in the current context is how the feminist insistence on dislocating classical film narrative should also be seen as part of a collective theoretical effort, enabled by Brechtian alienation, to pry open existing epistemic foreclosures. A deliberate estrangement of women's traditional role as beautiful objects, together with an elaboration of women's subjectivity as spectators, becomes, for Mulvey and subsequent generations of feminist critics, a means of staging – and hence subverting – the previously unproblematized vision constructed in accordance to masculinist interests.

These few examples have been brought up in an admittedly schematic fashion, but they suffice to help establish two points. First, if alienation may be understood as a demand to think in the terms I have outlined, it seems fair to conclude that contemporary theory may be seen as a systemic response to the key Brechtian contribution. It is, however, when the demand to think is entangled with specific artistic media – as for instance, theatre, painting, literature or film – that things become the most challenging: how is reflexivity possible when a particular form is involved, or how does thought's self-awareness take shape in conjunction with prescribed formal parameters? Staging, understood as a phenomenal rather than simply empirical process, is, I propose, one way in which this question has been answered. Notably, the epistemic space that is opened up from within an aesthetic spectacle, the space in which reflexivity can be staged, is also a steadily widening gap – and an intensifying non-correspondence – between the presence of a work as such and the way 'it' may be activated in reception. Precisely on account of its status as phenomenon rather than as actuality, therefore, staging remains an abstract operation. And it is such abstractness, which is also a quality of incompleteness and openness, which lends staging its political potential. At the same time that it signifies the mediatization of reflexivity, staging is the mark of theoretical practice *in process*.

Second, in Brecht's method, the leaning towards science and experimentation (in contrast to the fixity and fossilization of convention) goes hand in hand with the evacuation of empathy and identification as affects appropriate to reflexivity. This move, which may be called a move to de-sensationalize, is traceable in the analyses of drama, painting, literature and film as undertaken by theorists such as Althusser, Macherey and Mulvey. Even though their objects of inquiry remain sensuous, the sense that has become dominant as a result of the Brechtian way of mediatizing reflexivity is, one might say, rationality – that is to say, the capacity for cool-headed observation, logical explanation, didactic pedagogy and wisdom.[14] This leaves a fraught issue unresolved: what exactly is the status of the senses in relation to mediatized reflexivity? Walter Benjamin was still writing at a time when relaxation and distraction could be embraced as emancipatory sense modalities, as opposed to the absorption and contemplation necessitated by traditional cultural forms such as the novel and painting. But as alienation is followed to its logical conclusion, what becomes increasingly politically suspect is none other than pleasure. The heightened alarm of mystification and delusion (that is, false consciousness) sounded around aesthetic illusionism means that the Brechtian method, in spite of Brecht's own often entertaining stage productions, has led to the prevalence of a puritanical austerity as the hallmark of certain theoretical practices. As Mulvey sums it up revealingly in her landmark essay: 'It is said that analysing pleasure, or beauty, destroys it. That is the intention of this article' (ibid. 306).

These two intimately linked dimensions in the entanglement of reflexivity and aesthetic media – the phenomenon of staging and the increasing non-correspondence between production and receptivity on the one hand, and on the other, the residual ineluctability of the senses and with it the unresolved question of pleasure – are among the difficult issues confronting us in the days of 'theory after theory'. How viable might staging remain as a theoretical practice? How might the senses be (re)distributed after the critical censuring of illusionism, identification, empathy and other sensuous pleasures?[15]

By displacing the gravitational pull of dramatization onto the spectator as a thinking person, the Brechtian method has dethroned the transcendent mind and divided and distributed it among the ordinary masses. The point of the alienation effect is to make reflexivity political by making it *vulgar*: thought is no longer deep and refined but crude; it sticks out where you least expect it; it takes on unsubtle, obtrusive forms, like the petty, biased habits and behaviours of the uneducated classes (a good example: Brecht's Mother Courage). At the same time, the agency that accompanies this vulgarization of reflexivity – the ability to think otherwise, to reconceptualize, to stage a familiar object through the phenomenon of an alternative space – is increasingly faced with a certain impasse, namely, its own im-plication (in-folding), through the rational processes of division and distribution, in the endless fragmentation and reification of thought.

If reflexivity was, once upon a time, associated with freedom (think of the trajectory imagined by Hegel for the Western Spirit), in the days of hypermediatization it seems caught between becoming impotent under circumstances of ubiquitous technological surveillance and having to let the practice of staging multiply ad infinitum (in the sense of an infinite series of spatialization that breaks up the continuum of a mediatized spectacle into ever newer units). Staging defined in these terms now occurs not only in the form of the arrested tableau, collage, montage, conceptual art, installation art, and so forth but also in the form of various kinds of screening and framing possibilities, produced with sophisticated apparatuses and circulating everywhere as the daily fare of social interaction (consider the framing and cropping techniques of PhotoShop, for instance, or the multitasking capabilities of a device like the iPhone). In the days of proliferating, hypermediatized screens and frames, is staging, which belongs to an older, modernist way of objectifying reflexivity, still relevant? And even if it is, has not staging lost its once-utopian function now that it seems to have been thoroughly co-opted into facets of what Guy Debord has famously named society of the spectacle,[16] from museum art exhibits to television talent shows, to real estate marketing strategies? In terms of the senses, what has reflexivity, once staged/mediatized in the form of estranged thought and roughened perception, become in the new regime of the abstract touch – the flow, the click, the tap, the slide, the pinch and the finger swipe, all characteristic of digital technologies? Has not the speed and smoothness of the computer screen paradoxically reintroduced a sense of illusionism and automatism, exactly the kind of sensation that the earlier generations of media theorists such as Brecht and Benjamin were keen to dispel?

Pornographic intensities

Recall now how Benjamin describes the resilience of the Brechtian dramatic scene: 'It can happen this way, but it can also happen quite a different way' (Benjamin 1998: 8). The fundamentally empty, because open, nature of Brecht's epic theatre (as Benjamin writes, the wise man is a perfect empty stage) suggests that the most radical gestures of change, precisely because they are so radical, *can* turn into their opposites. Herein lies the danger of co-optation, whereby a different kind of revolution – capitalist, rather than socialist – overtakes the global scene with its invincible logic of exchange and substitution. Benjamin's '. . . this way, [or . . .] a different way' is, in this light, fully montage-able as a slogan for the consumer's choice, with as many spaces/breaks/gaps/variations introduced into a previously simple and restricted process. Nowadays, even the most basic selections to satisfy our daily needs often involve a limitless spectrum of options.

Beyond the spectre of capitalist consumerism, there is a larger epistemic conundrum underlying the mediatization of reflexivity through estrangement and alienation. To see this, we need to return briefly to a notion introduced by Shklovsky along-side that of art as device – namely, the notion of laying bare. While 'art as device' defamiliarizes an object in such a way as to make us notice its perceptible quality (the stoniness of a stone), 'laying bare' suggests, rather, a return to an original condition – behind a set of numbing habits or automatized conventions – in its *unadorned nakedness*. This is evident in Shklovsky's emphasis on the result of seeing something 'for the first time': 'Tolstoy makes the familiar seem strange by not nam-ing the familiar object. He describes an object as if he were seeing it for the first time, an event as if it were happening for the first time' (Shklovsky 1965: 13). 'The purpose of imagery in erotic art can be studied even more accurately; an erotic object is usually presented as if it were seen for the first time' (ibid. 18). Inscribed in Shklovsky's aesthetics of renovation and renewal is thus, ironically, a preoccupa-tion with the old and the timeless (what has been veiled or fogged up). With defamiliarization, it may be argued, comes the nostalgic longing for an implicit norm of authenticity, a 'first time' (both at the level of objects and at the level of perception), to which artists wake us from the mechanicity of repetitiveness. As Galin Tihanov writes:

> Any successful act of estrangement . . . rests on a paradox: the end product is meant as a piece of innovation – arrived at through various artistic devices – that serves, however, to revive and make more palpable the old (and constant) substance of things. To conduct the procedure of estrangement properly and to the desired end means to bring the old to the fore in and through the new, thus reasserting what is presumed to be the object's timeless substance.
>
> (Tihanov 2005: 686)

Critics who have explored the connections between Shklovsky and Brecht tend to see the former's concept of making strange as lacking in the dialogical possibility, embedded in the spectator's reaction, of historical change that is offered by Brecht's alienation effect.[17] While I share this view, a word in Benjamin's description of the family row – uncovering/discovering (*Entdeckung*) – gives me pause. The point is not to debate the instabilities of translingual traffic (in this case, among Russian, German and English) but rather to mark a predicament typical of the modernist gesture of making present and making new.[18] Like the notion of laying bare, the rhetoric of uncovering underlying conditions is intended to call attention to what has become unthinking (that is, mindless), but when examined closely, the potential for change and changeability (what is supposedly an endless and unpredictable proc-ess) that is attributed to art is also underpinned by an opposite kind of desire – that of exposing fundamentals, of restoring things to an absolute, as-yet untouched, state. This desire, which is in concert with a type of violent display – indeed, with display itself as a necessary form of violence and violation – may be termed por-nographic. A notable example along these lines is André Bazin's reading of the photographic image, whose 'aesthetic qualities . . . are to be sought in its power to lay bare the realities', as the cinematic lens strips from the object 'that spiritual dust and grime with which my eyes have covered it' and lets it be seen 'in all its virginal purity' (Bazin 1967: 15). A further example is Jacques Derrida's reading of Antonin Artaud's theatre of cruelty, which, in Derrida's description, 'lays bare the flesh of the word, lays bare the word's sonority, intonation, intensity – the shout that the articulations of language and logic have not yet entirely frozen, that is, the aspect of oppressed gesture which remains in all speech . . . ' (Derrida 1978: 240).

Such a tendency towards the pornographic seems at first quite at odds with the rational, cool-headed and experimental tone toward the production of thought that was intended by Brecht and Benjamin. Only when one ponders the evocative set of associations that runs from cruelty (and violence) to crudeness and primitiveness (as in Brecht's crude thinking [*plumpes Denken*] and Benjamin's 'crude' or 'primitive' example of the family row) and more recently, to what is termed 'bare life', whose transhistorical reality the philosopher Giorgio Agamben (1998) seeks to restore to global biopolitics, that the close affinity between pornography's denuding conventions and the logic of mediatized reflexivity becomes clear.

Could this be a reason the staging of reflexivity tends, in the hands of some contemporary artists, to become synonymous with the violence of medial exhibitionism?

As a brief example, consider the work of Austrian director Michael Haneke, whose self-conscious staging of mediality is often simultaneously a staging of physical violence. In films such as *Benny's Video* (1992) and *Funny Games* (1997), Haneke offers chilling portrayals of German-speaking bourgeois society through the most ordinary and peaceful settings. In *Benny's Video*, a teenager, obsessed with computers, invites a girl home to watch videos and ends up killing her and capturing the incident on camera. His parents, on discovering the crime, collaborate in covering it up so as to preserve the decorum of the status quo, only then to find themselves being reported to the authorities by their son, who has secretly taped their private conversations in which they reveal their culpability. In *Funny Games*, soon after a nuclear family arrives at its vacation home in an upscale countryside neighbourhood, two polite male adolescents, claiming to be house guests at a neighbour's, show up to borrow some eggs. The incident quickly spirals into a succession of viciously abusive acts inflicted on the family, whose members are trapped and tortured until they die. The two villains then move on to their next set of targets – another family on vacation. In both films, there is a conscious play on mediality, either involving the use of machines such as video cameras, computers, tape recorders, and the like or, as in the case of *Funny Games*, a literal rewinding of moments of the film itself in the midst of the disaster befalling the family.

Such medially self-referential citations are meant to draw attention to the saturation of contemporary life by media technology. Rather than staging a 'tableau' that in turn enables the audience to come in and complete the action, however, Haneke's display seems intent on exhibiting the extreme, yet pointless, nature of physical as well as ideological violence. This conjunction of the extreme and the pointless is fetishized precisely through its equation with reflexivity itself, as though critical thought must now not only be mediatized (through staging, as in the self-referentiality of the medium) but must also deliberately assault the audience's senses by stretching the mediality of the medium to its limits – *by ripping off the medium's clothes, as it were, and exposing its innermost secrets.* To my mind, it is such aggressive gestures of laying bare or uncovering – in what may be termed an aesthetics of subtraction – that put Haneke in the lineage of Shklovsky and Brecht, in a manner that magnifies the pornographic reasoning of modernist mediatized reflexivity. As is indicated by the title of Haneke's widely acclaimed film *Caché* (2005), what needs to be laid bare or uncovered is none other than the condition of aggression, a degree-zero 'reality' or 'ground' that is intimated as hidden because it has been repressed. Art-as-thought is thus, or so we are led to believe, a matter of stripping things naked, so as to return this reality or ground to its intact – that is, pure and authentic – place in history.

With an intellectual director like Haneke, the relationship of reflexivity to mediatization has become thoroughly tormented. As thought can no longer proceed without mediatization and yet mediatization cannot be trusted, an obsessive-compulsive dependency on media technologies now goes hand in hand with the coldness of suspicion, cynicism, and often denunciation of those technologies. Such intensities of sensation are at once moralistic and chic, and symptomatic of one dominant direction in which reflexivity as a modernist theoretical practice has mutated in postmodernity from its earlier and more optimistically utopian cast. It remains to be seen whether and how the philosophical capaciousness and playful adaptability of the latter, such as have been identified in the work of Brecht, can find some means of reasserting themselves against our era's pervasive metaphysical yearning for the purity of the void that is the ultimate lure of porn.

Notes

1 I am indebted to Jim Dennen and Julian Rohrhuber for some very engaging comments on the draft of this essay.
2 A somewhat different translation can be found in Benjamin (1969: 147–54). The quoted passage is on 150–1. See also Benjamin's slightly reworded versions of the same scene in 'What Is Epic Theatre? [First version]', in Benjamin (1998: 4–5), and 'The Author as Producer' in Benjamin (1998: 100). The original German versions of these texts can be found in Benjamin (1966).
3 Stanley Mitchell: 'There are . . . strong indications that the ideas and implications of "epic theatre" were common to them both [Brecht and Benjamin] before they met' (Benjamin 1998: viii).
4 This last point is made clear by 'The Author as Producer' (ibid. 100).
5 See also Brecht (1965).
6 My emphasis. Brecht is paraphrasing the epic writer Alexander Döblin's criterion for the epic.
7 For a helpful, informative discussion of the relationship between Shklovsky's term *ostranenie* and Brecht's term *Verfremdung*, see Mitchell (1974). For a discussion that argues the significance of World War I as the formative background behind Shklovsky's advocacy

of estrangement as artistic innovation, see Tihanov (2005). In his study, Fredric Jameson has argued that the term *Verfremdungseffekt* should be translated as estrangement effect rather than alienation effect; see Jameson (1998: 85–6, n.13).

8   See 'Alienation Effects in Chinese Acting' (Brecht 1964: 91–9).

9   For this important point, I am indebted to a conversation with Dr. Young-suk Kim on July 23, 2009.

10 Jameson writes that Barthes's Brechtian origins have often been neglected and that his classic *Mythologies* paved the way for the success of estrangement/alienation effect in French theory (poststructuralism); see Jameson (1998: 38, 40, 41, 49–51, 172–3).

11 In the context of French philosophy and literature, the phenomenological works on space and knowledge production by Maurice Blanchot, Gaston Bachelard, and the early Michel Foucault would be obvious interlocutors here. For reasons of word limit, a fully fledged exploration of this linkage will need to be deferred until another occasion.

12 The first two essays are found in Althusser (1971: 21–7 and 229–42); the third essay is found in Althusser (1977: 129–51).

13 See the chapter 'Lenin, Critic of Tolstoy' in Macherey (1978:105–35).

14 This point is thoroughly explored by Mitchell (Benjamin 1998) as well as by Benjamin himself.

15 I take the notion of the distribution of the senses from Rancière (2004: 7–45).

16 See Debord (1994). Debord's book was first published in the 1960s. By 'spectacle' Debord means not a collection of images but a society in which relations among people are mediated by images.

17 See Tihanov (2005: 686–91) for a discussion of how Brecht and Herbert Marcuse assessed and critiqued Shklovsky's aesthetic notion of estrangement as insufficient for coping with reification and alienation, which are complex and durable products of history.

18 Paul de Man's deconstructive analysis of modernity's desire for a new origin – a desire that is haunted by history – remains instructive at this juncture. See 'Literary History and Literary Modernity' (de Man 1983: 142–65).

Bibliography

Agamben, G. (1998) Homo Sacer: *Sovereign Power and Bare Life*, trans. D. Heller-Roazen, Stanford, CA: Stanford University Press.

Althusser, L. (1971) *Lenin and Philosophy and Other Essays*, trans. B. Brewster, London: Monthly Review Press.

Althusser, L. (1977) *For Marx*, trans. B. Brewster, London: New Left Books.

Barthes, R. (1977) 'Diderot, Brecht, Eisenstein', in *Music–Image–Text*, sel. and trans. S. Heath, Glasgow: Fontana/Collins.

Bazin, A. (1967) 'The Ontology of the Photographic Image', in *What Is Cinema?*, Vol. 1, trans. H. Gray, Berkeley: University of California Press.

Benjamin, W. (1966) *Versuche über Brecht*, Frankfurt am Main: Suhrkamp Verlag.

Benjamin, W. (1969) *Illuminations*, ed. and intro. H. Arendt, trans. H. Zohn, New York: Schoken.

Benjamin, W. (1998) *Understanding Brecht*, trans. A. Bostock, intro. S. Mitchell, London: Verso.

Brecht, B. (1964) *Brecht on Theatre: The Development of an Aesthetic*, ed. and trans. J. Willett, New York: Hill & Wang.

Brecht, B. (1965) *The Messingkauf Dialogues*, trans. and ed. J. Willet, London: Methuen.

Debord, G. (1994) *Society of the Spectacle*, ed. and trans. D. Nicholson-Smith, New York: Zone Books.

Derrida, J. (1978) *Writing and Difference*, trans., intro. notes A. Bass, Chicago: University of Chicago Press.

Jameson, F. (1998) *Brecht and Method*, New York: Verso.

Macherey, P. (1978) *A Theory of Literary Production*, trans. G. Wall, London: Routledge & Kegan Paul.

de Man, P. (1983) 'Literary History and Literary Modernity', in *Blindness and Insight: Essays in the Rhetoric of Contemporary Criticism*, 2nd edn, rev., intro. W. Godzich, Minneapolis: University of Minnesota Press.

Mitchell, S. (1974) 'From Shklovsky to Brecht: Some Preliminary Remarks Towards a History of the Politicisation of Russian Formalism', *Screen*, 15.2: 74–81.

Mulvey, L. (1985) 'Visual Pleasure and Narrative Cinema', in B. Nichols (ed.) *Movies and Methods*, Vol. 2, Berkeley: University of California Press. First published (1975) *Screen* 16.3 (Autumn): 6–18.

Rancière, J. (2004) *The Politics of Aesthetics: The Distribution of the Sensible*, trans. and intro. G. Rockhill, London: Continuum.

Shklovsky, V. (1965) 'Art as Technique', in L. Lemon and M. J. Reis (eds) *Russian Formalist Criticism: Four Essays*, Lincoln: University of Nebraska Press.

Tihanov, G. (2005) 'The Politics of Estrangement: The Case of the Early Shklovsky', *Poetics Today*, 26.4 (Winter): 665–96.

10

THE CANNY SUBALTERN

Eva Cherniavsky

> 'The Subject' implied by the texts of insurgency can only serve as a counter-
> possibility for the narrative sanctions granted to the colonial subject in the
> dominant groups. The postcolonial intellectuals learn that their privilege is
> their loss. In this they are a paradigm of the intellectuals.
>
> (Spivak 2000b: 287)

Subaltern Studies is one of the several contemporary knowledge projects where
the effects of poststructuralism (routinely aligned with postmodernism and
occasionally elided with it) have been descried and defended, in a debate whose
broad contours, at least, will certainly feel familiar whether or not one follows
Subaltern Studies. On one side, the antagonists worry that the critique of universality results in a celebration of the fragment, floating free from its historical context, and of performative identities, which now substitute for the study of class
formations. In this framework, poststructuralism and identity politics are routinely
run together, as (seemingly) cognate versions of the critique of universalism. This
conflation helps to sustain the charge that poststructuralism – and deconstruction
in particular – foil the progressive political aspirations of their advocates, surrepti-
tiously reasserting the essentializing categories they appear to assail. Over and
against an allegedly identitarian and essentialist poststructuralism, these critics array
historical materialism and a critical commitment to thinking social transformation,
a commitment all too readily brushed aside, they argue, by a critique of the
Enlightenment that perversely (if unwittingly) forecloses on *emancipation* by the same
token that it rejects universalism. Thus, for example, Sumit Sarkar points out how the
rejection of secularism (as a universalizing Enlightenment value) and the appreciation
of cultural differentiation makes Subaltern Studies (in its postmodernist variant)
oddly complicit with the ethno-nationalist politics of *hindutva* (Sarkar 2000: 311).

On the other side, poststucturalism's defenders (re)claim it as an ethics of incommensurability, indispensable for any reckoning with the epistemic violence of the colonial context and its legacies. Poststructualism offers a theory and a practice of supplementation, necessary to displace a singular narrative of capital (and its historical subjects), which is also a self-contained version of the West. As Gyan Prakash observes,

> If the West sentenced the otherness of the conquered to History, to recognize that project now as the work of a universal logic which used and produced difference without compromising its sovereignty is to repeat that act of incarceration. This leaves no room for the otherness and resistance that was not determined by the Western conquest; it denies that anti-colonial nationalism and subaltern struggles, while being constituted by dominant structures, could slip beyond and come back to haunt the conditions of their own constitution.
>
> (Prakash 2000: 236)

This essay ruminates on the ways in which we lose to the very terms of the debate a feel for the supple articulation of (among other things) Marxist political economy and poststructuralist critique of the subject that characterized Subaltern Studies *at the outset*. I am interested in why this articulation seems increasingly fraught and contested, and why poststructuralism's defenders appear oriented, not just to the deconstructive critique of domination, in the way Prakash suggests, but also to the idea of transformative contact with subalterns. In this context, I revisit the project of Subaltern Studies at the point of its emergence in the 1980s to suggest that its intervention in questions of subjectivity, agency and hegemony, staged originally as an intervention in (Eurocentric) Marxist historiography, also carries important implications for contemporary left academic work that situates itself in solidarity with subaltern mobilizations against the privatization of the (remaining) commons, IMF-imposed austerity measures, new (and not so new) regimes of labour discipline, and neoliberal governance more generally. While I share the political sensibilities that animate this scholarship – scholarship that cuts across American Studies, Ethnic Studies, Women's Studies, GLBT/Queer Studies and Postcolonial Studies more broadly, as well as Subaltern Studies itself – I will argue that this arena of 'theory after Theory' elides, at its peril, the critique of the non-representing intellectual so decisively urged in the essay from which my epigraph derives. The original title of 'Can the Subaltern Speak?' was 'Power, Desire, and Interest', Spivak tells us in the essay's opening line, and it is precisely the relation between the privilege to constitute our objects of study and the desires with which we invest them – to constitute our objects as commensurate to our investments – on which my essay presses (Spivak 1988a: 271).

I. Learning

Alongside a range of left-identified academic scholarship, which moves in and across the fields named above, Subaltern Studies seems marked today by the urgency of re-imagining a left political practice, we might say a socialism after socialism, cross-hatched with the political imaginary and symbolic systems of those who were historically marginal to (at the periphery or altogether displaced from) capital and capitalist social relations. This marginal position is subaltern by defini- tion. 'Since "subaltern" in the subcontinental use defines those who were cut off from the lines that produced the colonial mindset', Spivak observes, '*s/he did not emerge in the colonial cultural value-form*. Thus, considerations of cultural problematics in Subaltern Studies are not a substitute for, but a supplement to, Marxist theory' (Spivak 2000b: 325, my emphasis). With the dissolution of the Second World that represented, however imperfectly, an organized alternative to capitalism, such 'sup- plementation' has become the order of the day – and not just for those Subaltern Studies scholars seeking to recover from within the margins and lacunae of the colonial record the 'cultural value-forms' that it so meticulously effaced. Today it is the very possibility of a critical relation to capital (both a theory and a practice) that we vest in the subaltern, and it is her current political salience for the left, confronted by a moribund socialism on the one hand and an ever more predatory capitalism on the other, that feeds the urgency of reaching her, of a contact that would not reproduce at the outset the historical conditions of her silencing. Indeed, we might say that contemporary interest in the subaltern participates (tac- itly or otherwise) in a rejection of Spivak's famous assertion, wrought in her read- ing against the grain of Subaltern Studies in the 1980s, that the subaltern cannot speak. In Bart Moore-Gilbert's complaint,

> An insistence on the irreducible alterity and muteness of the subaltern, one might argue, paralyzes not just the subaltern, but the would-be ally of the subaltern – who is left in the double-bind of being required to show soli- darity with the subaltern without in any way 'selfing' that Other or 'assimilat- ing' her to the degree that solidarity perhaps inevitably demands . . . Indeed, possibly the greatest irony of an essay like 'Can the Subaltern Speak?' is that if its account of subaltern alterity and muteness were true, then there would be nothing but the West (and the native elite, perhaps) to write about.
>
> (Moore-Gilbert 2000: 464)

I will come back to this assessment later, which seems to me to mistake the import of Spivak's claim, even as it names the interest (of the would-be ally) that here runs together with that of the subaltern herself. For now, I want to consider how the alternatives to this 'paralysis' seem to converge or collate with a metaphorics of 'learning' – or of 'learning to learn from below'.

'Learning' in this sense signifies the possibility of a relation between elites and subalterns in which the terms of the exchange are set (at least partially) by subal- terns themselves: 'I am trying to think my way towards a subaltern historiography that actually tries to learn from the subaltern', writes Dipesh Chakrabarty, even as he concedes that learning is bound up in teaching: 'We write, ultimately, as part of a collective effort to help teach the oppressed of today how to be the democratic subject of tomorrow' (Chakrabarty 2000a: 272, 273). Chakrabarty is insistent that there is never parity – that the dialogue itself is never fully democratic – though it is nonetheless of use to the subaltern. A similar preoccupation marks Gayatri Spivak's recent work, although she prefers the formula of 'learning to learn from below', which marks, of course, the extent to which whatever might be transmitted from subalterns to elites in this exchange is not comprehended within elite determinations of educational value, so that it is first a matter of learning to recognize as knowledge and worth knowing what will appear as neither within the precincts of academic instruction:

> It is a narrative concerning a tiny group of one kind of subaltern. I have got to know them well in the last ten years, after I gave up my apologetic formula for Subaltern Studies (which the collective did not need anyway): strategic use of essentialism. I found instead a different one emerging from my own subaltern study: learning to learn from below. This one will have few takers.
>
> (Spivak 2000b: 333)

In Spivak's own gloss, 'learning to learn from below' is the alternative formula for a 'strategic essentialism' that has become the critical lynchpin of identity politics in the global North:

> In 'Deconstructing Historiography' I had suggested that the Subaltern Studies collective assumed a subaltern consciousness, however negative, by a 'strategic use of essentialism'. Subaltern Studies has no need of such apologetics. But the theoretically inclined metropolitan identitarians did. In the name of their own groups, they argued identity, claimed strategy, and sometimes gave me credit. No one particularly noticed what I have already mentioned, that Subaltern Studies never presupposed a consciousness for 'their own group', but rather for their object of investigation, and for the sake of the investigation.
>
> (Ibid.: 332)

In this account, strategic essentialism is mobilized, or perhaps more accurately co-opted, by those who write about themselves, and so 'learning to learn from below' is the critical rejoinder that refuses the conflation of investigator and investigated, and insists on the limits of the former's prerogative to know her objects – and by extension, herself. Yet it strikes me that 'learning to learn from below' is also Spivak's rejoinder to her own earlier emphasis on the intellectual's 'unlearning privilege', and the newer formula corresponds to what she argues is the contemporary importance, indeed the urgency, of 'activating' subaltern knowledges: '[T]he real effort should be to connect and *activate* the tribals' indigenous "democratic" structure to parliamentary democracy by patient and sustained efforts to learn to learn from below' (ibid.: 336, my emphasis). And again,

I have argued that in their current decrepitude the subaltern cultures need to be known in such a way that *we can suture their re-activated cultural axiomatics into the principles of Enlightenment*. I have argued that socialism belongs to these axiomatics. That socialism attempts to turn capital-formation into redistribution is a truism. It is by this logic that supplementation into the Enlightenment is as much the possibility of being the agent of the social productivity of capital as it is of the subjectship of Human Rights.

(Spivak 2008: 29–30, my emphasis)

The difference I mean to suggest between 'unlearning privilege' and 'activating' subalterns (or staging 'Enlightenment from below') is nicely marked in Spivak's own retrospective on 'Can the Subaltern Speak?', which here opens on a rather different agenda for the politically engaged intellectual than did her essay itself:

Indeed 'Can the Subaltern Speak?' is not really about colonialism at all. It is about agency; institutionally validated action. To put it as simply as possible, I will quote a recent piece, written by a woman, in *India Abroad*, a newspaper that has no intellectual pretentions: 'Spivak wrote a much-cited article called "Can the Subaltern Speak?" in which she argued that, unless validated by dominant forms of knowledge and politics, resistance could not be recognized ("heard") as such'. What kinds of politics can emerge from this, asks Neil Larsen. The politics of demanding and building infrastructure so that when subalterns speak they can be heard.

(Spivak 2000a: xx)

However, in 'Can the Subaltern Speak?' the intellectual's responsibility is to the history of the subaltern's silencing, a silence that cannot be 'filled' without repeating the original act of erasure (by representing her who cannot represent herself). Hence the imperative to 'speak to' (rather than 'speak for') the subaltern – to address the conditions of her muting (which are also the conditions of possibility of the intellectual's discourse). Here, by contrast, our obligation is to a *mobilization* of the subaltern subject – a suturing of subaltern difference to 'Enlightenment', broadly speaking, as it renders human emancipation a regulative political norm.

The project of 'demanding and building infrastructure' that allows subalterns to be heard involves orienting subalterns to participation in the public sphere, and facilitating access to it, although curiously, in Spivak's most recent writing, the contemporary public sphere seems continuous with its ideal instantiation, as the exercise of public reason. 'This is why an intuition of the public sphere, which ideally teaches democratic co-existence, is the point of the whole exercise. We should remember that the public sphere relates to unconditional hospitality as law to justice, heterogeneously' (Spivak 2008: 24), she writes. And again, 'We who are interested in alternative Development propose an ab-use (not abuse) of the Enlightenment (understood in shorthand as "the public use of reason"), a use from below' (ibid.: 133). The intellectual's mandate to activate subalternity within the domain of public reason is linked, one assumes, to what Spivak elsewhere cites as the changing condition of subalterns within the contemporary contexts of capitalist accumulation:

> Today the 'subaltern' must be rethought. S/he is no longer cut off from lines of access to the centre. The centre, as represented by the Bretton Woods agencies and the World Trade Organization, is altogether interested in the rural and indigeneous subaltern as source of trade-related intellectual properties or TRIPs. Many ways are being found to generate a subaltern subject asking to be used thus.
>
> (Spivak 2000b: 326)

If we can now imagine 'suturing subaltern axiomatics' into the operations of parliamentary democracy, this is possible because, unlike her colonial counterpart, the present–day subaltern *does* emerge in the value form of informational capital. This latest round of primitive accumulation then, or 'accumulation by dispossession' in David Harvey's resonant phrase, fosters the emergence of (certain, rural) subalterns into hegemony, in other words – as 'subjects *asking* to used thus' (Harvey 2005: 178–9). In this context, Spivak's project is to envision the 'reactivation' of subaltern *agency*, as it articulates – or might articulate – a *different* demand within the arenas of liberal democracy and mediatized public life.

At its core, however, Spivak's current preoccupation with subalterns' emergence into public reason returns us to the matter at the heart of Subaltern Studies: How do we reach subaltern subjects? How do we learn from them? Or, learn to learn when they are, by definition, heterogeneous to 'our' histories – when, as Spivak insisted in 1988, '[t]he historian must persist in *his* efforts in this awareness, that the subaltern is necessarily the absolute limit of the place where history is narrativized into a logic' (Spivak 1988b: 207)? Writing a decade later, Spivak's answer now hinges on considerations of scale, as she recommends the pursuit of 'one–on–one mind–changing contact' with individual subalterns, imagined as a singular, 'secret encounter', 'secret' not in the sense of hidden or private, but of a partial, fundamentally impossible communication, the attempted sharing of a 'secret' that can never go through fully in the exchange (Spivak 1998: 340). We find a similar emphasis on the simultaneous importance and (im)possibility of this exchange in Chakrabarty:

> The [historian's] investigation, in turn, must be possessed of an openness so radical that I can only express it in Heideggerian terms: the capacity to hear that which one does not already understand. In other words, to allow the subaltern position to challenge our own conception of what is universal, to be open to the possibility of a particular thought-world, however concerned it might be with the task of grasping a totality, being rendered finite by the presence of the Other: such are the utopic horizons to which this other moment of *Subaltern Studies* call us. Knowledge-forms produced at this end will not be tied to the state or governmentality for they will not reflect a will to rule. The subaltern here is the ideal figure of he who survives actively, even

joyously, on the assumption that the effective instruments of domination will always belong to somebody else and never aspires to them. What will history produced in this mode look like? I cannot say, for one cannot write history in this pure form.

(Chakrabarty 2000a: 275–6)

And, so he concludes,

This is why we need to go to a Derrida, or a Lyotard or a Levinas, not because they have become 'fashions in the West' (that's raising the question at the most superficial level) but because they are the philosophers of 'difference' and 'non-commensurability' for our times.

(Ibid.: 276)

In Chakrabarty's account, the difficulty of Spivak's 'secret encounter' – the necessary failures of that exchange – gives way to the celebration of a radical 'openness' to what we do not already understand. Yet, it is not the alterity of the subaltern *subject* evacuated in this celebratory invocation of an 'ideal figure', who appears not a *subject* at all, but a trope of *jouissance* (a joyous survivor) – or more exactly, as the figure of *the investigator's jouissance*? Indeed, *whose* jubilant emancipation if not our own is inscribed in this vision of a (non)subject without a will to domination? The undisclosability of the subaltern's assumptions and aspirations transmutes into a fantasy – but surely it is *our* fantasy – of ecstatic unmaking. Under the very auspices of Derrida and the philosophy of incommensurability, Chakrabarty envisions the subaltern as a *subject without loss*.

Here poststructuralism curiously falls in line with the strand of modernist idealism Rey Chow acutely notes, in which the oppressed resist on the basis of an essential integrity. Tracing this thought of 'subjectivity-in-exploitation' to the Lukács of *History and Class Consciousness*, Chow suggests how

numerous contemporary versions of identity-based critical thinking have, wittingly or unwittingly, been replicating Lukács's modernist narrative with its telos of self-ownership and self-affirmation in both individual and collective senses. Most of all, such critical thinking has frequently resorted to a similarly idealized assumption about humanity and subjectivity, *which are imagined as at once historically damaged and essentially beyond damage.*

(Chow 2002: 40, my emphasis)[1]

Moreover, how do we shift, within the terms of this imaginary, from ideality to injury? What is the relation between cathecting the 'ideal subaltern' and confronting in 'their current decrepitude' the subaltern cultures Spivak recommends we activate? Can we know where the desire for the former overwrites our encounter with the latter? How do we move from the scale of the secret encounter (and/the radical openness that is *perhaps* sustainable there) to that of mediatized social relations?

Indeed, whose project is 'Enlightenment from below?' Whatever its tactical value – its 'use' to the subaltern, in Chakrabarty's phrase – what Subaltern Studies teaches me (what I have learned from the volumes of *Subaltern Studies* and particularly the work of Ranajit Guha) is that the subject of this 'suturing' is *us*, just as, for instance, the subject of Indian nationalist narratives that championed peasant insurgencies was not the peasantry, but the comprador elite. The task of 'activating' subalterns answers to our own aspirations for organized resistance to the social relations of capital – and the aspirations *of subalterns* remain, as before, at the limit of our understanding.

II. Unlearning

This seems to me the central insight of Subaltern Studies in the 1980s: the subaltern is a site of discursive manoeuvre for the production of elite subjectivity, whether the production of the colonial rulers, of an all-India national elite – or of left academics struggling to retain a ground for political engagement in the academies of the global North. The subaltern is available to signify elite agency precisely because the subaltern subject herself is subjected to the epistemic violence of a radical designification. If the elite subject is split (between the signifier and a being that is never exhausted in language), the subaltern is split between the signifiers of subaltern life (that do not travel) and the language of colonial power in which she reduces to so much inert material (outside of history and prospects for becoming) – split, in other words, between the registers of family and community, on the one hand, and the 'fullness' of what I would call, borrowing from Hortense Spillers, a 'monumental' identity, on the other.[2]

However one imagines the subaltern in her fullness, as a radically debased or radically utopian figure, as lacking deliberative agency or as joyous survivor, the subaltern *subject* vanishes – and it is her 'blankness' that allows for the elaboration of a seemingly sovereign elite. The project of Subaltern Studies, in this view, is to undo this predication. Or, in Spivak's 1980s formulation,

> Thus do the texts of counter-insurgency locate, in the following description, a 'will' as the sovereign cause when it is no more than an effect of the subaltern subject-effect, itself produced through particular conjunctures called forth by the crises meticulously described in various *Subaltern Studies*. Reading the work of Subaltern Studies from within but against the grain, I would suggest that elements in their text would warrant a reading of the project to retrieve the subaltern consciousness as the attempt to undo a massive historical metalepsis and 'situate' the effect of the subject as subaltern.
>
> (Spivak 1988b: 204)

Similarly, for Prakash, Subaltern Studies seeks to trace the haunting presence of the 'otherness of the conquered' in the very text of the colonizers' self-narration.

At the level of historiographical practice, then, Subaltern Studies entails reading at the limits of the historical record, searching for the residues of subaltern imaginaries in the interstices of the value-laden metaphorics that negate both subaltern meaning and the meaningfulness of subaltern practices.[3] And it entails reading at the limits of a Marxist analytic that compels attention to the political life of the masses in the first place, even as it draws the limits of the political in a way that threatens to disappear the subaltern all over again. As Chakrabarty perceptively observes,

> Guha was prepared to suggest that the nature of collective action against exploitation in colonial India was such that it effectively stretched the imaginary boundaries of the category of the 'political' far beyond the territories assigned to it in European political thought. To ignore the problems that the political sphere could cause for a Eurocentric Marxism would lead, according to Guha, only to elitist histories, for one would then *not* know how to analyze the consciousness of the peasant – the discourses of kinship, caste, religion, and ethnicity through which they expressed themselves in protest – except as a 'backward' consciousness trying to grapple with a changing world whose logic it could never fully comprehend.
>
> (Chakrabarty 2000b: 473)

I take this as a second pivotal insight of Subaltern Studies that is intimately related to the first: *the subaltern is one whose agency is not legible within the field of the political – of political subject constitution – in which the investigator conceives his inquiry.* So Marxism – the Marxism of the Subaltern Studies group – requires supplementation by indigenous subaltern sign systems, but supplementation, it is vital to recall, involves a displacement of Marxist analytical categories by the (minimally reconstituted) signifiers of subaltern life (what Prakash calls 'haunting'), not any simple substitution of the subaltern signifiers themselves, even assuming this were possible. It is not only that we cannot think the subaltern's practice on her own terms – cannot retrieve or reconstitute what has been effaced – but that to do so leaves 'the political' intact, since this arena of hegemonic subject formation and (and counter-hegemonic struggle) is heterogeneous by definition to the sign systems that operate subaltern experience and sociality. On the side of Marxist analysis, then, we lose the 'object' of the inquiry (subaltern agency); but on the side of subaltern 'cultural axiomatics' (supposing that we could cross over), we lose the motive for an inquiry that is bound up at the outset in a critique of the political in modernity, as it arrays and delimits prospects for human emancipation. Against Moore Gilbert, I am suggesting that what is irreducible to Subaltern Studies (in Spivak's earlier accounts, as in the work of the group as a whole) is not subaltern alterity, *but rather the incommensurability between the terms of the investigator's analytic and the subaltern as 'object' of investigation.* This is what 'subalternity' means for the group – and what Spivak means in her initial, polemical assertion of the subaltern's muteness. *The statement 'the subaltern cannot speak' is a report on the condition of the intellectual.* The intellectual's privilege is her loss. Hence the aspiration to unlearning,

> In seeking to learn to speak to (rather than listen to or speak for) the
> historically muted subject of the subaltern woman, the postcolonial intel-
> lectual *systematically* 'unlearns' female privilege. This systematic unlearning
> involves learning to critique postcolonial discourse with the best tools it can
> provide and not simply substituting the lost figure of the colonized.
>
> (Spivak 1988a: 295)

'Unlearning', then, neither begins nor ends with the cultivation of alliance, but
demands our systematic scrutiny of the constitution of the political field in which
we produce our (dis)identifications and claim our agency – including our identifications with subalterns and our agency in 'activating' them. 'Unlearning' is not about
viewing the world from the subaltern standpoint, but understanding that our
present and historical implication in the discourses and institutions of world-
making renders that standpoint irretrievable.[4] 'Unlearning' requires us to know that
'Enlightenment from below', however valuable, however preferable to Enlightenment
tout court, or to international civil society, constitutes an elite project. It requires us
to know that our desire to be *freed by* subaltern agency (our desire for the subaltern
to break us *out* of hegemony) ultimately brings us no closer to subalterns' own
desires than any of the (variously inflected) projects to free subalterns (to break the
subaltern *into* hegemony), insofar as an elite 'we' are the subject of both emancipatory narratives. Most fundamentally, perhaps, the work of 'unlearning privilege' is *not
the same* as renouncing it. Such a renunciation, as Spivak brilliantly demonstrates in
'Can the Subaltern Speak?', is the prerogative of the privileged subject – and self-
repudiation, after all, is only a variation on the practice of discursive self-fashioning.

This is why 'Can the Subaltern Speak?' insists on the fundamental questions of
representation: who speaks? In whose name? Unthinking the sovereign subject, we
do not lay these questions to rest – as though the subject-effect, divested of presence, were no longer re-presented – no longer split because fully dispersed in the
signifier. On the contrary, Spivak suggests, to brush aside representation – to *refuse*
to represent; to assume that we *might* refuse – is to repeat the work of ideology in
the crudest sense (to render interest transparent),

> the intellectuals, who are neither of these S/subjects, become transparent in
> the relay race, for they merely report on the nonrepresented subject and
> analyze (without analyzing) the workings of (the unnamed Subject irreduc-
> ibly presupposed by) power and desire. The produced 'transparency' marks
> the place of 'interest'; it is maintained by vehement denegation . . . .
>
> (Ibid.: 279–80)

III. Solidarity

'This is the greatest gift of deconstruction' Spivak writes in another essay of the
same period, 'to question the authority of the investigating subject without para-
lyzing him, persistently transforming conditions of impossibility into conditions of

possibility' (Spivak 1988b: 201). But what, precisely, is the work of 'transformation'? Is unlearning an end in itself, or a way to set the conditions of possibility for learning (to learn)? To be sure, 'unlearning' is itself a form of learning, but is it not one that problematically forecloses on its object – that turns the investigator back on herself, in a posture of narcissistic self-contemplation? And what of the difference between the conundrums of subaltern historiography and our relation, in the present, to living subalterns? What is the bearing on Subaltern Studies of Spivak's claim that the subaltern today is no longer cut off from lines of access to the centre?

Today, as the insane forms of capital proliferate around us, and the field of political contestation seems given over to international civil society and the administrative rationality of 'risk-assessment', 'capacity-building', 'accountability' and 'compliance', the stakes seem high indeed in envisioning transglobal left alliances – or coalitions, by which name 'we' (left intellectuals in the academies of the global North) usually mean an alliance hospitable to heterogeneous identities and forms of political agency, including subaltern identities and agency. Against the prospect of 'speaking for', we assert the radical openness of coalition – its non-politically-normative character – and imagine these coalitional 'spaces' make possible something like the reciprocity Chakrabarty proposes, in which a left elite not only teaches democratic subjectivity to the oppressed, but also learns from subaltern interlocutors. At the same time, the very insistence on openness, contingency and emergence, on collectivity-in-difference, that underwrites the practice of coalition is forged from traditions of radical democracy that stand in dialectical relation to the modern political field. Within this field of political struggle, in other words, this 'openness' sets new conditions of possibility for collective action. But it is not absolute or unconditional. This is not to downplay the importance of coalitional politics, but simply to insist that coalition arrays a kind of collective political subject that is meaningful and transformative within a historically specific domain of modern political engagement. From this perspective, coalitions do not produce the conditions of receptivity to what we do not already know – to forms of subaltern knowledge that are not comprised within, *or assimilable to*, modern political traditions of radical democracy. This is why I suggest that 'unlearning' is not an episode, a moment in a process whose teleology is alliance, but that it sets as the form of our political obligation to subalterns the demand that we stay critically alert and accountable to the terms on which we inhabit the political and reconstitute it through our actions. No doubt, it is better to cultivate 'openness', the will to learn (to learn) from below, to seek out the 'one-on-one mind-changing contact', than to repudiate the aspiration that animates these projects. But my point is that the aspiration to learn – and its political instantiation in the form of coalitional organization – does not resolve the fundamental problem that Spivak so aptly and disturbingly casts as the subaltern subject's muteness – or more precisely, our incapacity to hear from her what we do not already know to know.

Of course, 'learning' can take rather different forms, not all of which depend on intersubjective relations. Partha Chatterjee also advocates for the value of learning, though his formulation ('educating ourselves') already sets apart this view of subaltern pedagogy. 'At the same time, in carrying out their pedagogical mission in political society, the educators – enlightened people like us – might also succeed in educating themselves,' he notes. 'That, I submit, would be the most enriching and historically significant result of the encounter between modernity and democracy in most of the world' (Chatterjee 2004: 51). In a study that centres on the interaction of subalterns and the state in the realm of what he terms 'political society' – which he distinguishes from civil society, defined (by contrast) as the formative ground of the rights-bearing citizen – Chatterjee locates the possibility of 'educating ourselves' in forms of subaltern publicity. Publicity in this sense has no traffic with 'public reason', nor is it a matter of our facilitating access, by cultivating 'an intuition of the public sphere, which ideally teaches democratic co-existence'. On the contrary, the subalterns that Chatterjee studies have sufficiently intuited the public sphere, precisely because it is no longer (if indeed it ever was) the arena of 'public reason'. Surely, this is what it means to posit a 'new subaltern', no longer cut off from lines of access to the centre: the new subaltern, like the old, remains caught between exclusion from the field of political subject constitution, or emergence into its norms. But the contemporary degradation of publicity, its disconnect from the norms of rational (enlightened) public debate, its dedication to the spectacle and sensations of embodiment, mean that the subaltern can hardly escape her public embodiment.[5] In Michael Warner's terms, we might say that subalterns, too, are possessed of an 'iconicity', or virtual public body (Warner 1992: passim). And while subaltern iconicity routinely codes as atavistic, sectarian, fanatical, massified or monumental, this encoding (like any other) remains open to slippages and resignifications, to performative eruptions (or, perhaps, to incremental insinuations) of what we might call, following Guha, subaltern consciousness.

This is perhaps something of what Sumit Sarkar has in mind, when he asks after the continuing investment in the critique of Enlightenment – why target Macaulay, he muses, rather than multinationals?[6] Along these lines, I am suggesting that the retrenchment of public reason – what we might apprehend, in another context, as the contemporary crisis of the democratic public sphere – opens possibilities for the elaboration of a still-not-legible – not yet 'political' – but no longer immobilized (death-bound) subaltern agency. In this context, the education of the educators requires our critical alertness to tactics of subaltern publicity at the limits of the political – in the place, as Chatterjee suggests, where the dispossessed and disenfranchised negotiate with power. This 'self-education' entails no assumptions about subaltern desires – not even, minimally, the imputation of a desire to educate us. As a practice of learning, it corresponds with the ethos of 'speaking to' rather than 'for' or 'with' subalterns.

Indeed, if left solidarity – the prospect of 'speaking with' – beckons as the shape of our own political desire, the subaltern is not – cannot be – the place where we already know to invest it.

Notes

1 In a related discussion, Antonio Viego suggests how the attribution of a core integrity to ethnic subjects (somehow inured to historical damage) further plays out in the imputation of full legibility. *Dead Subjects* is especially concerned with the claim that psychoanalysis is not germane to the work of Ethnic Studies. 'To continue arguing that certain theories are, to use Rowe's works, overly "esoteric" in their "psycholinguistic" excess', Viego contends, 'is to occlude a very significant mechanism in the production of racist thinking that renders some subjects potentially fully calculable through the medium of language' (Viego 2007: 67). The subject without loss, 'essentially beyond damage', as Chow puts it, appears *alternately* as fully elusive, an ideal figure on the utopian horizon of Subaltern Studies, and as fully knowable, the ideal object of positivist social science (Chow 2002: 40).
2 See Spillers (2003, ch. 8).
3 Guha (1988b) both theorizes and exemplifies this reading method in 'The Prose of Counter-Insurgency'.
4 Chandra Mohanty's willingness to embrace the language of 'standpoint' sets her somewhat apart from others working on subalterns today, but her investment in subalternity as the privileged site for the production of critical knowledge constitutes something like the common sense of contemporary left academic work. See *Feminism Without Borders* (2003).
5 This seems central to the context Chow has in view when she observes that,

> [i]n this context, *to be ethnic is to protest* – but perhaps less for actual emancipation of any kind than for the benefits of worldwide visibility, currency, circulation. Ethnic struggles have become, in this manner, an indisputable symptom of the thoroughly and irrevocably mediatized relations of capitalism and its biopolitics.
>
> (Chow 2002: 48)

6 Or, more fully,

> The decisive shift in critical registers from capitalist and colonial exploitation to Enlightenment rationality, from multinationals to Macaulay, has opened the way for a vague nostalgia that identifies the authentic with the indigenous, and locates both in the pasts of an ever-receding community, or a present that consists of fragments alone.
>
> (Sarkar 2000: 318)

Bibliography

Chakrabarty, D. (2000a) 'Radical Histories and Questions of Enlightenment Rationalism: Some Recent Critiques of *Subaltern Studies*', in V. Chaturvedi (ed.) *Mapping Subaltern Studies and the Postcolonial*, London: Verso. 256–80.

Chakrabarty, D. (2000b) 'A Small History of Subaltern Studies', in H. Schwarz and S. Ray (eds.) *A Companion to Postcolonial Studies*, Malden, MA: Blackwell. 467–85.

Chatterjee, P. (2004) *The Politics of the Governed: Reflections on Popular Culture in Most of the World*, New York: Columbia University Press.

Chow, R. (2002) *The Prostestant Ethnic and the Spirit of Capitalism*, New York: Columbia University Press.

Guha, R. (1988a) 'On Some Aspects of the Historiography of Colonial India', in R. Guha and G. C. Spivak (eds.) *Selected Subaltern Studies*, Oxford: Oxford University Press. 45–84.

Guha, R. (1988b) 'The Prose of Counter-insurgency', in R. Guha and G. C. Spivak (eds.) *Selected Subaltern Studies*, Oxford: Oxford University Press.

Harvey, D. (2005) *A Brief History of Neoliberalism*, Oxford: Oxford University Press.

Mohanty, C. (2003) *Feminism Without Borders: Decolonizing Theory, Practicing Solidarity*, Durham, NC: Duke University Press.

Moore-Gilbert, B. (2000) 'Spivak and Bhabha', in H. Schwarz and S. Ray (eds.) *A Companion to Postcolonial Studies*, Malden, MA: Blackwell. 451–6.

Prakash, G. (2000) 'Can the "Subaltern" Ride? A Reply to O'Hanlon and Washbrook', in V. Chaturvedi (ed.) *Mapping Subaltern Studies and the Postcolonial*, London: Verso. 220–38.

Sarkar, S. (2000) 'The Decline of the Subaltern in *Subaltern Studies*', in V. Chaturvedi (ed.) *Mapping Subaltern Studies and the Postcolonial*, London: Verso. 300–23.

Spillers, H. (2003) *Black, White, and in Color: Essays on American Literature and Culture*, Chicago: University of Chicago Press.

Spivak, G. C. (1988a) 'Can the Subaltern Speak?', in C. Nelson and L. Grossberg (eds.) *Marxism and the Interpretation of Culture*, Urbana: University of Illinois Press. 271–313.

Spivak, G. C. (1988b) *In Other Worlds: Essays in Cultural Politics*, New York: Routledge.

Spivak, G. C. (1998) 'Cultural Talks in the Hot Peace: Revisiting the "Global Village"', in P. Cheah and B. Robbins (eds.) *Cosmopolitics: Thinking and Feeling Beyond the Nation*, Minneapolis: University of Minnesota Press. 329–48.

Spivak, G. C. (2000a) 'Foreword: Upon Reading the *Companion to Postcolonial Studies*', in H. Schwarz and S. Ray (eds.) *A Companion to Postcolonial Studies*, Malden, MA: Blackwell. xv–xxii.

Spivak, G. C. (2000b) 'The New Subaltern: A Silent Interview', in V. Chaturvedi (ed.) *Mapping Subaltern Studies and the Postcolonial*, London: Verso. 324–40.

Spivak, G. C. (2008) *Other Asias*, Malden, MA: Blackwell.

Viego, A. (2007) *Dead Subjects: Towards a Politics of Loss in Latino Studies*, Durham, NC: Duke University Press.

Warner, M. (1992) 'The Mass Public and The Mass Subject', in C. Calhoun (ed.) *Habermas and the Public Sphere*, Cambridge, MA: MIT Press. 377–401.

11

THEORY AFTER POSTCOLONIAL THEORY

Rethinking the work of mimesis

Simon Gikandi

As a critical practice that emerged in what has come to be known as the post-philosophical moment, postcolonial theory has been defined by a radical gap between its central conceptual claims, often focused on issues of cultural hybridity and difference, and its objects of analysis or reference, including the histories, texts and social worlds of former European colonies in Africa, the Caribbean and Asia.[1] The most obvious sign of this gap is the persistent difficulties postcolonial theory has accounting for, and providing us with, a critical language that can adequately speak about the literature of decolonization as a distinctive event in literary history. Indeed, it could be said that postcolonial theory has had greater success in addressing the figuration of colonialism in the discourse of European modernity, or explicating the representation of minorities in the metropolis, than accounting for the worlds of the decolonized. As a result, the institutional authority of postcolonial theory often appears divided: it is celebrated in European and North American institutions of interpretation as a significant addition to poststructuralist or postmodern conversations, but it is treated with hostility or benign neglect in the postcolonial world. Even among its most prominent practitioners, there is a lingering suspicion that postcolonial theory is the discourse of the émigré intelligentsia or that it is used as much as a 'strategy of differentiating oneself from the racial underclass as it is to speak in its name' (Spivak 1999: 358).

The bifurcated identity of postcolonial theory is, of course, part of its functional history: the moment of emergence of postcolonial theory in the early 1980s was defined by a well-known paradox – the need to undertake a systematic deconstruction of what Gayatri Spivak has called 'the millennially cherished excellences of Western metaphysics' while recovering or inscribing postcolonial testimony (Spivak 1987: 136). Homi Bhabha further elaborated this paradox in a forceful attempt to synchronize the agenda driving postcolonial theory with the so-called postmodern condition:

> Postcolonial criticism bears witness to the unequal and uneven forces of
> cultural representation involved in the contest for political and social author-
> ity within the modem world order. Postcolonial perspectives emerge from
> the colonial testimony of Third World countries and the discourses of
> 'minorities' within the geopolitical divisions of East and West, North and
> South. They intervene in those ideological discourses of modernity that
> attempt to give a hegemonic 'normality' to the uneven development and the
> differential, often disadvantaged, histories of nations, races, communities,
> peoples. They formulate their critical revisions around issues of cultural dif-
> ference, social authority, and political discrimination in order to reveal the
> antagonistic and ambivalent moments within the 'rationalizations' of modernity.
>
> (Bhabha 1994: 171)

On its inauguration, postcolonial theory could not assert its critical authority or
distinctive identity in relation to other forms of poststructuralism merely through
the subversion of the descriptive or normative claims of Western systems of representation; it also needed the agency of 'colonial testimony'. This testimony could
be drawn from the colonial library, the 'Third World', or from the experiences of
racial and ethnic minorities in the global North who would come to constitute
both a cultural geography and politics of identity. But when postcolonial theorists
invoked colonial or 'Third World' testimony, they were confronted by a certain
ambiguity in relation to the dominant institutions of interpretation. For one, it was
not clear what role postcolonial theorists were being asked to play in the institutions that scrambled for their services: were postcolonial critics new native inform-
ants who derived their aura from identification with 'other racial and ethnic
minorities in the metropolitan space' or were they involved in the manufacture of
'a new Third world'? (Spivak 1999: 360).

These issues went beyond the claim that postcolonial theorists had a tendency
to homogenize the 'Third World' or to supplement the global South with a
European simulacrum going by that name. Much more perplexing for literary
historians was that postcolonial criticism was driven by the imperative to inscribe
'Third World' testimony without accounting for the process of decolonization –
and the narratives it generated – as a literary event, that is, as a recognizable pattern
of an experience worthy of narration, of negation, or registration in language and
as the source of a tradition whose ambition was the representation of time in narrative form. Except in very rare cases, postcolonial theory showed little interest in
the literature of decolonization or its histories. Many monographs influenced by
postcolonial theory were, of course, written on the founding texts of the postcolonial world, but in many reputable circles, these works and their critics were not
considered postcolonial enough. It is as if postcolonial literature began with Salman
Rushdie.[2]

In the circumstances, thinking about a postcolonial criticism after postcolonial
theory must begin by raising a number of questions: why did the works of leading
writers such as Peamoedya Ananta Toer, R. K. Narayan, Chinua Achebe, George

Lamming, V. S. Naipaul and Flora Nwapa, to just mention a few writers, disappear from the postcolonial institution of interpretation? Why was postcolonial criticism afraid of literary traditions that insisted on the priority of history and referentiality? Why was postcolonial theory, in its moment of emergence, afraid of realism and modernism, the two economies of representation that enabled a literature both inside and outside colonialism?

It could be said, of course, that a postcolonial project was not interested in the literature of decolonization and its forms of representation because its mandate, as Bhabha put it after Jürgen Habermas, was 'to explore those social pathologies – "loss of meaning, conditions of anomie" – that no longer simply "cluster around class antagonism, [but] break up into widely scattered historical contingencies"' (Bhabha 1994: 171). Postcolonial criticism often attracted emergent critics of nationalism and post-imperial cultural geographies because it seemed fine-tuned to account for forms of fiction whose ambition was to delegitimize the nationalist project and its literary forms. From this perspective, postcolonial theory was attuned to novels that appeared to be postmodern in form and to be driven by what Appiah aptly described as the imperative to reject both the 'Western imperium' and 'the nationalist project of the postcolonial nationalist bourgeoisie' (Appiah 1992: 152). Postcolonialism may not have been the equivalent of postmodernism, but it too set out to challenge 'earlier legitimating narratives' (ibid.: 153).

And yet, a literature of delegitimation did precede the emergence of both post-modernism and postcolonial theory. Indeed the novels that buttress Appiah's argument – Yambo Ouologuem's *Le Devoir de violence* (1968) and Ahmadou Kourouma's *Les soleils des indépendances* (1968) – were published before the advent of postcolonial discourse. More significantly, while this literature sought to go beyond the narratives of national legitimation, which spoke the language of realism, the task of delegitimation was enabled by a turn to another form of mimesis – the language of high modernism, realism's historical contra-term. In Anglophone Africa, for example, writers questioned the nationalist project through the highly interiorized world of the alienated subject, its stream of consciousness and rhetoric of failure. This is evident in the works of leading writers from the late 1960s, including Wole Soyinka (*The Interpreters* [1965]), Ngugi wa Thiong'o (*A Grain of Wheat* [1967]) and Ayi Kwei Armah (*The Beautyful Ones Are Not Yet Born* [1968]).

Going by the dates of publication alone, the emergence of these delegitimizing narratives cannot solely be explained by the theoretical revolution in Europe associated with the events of May 1968.[3] Many of the novelists were aware of that European event and some of them were associated with the student movement in European or American universities, but the turn to modernism was generated by the crisis of the nationalist project in the first decade of African independence. The events of May 1968 simply provided further theoretical clarification of the conditions of possibility of these narratives.

Now, if the task of reading narratives of delegitimation was the impetus for a postcolonial criticism, then one has to ask why the emergent postcolonial discourse seemed oblivious to these modernist works or the realist works that preceded them.

Part of the reason is that practitioners of postcolonial theory took the terms implied by their project – 'post' and 'theory' – seriously and fell back on both categories as a way of differentiating their project from the interpretative institutions that had preceded them. More significantly, the postcolonial desire for a transcendental moment – one beyond the nationalist project and its narratives styles – seemed to coincide with the poststructuralist preposition that the literary text could only perform its subversive function by being relieved of the burden of mimesis, one based on identity, analogy and resemblance. Was not mimesis after all considered to be the quintessential figure of white mythology, the hitherto uncontested unity of 'natural necessity, of analogical participation, of resemblance'? (Derrida 1982: 215). Was not the authority of the 'post' premised on the imperative to go beyond the representable and visible and 'to activate the differences' as a way out of the terror of 'the transparent and the communicable experience'? (Lyotard 1984: 82).

These questions presuppose the understanding of a certain moment of emergence of postcolonial criticism within the moment of theory. Simply put, postcolonial theory emerged at a time when the most contentious debates in literary studies revolved around one central problem – what Gerald Graff called the 'propositional function of art' (Graff 1979: 71), its ethical and political function. In literary studies, the identity of 'theory' came to depend on what was seen as the incommensurability of the rhetorical function of language and its referential claims. For Paul de Man, one of the most influential figures in American literary circles in the 1980s, the authority of theory, and the presumed resistance to it, was pegged on a separation of rhetoric and referentiality, allegory and symbol:

> Literary theory can be said to come into being when the approach to literary texts is no longer based on non-linguistic, that is to say historical and aesthetic, considerations or, to put it somewhat less crudely, when the object of discussion is no longer the meaning or the value but the modalities of production and of reception of meaning and of value prior to their establishment – the implication being that this establishment is problematic enough to require an autonomous discipline of critical investigation to consider its possibility and its status. Literary history, even when considered at the furthest remove from the platitudes of positivistic historicism, is still the history of an understanding of which the possibility is taken for granted.
>
> (de Man 1986: 7)

De Man (1986: 7) went on to argue that what distinguished literary theory from literary history and criticism was 'the introduction of linguistic terminology in the metalanguage about literature'. More specifically, a linguistic terminology would designate 'reference prior to designating the referent'; the turn to theory would not abrogate referentiality, but it would position 'reference as a function of language and not necessarily as an intuition' (ibid.: 8).

In the popular version of theory enabled by de Man and his reading of the post-philosophical or poststructuralist tradition, the theoretical enterprise was one in which literal meaning was not invested in the referent or consciousness, where identity and identification in symbolic language was called into question by alle-gory and irony, and rhetoric had preference over semiology. Above all, to be theo-retical was to call into question a mode of criticism and interpretation that was preoccupied with what de Man dismissed as the 'external politics of literature', one that strove to reconcile 'the internal, formal, private structures of literary language with their external, referential, and public effects' (de Man 1979: 3). Under the rubric of theory, literature would shift from the task of understanding rooted in historicism – formal, hermeneutical, structural or phenomenological – and end up in a state of 'suspended ignorance': 'Literature as well as criticism – the difference between them being delusive – is condemned (or privileged) to be forever the most rigorous and, consequently, the most unreliable language in terms of which man names and transforms himself' (ibid.: 19).

This kind of relentless critique of the referential function of language could very well be said to have triggered the postcolonial turn, for almost every major document of postcolonial criticism published in the early 1980s pegged its author-ity on the critique or renunciation of the intuitive or historicist basis of criticism. Historicism was often associated with colonial power and governmentality and was thus seen as the enemy of theories that sought to go beyond the prison house of colonialism. In Edward Said's pioneering work, *Orientalism*, for example, the target was not simply European colonial policies in the Levant, but 'Orientalism', a hege-monic system of representation that assumed that its objects of analysis were syn-chronic, fixed in time and space, and intelligible (Said 1979: 20–1). Against this synchronic system of representation and the referential power that it had acquired through writing, Said turned to a method of displacement in which the power of historicism and its 'synchronic essentialism' was countered by the instability of diachrony. Introduced into what appeared to be a fixed system of representations, diachrony would destabilize history and its narrative; this instability would suggest that 'history, with its disruptive detail, or dramatic movement, is possible in the Orient and for the Orient' (ibid.: 240).

While Said was content to invoke the power of narrative to destabilize 'the permanence of vision' associated with historicism, other critics were beginning to deploy theory to deconstruct what Bhabha described as 'an undeniable collabora-tion between historicism and realism' (Bhabha 1984: 98). For Bhabha this collabo-ration was problematic for three reasons: first, the conception of the relationship between the novel and history 'in terms of an organic, progressive approximation of reality' and the insistence on 'accuracy of reflection' negated the function of writing as the very sign of the unreliability of language (ibid.: 94). Second, the assumed link 'between the order of literary history and the unmediated originality of the texts' (ibid.: 94) negated the function of language in a colonial situation. Bhabha's contention was that the representation of the colonized subject at a mimetic level could only be achieved by forcibly harmonizing the historical deter-minant of the Western narrative of identity with the alienated condition of the colonized. Within the logic of this harmonization, the bringing together of signs and signifiers as it were, the discourses and institutions of English literature could only provide 'a dim and refracted light, that casts a shadow on an alien culture' (ibid.: 95).

Third, the assumed collusion between historicism and criticism was that the project of literary criticism itself, driven by a redemptive hermeneutics, was at odds with the subversive cultural work of the 'Third World'. Indeed, literary criticism as it existed within the so-called Commonwealth tradition was seen as nothing but the obliteration of colonial difference in the name of universal culture. Under this regimen, differences of 'genre, mode, structuralism', the diversity of 'cultural and social practices', and even 'the changing institutions and discourses of Literature' (ibid.: 98) would be subsumed under the authority of a transparent historical determinant. Postcolonial theory was thus promoted as a turn to difference.

It is, however, significant to note that although this turn to difference was prompted by the need to undo the assumed collaboration between historicism and realism, its targets were not initially philosophical but critical. The first target of the critique of existing systems of thought and modes of reading was a discursive formation through which, to use Bhabha's apt phrase, texts were 'systematized, synthesized, and signified' (ibid.: 99). At the centre of these discourses, indeed the force against which postcolonial theory came to define itself, was the project of literary criticism associated with F. R. Leavis at Cambridge and his disciples in the outposts of the former British empire. Thus when emergent critics such as Bhabha claimed that they were questioning presuppositions of 'mimetic adequacy' (Bhabha 1994: 134) and the 'normative knowledge of the text' (Bhabha 1984: 100), or the universal claims of literary criticism, they were in essence trying to dislocate Leavisian criticism from its unquestioned pedestal in the field of English studies.

And if Leavisian criticism presented postcolonial theorists with their most intractable problems, it was because, unlike American new criticism, it could not simply be dismissed as pure formalism; on the contrary, its moral and cultural authority depended on the assumption that it was rooted in deep history. While Leavis's method was premised on the notion that the value of literature lay in its language, he also took it for granted that the literary, more specifically the poem, was 'a pregnant hint of the way in which the Human World is created and, in constant renewal, maintained' (Leavis 1975: 36). For Leavis, language was not simply rhetorical; rather, it manifested 'livingness in human life'; it was more than a means of expression; it was 'the heuristic conquest won out of representative experience, the upshot or precipitate of immemorial human living, and embodies values, distinctions, identifications, conclusions, promptings, cartographical hints and tested possibilities' (ibid.: 44). The key terms in Leavis's lexicon – experience, tradition and moral consciousness, for example – were inconceivable outside the lexicon of a parochial Englishness. How could this edifice of universal culture and civilization concealed behind the walls of an intuitive reference be challenged?

For a generation of scholars and students trained in the colonial university, one way of undoing the moral economy of English was to expand its boundaries in order to incorporate the cultural geography of the colonized and their modes of consciousnesses. Alternatively, one could dilate English and Englishness by genres that had developed in England in the nineteenth century and had been transformed by colonial spaces. Fashioned after Leavis's literary criticism, the study of what was known as Commonwealth Literature sought to identify literary language as essentially historicist. Novels produced in English in the colonies were seen as analogous to the tradition of the genre as it had evolved in England. Indeed, leading critics in the Commonwealth mould assumed that novels spoke the critical language privileged by Leavis. For Kenneth Ramchand, to use one prominent example, West Indian novelists applied

> themselves with unusual urgency and unanimity to an analysis and interpretation of their society's ills, including the social and economic deprivation of the majority; the pervasive consciousness of race and colour; the cynicism and uncertainty of the native bourgeoisie in power after independence; the lack of a history to be proud of; and the absence of traditional or settled values.
>
> (Ramchand 2004: xxxiv)

This form of criticism took Leavis's lexicon for granted: the novel, like criticism, was a mode of analysis and interpretation; history was mediated by consciousness, and the thing wanting was values and traditions.

One could argue, of course, that the criticism that was developed to explain the emergence of a Commonwealth Literature sought to inscribe colonial difference even as it rehearsed Leavis's language. Indeed, Ramchand's work was unique in its meticulous mapping of the West Indian cultural library and the colonial archive. A key starting point in his project was that the peculiar nature of West Indian society had transformed the novel as a genre in the islands:

> If, however, the social consciousness of writers from the islands draws attention to itself as a peculiarly interesting matter, it is worth pointing out at once that this social consciousness does not operate in the way that class consciousness operates in some English novels. This is one respect in which the West Indian novel naturally differs from the nineteenth century English novel to which it is, by colonial education, affiliated. The social consciousness of West Indian writers is not as concerned with consolidating or flattering particular groups.
>
> (Ibid.: xxxiv)

But this invocation of difference was still analogical; the language of social consciousness remained intact. There was hence the need for another mode of discourse that would challenge the identitarian logic of literary criticism.

What made Bhabha's early work, especially the essay on 'Representation and the Colonial Text', significant, then, was that it sought to question the key terms in the lexicon of literary criticism and to institute 'the subject of difference' as the fulcrum of textuality.[4] Indeed, this invocation of difference as the informing condition of the colonial text was intended to displace the logic of mimesis within the existing critical discourse. Where the Commonwealth school had sought continuities with the English literary tradition and had taken Leavis's terms for granted, hoping to translate the institution of literary criticism to account for colonial situations, the new theoretical approach would work with the de Manian notion that literary theory had the capacity to upset 'rooted ideologies by revealing the mechanics of their workings' (de Man 1986: 11).

This unmasking of rooted ideologies could be directed at what Bhabha construed to be the foundation of Commonwealth literary history and criticism – its mimetic contract. In fact, at the heart of Bhabha's manifesto was the need to transform the terms of representing difference.

> 'Distortion' is the recognition of 'difference' in relation to the pre-giveness of an affirmative image which constitutes the primary cognition of which the literary text is only a secondary elaboration. The demand is then for the replacing of one content with another, until through a process of 'correction' the right image is produced. Literature as a discourse or practice, engaged in a form of transformative 'work' is effaced, and the succession of images – a question of the *history* of textual signification and ideological struggle – becomes the moralist rectification of a 'given' essence. The construction of the colonial as a sign of difference within the production of literary discourses is a perspective denied within this critical tradition. The problem of *representing difference* as a problem of narrative can only be seen, within this kind of critical discourse, as the demand for *different representations*.
>
> (Bhabha 1984: 106)

But the strategy of undoing mimesis through the reading of difference in the colonial text was bound to run into a set of problems that highlight the tension between postcolonial theory and the texts of decolonization that opened my reflections. If colonialism, as a system of power, was built on the manufacture of difference, and if the production of the colonial subject as the 'other' was essential to its systems of rule and control, as numerous scholars have argued, then what was the nature of the difference that could undo the dominant system of representation? What would happen if the ideologies being unsettled were the operative mechanism of the text under interrogation? What if the text, instead of providing its readers with an account of its difficult or impossible relation to its referent, or even gesturing towards what Werner Hamacher has called 'the impossibility of thematization', was invested in the measurability of 'the referential relation'? (Hamacher 1989: 173). This was the question that would emerge when Bhabha turned his attention to the reading of V. S. Naipaul's *A House for Mr Biswas*. Here, Bhabha's tactic was to deploy a theory of reading, one pegged on the textualization of difference, in order to relieve the text of its burden of referentiality.

Now, prior readings of *A House for Mr Biswas* had sought to account for its standing as a mirror of the crisis of colonial society in the West Indies and to illuminate what Ramchand described as 'the outer sociohistorical situation' (Ramchand 2004: 157) from which the novel drew its materials and characters. For many critics in the Commonwealth school, Naipaul's novel was a mirror of the precariousness of the East Indian subject in the West Indies. Even among the harshest critics of Naipaul's politics, there was a consensus that the author had succeeded in giving form and meaning to the crisis of his subjects and that his novel had drawn on the chaos and disorder of colonial society as it sought to transcend objectification and radical difference. Naipaul's success was explained both in terms of his ability to provide visible representations of the alienation of the colonial subject in the form of Mr Biswas and his capacity to give the resulting crisis a determinate meaning. For Ngugi wa Thiong'o, for example, Naipaul's success as a novelist lay in his ability to represent Mr Biswas's search for security and identity in the concrete and 'specific terms of a definite social struggle' (Ngugi wa Thiong'o 1973: 94). Imagined in 'the concreteness of time and place and action' Mr Biswas would be recuperated as 'Caribbean man in search of himself and his place in the world' (ibid.: 94).

Going against this kind of redemptive reading, Bhabha's goal in 'Representation and the Colonial Text' was to show that far from thematizing a referential relation or seeking a reality effect, Naipaul's novel exposed the incommensurability of a given history and its textual signification. Rejecting metaphor as the figure of 'pre-given' relationship between the text and its referent, Bhabha would turn to metonymy, the figure of difference, in a reading whose goal was nothing less that the exposure of the duplicity at work in Naipaul's text in relation to its West Indian referent (Bhabha 1984: 115). Bhabha's tactic – the theoretical gesture, as it were – was to show how the textualization of history (as difference) and its metonymic displacement negated a historicist reading of the novel and became a form of anti-mimesis. In other words, he would demonstrate how Naipaul's novel resisted its incorporation into literary realism through 'the tropes of the text as metonymy and repetition instead of metaphor, and its mode of address as the "uncanny" rather than irony' (ibid.: 115).

Other critics had, of course, recognized loss as the central motif in *A House for Mr Biswas*; but this loss, and the structure of displacement that it generated, had been read as part of Naipaul's 'realistic' understanding of colonial society; the modes of repetition that structure the novel were read as reflections on the alienated consciousness of the colonial subject. Alternatively, the prevalence of loss in the novel and the modes of repetition it engendered were explained in terms of Naipaul's hostility towards colonial subjects. Bhabha's essay was radical in its recuperation of the text's negative temporality – its constant reference to 'loss, circularity and the demoniacal' (ibid.: 115) – as part of its operating mechanisms rather than problems to be overcome. Focusing on marks of displacement and disavowal in Naipaul's novel, Bhabha would assert that the role of colonial fantasy was to undermine 'the myth of the realist narrative – its grand syntagms and sequentiality, its pleasure, irony, comedy, characters and consolations, its historic utterances and easy identifications between I and you' (ibid.: 119). But was this mode of reading endorsed by Naipaul's text?

It is, of course, true that a significant turning point in Naipaul's novel is when Mr Biswas comes to recognize his condition as a colonial subject as essentially one of loss:

> Change had come over him without his knowing. There had been no precise point at which the city had lost its romance and promise, no point at which he had begun to consider himself old, his career closed, and his visions of the future became only visions of Anand's future. Each realization had been delayed and had come, not as a surprise, but as a statement of a condition long accepted.
>
> (Naipaul 1984: 494)

But this moment of negative recognition does not displace mimetic irony or ethical realism as the dominant modes in Naipaul's text; on the contrary, Mr Biswas's inadequacy is represented as a consequence of both the colonial and the Hindi structures that have stacked the deck against him. To the extent that metonymic displacement and repetition reinforce the reader's sense of the gap between Mr Biswas' desires and his social condition, they reinforce the novel's claim to a reality effect. And far from being the measure of a mimetic absence, colonial fantasy and the narrative disturbances it generates come to function as part of the text's claim to a certain kind of historicity and its auto-referential purpose.

We can better understand the centrality of historicity and referentiality in the tradition that produced writers such as Naipaul if we recall the affinity between the theories and literatures of decolonization and the recalibration of the politics of representation in a colonial situation. In the work of Fanon, to cite one example, the narrative of liberation was conceived as nothing less than the transformation of a 'Real' held prisoner by colonial governmentality into a space of freedom. Seeking an alternative mimesis, the work of literature was inseparable from the quest for freedom. This freedom, or rather the ideal of sovereignty informing it, was part of what Fanon famously called an 'illuminating and sacred communication', which was, in turn, nothing less than 'an invitation, an encouragement, and a promise' (Fanon 1967: 45).

For Fanon, the aesthetic of colonialism was predicated on the division of the world into the zones of the self and the other and the imprisonment of the latter in an order of deception, alienation and colonial command. Under colonialism, aesthetic expressions were intended to reinforce the authority of 'the established order' and to create 'an atmosphere of submission and of inhibition which lightens the task of policing considerably' (Fanon 1963: 38). The imperative for a narrative of liberation was the decolonization of the emblematic colonial city (underwritten by an enforced sense of order) into a new, self-engendered pact between colonized writers and audiences. Under these terms, the narrative of decolonization could not be conceived as emerging out of 'the ambivalence of colonial inscription and identification', as Bhabha has argued, but as a gesture of restitution and redemption; a naming of the constitution of the Other in the discourse of colonial power was the first gesture in the rewriting of the narrative of colonial imprisonment to one of liberation.

Decolonization was a writerly gesture that established new subjectivities and affiliations. Indeed, Fanon took it for granted that the epistemology of decolonization was predicated on the validation of a liberated factum, one brought into public consciousness by a new sense of the real. Any legitimate claims to national sovereignty had to start 'from living reality and it is in the name of this reality, in the name of the stark facts that weigh down the present and the future of men and women, that they fix their line of action' (ibid.: 207). This, then, was Fanon's mimetic mandate:

> The artist who has decided to illustrate the truths of the nation turns paradoxically toward the past and away from actual events. What he ultimately intends to embrace are in fact the castoffs of thought, its shells and corpses, a knowledge which has been stabilized once and for all. But the native intellectual who wishes to create an authentic work of art must realize that the truths of a nation are in the first place its realities. He must go on until he has found the seething pot out of which the learning of the future will emerge.
>
> (Ibid.: 225)

Our theoretical instincts may now work against realism and all the historicist claims associated with it, but if the texts that heralded the emergence of a postcolonial temporality insisted on a referential code as part of their own condition of possibility, it is difficult, if not impossible, to consider the reality effect invoked in postcolonial texts as 'the platitudes of positivistic historicism' (de Man 1986: 7). Thinking about the status of postcolonial literature after theory, then, is perhaps an invitation to recognize this reality effect itself as the informing condition of a postcolonial literature. The first step in this process is to insist on historicism and the mimetic codes associated with it as already written into the postcolonial text as a problem to be represented in narrative. In this context, the work of criticism should start not by dismissing the ideologies and narrative codes of colonialism or nationalism but by recognizing how postcolonial texts sought to inscribe the mimetic order of colonialism and to figurate the alienated temporality that had produced the colonized as subjects.

But the task of criticism cannot stop at the recognition and recuperation of historicism as a problem of representation in postcolonial literature. A second step is necessary; and it entails an acknowledgement of the fact that if history or realism were summoned to authorize the imagination of a postcolonial subjectivity and polity, they were compromised terms, heavily associated with the colonizing order. As Timothy Mitchell has put it in his powerful study of colonialism in Egypt, the symbolic representations of colonial order were 'the mark of a great historical confidence' (Mitchell 1988: 7). Postcolonial literature would ultimately have to thematize the limits and failure of this colonial mimesis; the engagement with historicism and the deployment of mimetic economies would then become modes of both making sense of colonialism but also of marking the limits of its representative systems and inscribing a new politics of time and space.

Postcolonial criticism has to start reading its primary texts carefully and to understand the theoretical work that was embedded in the foundational novels of decolonization. Consider, for example, the problem of closure in the classical texts of decolonization, especially the gap between the subject's desire for resolution through the transcendence of the colonial situation and the novelists' recalcitrance: why does the narrative drive for freedom always fall short of the goal of transcending the objective and objectifying world of colonialism? Achebe's *Things Fall Apart*, to cite a now classic example, ends with the death of its hero, Okonkwo, his history erased, his cultural texts denuded and his life history reduced to a paragraph in the colonial library:

> The story of this man who had killed a messenger and hanged himself would make interesting reading. One could almost write a whole chapter on him. Perhaps not a whole chapter but a reasonable paragraph, at any rate.
>
> (Achebe 1994: 208–9)

Here one can see th1e historical confidence that enables the colonizer to reproduce the colonized in objective form. But when Achebe reduces this grand gesture of objectification to a mere paragraph in his anti-colonial novel, we can see how irony enables a counter-mimesis. Irony, rather than allegory, is perhaps the key code in the production of what I have called an early postcolonial style.

Achebe's *Arrow of God*, clearly one of the most important counterpoints to the colonial text, ends with the madness of Ezeulu, the high priest who misjudges the meaning and economy of modern time. Isolated from his community and exiled from colonial history, Ezeulu is condemned to spend his last days 'in the haughty splendour of a demented high priest' (Achebe 1969: 229), spared the final outcome of the phenomenology of colonial conquest. The ironic reversal here works in two directions: it rejects the reduction of the colonized into objects enabled through the simulation of their world as an extension of the colonizer's imagination; but it also rejects Ezeuru's attempt to deploy symbolism to invoke an immutable truth.

There are, of course, novels in which irony seems to be superseded by powerful allegories of postcolonial self-making, but even here, the moment of closure is remarkable for its inscription of the failure of what one may call a postcolonial wish fulfilment rather than the phenomenology of a happy ending. In Flora Nwapa's *Efuru*, the title character has to give up on her desire to have a child, choosing instead to dedicate her life to her deity, but Efuru's choice is the melancholic acceptance of necessity rather than an embracement of freedom:

> Efuru slept soundly that night. She dreamt of the woman of the lake, her beauty, her long hair and her riches. She had lived for ages at the bottom of

the lake. She was as old as the lake itself. She was happy, she was wealthy. She was beautiful. She gave women beauty and wealth but she had no child. She had never experienced the joy of motherhood. Why then did the women worship her?

(Nwapa 1966: 221)

The rhetoric of doubt ironizes the search for symbolic closure.

In other instances, what is plotted as the colonial subject coming into an awareness of itself in a temporal space defined by freedom exposes the symbolic order of decolonization, the time and space of the new nation, as a time of disorder and emptiness. At the end of Mulk Raj Anand's *Untouchable*, the spell of Gandhi's voice triggers an epiphany in Bakha, the untouchable, prompting his self-recognition of himself as a free subject in a decolonized *polis*, but he still feels torn between 'his enthusiasm for Gandhi and the difficulties in his own awkward, naïve self' (Anand 1945: 156). Similarly, the moment of decolonization in Ngugi's *A Grain of Wheat* is dominated by the melancholy that arises when the colonized discover that their whole narrative of decolonization revolves around a false hero, a phantasm who must now become a scapegoat. The lived experience of the decolonized is placed at odds with its symbolism as Gikonyo, who has suffered through colonial terror, now finds that it is only in art – the stool that he will carve for his estranged wife – that he can find recompense (Ngugi wa Thiong'o 1967: 247).

The belief that the work of art can provide utopian compensation for painful histories is a reminder of the tenuousness of the terms by which colonial subjects are asked to come into being as modern subjects. At the end of Narayan's *Waiting for the Mahatma*, for example, the coming of Indian independence is supposed to ensure the happiness and fulfilment of Sriram and Bharati, the young nationalist couple who have been asked so often in the novel to postpone their wedding until the arrival of the new symbolic order represented by decolonization. Narayan's Gandhi makes the connection between *Polis* and *Eros* when, at the end of the novel, he promises to officiate at the young couple's wedding, giving private desire precedence over public duty for the first time in the novel:

Tomorrow morning, the first thing I do will be that. I will be your priest, if you don't mind. I've been a very neglectful father; I'll come and present the bride. Tomorrow, the very first thing; other engagements only after that. I already have here all the fruits and flowers ready, and so after all you can't say I have been very neglectful.

(Narayan 1955: 253)

But irony, the signature figure of mimesis, is quickly deployed to undo the marriage of convenience between the political and erotic, for no sooner has Gandhi made his promise to temporarily sacrifice public duty for private morality, than he has a premonition: 'Bharati, I have a feeling that I may not attend your wedding tomorrow morning . . . I seem to have been rash in promising to officiate as your priest' (ibid.: 253). And soon after, in a classical reversal of the phenomenology of the happy ending, Narayan's novel turns to history to play out one of the most hallowing scenes of postcolonial tragedy. As the Mahatma is about to step on the dais, a man steps forward, pulls a revolver out of his pocket, takes aim and fires: 'The Mahatma fell on the dais. He was dead in a few seconds' (ibid.: 254).

The moment of closure in all these novels denotes what Ross Chambers, writing in a different context, has called 'a consciousness of lack' (Chambers 1993: 206), of a mimesis of empty time, of exclusion from the law, the word, and desire. And yet, these melancholic moments – and the pathos of lack that define them – are the signatures of what I would like to call a postcolonial mimesis. They are marks of a temporality stranded between the time of a dying colonialism and a stillborn nationalism. My conclusion is that if we are now in a theory after theory moment, as the editors of this volume propose, the literary text of decolonization must be recognized as creating the spaces in which postcolonial criticism would emerge, rather than an insignia of a failed politics of representation. These works were the products of a time when the imperative for a postcolonial order was pegged on the desire and demand for narratives that would enable the colonized to interrupt and disrupt colonial history but also claim a space of experience and knowledge in the discursive formation of modernity. In this sense, the foundational texts of postcoloniality would incorporate the mimetic register in what Derrida would call its '"internal" duplicity' (Derrida 1981: 186): one form of mimesis would recover the experiences of the colonized from the objective and totalized regimen of the imperium; another mimetic gesture could call attention to the limits of any attempt to contain this world in literary form. Late postcolonial literature, and the theories developed to account for it, have continued this project using the tools of poststructuralism and under the sign of postmodernism. Perhaps the work of theory after theory is to reconcile theories, texts and experiences under the sign of a postcolonial mimesis.

Notes

1   This essay is an excerpt from a work in progress tentatively entitled *Early Postcolonial Style*. I use 'early' and 'late' postcolonial style to periodize the literature of the former British colonies and to call attention to the shifts and transformations that take place within its institutions of production and styles. In general, an early postcolonial style starts with the search for a literature that imagines decolonization beginning around the 1890s and continuing to the period of political decolonization after the Second World War. A late postcolonial style is evident in the literature and theories produced after the 1960s in the former colonies and their diasporas in Europe and North America. For the concept of an early style, see Chambers (1993); a compelling idea of a late style can be found in Said (2007).

2   This is a very broad generalization and there are obviously exceptions to this rule, but many critics seem to have taken seriously or at least misconstrued Rushdie's claim that 'Commonwealth Literature' did not exist. As my discussion below indicates, there were

compelling reasons to escape the conceptual prison house of 'Commonwealth Literature', but not to dismiss the literary texts that had been produced under this rubric. See also Rushdie (1991).

3 For the significance of the events of May 1968 to the poststructuralist revolution, see Young (1990: 1–20).

4 During this time other postcolonial critics like Said and Spivak were redeploying difference toward anti-imperial ends, but they were based in American institutions where a mode of formalism, operating under the name of New Criticism, did not have any powerful historical claims or interest in the narratives of the colonized.

Bibliography

Achebe, C. (1969) *Arrow of God*, New York: Anchor Books.

Achebe, C. (1994) *Things Fall Apart*, New York: Anchor Books.

Anand, M.R. (1945) *Untouchable*, London: Penguin.

Appiah, K.A. (1992) *In My Father's House: Africa in the Philosophy of Culture*, Oxford: Oxford University Press.

Armah, A.K. (1968) *The Beautyful Ones Are Not Yet Born*, London: Heinemann.

Bhabha, H.K. (1984) 'Representation and the Colonial Text: A Critical Exploration of Some Forms of Mimeticism', in F. Gloversmith (ed.) *The Theory of Reading*, Brighton: The Harvester Press. 93–122.

Bhabha, H.K. (1994) *The Location of Culture*, London: Routledge.

Chambers, R. (1993) *The Writing of Melancholy: Modes of Opposition in Early French Modernism*, trans. M. Seidman Trouille, Chicago: University of Chicago Press.

de Man, P. (1979) *Allegories of Reading*, New Haven, CT: Yale University Press.

de Man, P. (1986) *The Resistance to Theory*, Minneapolis: University of Minnesota Press.

Derrida, J. (1981) *Dissemination*, trans. B. Johnson, London: Continuum.

Derrida, J. (1982) *Margins of Philosophy*, trans. A. Bass, Chicago: The University of Chicago Press.

Fanon, F. (1963) *The Wretched of the Earth*, trans. C. Farrington, New York: Grove Press.

Fanon, F. (1967) *Toward the African Revolution*, trans. H. Chevalier, New York: Monthly Review Press.

Graff, G. (1979) *Literature Against Itself: Literary Ideas in Modern Society*, Chicago: University of Chicago Press.

Hamacher, W. (1989) 'LECTIO: de Man's Imperative', in L. Waters and W. Godzich (eds) *Reading De Man Reading*, Minneapolis: University of Minnesota Press.

Kourouma, A. (1968) *Les soleils des indépendances*, Montreal: Les Presses de l'Université.

Leavis, F.R. (1975) *The Living Principle: 'English' as a Discipline of Thought*, London: Chatto & Windus.

Lyotard, J-F. (1984) *The Postmodern Condition: A Report on Knowledge*, trans. G. Bennington and B. Massumi, Minneapolis: University of Minnesota Press.

Mitchell, T. (1988) *Colonising Egypt*, Cambridge: Cambridge University Press.

Naipaul, V.S. (1984) *A House for Mr. Biswas*, New York: Vintage Books.

Narayan, R.K. (1955) *Waiting for the Mahatma*, Chicago: The University of Chicago Press.

Ngugi wa Thiong'o (1973) *Homecoming: Essays on African and Caribbean Literature and Politics* (1972), Westport, CT: Lawrence and Hill.

Ngugi wa Thiong'o (1967) *A Grain of Wheat*, Oxford: Heinemann Educational Books.

Nwapa, F. (1966) *Efuru*, London: Heinemann.

Ouologuem, Y. (1968) *Le Devoir de violence*, Paris: Le Serpent à Plumes.

Ramchand, K. (2004) *The West Indian Novel and Its Background*, Kingston, NY: Ian Randle Publishers.

Rushdie, S. (1991) 'Commonwealth Literature Does not Exist', *Imaginary Homelands*, London: Granta.

Said, E. (1979) *Orientalism*, New York: Vintage.

Said, E. (2007) *On Late Style: Music and Literature Against the Grain*, New York: Vintage.

Soyinka, W. (1965) *The Interpreters*, London: Deutsch.

Spivak, G.C. (1987) 'French Feminism in an International Frame', *In Other Worlds: Essays in Cultural Politics*, New York: Methuen.

Spivak, G.C. (1999) *A Critique of Postcolonial Reason: Toward a History of the Vanishing Present*, Cambridge, MA: Harvard University Press.

Young, R. (1990) *White Mythologies: Writing History and the West*, London: Routledge.

PART IV

Biopolitics and ethics

12

AFTER LIFE

Swarms, demons and the antinomies of immanence

Eugene Thacker

Life after life

In philosophy – as in the world – 'life' is a perplexing phenomenon. In ways that betray our anthropomorphic biases, we are accustomed to 'concept' and 'life' being separated by a clear boundary: when we stop thinking, we start living; and in order to begin thinking, one must bracket living. At a certain point, the most adequate concept of life simply becomes 'life itself' – with the 'concept' part then receding behind a haze of affective immediacy. In such instances, the visceral nature of life would exchange places with life as a speculative phenomenon (a pre-philosophical boundary that conditions both the analytical and continental traditions . . .). If this is the case, then in what way does the thought-of-life imply a correlative life-of-thought that is isomorphic with it?

The concept of life encompasses so much, from the most reductive biological viewpoint to the most open-ended ethical viewpoint. Today, in an era of biopolitics, it seems that life is everywhere at stake, and yet it is nowhere the same. The question of how and whether to value life is at the core of contemporary debates over bare life and the state of exception. At a more basic level, in our techno-scientific world view, it seems that life is claimed of everything, and yet life itself is nothing. While scientists continue to debate whether a virus is living, the advances in bio-technology and artificial life have, in different ways, questioned the idea that life is exclusively natural or biological. We also live in a time in which events at the micro-level are also events at the macro-level: the increasing frequency of global pandemics, new biopolitical modes of production and the prevalence of natural disasters are events that are at once local and global, molecular and planetary. While human beings or human groups are obviously involved in such events, there is also a sense in which such events are beyond human comprehension. In short, life is human centred and yet non-human oriented.

This invites us to consider a series of questions concerning the concept of life today. What must be already given for the concept of life to be thought at all? In short, is there an *a priori* idea of life that signals both the moment it becomes a matter of ontology, and the moment it slips beneath the radar of ontological thinking? When does philosophical reflection on life simply become a matter of regional philosophies, such as natural philosophy or the philosophy of biology, and when does life become a concern of fundamental philosophy – the being of life, as it were? In other words, if 'life' is a problem *of* philosophy, is it also a problem *for* philosophy?

Swarming life

If anything characterizes contemporary thinking about life, it is that life ceases to be exclusively thought in terms of a fixed transcendent essence, determinately inscribed within the spirit, the organism or the cell. In its place, what has gradually emerged is the idea of a life that is radically distributed and disseminated, both in terms of its spatial topography, and in terms of its temporal causality. Here life is not simply this or that particular living organism, nor is it reducible to this or that life substance (be it an immaterial soul or the molecule of DNA). Above all, life is not limited to the Aristotelian and Darwinian hierarchy, which places the human at its pinnacle. In short, what characterizes much thinking about life today is a pervasive non-anthropomorphic quality that resonates with our current vernacular of networks, complexity and globalism.[1]

Arguably, the emblem of this anti-anthropomorphism is the phenomenon of swarming, so common today in popular science fiction and horror. The swarm is distributed and horizontal, but also driven by an invisible, intangible life force – 'life' is at once transcendent and immanent to its particular manifestations. Something drives the swarm, but this something is also nothing – at least nothing that stands above and apart from the singular phenomenon of the swarm itself. One discovers clear examples of this in modern philosophy. Deleuze, in one of his last writings, would call this purely immanent anonymity 'a life', Bergson would refer to a dynamic, processual, *élan vital*. Spinoza would take up the language of pantheism by talking about a single substance pervading the world, as 'God or Nature'. At the core of this concept of life is a long-standing issue in philosophy: the relation between life and immanence.

This type of distributed vitalism thinks of life as a complex mode of collective organization, which is often granted attributes of life or, alternately, vitalistic properties that in turn question the very concept of life. One of the earliest systematic descriptions of such phenomena comes from Aristotle. In the *Historia Animalium*, he describes an insect swarm:

> The drones, as a rule, keep inside the hive; when they go out of doors, they soar up in the air in a stream, whirling round and round in a kind of gymnastic exercise; when this is over, they come inside the hive and feast themselves . . . They say that, if a swarm goes astray, it will turn back upon its route and

by the aid of scent seek out its leader. It is said that if he is unable to fly he is carried by the swarm, and that if he dies the swarm perishes; and that, if this swarm outlives the king for a while and constructs combs, no honey is produced and the bees soon die out.

(Aristotle 1984: 624a, 22–32)

What is interesting here is the ambiguity of the passage with respect to the phenomenon of swarming. On the one hand, Aristotle is intent on granting a purpose to swarming, be it in terms of foraging for food or in terms of a war-like competition among species. On the other, his descriptions often slip into poetic flourishes, as in the image of the dancing, spiritual gymnastics of the swarm – which is immediately followed by the more bestial image of a feeding-frenzy. Added to this are the obvious political tropes Aristotle uses, not only in designating a king, but also in the existence of a 'centre' that directs, controls and conducts the swarm from a position transcendent to the swarm itself.

This ambiguity is reflected in the scientific study of swarms – flocking behaviour in bats, schooling or shoaling in fish and of course the numerous examples of insect swarms (ants, wasps and locusts). An important move towards the biological study of swarms was made in the work of William Morton Wheeler (1865–1937), an entomologist who used the term 'superorganism' to describe ant swarms. Wheeler's writings on insects repeatedly describe a kind of life that is not just that of the individual organism, but that of the collective organization of organisms. Wheeler's terminology was also used by Herbert Spencer to describe the 'organismic analogy' for social organization. This type of thinking extends into contemporary biology, where the study of insects has been a privileged site for understanding swarming behaviour, as exemplified in the work of E. O. Wilson (who argues that swarms are a 'top-down' phenomenon) and Deborah Gordon (who argues, against Wilson, that they are more 'bottom-up').

But the swarm – as a concept – is neither exclusive to nor determined by biology. For instance, the study of swarms has had an equally profound impact on computer science and mathematics. Here are the authors of the textbook *Self-Organization in Biological Systems* describing the swarming behaviour of army ants: 'In self-organizing systems, pattern formation occurs through interactions internal to the system, without intervention by external directing influences' (Camazine *et al.* 2001: 8). This more abstract perspective has led to the greater mathematization of swarms in computer science, in new sub-fields such as 'Ant Colony Optimization' or 'Swarm Intelligence'. It has also found application in other areas such as telecommunications routing and military strategy. RAND researchers John Arquilla and David Ronfeldt present an entire swarming strategy they call 'BattleSwarm'. They define a swarming as 'the systematic pulsing of force and/or fire by dispersed, internetted units, so as to strike the adversary from all directions simultaneously' (Arquilla and Ronfeldt 2000: 8).

This brings us to the presence of swarms in many treatises of political philosophy. Aristotle makes collective behaviour the ground of his political philosophy. He notes, in a rather well-worn passage:

> that man is more of a political animal than bees or any other gregarious
> animals is evident . . . But he who is unable to live in society or who has no
> need because he is sufficient for himself, must be either a beast or a god: he
> is no part of a state.
>
> (Aristotle 1984: 1253ª7, 28–31)

For Aristotle, collective behaviour differentiates the political from the natural –
though, as we have seen, he cannot help but to employ political tropes in his
descriptions of swarming in nature. However, it is Marx who adds a further refinement to the idea of the political swarm, and that is in terms of the idea of production and labour. 'We presuppose labour', Marx notes, 'in a form in which it is an
exclusively human characteristic'. For instance, we analogize a spider's weaving a
web to that of a textile weaver, and the construction of a bee nest to that of the
architect building a house. But there is a crucial difference, according to Marx, for,

> what distinguishes the worst architect from the best of bees is that the architect
> builds the cell in his mind before he constructs it in wax. At the end of every
> labour process, a result emerges which had already been conceived by the
> worker at the beginning, hence already existed ideally.
>
> (Marx 1976: 283–84)

Here it is the speculative labour of thought itself that distinguishes the human from
the insect, and the political from the natural. This speculative pre–existence not
only accounts for the causal relations between an ideal and a manifested form, but
it inadvertently points to one of the great puzzles of swarming in nature – the issue
of governance, control and causality. The question of whether collective behaviour
is governed transcendently or immanently is, in a way, foreclosed by a reliance on
anthropocentrism, either in terms of the speculative labour of planning or in terms
of a rational decision based on mutual benefit.

Thus swarming, which we may initially take as a biological concept, also has a
technical and a political dimension as well. In each case, swarms have certain elements in common. There are multiple, individuated units, which exist in some sort
of coordinated group formation, that then sustains itself for a certain period of time
through the interplay of 'simple' local actions and 'complex' global patterns. But
how does global organization occur without centralized control? There must be
some principle or condition that enables the emergence of global organization. It
is for this reason that concept of 'life' enters the frame. And it is Henri Bergson
who best encapsulates this attitude:

> When we see the bees of a hive forming a system so strictly organized that
> no individual can live apart from the others beyond a certain time, even
> though furnished with food and shelter, how can we help recognizing that
> the hive is really, and not metaphorically, a single organism, of which each
> bee is a cell united to the others by invisible bonds?
>
> (Bergson 1998: 166)

What Bergson highlights here is a distinction that has become crucial for thinking about life in terms of the swarm. That distinction is between the life *in* the swarm and the life *of* the swarm. In the former instance, one considers life in terms of the individual and individuated organisms that constitute the phenomenon of collective behaviour (this ant, this bird, this zombie). But this type of life cannot simply be ratcheted up to account for the phenomenon of collective behaviour in itself; thus another concept of life is required, one which basically follows a familiar maxim: the whole being greater than the sum of its parts. In this distinction, thinking about life is predicated on a key relationship between the concrete manifestations of life, and an abstract principle of life. The former refers to all those instances of life that can be placed into species, categories and sets, whereas the latter is what is referred to when we hear talk of 'life itself'.

The life 'in' the swarm is comprehensive, precisely because one is always looking at and thinking about a swarm from the vantage point of an observing, thinking subject. But the life 'of' the swarm is more difficult. All of the above examples of swarming – scientific, technical, political – present us with not only an instance in which the whole is greater than the sum of its parts, but also with an instance in which the parts seem to be related to each other in a way that exceeds any totalistic whole. Such examples are 'too big', in that we strain to find the edges of such phenomena – they are, in Kant's terms, dynamically sublime. But they are also 'too small', in that we again strain to discern the minute multiplicity of interactions – what Kant calls a mathematical sublime. If swarms in themselves are indeed alive, then there is a sense in which their being alive puts 'life' itself into question. If thought requires a certain orientation towards its object of thought, and if the idea of life-as-swarming effaces this relationship, then how should the concept of life be thought at all? Put differently: if thought presumes a certain exclusivity to the human, and if the concept of life is thought in ways that are decidedly non-human, then how is life to be thought at all, existing as it does above and below the scale of the human being? Addressing these questions will require that we think this contemporary concept of life-as-swarming in a different light – that of demonology.

Towards a demonology of swarms

As we have mentioned, representations of swarms outside of science are most commonly found in genre science fiction and horror, where the swarm is often associated with the demonic, or some unnamed, malefic force. Sometimes the swarms are actually composed of animals, as in the numerous 'revenge of nature' films that feature insect swarms: *Them!* (1954), *The Swarm* (1978) and *Locusts: The 8th Plague* (2005). But examples such as these take up an earlier motif, that of demonic possession as swarming – the climactic scenes in Goethe's *Faust* and in gothic novels such as Lewis' *The Monk* inaugurate a tradition that can be found in twentieth-century science fiction and fantasy works, such as Fritz Leiber's *Gather, Darkness!* and James Blish's *Black Easter*. More recently, the demonic swarm has found expression in video game culture. The series *StarCraft*, for instance, features a species known as the 'Zerg': an alien, totalitarian, hive-mind, warring species of gene-traders. If ever there was a candidate for the ultimate 'Other' then surely this would be it.

In these and other examples the Judeo-Christian demon is intimately linked to the insect-animal through this dynamic, amorphous topology that we have been calling the swarm. The point here is not just that the swarm is coded as evil or malefic; rather, it is how the swarm, as a certain form-of-life, puts forth certain limits to thinking 'life' at all.

This idea is brought forth with great clarity in Dante's *Inferno*, one of the classic depictions of the demonic. The *Inferno* carefully stratifies different types of demonic life. One could even say that the *Inferno* represents a kind of Scholastic demonology, in which one finds an indistinction between Aristotelian forms of life: there are human bodies melting into dead trees, rivers flowing with blood, and entire cities populated with the living dead. In the *Inferno* there is little to separate life as natural-biological from life as political-theological. The motif of possession in the *Inferno* demonstrates this: demonic possession is not just the possession of the living, but a sort of plasticity of the living to include the non-living. Demons possess not only human beings and animals, but the very landscape, the very terrain of the underworld. Demonic possession is geological and climatological, as well as teratological.

Consider the Second Circle, the Circle of the Lustful. In a dramatic passage, Dante-the-pilgrim is lead by his guide Virgil to a precipice where, for the first time in the narrative, he encounters the strange vitalism of the demonic:

> I came to a place where no light shone at all, bellowing like the sea racked by a tempest, when warring winds attack it from both sides. The infernal storm, eternal in its rage, sweeps and drives the spirits with its blast: it whirls them, lashing them with punishment. When they are swept back past their place of judgment, then come the shrieks, laments, and anguished cries; there they blaspheme God's almighty power. I learned that to this place of punishment all those who sin in lust have been condemned, those who make reason slave to appetite; and as the wings of starlings in the winter bear them along in wide-spread, crowded flocks, so does that wind propel the evil spirits; now here, then there, and up and down, it drives them with never any hope to comfort them – hope not of rest but even of suffering less. And just like cranes in flight, chanting their lays, stretching an endless line in their formation, I saw approaching, crying their laments, Spirits carried along by the battling wind. And so I asked, 'Teacher, tell me, what souls are these punished in the sweep of the black wind?'
>
> (Dante 2003:V: 30–51)[2]

Keeping with our idea of swarming life, we can pose a simple question: what is it that swarms in this scene? The allegorical underpinning of the scene makes it unclear whether it is the 'storm' that causes the bodies to swarm, or if it is the storm that is itself this swarming. The image of the starling flocks underscores the dynamic interplay of body and space that is akin to the self-organizing capacity of

FIGURE 12.1   Dante's *Inferno*, Canto V, the Second Circle, from an engraving by
Gustave Doré.

swarms, flocks and the like. In addition, the image of the starlings is subtly contrasted
with that of the cranes, whose formation seems much more linear and rigid, as if
their 'line' of flight is mirrored in the song lines of their chanting.

This passage is visualized with great drama by Gustave Doré's engravings of the
Commedia. One of the images depicts the famous scene in which two of the figures –
Paolo and Francesca – emerge from this swarm of bodies to tell their tragic tale.
Dante-the-pilgrim, moved by the scene and their story, is overcome and faints next
to Virgil who is by his side. But what is equally interesting in this image is the way
that Doré makes the bodies of Paolo and Francesca barely stand out from the
amorphous background of swarming spirits, which seems to recede to infinity.
Indeed, in certain areas, the bodies appear to merge into the backdrop of the storm
itself (Figure 12.1).

Using Doré's images as guides, it is instructive, from a topological point of view,
to juxtapose the different types of demons in the *Inferno*. What one discovers is a tension
within the *Inferno* itself, within the stratifications of the demonic. One can identify at
least three types of demonism in the *Inferno*. First there is, at the centre and lowest point
of the underworld, the figure of Lucifer. Here we have the counter-sovereign, who is,
like the divine sovereign, centralized and transcendent with respect to that which he

governs. Further from this, there are the multitude of demons, such as the so-called Malebranche demons found in the Eighth Circle. These are 'demons' in the more familiar, Faustian sense – they are torturers, tricksters and tempters. They operate according to the rule of the underworld, and are more decentralized, their power emanating from the counter-sovereign. Contrasted to these two types of demons there is a third, which is the type we previously encountered in the Second Circle. But here there is neither an embodied counter-sovereign, nor a multitude of demons. There is only the immanent, fully distributed life force of swarming itself. The bodies of the Lustful are also spirits, and the spirits also dissolve into the 'elemental' or climatological swarming of the storm and the wind. It is the most manifest form-of-life (indeed, Dante faints before its force), and yet, it is also the most empty (the swarm of the storm is not a discrete thing, much less an individuated body). Arguably, this last case puts forth the most difficult view of life – not transcendent, governing cause, and not an emanating, radiating flow, but a concept of life that is fully immanent, and yet never fully present. This concept of life is at once overflowing and productive, but, not being a discrete thing in itself, it is also pure emptiness.

This concept of life in the *Inferno* – at once immanent and yet empty – is elaborated in the demonology of the period as well. Thomas Aquinas' treatise *De Malo* (*On Evil*), written in the 1270s, serves as the blueprint for Scholastic demonology of this period. Aquinas considers demons to be intermediary beings like angels, lacking the absolute omnipotence of God but also lacking the limits of mortality of human beings. The onto-theological status of spiritual creatures is, in effect, an act of boundary-management between the natural and supernatural. Aquinas' treatise places the demon within an ontological framework of 12 questions, examining the demon itself as a kind of life form – or, more accurately, as a perturbation within the 'flow of life', the *spiritus*. As he notes, demons have the ability to perturb or intervene in normative life processes 'and in the case of those awake, devils can sometimes indeed move internal vapours and fluids (*spiritus et humores*) even to the point that the use of reason is completely fettered, as is evidently the case with the possessed' (Aquinas 2003: 156).

Spiritus is precisely that which mediates the natural and supernatural, earthly and divine – as well as managing the distinction and separation between them. Aquinas makes a key point here, however – the demon does not possess the power to create life, though it may give the impression of animating and re-animating. This is because, for Aquinas, the demon itself is not living, and is not animated. Here we must presume that the demon does not have animation in the Aristotelian sense of living, natural beings – and yet it can have the effect of animating. The demon, then, seems to be that which can animate but which is not itself animated; that which perturbs and disturbs the flow of life but which is not itself living.

The discourse on the demon, and in particular the depiction of the demon in terms of swarming, raises another difficulty with regard to the concept of life. With the swarm, the primary conceptual challenge was how to account not just for the life 'in' the swarm, but for the life 'of' the swarm. That is, the problem was how to think the swarm as a fully immanent phenomenon. With the association of the swarm with the demon, another problem emerges. The concept of life is most often assumed to be a concept of presence – this is, arguably, what enables life to become an object of philosophical reflection. Life is defined by its flux and flow, by its givenness and the 'gift' of its pouring forth. All of this presumes an ontology of generosity – that life 'is' and life 'does'. But the demonic swarm puts forth another concept; or, really, it highlights a lacuna already existent within the ontology of generosity. That lacuna is the degree to which a concept of life as immanence requires an insubstantial, 'empty' concept of life. Hence the problematic of the demonic swarm: is the limit of our thinking about life this contradiction of an expressive void, an immanent emptiness?

The logic of life

Addressing this question requires that we move back further. In short, the various and often competing epistemologies of life in the end point back to a more fundamental question concerning an ontology of life . . . and to what extent such an ontology is possible. It is for this reason that a return to Aristotle's project is worthwhile, for Aristotle sets out a framework for thinking about life whose influence can still be discerned to this day. That framework is really a limit and one worth investigating given the current interest in biopolitics, bare life, neo-vitalism and so forth.

The *De Anima* – whose Greek title is *Peri Psukhē* – is divided into three parts. At its core is this term *psukhē*, which can be roughly translated as 'life-principle' or 'principle-of-animation'. The Medieval Latin translation of *anima*, as well as the unfortunate English translation of 'soul', illustrates the difficulties that even the most basic translations of the text must confront. The text contains comments on the hierarchy of life (plants, animals, humans), the role of sensation, imagination and cognition in human beings, and an infamously opaque section on the immortality of the life-principle, which would bring accusations of heresy during the Scholastic era. Thus, the *De Anima* is relevant for its attempt to establish a framework within which 'life' generally speaking can become the object of philosophical speculation.

The Aristotelian problematic is actually quite simple. To understand this we need to bear in mind that there are two Aristotles: Aristotle-the-metaphysician, reflecting on essence-concepts such as form, substance and cause, and Aristotle-the-biologist, travelling through the eastern Aegean, observing the biodiversity of plants and animals. Aristotle-the-biologist observes a set of characteristics unique to what he calls life. These include form and causality (life is creative, inventive and productive), time and temporality (life is becoming, change and movement) and spirit and teleology (life as that which is common among all the living).

But Aristotle-the-metaphysician struggles to articulate a coherent concept to encompass these diverse characteristics of life. On the one hand, any concept of life must be transcendent to life in order to account for its propensity for change. But this means that such a concept cannot itself be a part of life, cannot be a kind of life, or one among many instances of life, for otherwise this simply begs the question, in an infinitely-deferred search for a first principle. On the other, any concept of life must be immanent to life in order to demonstrate the non-separation between essence and existence. Any concept of life must account for life in a way that acknowledges the internally-caused, auto-animating and self-organizing capacities of life. Thus any concept of life must account for the principle characteristics of life, without itself being part of them; and any concept of life must be inseparable from actual instances of life – while not being determined by them.

In the *De Anima*, Aristotle takes up and reworks the pre-Socratic term *psukhē* to function as this concept of life. Throughout the treatise he attempts numerous formulations: 'The soul (*psukhē*) is the cause and the first principle of the living body' (Aristotle 2000: 415b); 'the soul is in a sense the principle of animal life' (ibid.: 402a); 'that which has soul is distinguished from that which has not by living' (ibid.: 413a). If the term *psukhē* cannot be understood in terms of the Christian 'soul', at the same time, it cannot simply be translated as 'life' in a biological sense, since there are other terms in Greek that denote this (for instance, the term *zoē*, also frequently used by Aristotle). From a modern perspective, the term *psukhē* itself seems caught between theology and biology. In its simplest form, Aristotle's term *psukhē* denotes a life-principle, or 'that by which the living is living'.

Aristotle's concept of life *psukhē* must account for life without itself being life, though it cannot be separate from life; it must be at once external and internal to life. How does Aristotle smooth over this contradiction? He does this by stressing a key distinction within *psukhē*. Of his intention in the *De Anima* Aristotle states that 'we seek to examine and investigate first the nature and essence of the soul, and then its attributes'. Continuing, he notes that, of the attributes of the soul, 'some seem to be affections peculiar to the soul, and others seem to belong to living things also, by virtue of the soul' (ibid.: 402a). Thus, we can say that Aristotle's concept of life differentiates between *psukhē*-as-principle and *psukhē*-as-manifestation. On the one hand, we have an abstract principle of life and, on the other, a set of concrete manifestations of life. Whereas the former is abstract and never present in-itself, the latter is concrete but reliant on the former for its existence. If *psukhē*-as-manifestation is that-which-is-living, then *psukhē*-as-principle is that-by-which-the-living-is-living.

We might refer to this distinction in less verbose terms as that between 'Life' (with a capital L) and 'the living'. The concept of life is thus divided by Aristotle between an onto-theological notion of Life ('life itself') and an onto-biological notion of the living (particular manifestations of Life). Life is that through which the heterogeneous domains of the living are alive; and Life is that by which the domains of the living can be said to be alive. Hence Aristotle's ontology of life sets out to address both the concept of life and its manifestations. The term *psukhē* signifies that which is held in common among all the living, while the internal distinction between Life and the living accommodates stratifications within life.

Immediately one notices a number of contradictions within this Aristotelian framework. For instance, while we can point to numerous instances of the living, Life, in itself, is never existent as such. That is, what is common among the living is Life, but Life in itself has no properties or characteristics. This would imply that, while the living is characterized by process of production, growth and development, Life, since it has no existence, is void of any content, biological or otherwise. Finally, Life and the living become increasingly incommensurate with each other on the issue of their intelligibility: one cannot think Life without also thinking the living; one cannot think Life while also at the same time thinking the living. In short, there must be a conceptual guarantee, something 'in' each instance of the living that allows us to say that each of those instances is an instance of Life. In other words, while we can think the multiple instances of the living, the thought of Life remains a horizon for thought itself. And yet this absence, this void, also guarantees the proliferation of instances of the living.

In the split between Life and the living, so central to Aristotle's ontology of life, and so necessary in order for him to begin to think life at all, we see that contradiction appears to play a central role. Contradiction is, of course, important for Aristotle. What has come to be known as the Law of Non-contradiction makes the absence of contradiction central to any adequate concept – indeed to thought itself (Aristotle 1984: 1005b, 18–20) However, as we have noted, the Aristotelian distinction between Life and the living opens onto a series of unavoidable contradictions, contradictions that, in effect, must be affirmed if one is to grant life the status of an ontology. The relation between 'life' and 'logic' is implicitly posed by the *De Anima* as one of contradiction. This puts Aristotle in a difficult position: to what extent is there something like life-in-general, or a common principle of Life that cuts across all the instances of the living? To what degree does the affirmation of such a life-principle (*psukhē*) also entail the affirmation of the sort of contradictions Aristotle notes above?

The entelechy of the weird

Perhaps, instead of attempting to resolve such contradictions, we can actually develop them further. Let us suppose that contradiction is not an accidental or derivative by-product, but that it is in some way significant, if not foundational, to any ontology of life in the Aristotelian framework.

If we shift our position a little, we realize that this is what the eclectic tradition of supernatural horror or 'weird fiction' often does, presenting us with strange creatures that occupy the horizon of thought itself. The horror that is expressed in the tales of H. P. Lovecraft, for example, does not result from the threat of a monster – indeed, there are rarely 'monsters' in the traditional sense in Lovecraft's stories. Rather, the 'cosmic horror' in Lovecraftian stories results from the possibility of a logic of life that is *absolutely* inaccessible to the human, the natural and the earthly. In Lovecraft's stories creatures such as the Shoggoths can barely be named, let alone adequately described *or thought*. This is the crux of supernatural horror. It is not the monster that causes horror, that which threatens existing categories of knowledge. Rather, it is the 'nameless thing', which presents itself as a horizon for thought itself – it is formless and yet all shapes; it is so ancient it is alien; it is alive only insofar as all human concepts of 'life' are irrelevant. In short, in supernatural horror 'life' cannot be thought because it can only be thought through a logic of contradiction.

If we were to develop the contradictions at the centre of Aristotle's ontology of life, we could then ask what conclusions follow – however aporetic or 'weird' – when this logic of contradiction is applied to *psukhē* and the distinction between Life and the living. What we could do, then, is to take this *conjunction* of Life and the living, and then consider three *disjunctions* between them, and thereby test the Aristotelian logic of life. We could consider, for example, Life as subtracted from the living. Would this not give us a sort of formless life, an amorphous life, the kind that one finds in films such as *X: The Unknown*, *The Blob* or *The Mist*? Similarly, we could consider the living as subtracted from Life. Would this not give us something like a purely non-actualized life, a bestial spectre or spiritual creature, as one finds in films such as *Fiend Without a Face* or *Cure*, or Ambrose Bierce's story 'The Damned Thing'? Finally we could consider the ultimate disjunction, a double disjunction of that which is 'animate' but which is neither Life nor the living – something like the purely negative life, as one finds in William Hope Hodgson's *The Night Land*, Fred Hoyle's *The Black Cloud* or the manga *Uzumaki*.

Let us, a bit tongue-in-cheek, refer to this approach as 'Aristotelian biohorror'. Beginning from the premise that any ontology of life must confront the limitations of the Aristotelian framework, Aristotelian biohorror then entertains the idea that such contradictions must in fact be affirmed in order to think 'life' at all. In short, Aristotle's ontology of life suggests that there is an essential relationship between logic and life. But this relation is grounded in the contradictions that themselves form the relation between logic and life – in short, the logic of life in the Aristotelian framework requires the affirmation of contradiction. It results in a series of improbable, unlikely instances of the living that are at once logical and bio-logical monsters. We can refer to this as the 'vitalist antinomy'.

In closing, we can set out the problem in a plain way: there is no philosophy of life that is not also partially, or even fully, a biology of life and a theology of life. To consider a philosophy of life, then, is also to consider a non-philosophy of life, or the ways in which the very concept of life forms a kind of limit-concept for philosophy. If every philosophy is shadowed by a non-philosophical domain that at once conditions its possibility and its horizon of thought, then 'the nonphilosophical is perhaps closer to the heart of philosophy than philosophy itself' (Deleuze and Guattari 1994: 41). This is tantamount to saying that to think the concept of life philosophically, one must have recourse to non-philosophical discourses. In this sense, every 'philosophy of life' presupposes a non-philosophical vantage point from which 'life' as such can continue to be thought.

Notes

1 For an expansion of this theme see Galloway and Thacker (2007) and Thacker (2004).
2 The key passage reads, 'E come li stornei ne portan l'ali / nel freddo tempo, a schiera larga e piena,/così quel fiato li spiriti mali.'

Bibliography

Aquinas, T. (2003) *On Evil*, trans. R. Regan, Oxford: Oxford University Press.

Aristotle (1984) *The Complete Works of Aristotle*, ed. J. Barnes, Princeton, NJ: Princeton University Press.

Aristotle (2000) *De Anima*, trans. W.S. Hett, Cambridge: Harvard University Press.

Arquilla, J. and Ronfeldt, D. (2000) *Swarming and the Future of Conflict*, Santa Monica, CA: RAND.

Bergson, H. (1998) *Creative Evolution*, trans. A. Mitchell, Mineola, NY: Dover.

Camazine, S., Deneubourg, J.L., Franks, N.R., Sneyd, S., Theraula, G. and Bonabeau, E. (2001) *Self-organization in Biological Systems*, Princeton, NJ: Princeton University Press.

Dante Alighieri (2003) *Inferno*, trans. M. Musa, New York: Penguin.

Deleuze, G. and Guattari, F. (1994) *What is Philosophy?*, trans. H. Tomlinson and G. Burchell, New York: Columbia University Press.

Galloway, A. and Thacker, E. (2007) *The Exploit: A Theory of Networks*, Minneapolis: University of Minnesota Press.

Marx, K. (1976) *Capital, Volume I*, trans. B. Fowkes, New York: Penguin.

Thacker, E. (2004) 'Networks, Swarms, Multitudes', in *Ctheory*, available at: http://www.ctheory.net/articles.aspx?id=422 and http://www.ctheory.net/articles.aspx?id=423.

13

INCLINING THE SUBJECT

Ethics, alterity and natality

Adriana Cavarero

Various are the attempts to attack the modern notion according to which philosophical knowledge can unambiguously account for the world and the self. As it has been noted,

> the status of theory today, both within the fields of social sciences and humanities, is testimony of the existence of a multifaceted landscape of positions that is often quite critical toward the claims of a comprehensive and neutral possibility of (theoretical) knowledge.
>
> (Guaraldo 2001: 24)

To simplify, however, one could say that the complex and articulated contemporary theoretical landscape, in its critical attempt to question modern notions of the subject, can be divided into two opposite yet equally specular endeavours. The first corresponds to the perspective that, by endorsing the postmodern and post-structuralist discourses on multiplicity and fragmentation, aims primarily at destabilizing the conceptual frameworks through which the subject constructs itself as a self-sufficient and impermeable ego. In as much as a number of different scholars share a speculative interest in questioning the 'being' of human beings and, therefore, in ontology, the second corresponds to the perspective that aims at contrasting the ideology of individualism through an essential focus on relationality and dependence. From a certain point of view, in order to unmask the delirium of omnipotence of the ego, both perspectives give the *other* – whatever the 'other' can mean in the diverse geo-linguistic contexts here at stake – a fundamental role. There is a crucial difference, however. While the first perspective causes the isolated, perfect, sealed shape of the ego to collapse into the vortex of multiple fragments that succeed in nullifying all of the possible spatial patterns of the scene (there is no centre nor periphery any longer), the ontological perspective, by insisting on a constitutive relationality, tends to re-orient the scene from its vertical axis to a horizontal one. In both cases the Cartesian prototype of the subject is removed from its solid pedestal, by virtue of a theoretical gesture that refuses the traditional philosophical appeal to a vertical, linear direction of truth and good. In the first case, though, the subject is deconstructed and fragmented, resulting in the joyful experience of its own infinite dissolution. In the second case it rather encounters its human sharing in finitude, insufficiency and dependence. In other words, the notorious self-referential ego that stands up on the arrogant act of its own founda-tion, displaced by relational ontology from the verticality of its posture, eventually finds out not only that it must be there with others but also that others are perhaps necessary and constitutive for itself to be. The question, after all, regards precisely the role of the other in this 'being' which, contextually, is already a 'being there'. For many reasons – that engage in vital problems of ethical and political order – it is a crucial question indeed. Although the issue of relational ontology cannot but affect the vertical posture of the modern subject, the horizontal reorienting of the scene is, in fact, open to diverse configurations. It could resolve in the paradigm of a flat horizontality thought in terms of interdependence and ideal reciprocity. But it could also resolve in the much more radical gesture of giving every self – not necessarily in turn and on a mutual basis – to the unilateral 'inclination' of the other. The horizontal metaphor can be further displaced, so to say, and the self located in a slightly different position, neither vertical nor horizontal, yet given over, exposed, offered, *inclined* to the other. Within feminist theory this unbalancing gesture nestles, more or less explicitly, in the imaginary of the ethics of care.

Launched by Carol Gilligan's seminal book *In a Different Voice* (1982) and reart-iculated by Jean Tronto's work on *Moral Boundaries* (1993), the issue of 'care' has widely influenced the feminist debate and the contemporary discourse on ethics. The ontological problem that lies at the core of it, however, has been largely either neglected or, at least, partially undervalued. To introduce the complexity of the problem, I will begin by quoting an interesting statement from Tronto's book, who crucially remarks that if we focus

> on an integral concept of care we will also need to alter other central aspects of moral and political theory; we will need to shift from the dilemma of auton-omy or dependency to a more sophisticated sense of human interdependency.
> (Tronto 1993: 101)

Decisively centred on the question of ontology, the second part of the statement is worthy of attention indeed. By looking at the condition of being human from the perspective of care, it essentially claims that this condition consists of interdepend-ency rather that dependency. In particular, the thesis suggests that, in as much as dependency is entrapped in the dilemma that opposes it to the notorious ontology of the autonomous individual professed by modernity, dependency results in a cate-gory that is too compromised and too 'simple' to be useful. On the contrary, claims Tronto, by getting rid of the binary and compromising logic of this contraposition, it becomes possible to glimpse a form of interdependency that looks more 'sophisticated' and effective. In other words, according to Tronto, the focus on an 'integral' concept of care, beyond endorsing an ontology thought in terms of relationality, also demands our effort to overcome the limits of a certain representation of care, dear to feminist theory, in which relationality means dependency.

At least semantically, if not conceptually, interdependency has, of course, a very strict connection with dependency. Especially if conceived as a net of reciprocal dependency, interdependency, so to speak, ought to admit that dependency comes first. Tortuous as it seems, from a perspective that aims at problematizing the general model of relational ontology through the issue of care, the question of the relationship between interdependency and dependency discloses a number of important speculative knots.

One of them, capable perhaps of standing in for all of the others, could be put in the following terms: while the phenomenological scenario of care hints at a relationality materialized in dependency, the theoretical option for interdependency does not solicit, necessarily, the framework of care. As a matter of fact, in the history of ontology, interdependency can count on the speculative authority of various scholars who are not concerned with care at all. This success, moreover, within the discussion on democracy, often results from an increasing propensity to conceive relationality in terms of horizontal reciprocity. Hannah Arendt and most of the contemporary philosophers who are inspired by her thought fit perfectly in the picture. Namely, her insistence on the relational feature of the human condition, even more if it is understood as a mutual exposure of everybody to the other, evokes an horizon of ideal reciprocity rather than unbalanced dependency. Symptomatically, this is a coherent effect of what I would define as an evident discrepancy within the principal category of Arendt's speculation: although she focuses on natality, she does not focus on care.

In spite of Arendt, it is easy to argue that while one could, perhaps, conceptualize care without immediately involving the category of natality, nobody can seriously look at natality without seeing care. The scene of birth presents us, inevitably, with the absolute exposure of the child, the newborn, the one who announces the human condition as substantially vulnerable (Butler 2004: 31, Cavarero 2009: 20–4). Even if the target remains the abstract, autonomous, self-referential individual of modernity, natality allows for neither an imagery of interdependency nor the horizontal pattern that sustains it. It rather upholds a relational ontology consisting of unbalanced and even unilateral exposures.

Natality speaks of dependency and vulnerability, and, on a regular phenomenological basis, it speaks of relationships between mother and child. Differently told, if natality is the category at stake, there is a child depending on the other – ordinarily a mother – and needing care. Although time and again they caution against the stereotype of oblative maternity, namely the traditional model of the mother as giver and carer, feminists are familiar with the topic. And artists too. In the Louvre Museum there is an oil painting by Leonardo da Vinci: *Sant'Anna, la Madonna e il bambino con l'agnello* [*Virgin and Child with St. Anne*]. The structure of the painting

FIGURE 13.1   Sant'Anna, la Madonna e il bambino con l'agnello [Virgin and Child with St. Anne], Leonardo da Vinci.

is remarkable for the conspicuous *inclination* of the figure of the Virgin Mary (Figure 13.1), who stands in the centre and, leaning forwards, bends over the child. The Virgin sits in the lap of her mother Anne, who slightly bends her head towards Mary and thus, according to the axis of the glances that crosses obliquely the painting, towards the Child Jesus. The Child is grappling with a lamb, an evident symbol of the passion and sacrifice that await him. The pictorial evocation of the future *vulnus* (injury or wound, in Latin) comes thus to emphasize the condition of vulnerability that the Christ shares with the humans, by representing it in that exemplary time of childhood which identifies the vulnerable with the helpless. Bent over him, as if she wanted to save him from his destiny, the Virgin stretches out her arms and holds his body, in an ordinary gesture of care. Imbalanced on her axis, she leans out conspicuously.

It is commonly understood that the maternal is, for women, an *inclination*. Which is plausible. Not, however, in the sense, usually invoked, that feminine nature is inclined to maternity; but rather in the sense, truer to the etymology of the term, that 'every inclination turns outwards, it leans out of the self' (Arendt 2003: 82). With no reference to the figure of the mother, this definition appears in a minor text by Hannah Arendt, *Some Questions of Moral Philosophy*. Among these questions, as she emphasizes, stands out the fact that moral propositions 'all take as their standard the Self and hence the intercourse of man with himself' (ibid.: 76). According to Arendt, moral propositions are, in this sense, egoistical even when they intend to be altruistic. This is true for Kant's categorical imperative as well as for the Christian precept 'Thou shalt love thy neighbour as thyself'. Thus, in various ways, the centrality of the self frames the conceptual and problematic structure of moral philosophy. No inclination that leads the self outwards and bends it over the *other* disturbs, in short, the solid egoistic foundation of the system. To put it differently, moral philosophy has never been disturbed by the complex ontological issue of *inclination*.

I should make clear that I am here transgressing, robbing and exploiting the text of Hannah Arendt in a very free and philologically disrespectful way. Aimed at reconsidering the problem of ontology nestled in the issue of care, my strategy consists of both taking advantage of her definition of inclination and mobilizing it versus the vertical or horizontal axis on which philosophy generally counts. But Arendt deals with the category of inclination only occasionally – almost accidentally I should say – in the text mentioned above and, as it is worth repeating, she does not connect it at all with either the topic of maternity or with that of care. Her principal issue – to put it in Judith Butler's words – is substantially that of dislodging 'the subject as the ground of ethics in order to recast the subject as a problem *for* ethics' (Butler 2005: 110). But Arendt's solution, though it endorses the idea of a relational, anti-narcissistic ontology, does not take *maternal inclination* into account.

Yet, the figure of the mother presents us with an immediate ethical tone that diverse streams within feminist theory have never failed to perceive and emphasize. At the head of the list lie, of course, those who see in the mother the primary instance of a *care* of the *other*. The literature on the topic (Held 2007; Larrabee 1992) is worth discussing, beginning with the works of Carol Gilligan and Joan Tronto quoted above. Here, however, my task is not that of participating in this discussion, but rather of reorienting the critical perspective from ethics to ontology, in order to investigate more carefully the *other* who appears on the maternal scene of care. Irreconcilable to the other in general or, even worse, to the indeterminate Other, encumbered by its enigmatic capital letter, this other is, and in the first place, the one who lies in the warm fold of the embrace and is still infant, vulnerable creature, tender child. Bent over him, as in Leonardo's painting, the mother leans out. The fact that the child in question is a son and not a daughter depends, of course, on the iconographic power of the Virgin Mary within Western culture. Like all crucial articulations of the symbolic order, the maternal lives in the intensity of its images and representations which, in this case, can count on a great artist. Well known to feminist critique, the celebrated stereotype of the oblative woman rests, in fact, on a wide consensus between art and religion, which Leonardo's genius exemplarily represents. The patriarchal tradition does not reject the feminine virtue of caring for the other; on the contrary, it praises and exalts it, persuaded that each gender has, by nature, its role. Naturally destined to care, as the phallocentric story goes, women express in this task their own specific essence. Because of their congenital rationality, men enjoy, instead, a wider sphere of expression. According to a scheme already working in Aristotle, man exists in fact *for himself* and for the political community, whereas woman, confined within the domestic sphere, exists *for the other*. That is, in the final analysis, she exists for him.

Stereotypes – we could call them 'conceptual frames', or, according to a certain feminist lexicon, 'culturally constructed gender identities' – are notoriously hard to dismantle. Even the critical discourse that aims at demolishing them must necessarily feed on the very same language in which they are incorporated. The impetus of frontal demolishing is, however, rare within feminist theory. Well aware of the fact that language cannot be transcended, contemporary feminism prefers to undo and unravel its web. While showing a certain sympathy for postmodern styles or ontological approaches, the most prevalent strategy is to deconstruct, dismantle and disconnect gender stereotypes in order to recombine them according to unexpected modalities of signification. As far as the stereotype of maternity is concerned, this strategy seems to work particularly well if the enterprise involves one of the fundamental issues of its conceptual constellation; this is the case of birth – and this is why, more or less against her intentions, Hannah Arendt ends by being a very precious guide and accomplice.

In one of her major works, *The Human Condition*, Arendt regards natality as a fundamental aspect of our being human and therefore identifies it with the 'naked fact of our original physical appearing' (Arendt 1958: 176). The theoretical context, in this case, is a critique of metaphysics, and her central thesis is that human beings exist insofar as they appear in the world and are constitutively exposed one to the others, beginning with the initial phase of this appearance: birth. This means – in spite of Arendt's usual reticence in regard to this subject – that each human being is, first of all, exposed to the mother. As it is worth repeating, a mother is actually necessary here, at least if what eventually matters is the liquidation of the self-referential ego standing on its vertical axis. However, by embodying the other of the newborn, the mother not only confirms the relational frame of Arendt's ontology, but also, by predisposing it towards an altruistic ethics, cautions against dreams of horizontal reciprocity and compels us to understand it in terms of dependency. The problem is indeed not only that of unmasking the individualistic ontology of modernity, but also that of compelling the self to renounce its arrogant pretensions of autonomy and independence.

When confronted with the primary roots of our being there, the transparent and self-referential subject of modernity wavers and reveals all its vanity. As a matter of fact, imprisoned as it is in its own narcissism, the modern self neither exposes itself nor leans out: it aims rather at making itself immune from the other through a gesture of vertical self-foundation that pretends not to need the other's inclination. Disproving this immunitary connotation of the self (Esposito 2002), the newborn, on the contrary, while he exposes himself totally and irremediably, declares a congenital vulnerability as his constitutive condition. Already owing to the *other* his coming into the world and his subsisting there in vulnerability, he belongs to a scene where he depends on her, and she, by leaning out and thus thrusting herself outwards, bends over him.

From this perspective, the contraposition between a feminine ethics of care and the masculine disposition to pronounce abstract moral judgements (Gilligan 1982), although interesting, is therefore only a premise. We are not dealing with the generic contrast between a relational ontology and one that keeps founding itself on the paradigm of the individual. Since it implicates a relationality that is originally dual, and is furthermore characterized by a relation that is unbalanced between inclination and dependence, the scene of natality appears, indeed, more complex: neither verticality nor horizontality describes its frames. Two figures are involved: the mother and the infant. If the former is haunted by the stereotype of the oblative woman, the latter seems to demand this very oblativity, since he exists in the condition of extreme vulnerability and dependency. Interdependency would be, in this context, unthinkable; namely, it would appear as an intellectual abstraction from the reality of the context.

Given that the discourse here insists on the reality of the context, this is perhaps the right moment for providing a short justification regarding my disputable choice of denoting the child as a 'he' and not, as the English syntax would require, as an 'it'. From a certain point of view, 'he' is the correct word because, through Leonardo's genius, we are actually observing a scene where the child is a male: Jesus. Raised in the name of a radical ontology, the choice of a sexed pronoun, however, does not depend on this particular painting but rather stems from a speculative necessity. Although, usually language refers to the infant as a neutral being, the mother knows he or she is gendered. Their relation, from the point of view of her maternal inclination, is already a sexed knowledge.

For the infant, however, this very relation is one of crucial dependence, which is moreover unconscious and unidirectional. Vulnerable creature, the child is totally given to the action, benign or malign, of the one bending over him. In this sense, the infant embodies in an exemplary way the other as helpless. And in this sense, it is symptomatically indifferent whether the child in question is a boy or a girl. Precisely because he or she is an embodied singularity, an incarnated being, and not the fictitious entity thought by metaphysics – call it man or the individual or the subject – the infant is always gendered. His or her vulnerability, as the primary mark of the human condition, however, is regardless of gender.

This does not mean, of course, that the scene too is regardless of gender. In the dual relation we are analysing here, an *other*, predictably gendered as female, is indeed always part of the picture and, even if substituted by someone else, she inhabits, under the name of 'mother', its imaginary. Generated by an infinite chain of other mothers that goes back to the beginning of time, she generates vulnerable beings and, above all, as well as beyond the act of procreation, she plays the role, never symbolically superseded, of the one who is responsible *for them*.

Interestingly enough, if we continue to follow Arendt and attend to her description, we are invited to observe the scene of natality as separated from the event, still fundamental, of the delivery. She warns us, in fact, that there is always more at stake in life than 'the procreation of individual living organisms' (Arendt 2003: 51). This means, in Arendtian terms, that human beings exist, and live as irremediably unique beings, insofar as they belong to the world and appear in it. That is, not only are they *already there*, but they are there in a way that no previous stage, let alone the embryo, influences the meaning, ontologically contextual, worldly and material, of their actual and real being there. In this sense, the infant represents the initial phase, particularly fragile because of his unilateral exposition to the others, of the coincidence – that can never be separated – of life and appearance. And, in the same sense, the mother is a necessary part of the picture, but not due to the title she earns from the act of generation. Rather, she plays the role – attested by ordinary experience and exemplarily depicted by Leonardo – of the one who, bending over the infant, is *par excellence* responsible for his vulnerability in the context of the relation. Mother – it is worth repeating it – is thus above all the *name* of an inclination over the other; or, differently told, the function that evokes the figure of responsibility engendered on the inaugural scene of a human condition in which helplessness is the mark of the beginner.

Mother, however, even if assumed as a name denoting an unbalanced inclination towards the other, does not coincide, necessarily, with the self-renouncing, oblative figure of the good mother. As feminist theorists know for sure, within the history of the Western imaginary the general catalogue of the stereotypes of maternity displays evil mothers too. One of them, almost perfect in her dramatic contraposition to the Virgin Mary, is Medea. A creature of the myth, she is notoriously constructed by Euripides as a character symbolizing infanticide, that is, as the icon itself of an evil response to the essential exposure of the helpless. We know how the story goes and how the tragedy recounts that Medea, reacting to Jason's betrayal, murders her own children in revenge. From then on, among the mothers of death, assassins who only murder their male offspring (Loraux 1998: 51), the criminal deed that remains linked to the name of Medea, more than any other in the Western imaginary, is infanticide. The legend also recounts how she killed and tore into pieces her newborn brother Absyrtus. Other homicides follow. Alien sorceress who comes from elsewhere, from the distant regions of the Caucasus, Medea knows many ways of perpetrating murder. In her story, framed by a mysogynist imaginary – very evident in the text of Euripides – the sequence of crimes functions as an accumulation of excess that succeeds in emphasizing the cruelty of the infanticidal woman. The murderer of her own children, *paidoleteira*, repeatedly qualified as *deine*, uncanny, Medea is an outsider who brings her deed of horror from elsewhere, that is, according to the ideological geography of origins, from a space both barbaric and uncanny. Apparently, Greece cannot bear this crime of atrocious perfection. Horrorist violence (Cavarero 2009) demonstrates, here, that its aim is to destroy the vulnerable, indeed the helpless, going so far as to 'undo' its corporeal singularity in the early years of life. We are in Greece, but the killing fields familiar to Homer are very far. The victim, here, is not the hero, the warrior at the height of his virility, the champion of reciprocal massacre prepared to suffer wounds on his own body, but rather the infant, the child. 'You could endure – a mother! – to lift sword against your own little ones' exclaims Jason on the stage (Euripides 1963: 58). Centred on the mother, the circle of the ontological crime completes itself. She who responds with a wounding blade to the exposure of the vulnerable as the absolutely helpless is also she who manifests a propensity to cut bodies 'to pieces', who aims to destroy that uniqueness that every mother immediately recognizes in her child. And, on the other hand, the violent response stands out more forcefully because it is from the mother that care is expected.

Good mother, evil mother: if observed through the paradigm of inclination illustrated above, the stereotype of maternity narrated by the Western encyclopaedia appears disquieting indeed. The icon of the Madonna and child, the representation of a maternity that exalts the sole response of care, seems to frame the context. Medea, in appearance at least, occupies the opposite pole. In appearance: because there is also the story of a loving mother – 'though you kill them, they were your beloved sons' (Euripides 1963: 55). Euripides has her say to herself. And even if we know that, already in Homeric language, 'never is the insistence on the skin's softness so great as at the moment that it is injured' (Loraux 1995: 98), there is always a melting maternal sensibility in her that notes, as she embraces her sons, that the 'children's skin is soft, and their breath pure' (Euripides 1963: 50). Though she kills them with a blade that cuts and plunges into their flesh, Medea has nothing in common with the warriors of the *Iliad* and their world. Given that she is a mother, the vulnerable ones whom she wounds, even at the very moment of the homicidal act, are also recognized by her on the side of care. And it is precisely this 'necessary side' that makes the violence perpetrated on this scene a peculiar form of horror.

As a matter of fact, if we restrict the maternal merely within the sphere of care, we not only reinforce over again the stereotype of oblativity (which, as Lacan says, means 'everything for the other') but most of all we obscure the alternative between care and wound of which inclination properly consists. Though outlining a relational structure that frees ontology from the centrality of the self and focuses on the other, the scene of the mother who bends over the infant, actually, is not yet a response, but only a predisposition to respond. Differently told, it is a leaning out over the helpless creature who, just because of his unilateral exposition, becomes himself a request.

In this sense, not to lean out, to hold oneself upright and turn around to go elsewhere, means to avoid, and escape from, the request; that is, it means to deny a human condition that singularly interrogates and summons each of us in so far as we are human. It corresponds, in other words, to evil as expression of irresponsibility, structurally different from that evil which concerns instead the very act of wounding specifically chosen as a response. Feeding on the drama of this irresponsibility, the vast and moving narrative of the abandonment of the infant gives evidence precisely to this prejudicial form of violence, certainly atrocious but still ascribable to the actions of an inflexible and self-referential self standing on its vertical axis. The alternative between care and wound, between love and violence, is instead entirely inscribed within the inclination as always already predisposed, or more, disposed to answer. Turned outwards, bending over, responsive, this alternative is typical of a self that leans out over the other, conspicuously abandoning its own balance.

Our short investigation on the Virgin Mary and Medea attests that the alternative can count on powerful images. A shocking figure, the latter is precious because she warns us that, in the maternal inclination, care is not an automatic or inevitable response; it is, rather, and after all, the ordinary as well as desirable side of that violence, equally plausible, which the vulnerable includes in its name. *Vulnus* is, in fact, the Latin word for wound. The very possibility of receiving the wound is what the vulnerable first announces and, perhaps, like the 'face of the other' (Levinas 1980: 198) described by Levinas, expects. This does not mean, of course, that the maternal inclination, responding to the vulnerable, leans towards infanticide. It rather testifies that infanticide can be passed down the centuries as the most scandalous crime precisely because, by denying care in a contextual and direct way, it comes to confront care itself as the other side – the ordinary one – of the response. It is at any rate a helpless creature, the paradigm of absolute human vulnerability, that demands here a response. To lean out over this creature corresponds to lean out over an other who exposes him- or herself completely to the wound and has no weapons, that is, does not defend him- or herself and in turn does not wound. Maternal inclination does not resolve for Good or Evil; it simply bends over the infant, outlining a scenario in which good and evil, performed with full and unilateral power, envisage no retaliation.

In this sense, the figure of the infant ends with embodying the more significant archetype of all the helpless as such, that is, of all human beings stricken unilaterally by a non-reciprocable violence. Such a violence – as attested by the history of genocides and massacres, as well as other old and new forms of horrorism (Cavarero 2009) – rarely envisages a mother in the role of slaughterer. Nevertheless we need perhaps the maternal inclination in order to reveal the extreme crime of which this very violence consists. After all, without renouncing the care, on the contrary, by founding it on the inclination, the maternal figure can enlighten the radicality of this violence just because the ontological crime is here emphasized in the form of scandal.

In Leonardo's painting, the Virgin sits on the lap of her mother Anne. The triangle outlined by Mary's body leaning forward finds in Anne's body a support, almost an anchorage that permits the daughter to thrust herself outwards in the inclination. More than holding her back so that Christ is not subtracted from the salvific necessity of his sacrifice – and in this case she would represent the Church – Anne allows Mary to lean out. The image, in a sense, suggests that every mother had a mother, according to a potentially infinite series of unilateral inclinations first received and then given. Does interdependency fit the picture? If we maintain the ontological primacy of unilateral dependency, whose contingent evolution can but also cannot result in a series of unilateral dependencies, it does. Anyhow, here, in this amazing painting that trusts in continuity but not in horizontality, we see only a portion of the series, of which Jesus genealogically represents the end. Conspicuous for the absence of Joseph, Leonardo's anomalous version of the Holy Family allows that the helpless, precisely because fated to the *vulnus*, turns back his gaze to the theory of the oblique mothers on whom he depends.

Bibliography

Arendt, H. (1958) *The Human Condition*, Chicago: The University of Chicago Press.

Arendt, H. (2003) 'Some Questions of Moral Philosophy', in *Responsibility and Judgment*, New York: Schocken Books.

Butler, J. (2004) *Precarious Life: The Power of Mourning and Violence*, London: Verso.

Butler, J. (2005) *Giving an Account of Oneself*, New York: Fordham University Press.

Cavarero, A. (2009) *Horrorism: Naming Contemporary Violence*, New York: Columbia University Press.

Esposito, R. (2002) *Immunitas. Protezione e negazione della vita*, Torino: Einaudi.

Euripides (1963) *Medea*, in *Medea and Other Plays*, trans. P. Vellacott, Harmondsworth: Penguin.

Gilligan, C. (1982) *In a Different Voice: Psychological Theory and Women's Development*, Cambridge, MA: Harvard University Press.

Guaraldo, O. (2001) *Storylines: Politics, History and Narrative from an Arendtian Perspective*, Jyvaskyla, Finland: SoPhi Academic Press.

Held, V. (2007) *The Ethics of Care: Personal, Political, Global*, Oxford: Oxford University Press.

Larrabee, M.J. (ed.) (1992) *An Ethics of Care: Feminist and Interdisciplinary Perspectives*, New York: Routledge.

Levinas, E. (1980) *Totality and Infinity*, New York: Springer.

Loraux, N. (1995) *The Experiences of Tiresias: The Feminine and the Greek Man*, Princeton, NJ: Princeton University Press.

Loraux, N. (1998) *Mothers in Mourning*, Ithaca, NY: Cornell University Press.

Tronto, J. (1993) *Moral Boundaries: A Political Argument for an Ethic of Care*, New York: Routledge.

14

THE PERSON AND HUMAN LIFE

Roberto Esposito

TRANSLATED BY DIANA GARVIN AND THOMAS KELSO

The paradox of the person

1

In 2006, the cover of the December edition of *Time* magazine, traditionally dedicated to the person of the year, showed a photo of an illuminated computer, with instead of the monitor, a reflective, mirror-like surface, and in its center enormous letters spelling the pronoun 'you'. In this way, whoever looks at it sees his or her own face reflected, promoted in fact, to 'person of the year', as the text above it assures the reader. The intention of the magazine is that of certifying, in this hyperrealistic way, the fact that in contemporary society, no one exercises greater influence than Internet users, with their photos, their videos and their statements. However, on a deeper level, the message lends itself to another, more unexpected interpretation, since it splits onto two mutually opposed planes. On the one hand, declaring them 'person of the year' situates readers in the space of absolute centrality reserved for exceptional individuals, until now. On the other, and at the same time, it places them in a series that is potentially infinite, to the point of making every one of their singular features disappear. It is as if lending everyone the same 'mask' ends up making of it the valueless sign of a pure repetition. It is as if the inevitably contradictory result of an excess of personalization were to remove the subject from his place through the contraption of a machine that replaces him and pushes him into the faceless dimension of the object. After all, this exchange of roles, ingenuously or maliciously staged on the cover of *Time*, is nothing but the most explicit metaphor for a much broader and more general process. In times when even political parties strive to become 'personal' in order to make voters identify with the figure of the leader, any old gadget is sold by advertising as maximally 'personalized' – adapted to the personality of the buyer, destined, even, to highlight it even more. Naturally, in this case, too, this results in reconciling the tastes of the public with models that are scarcely differentiated. The same paradox returns: the more one tries to extract the unmistakable characteristics of the person, the more one determines the opposite, specular effect of depersonalization. The more you want to impress the personal seal of subjectivity, the more you seem to produce the contrary result of subjection to a reifying apparatus.

Such a paradox acquires much more importance when, as happens today, the normative reference to the notion of the person spreads like wildfire to all the domains of our experience. From juridical language, which deems it the only thing able to give form to the otherwise ineffective imperative of human rights, to politics, that has long substituted it for the insufficiently universal concept of the citizen, to philosophy, which found in it a rare point of convergence between its analytical and its so-called continental components. In this sense, the appeal to the category of the person goes well beyond the personalist tradition, from Jacques Maritain (1882–1973) to Emmanuel Mounier (1905–50) to Paul Ricoeur, who deployed it in a variety of ways, to include post-Husserlian phenomenology (in particular, that of Edith Stein [1891–1942]), neo-Aristotelian ontology, and, finally, the Oxford philosophical school's research on personal identity. After all, the transversal character of that which is personal versus that which is not declared such is capable of linking even opposed ideological and cultural fronts, and is even more evident in the set of discourses recognized today on the horizon of bioethics. However much divided over everything – over the moment when life, qualified life, starts and when it finishes, and above all over whom its legitimate proprietor may be – laypersons and Catholics agree on its ontological supremacy. Whether human life acquires personhood at conception, as Catholics maintain, or only later, as laypersons argue, it is the symbolic threshold and, as such, it is declared sacred or at least intangible.

2

Before examining the antinomy that this causes, let us note the extraordinary success that makes the notion of the person one of the most privileged of keywords – equalled only by democracy, perhaps – in our conceptual lexicon. Meanwhile, at its root there is an uncommon semantic richness, due to its triple matrix of theological, juridical and philosophical character. But to this first, as it were intrinsic, reason, a second, perhaps even more cogent, historical reason may be added. It can be no surprise that the language of the person knew a moment of distinctive growth at the end of the Second World War to such an extent that it became the linchpin of the 1948 Universal Declaration of Human Rights. This was a reaction to the attempt made by the Nazi regime to reduce human being to its naked, somatic component, which however it interpreted in a violently racist key. Without establishing any direct filiation, such a political ideology, or better, political biology, constituted the paroxysmal point of fulfilment, and at the same time, the fatal twisting of a cultural strand that differs from, and is also an alternative to, the prevailing line of modernity's philosophico-political tradition, a strand we may define as 'biopolitical'. If the tradition had located thought and political action's centre of gravity in the free and rational nucleus of human existence, already from the beginning of the nineteenth century another thread of thought tended to valorize the unthinking corporeal element that constitutes its deep and unavoidable substrate. At its origin we can place the clear distinction made by the great French physiologist, Xavier Bichat (1771–1802), between a vegetative, unconscious life and another cerebral, rational type inside of every living thing. When a succession of authors, such as Arthur Schopenhauer, Auguste Comte and August Schleicher (1821–68), would translate the biological researches of Bichat into different registers – philosophical, sociological and linguistic, respectively – variously maintaining the primacy of unconscious life over conscious life, they would open the door to a mode of thought that radically disputes the philosophical and political primacy of the component that is subjective, indeed, personal.

This mode of thought maintains that political organization depends, not on the voluntary and rational choice of individuals united in a foundational pact, but on the inextricable knot of strengths and instincts that are innervated in the individual body, and even more, in the ethnically determined traits of different populations. This cultural current was sustained first by comparative anthropology and later, from the second half of the century on, by a Social Darwinism that was inspired by hierarchy and exclusion. Naturally, for it to encounter the Nazis' murderous racism, a series of non-linear transfers, impossible to reconstruct here, were necessary. The most relevant is the displacement of the 'double life' principle from the level of the single, living individual, where Bichat had located it, to the entire human species, which was thus divided by thresholds, with different values assigned to them, between one zone for human characteristics and another, assimilable to the nature of beasts. In this way the animal was to become, rather than our common progenitor, that which violently divides man from himself, consigning a section of humanity to death in the same moment that it assigns another section of it to qualified life. It was this moment, in the thanatopolitical reversal of the biopolitical tradition, that determined a catastrophic turning point in the idea, and above all, in the practice, of politics, and the notion of the person was the first victim: rather than being inhabited by a spiritual nucleus that renders it intangible, the human body, now coinciding only with itself and with its own racial code, could be entrusted to surgery *en masse* in the extermination camps.

3

This is the lethal drift that the philosophy of the person opposed in the aftermath of the Second World War. Against an ideology that had reduced the human body to its hereditary bloodline, this philosophy intends to recompose the unity of human nature by reaffirming that its character is irreducibly personal. However, such a reunification of the life of the body and the life of the mind turned out to be difficult to achieve, because it subtly contradicts the category designated to realize it: the category of the person. Here is where the antinomies have been lying in wait since the beginning, continuously distancing the first goal proposed by the Declaration of

1948, that is to say, the effectuation of human rights valid for everyone. In fact, these rights remained largely unheard of for an entire part of the world's population, still exposed to poverty, hunger and death. Without calling into question the subjective commitment of the authors of the Declaration or that of all their personalist heirs, the underlying problem relates to something we have hinted at already, the separating and reifying apparatus implicit in the very notion of the person.

To recognize this apparatus, its genesis and its effects, it is necessary to go back to its roots in the juridical and philosophical. What gives them a common logical structure, despite the obvious differences in their vocabularies and intentions, is an insoluble and contradictory combination of unity and separation, in the sense that the very definition of that which is personal, in the human race or in the single human, presupposes an impersonal or less than personal zone, from which the former draws its importance. In sum, as the biopolitical current inscribes the behaviour of man in the density of his somatic nature, so too the personalist conception, rather than contesting the absolute prevalence of the body over the rational–spiritual element, limits itself to reversing the relation in favour of the latter.

4

The Christian tradition, both in Trinitarian dogma and in the doctrine of Christ's double nature, not only locates unity in the framework of distinction – in the first case, between persons, in the second, between the same person's differing substances – but also presupposes the fixed primacy of the spirit over the body. It is difficult to measure with precision the influences, probably reciprocal, that, in terms of the concept of the person, connect the first dogmatic Christian formulations and the Roman juridical conception. It is a fact that the theological dualism of soul and body (in turn, of mediated Platonic derivation) assumes an even more cogent sense in the distinction, presupposed in all Roman law, between human and person. In Rome, *persona* not only does not coincide with *homo* (a term frequently used to identify slaves), but also constitutes the device used to divide mankind into well-defined categories and rigidly subordinates some of them to others. On one hand, the *summa divisio de iure personarum*, framed by Gaius and reformulated in the Justinian *Institutiones*, includes every type of man, including slaves, who are technically assimilated to the regime of the thing. On the other, it operates by means of successive, linked divisions, initially between *servi* and *liberi*, and then within the latter term, between *ingenui* and *liberti*, divisions that have the task of setting human beings in a condition defined by reciprocal hierarchical difference. Within this juridical mechanism, which unifies men through their separation, only the *patres*, that is to say, those who have the faculty of ownership on the basis of their triple status as free men, Roman citizens and individuals who are not dependent on others (*sui iuris*), turn out to be *personae* in the full sense of the term. Meanwhile, all the others, situated on a scale of descending value from wives, to children, to creditors, down to slaves, are located in an intermediate zone that continually oscillates between person and non-person or, more bluntly, the thing: *res vocalis*, the tool with the ability to talk, is how the *servus* is actually defined.

To get to the bottom of this apparatus's functioning we do not need to fix our attention on only the distinction, or even the opposition, that in this way comes to distinguish between different types of human beings, some placed in positions of privilege, others crushed in a regime of absolute dependence, but more so on the consequential relationship that passes between the one situation and the other: to be able to rightfully fall within the category of person one must have power, not only over one's possessions, but also over certain beings, themselves reduced to the dimension of the possessed object. The fact that this holds true even for children, and thus for every human being on his or her birth certificate, on which, at least in archaic law, is borne the law of life and death on the part of the father, therefore authorized to sell him, lend him, abandon him, if not to kill him, means that no one in Rome possesses the qualification of person throughout the course of his entire life. Some can acquire it, others are by principle excluded, while the majority pass through it, entering it or exiting it according to the wishes of the *patres*, as codified in the performative rituals of the *manumissio* and the *emancipatio*, which regulate the passage from the state of liberty to slavery and vice versa.

From this perspective, the Roman apparatus of the person clarifies not only the role of a certain juridical figure, but also something that pertains to the general functioning of law, that is to say, the power to include by means of exclusion. As far as it can be enlarged, the category of those who enjoy a certain right is defined only by contrast with those who, not falling within it, are excluded from it. If it belonged to everyone, like a biological characteristic, language or the ability to walk, for example, a right would not be a right, but simply a fact with no need for specific juridical denomination. In the same way, if the category of person coincided with that of human being, there would have been no need for it. Ever since its original judicial performance, personhood is valuable exactly to the extent to which it is not applicable to all, and finds its meaning precisely in the principled difference between those to whom it is, from time to time, attributed and those to whom it is not, or from whom, at a certain point, it is subtracted. Only if there are men (and women) who are not completely, or not at all, considered persons, can others be or become such. From this point of view, to return to the paradox we began with, the process of personalization coincides, looking from the other side of the mirror, with the depersonalization or reification of others. In Rome, *persona* means whoever can reduce others to the condition of the thing. Just as, correspondingly, a man can be pushed into the status of the thing only in the presence of an other who is proclaimed to be a person.

Subjected subjects

1

For a very long period, lasting essentially until Leibniz, the meaning of the word *subiectum* is not dissimilar to what today we usually define as an 'object'. Indeed, beginning with Aristotle, this designates something like a support or substrate of essential or accidental qualities equipped with a receptive capacity: thus the exact opposite of a mental reality, that is, an agent of thought and action. From this point of view the subject, in the ancient and medieval sense, not only does not oppose the object, like the perceiver and the perceived, or like the inside and outside of a sphere, but is from the start taken in the sense of 'subject to', rather than of 'subject of'. Now this is precisely the point of convergence where the philosophical definition of the subject intersects with Roman juridical semantics, although modern juridical semantics is totally incapable of assimilating this due to its preoccupation with an objectivist notion of law. A passage by Gaius (*Institutiones*, I, 48) confirms this in a form that reintroduces the relationship to the category of the person: '*Quaedam personae sui iuris sunt, quaedam alieno iuris subiectae sunt.*' With this proposition, Gaius intends to say that in Rome some, properly defined people, are endowed with their own statute, while others are submitted to an external power. *Subiecti*, in this case, has the modern meaning of 'subjected' (*assoggettati*), from which the term 'citizen subjects' (*sudditi*) was derived during the formation of the absolutist States: unlike slaves, citizen subjects consciously agree to obey the sovereign power that renders them such.

Here we have already exposed that dialectic, elaborated analytically above all by Michel Foucault, between subjectivity and subjection, which takes us back by another route to what we defined as the apparatus of the person. It is as if this dialectic, at a certain point, incorporated the difference, and also the contrast, between the traditional passive meaning of *subiectum* and the nascent active meaning of *subiectus*. We may say that, inside every living being, the person is the subject destined to subject the part of himself not endowed with rational characteristics, which means the corporeal, the animal. When Descartes, who also had yet to inaugurate the modern semantics of the ego in the transcendental sense, contrasts *res cogitans* and *res extensa*, likening the mental sphere to the former, and the body to the latter, he reproduces, from yet another angle, the same effect of separation and of dominance that we have already individuated in the theological and juridical logic of the person. At that point, not even the passage initiated by Locke and brought to completion by Hume, of the concept of the person from the sphere of substance to that of function, will be able to change things. Personal identity continues to reside in the mind, in the memory, or in a simple, subjective autorepresentation, and its qualitative difference from the very body in which it is installed is increasingly accentuated.

2

The relationship between subjectivity and subjection, implicit in the juridical and philosophical declension of the person, was rendered quite transparent by Hobbes through his decisive transposition of its apparatus on the terrain of politics. This passage, oriented by the absolute foundation of sovereignty, occurs along two argumentative trajectories that at a certain point intersect in a similar effect of separation. The first concerns the disjunctive relationship between 'natural people' and 'artificial people'. While the first autorepresent themselves using their own words and actions, the latter represent the actions and words of another subject, or even of another non–human entity. As always happens in Hobbes, the logical conclusion entailed turns out to disrupt the preceding tradition: not only does the insoluble relationship inside every human being that forever held the physical body in relation with the 'mask' that it wore – that is to say, with the juridical qualification that was from time to time attributed to it – fail, but even the necessarily human character of the person is revoked. If the juridical constitution of a person is nothing other than its function of representation, this qualification can be granted to collective associations, too, and to entities of varied character such as a bridge, a hospital or a church. Hence the rupture, by now complete, with the biological referent, from the moment that the representative mechanism allows, or rather foresees, the material absence of the represented subject. And even the logical primacy, asserted by Hobbes, of the artificial over the natural person.

But the even more meaningful element in the dialectic of personalization and depersonalization, to which we have often referred, is that, in the Hobbesian analytical system, not only can things be transformed into persons, but persons can also be pushed towards the dimension of the thing. This happens at the crucial moment in which we pass from the state of nature to the civil state, when the Person destined to represent all the others enters the scene, that is to say, the sovereign, understood as the unity of all 'in one and the same person' (Hobbes 1999: 118). Elsewhere defined as the 'soul' of the body constituted by the subjects (*sudditi*), on one hand, this soul transforms them from simple living beings into personal subjects (*soggetti*) capable, at least once, of deciding their own condition. On the other hand, and at the same time, it totally deprives them of personal autonomy, incorporating the rights that they had in the state of nature in exchange for the protection of their life. From that moment on the sovereign is the only one who can legitimately represent them, and thus, the only one who can technically define himself as a person. This process, bifurcated by the acquisition and confiscation of political personhood, finds its own epicentre in the paradigm of authorization, where each person authorizes the sovereign person, aptly defined by the ancient theatrical term, actor, to represent him. From that moment on not only is every person placed under the imperative of their own subjection (*sudditanza*), but, as the author of it, they may not even complain should they suffer an injustice, which is also the case due to the only criteria for defining that which is just being provided by the same sovereign. The fact, then, that this subjection concerns the public sphere of the citizen and not the private sphere of the human proves, from another point of view, how the mechanism of the person cannot function without dividing the unity of the living being in two: if the person has lost his own body, the body, in its turn, will not recover its own person (*persona*).

3

It is the emancipation from the corporeal substrate that indisputably makes the body the property of the person who inhabits it and in no way coincides with it.

For both Locke and Mill, the person, not by being but rather by having a body, is its sole proprietor, and is authorized, therefore, to use it as it pleases. Our starting point, the paradox of a subject that can only express its personhood (*qualità personale*) by objectifying itself returns, breaks down into a fully human, because rational, moral and spiritual nucleus, and an animal, or even objectal (*oggettuale*), stratum, exposed to the absolute discretion of the former. The culmination of this parabola is singularly close, in its extreme results, to the negative biopolitics that it, too, starts by rejecting, and is recognizable in the bioethics, liberal according to its own self-definition, that finds its greatest representatives in Peter Singer and Hugo Engelhardt. For both of them, not only are all human beings not persons – since no small portion of them are situated in a descending ladder that goes from the quasi-person or infant, to the semi-person or old man, to the non-person or patient in a vegetative state, to the anti-person, represented by the mad man, but what matters even more is that all of them are exposed to their custodians' right of life and death over them, on the basis of social, and even economic, considerations. Nor is it a coincidence that Engelhardt, in particular, deduces such conclusions from an explicit comparison with the *ius personarum* of Gaius. As a captured wild animal is the hunter's prey, so too is the defective child or the almost incurable old man 'under the hand' of his or her custodian, who is legitimately free to keep him alive or to abandon him to death. Once again, the apparatus of personhood reveals itself as a terrible thing that, separating life from itself, can always push it into a zone of indistinction with its opposite.

For a philosophy of the impersonal

1

If these are the results of the personalist paradigm, the least that one can say of it is that it did not succeed in welding spirit and flesh, reason and body, right and life, into a single block of meaning. Despite the constructive intention and the meritorious commitment of its many interpreters, at the very moment it predicates the equal dignity of every human being, this paradigm is unable to erase the thresholds with which it divides them. It can only move them, or redefine them, on the basis of historical, political or social circumstances. And this is because the very category of the person is constituted around a diaphragm that, ever since its original theatrical meaning, separates it from even the face that wears it. The same principled contrast with the biopolitical perspective needs to be reread in light of this antinomy, not to dissolve it, but to transpose its terms to a different logic. That Nazi thanatopolitics brought the primacy of the ethnic body to an apocalyptic point of no return, as opposed to what a long and glorious tradition had defined as the person, does not entail that we should, or even that we could, return to this tradition as though nothing had happened. After the two world wars the modern conceptual lexicon, so strongly imbued with theologico-political categories, can no longer untie the knots tightening around us on all sides. This implies neither refusing it *en masse*, nor in its single segments, such as the person, but inscribing them in a horizon from which their most glaring contradictions may finally come to light, rendering possible, and necessary, the opening of new spaces for thought.

Nietzsche, from a position that today is certainly impossible to assume in its entirety, had already understood the irreversible decline of this lexicon, refusing its traditional dichotomies, starting with the metaphysical separation of soul and body. Maintaining that the mind, or soul, is an integral part of an organism that has the body as its only expression, he breaks decisively with the apparatus of personhood. After two millennia of Christian and Roman tradition it is impossible for him to continue to separate the unity of the living being in two juxtaposed, and superimposed, strata, one spiritual and the other animal. The animal side, understood as both the pre-individual and post-individual element of human nature, is not our ancestral past, but rather our richest future. That Nietzsche would subsequently confer a highly problematic declension to such intuitions, pushed by his self-appointed inheritors in a racist direction where he had never intended to head, does not revoke the explosive force in question. Affirming, as in fact he did, his desire to reread all of European history with 'the guiding thread of the body' meant inscribing his discourse in an expressly biopolitical frame with an awareness that until then no one else had demonstrated. Against every spiritualism, old and new, and with a categorical apparatus system profoundly marked by the Darwinian turning point (more than he himself was willing to recognize), what he grasped was the essential link between politics and biological life. When, using the ambiguous formula of the will to power, he recognized that politics, like knowledge, too, always has something to do with the body, Nietzsche foresaw something that only today is obvious to everyone. Namely, that at the centre of present and future conflicts there would not only be a different distribution of power, and not even the choice of the best regime or the best political party, but rather, and foremost, the definition of what human life is today and what it may become tomorrow. Whatever the meaning that he gave to the expression 'great politics' was, clearly this implied a total deconstruction of the paradigm of the person, which was fully involved in the crisis of the double tradition, theological and juridical, whence it derived. If, as opposed to the vital powers that traverse and constitute it, a preformed individual subject does not exist; if the system of law, with its promise of equitable distribution, does nothing but express and sanction, and thus legitimize, the result, at times provisory, of relationships of force arising from past clashes; if even the institution of the State, as is thought by theorists of sovereignty, is nothing but a prophylactic envelope destined, not so much to protect, as to subject (*assoggettare*) its own subjects (*sudditi*) to an order that sometimes contrasts with their own interests. If all this is true, then the relationship between humans must be submitted to a process of radical revision that the modern political dictionary is completely incapable of putting into focus.

2

The second powerful deconstruction of the paradigm of the person is owed to the work of Freud. If this is recognized in the presupposed primacy of the rational and voluntary choice of the subject agent, it is all too evident that the importance assigned by the father of psychoanalysis to what he would define as the unconscious constitutes a radical rebuttal. But what must be underlined is the precocity of his critical intention, already operating in his 1901 essay, *The Psychopathology of Everyday Life*. The writing revolves entirely around the dialectic between the person and the impersonal in a form that makes one simultaneously the content and the negation of the other. It is no accident that the book opens with the phenomenon of forgetting personal names and substituting them with others that have the function of covering something that disturbs the subject in question to the extent of finally causing him to lose the memory of all proper nouns. Here the loss clearly concerns, even before the noun or the nouns, the 'proper' as such: the self-presence of he who, in order to escape the pressure of the disturbing thing, is struck by an amnesia that dispossesses him of his own mnemonic capability, entrusting it to an alien power. The conclusion that Freud draws from this identifies the impersonal ground of what we usually define as personality in a vertiginous exchange between identity and alterity, the proper and the extraneous: 'It is as if I were obliged to compare everything I hear about other people with myself; as if my personal complexes were put on the alert whenever another person is brought into my notice' (Freud 1966: 24). The element that characterizes daily experience lies in the enigmatic overlap between the person and the impersonal determined in everyday life. In this sense, the book's title, *The Psychopathology of the Everyday Life*, needs to be taken literally. That everyday life is the subject, not simply the frame or the background, of the psyche's pathology implies that every preceding or ulterior subjective figure gives way to the event that it lives, or rather, by which it is lived, and which it can never appropriate. The episodes that Freud's text recounts in such detail are not the acts, realized or failed, of a personal subject, but anonymous pieces of life that always fall short of, or lie beyond, the person. In fact, what is missing is not the act, but the one – that is, the conscious intention of the one – who brings it into being, which is always traversed, and disfigured, by its own negative. Each person, sick or healthy, is invested with a psychic current that is heterogeneous to it and disturbs its behaviour. The even more meaningful element of the analysis is that this heterogeneity, far from being external, emerges from the same unconscious ground that gives rise to consciousness. As Freud himself would explain elsewhere, what is disturbing is not what opposes us, but the folding onto itself of that with which we have always been most familiar. Of course, not all of Freud's work follows this deconstructive line. And yet, the theoretical passage into the enclosure of what modern philosophy sequestered within the apparently impassable borders of the personal subject, is almost open.

3

Simone Weil is the one who decisively penetrated its interior. One is struck by the clarity of her position during the last years of the war, the Nazi defeat already foretold, at the very moment when Maritain and Mounier rally the European

intelligentsia around the banner of a new personalism. When she, in the most absolute solitude, finds the courage to write: 'the notion of rights [*droit*], by its own
mediocrity, leads on naturally to that of the person, for rights [*droit*] are related to
personal things', she grasps the issue's central point: person and right (*diritto*), in the
seductive formula of the right of the person, are welded together in a doubled
distancing from the community of humans and from each of their bodies (Weil
2000: 64). As for the first, this is attainable only by a justice capable of putting the
commitment of obligation towards others, the law of the *munus*, ahead of the
claiming of determined prerogatives. It certainly cannot be achieved by a juridical
apparatus that functions by excluding those who remain outside of its categories,
beginning with the category of the person, which is only apparently universal. The
critical reference to Roman history, compared with Nazism with obvious hermeneutic forcing, needs to be situated in this line of thought. It is precisely in Roman
civilization that the law is indissolubly linked to the possession of people reduced
to things. The original distinction between free men and slaves, specified from the
beginning by the *ius personarum*, is the architrave where Roman power rests, a figure of exclusion that, despite profound discontinuities, seems to return, always in
different modalities, to characterize the history of the West. But Weil's challenge to
the category of person does not end here. To maintain, as the author does, that 'So
far from being his person, what is sacred in a human being, is the impersonal in
him' seems to inaugurate a radically new discourse, and for the moment we cannot
help but sense its urgency, even if we are still unable to define its contours (ibid.:
54). Part of it is, in any case, already recognizable in Weil's analysis. In particular, in
a passage that concerns the two faces of the relationship between body and person,
the sovereign dominion of the latter over the former, and the indifference that the
ideology of the person reserves for the sufferings of the body and of bodies unpro-
tected by this qualification, she argues,

> I see a passerby on the street. He has long arms, blue eyes, and a mind whose
> thoughts I do not know, but perhaps they are commonplace. . . . If it were
> the human personality in him that was sacred for me, I could easily put out
> his eyes. As a blind man he would be exactly as much a human personality
> as he was before. I should not have touched the person in him at all. I should
> have destroyed nothing but his eyes.
>
> (Weil 2000: 50–1)

What these sentences delineate, and what their inverse or affirmative side assumes,
is the possible and necessary detachment of right and person. What should be
thought is a right thus oriented towards justice, not of the person, but of the body,
of all bodies and of every body taken individually. Only if rights, as pompously as
uselessly called 'human', were to adhere to the bodies, drawing from them their
own norms, no longer the transcendental type, fallen from on high, but immanent
to the infinitely multiple movement of life, only in this case would they speak with
the intransigent voice of justice. Then even a body, artificially fed or kept alive

without hope, that can no longer bear to suffer uselessly, could claim the last of its rights, escaping from the irrevocable decrees of the person.

4

If in reflections on justice the reference to the impersonal is still confined to being the inverse of the person, for some time it has constituted the semantic horizon of great literature, as it does for all contemporary art, from non-figurative painting to dodecaphonic music, to cinema. When Maurice Blanchot asserts: 'to write is to pass from "I" to "he/it [*il*]"', invoking the figure of the 'neutral' that subtends, like an elusive margin, his entire oeuvre, he is referring to precisely that underground movement which displaces the nineteenth-century literary experience towards the harbourless land of the impersonal (Blanchot 1993: 380). There, in its most extreme trials, what is at stake is something of a 'relation of the third kind' as the author puts it, situated well beyond the dialogical relationship and even beyond any form of verbal interaction between characters endowed with a stable consistency. From a certain moment on, between the end of the nineteenth century and the beginning of the next, none of these, and even what is termed the narrative voice, would retain the capacity, or the intention, to say, 'I', to speak in the first person, addressing a second, ultimately specular, person. What characterizes all of them, emptying them of their traditional subjective characteristics, is that passage to the third person to which Emile Benveniste had assigned the peculiar role of the 'non-person', or precisely, the impersonal, in the pronominal system of the Indo-European language.

Already the first, and most famous, character 'without qualities', that is to say, Robert Musil's Ulrich, had claimed: 'What with laws being the most impersonal thing in the world, the personality becomes no more than the imaginary meeting point of all that's impersonal' (Musil 1995: 516). What he meant to say is well known: since the subjective unity of persons failed, exploded into a thousand fragments, so much so that, with a few years' distance, we are at times more similar to another than we are to ourselves, the world in which we move escapes from our control and from our ability to intervene in order to position ourselves on trajectories the origin and results of which are unknowable. Naturally this dislocation has precise consequences, not only on the ethical, but also on the juridical plane: once what a valorous tradition defined as the person, equipped as such with moral reason and with freedom of choice, was called into question, the delicate problem of the imputability of action was opened, and thus, the problem of the agent's responsibility. But precisely because it is not imputable to anyone, and situated at the point of convergence between pure contingency and pure necessity, action offered Musil the possibility of experiencing absolute perfection.

Later, for Kafka, the impersonal is no longer an option to be adopted, but the general form within which every choice is inevitably subtracted and expropriated from us. In this case, the neutral is not understood as something that occupies the place of the person, not even as its exterior inverse. It is that which, while severing every relation between author and text, giving the story the impenetrable character of absolute objectivity, puts every character, by now no longer definable as such since they are deprived of any fragment of subjectivity, in a relationship of non-identification with themselves. From this point of view, not only have the pre-emptively disfigured figures that move without direction or goal in Kafka's texts lost the power to determine what happens to them, but also what happens is nothing other than the inexorable repetition of that which has been happening all along. The source of the problem's impression of insurmountability is that they believe it lies before them, when it is actually always behind them. People cannot realize this, because they do not have memory, necessarily linked to a certain principle of personal identity, and they perceive only indirectly what they are or are not. But they grasp, opaquely, that in such an absence of transparency, in the destitution of their own subjective consciousness, it is best to gamble their only possible destination, the possibility, if not of redemption, at least of having, or better, being, a destiny. In any case, Kafka's texts certify that it is no longer permitted, nor would it make sense, to pass back through the mirror – to re-enter that same world of rational subjects and of shared values that started the machination that grips us now.

5

Even if one cannot say that the collective vision of twentieth-century philosophy was as profound as that of its literature, at least one of its most innovative veins found itself productively contaminated. I refer to the frayed line from Henri Bergson to Gilles Deleuze, through Maurice Merleau-Ponty, Gilbert Simondon, Georges Canguilhem and Foucault himself, which thought human experience, not in the transcendental prism of the individual consciousness, but in the indivisible density of life. For all of them, despite profound differences in approach and vocabulary, what we call the subject, or person, is nothing but the result, always provisory, of a process of individuation or subjectification, quite irreducible to the individual and his masks. Nevertheless, to identify this process with the first or second of these terms, individuation or subjection, is not a matter of indifference for the direction that the discourse intends to assume. In both cases what is at stake is a radical criticism of the category of person and of the separating effect it inscribes in the configuration of the human being. And in both cases this criticism is conducted with the paradigm of life understood in its specifically biological dimension as its point of departure. But if in Deleuze, in accordance with his Bergsonian genealogy, life relates only to itself, on its own plane of immanence, in Foucault it is grasped in the dialectic of subjection and resistance in relation to power. While in the first case the result is a sort of philosophical affirmation of life, much more radical than the philosophies of life that marked the first decades of the twentieth century from variously historicist, phenomenological or existentialist viewpoints, the latter delineates the sharpest profile of what has been given the demanding name of biopolitics. What remains to be considered is the possible conjunction of these two trajectories in something that could become an affirmative biopolitics, no longer defined by power over life, such as the last century knew in all its tonalities, but of a power of life.

At its centre, but also at its extremes, there can be nothing but a clear distancing from the hierarchical and exclusionary apparatus of the category of the person, in any of its declensions, theological, juridical or philosophical. Both the Deleuzian notion of immanence and the Foucauldian notion of resistance move in this direction: a life that coincides to the very last with its simple mode of being, with its being such as it is, a life that is precisely, 'a life', singular and impersonal, and cannot but resist whatever power, or knowledge, is arranged to divide it into two reciprocally subordinated zones. This does not mean that such a life would not be analysable by knowledge, without which, after all, it would remain muted or indistinct, or irreducible to power, but life in a modality capable of modifying both, transforming them on the basis of its own requirements, producing, in turn, new knowledge and new power as a function of its own quantitative and qualitative expansion. This possibility, but we could certainly just as well say this necessity, is rendered clear in the double relationship that connects life to right (*diritto*) on one side and to technology (*tecnica*) on the other. In no case is a loosening of the millennial knot that history has tied between these terms imaginable. What a biopolitics that is finally affirmative can and must signal is, rather, the reversal of their relations of force. It cannot be law (*diritto*), the ancient *ius personarum*, that imposes its laws from without and from on high on a life separated from itself; but both the corporeal and immaterial grain of life must make its own norms the law's constant reference, always increasing its consistency with the needs of all and of each. The same applies to technology, which has become in this third millennium the most direct interlocutor of our bodies: of their birth, their health and their death. Against a nineteenth-century tradition that saw in technology an extreme risk from which the specificity of the human being needed to be saved – by covering it with the enigmatic mask of the person – we need to make it functional for a new alliance between the life of the individual and the life of the species.

Bibliography

Amato, P. (ed.) (2004) *La Biopolitica*. Milan: Mimesis.

Bazzicalupo, L. (2006) *Biopolitica e bioeconomia*. Rome–Bari: Laterza.

Bazzicalupo, L. (ed.) (2008) *Impersonale*. Milan: Mimesis.

Blanchot, M. (1993) *The Infinite Conversation*. Trans. Susan Anderson. Minneapolis: University of Minnesota Press.

Bodei, R. (2002) *Destini personali*. Milan: Sansoni.

Cutro, A. (ed.) (2005) *Biopolitica*. Verona: Ombre Corte.

Esposito, R. (2007) *Terza persona. Politica della vita e filosofia dell'impersonale*. Turin: Einaudi.

Esposito, R. (2008) *Bíos: Biopolitics and Philosophy*. Trans. Timothy Campbell. Minneapolis: University of Minnesota Press.

Freud, S. (1966) *The Psychopathology of Everyday Life*. Trans. James Strachey. New York: Norton.

Hobbes, T. (1999) *Leviathan*. Trans. Rod Hay. Hamilton, Ont.: McMaster University Archive.

Maritain, J. (1943) *The Rights of Man and Natural Law*. Trans. Doris Anderson. New York: Charles Scribner's Sons.

Marzocca, O. (ed.) (2006) *Lessico di biopolitica*. Rome: Mimesis.

Montani, P. (2007) 'Filosofia politica' *Bioestetica*. Rome: Carocci.

Musil, R. (1995) *The Man Without Qualities*. Trans. Sophie Wilkins. New York: A.A. Knopf.

Rodotà, S. (2006) *La vita e le regole*. Milan: Feltrinelli.

Weil, S. (2000) *Simone Weil: An Anthology*. Ed. Siân Miles. New York: Grove Press.

PART V

Renewing the aesthetic

15

THE WRONG TURN OF AESTHETICS

Henry Staten

In its original use, the word *art* refers not to artworks but to the skill and know-how by means of which artworks are made. The phrase 'work of art' testifies to the primacy of this use; a work *of* art is a thing that has been made by art, an 'artefact'. In contemporary usage, however, the sense of art as know-how has been thrown into the background; most of the time, in most contexts, we hear 'art' as referring to art's products. This shift makes the question 'what is art?' (asked as one looks at a painting, or Duchamp's urinal) an endlessly tantalizing riddle rooted in mystery. The decisive turn towards this modern mystification of art was taken by the Romantic theory of genius, according to which arthood is infused into the art product by the breath of the creator's inspiration. Romantic thought, however, never entirely forgot about art in the traditional sense; thus Kant, who gave the Romantic theory its most influential form, tortuously reconciled the old value of art as maker's knowledge, derived from previous models of art making, with the ascendant value of genius. But the last vestiges of regard for art as techne were erased in the modern notion, purportedly inspired by Duchamp, that art is basically conceptual – a matter of bestowing the name of art on an object, any object whatever, and framing it as such.

Duchamp's opening up of the notion of art to admit 'anything whatever' was supposed to be counter-institutional, a step away from the monumentalization of the masterwork and its creator and towards the democratization of art (de Duve 1996). But it has not worked out that way; rather, the old, mystified value of the art object has not only survived but flourished, as the new kinds of objects defined as art are shown in the same exhibition spaces, with the same price tags, as the old ones. And the process of mystification at the level of theory, with its continued fetishization of the art object, proceeds in combination with the evolution of the power of the art market.

Among the most culturally pernicious effects of this mystification is what the radical anthropological theorist Alfred Gell called the 'mismatch' between 'the spectator's internal awareness of his own powers as an agent' and the conception the spectator forms of 'the powers possessed by the artist' (Gell 1992: 53–4). No doubt we should be impressed by another human being's know-how that exceeds our own; but the more the nature of a know-how is hidden behind an ideological curtain, the more likely it is to stymie the spectator's sense of their own agency, and the more serviceable it becomes to the power interests to which art is so easily wed. By contrast, to the degree that the spectator learns *what art is* – productive know-how that human beings learn as they learn any other social practice, and which, like any other social practice, some people are better at than others, in large part thanks to a combination of hard work and favourable circumstances – the visible work loses its aura of mystery, and the cowing of the spectator by the feeling of mismatch correspondingly diminishes.

I

From the ancient Greeks and Romans, through the Middle Ages and Renaissance, down to Kant, the word art (along with those other words such as Kunst that we translate as art) refers primarily to the skill and know-how by which artworks are made. At the beginning of this entire historical sequence lies the Greek word techne; and the difficulties that arise in attempting to translate techne as 'art' alert us to the conceptual confusions that afflict our modern usage. The Greeks did not, in fact, have a word that can be adequately rendered by our word 'art', and trying to reconstruct our concept from the words they did use is not an easy matter.

In its narrowest focus, an investigation of 'the ancient Greek concept of art' would have to take into account at least three words/concepts – techne, poiesis and mimesis – that divide the field of our 'art' among them, but bring in other things that do not belong to this field. Poiesis means 'making' in general, whether of a 'fine art' or 'craft' variety, but by the fifth century BC, it had come to refer pre-eminently to one kind of making, that of the poet; thus when Aristotle says at the outset of *Poetics* that he will treat of 'the art of making', poietike, *as a whole and in its genres*, he is referring only to the poem-making art. Techne, the Greek word that is most commonly translated as 'art', by contrast, carried no such lustre, because down through the classical period, long after poiesis had glamorized and specialized its meaning, techne retained the sense of reference to productive knowledge in general, regardless of how low a type. The third term, mimesis, unlike poiesis and techne does not refer to making as such, but rather points to the function for which a certain subset of makings is designed, the function of 'representation'. Like poiesis and techne, mimesis refers to the act of the artist, in this case, the act of miming (not the mimetic object by which this act is carried out), but the set of what the Greeks defined as mimetic objects is pretty close to what in our culture has traditionally been thought of as fine art. Yet no one translates mimesis as art; it is almost exclusively techne that gets translated this way.

Because *art* in modern usage no longer means *techne*, the attempt to translate techne as art produces considerable confusion, in particular when we are given to understand, in the old, but still widely disseminated, translations by Benjamin Jowett or Lane Cooper, that Socrates in the *Ion* denies poetry the status of art. Since Socrates actually argues that poetry is divinely inspired, and therefore not like the techne of the fisherman or the charioteer (among others, but I choose the two lowliest to underline the point), for the naïve reader it can be misleading in the extreme to read in English that he is denying that poetry is art. Socrates is interested only in the question of *how poetry is brought about*; he means by 'art' (i.e. techne) neither art objects nor some higher power of art creation but the systematic, culturally acquired knowledge by means of which human beings organize their activity towards the achieving of an end; that is why he can cite fishing and charioteering as exemplars of real 'art'. Even through the obscurity created by the modern concept of art, careful reading of the dialogue reveals that this is indeed what he means; but one does have to cut through the obscurity.

The Greek notion of techne is in fact typical of the way in which 'art' is viewed in traditional, pre-industrial cultures, and continuous with the way in which, anthropologists tell us, it is viewed in indigenous cultures of the present day. In such cultures, according to Raymond Firth, 'Pleasure in deft arrangement of formal qualities is not absent. But it tends to find expression in technical judgment' (Firth 1992: 24). Anthropologists have tended to see this propensity for 'technical judgment' as too limited, and have tried to descry 'the same kind of aesthetic sensibilities and judgments' as those of 'Western peoples' behind the mere technical judgement of the indigene (Firth 1951: 156). There is in this a benevolent desire to dignify the natives by extending the mantle of aesthetics to them; but this desire may well, as Gell says, tell us more 'about our own ideology and its quasi-religious veneration of art objects as aesthetic talismans' (Gell 1998: 3) than it does about these other cultures. However that may be, when we learn to see art as techne we need no longer feel that the technical judgement of indigenes requires dignifying.

It is telling that, while the Western art-viewing public, including most of our anthropologists, is wedded to aesthetics, our *artists* are not. An artist cannot afford the theorist's or spectator's detachment from the technical processes by which art is made; thus, when an artist views the work of another artist, they tend to react in the way that Firth's indigenes do, with an 'expression of technical interest', because the artist thinks, first and foremost, in terms of their own knowledge and practice of art production. As an arrant non-artist, I remember being struck, and chastened, by this on my first visits to artists' studios. Artists are, as Paul Valéry said of himself, 'much more attentive to the formation or fabrication of works than to the works themselves' (Valéry 1958: 69).

II

But how *does* art get made? Is the nature of the art-making process any less mysterious and controversial than that of art objects? I have been promoting the notion of techne, and I have claimed that techne is related to Gell's concept of the 'technology' of art. The concept of art as techne is, however, only a thin cross section of the 'technology' of the total social process that Gell studied. Techne does not include, for example, the technology of magic that is involved in the making of a work like the canoe prows Gell analyzes; techne is only the part of the technology that is directly involved in the shaping of the work – the part involving tools, materials, the skilful wielding of the tools to shape the materials and, encompassing this entire ensemble, the knowledge that bears directly on skilful wielding, including, prominently, the idea of the kind of finished, organized object or state of affairs at which the demiourgos is aiming, based on a sense of what an excellent exemplar of the kind looks like.[1]

The most crucial fact about techne is that it is in the first instance a social, not an individual, possession, a practical knowledge that has been accumulated across generations within any given culture, and the individual's power to make something, whether a craft artefact or a fine art work, is a derived or delegated power that resides primarily in the art itself. We are, however, so inured to the idea that 'fine art', as opposed to craft work, requires a special, indefinable intervention on the part of the artist, that the definition of art as techne seems to leave out precisely the most essential thing about art. *Of course* in art of the traditional kind the artist must have a certain acquired art-making knowledge, which they use to hack away at the marble, *but* presiding over this skilled hacking away is something that critical analysis can point to but never pin down, and which is manifested in the particularity of the individual work – its grazia, je ne sais quoi or aura – and which cannot be the product of 'mere' techne.[2] To this way of thinking, it seems self-evident that the technology of art can produce only conventional, generic or, in Kant's formulation, 'mechanical' work.

Making war against this way of thinking, structuralism in its most polemical 'death of the author' phase posited all artworks from the lowest to the highest as the product of a strictly mechanical combinatory of pre-existing elements – a notion that had great appeal at the time for many of us who were sick of aesthetic mystery. The work done by the structuralists on the theory of art was, however, primarily negative; they did not produce a convincing new account of art as such and, in particular, none of them ever quite grasped art as techne. Instead, they paved the way to a general loss of interest (in departments of literature, and to a considerable degree in departments of art and music as well) in the specificity of the work of art, so that the study of art, in those venues at least, in the 1980s and well into the 1990s was dominated by larger questions of culture and the political. For anyone interested in the question of art 'as art', whether as product or as production, and not in leaving it behind, the structuralist 'death of the author' thus left the question of how art is made shrouded in deeper darkness than before. The question of art, in any sense of the term, is a question of value: either of where value resides in the art object or, in the techne view, the radically different question of how, out of the infinity of forms that can be mechanically generated, a particular individual in a particular concrete situation makes judgements of better and worse resulting in a work that is a candidate for appreciation as art by the relevant valuing community (see Dickie 1984). The structuralist combinatory generates an indiscriminate pro-liferation of forms; but how does an individual artist make the judgements of value that select the good ones out of this wilderness? Indiscriminate proliferation of forms does not produce Foucauldian carnival; well before structuralism, Jorge Luis Borges saw that the mechanical combinatory produces only the nightmare vision of the library of Babel.[3]

Borges's nightmare vision confirms the structuralist insight that something very far removed from the form-creating power of genius is the basis of the creative process, while alerting us to the fact that the structuralist combinatory cannot be the whole picture.

That *genius* cannot be the whole picture was already recognized by Kant, and in those same pages in which he argued that 'beautiful art is possible only as a product of genius' (Kant 2000: 186, §46). Even conscientious readers of Kant have had trouble recognizing just how fundamental, and how shocking, is the limitation that Kant places on the sovereignty of genius: genius as such does not and cannot produce the *form* of the finished art work, but only 'rich *material* [Stoff] for products of art'; left to itself, in the absence of the 'slow and painstaking', mechanical pursuit of form, genius produces 'nothing but nonsense' (ibid.: 197, §50). I underline: Kant says that *genius is not the origin of aesthetic form; genius as such produces nothing but nonsense.*

Coming from the diametrically opposite position, Kant arrives at the same impasse as Borges. The 'productive' faculty, whether genius or the universal combi-natory, cannot account for the crucial factor in art: the *form* of the individual work.

Kant proceeds to give a sober, and within its limits, entirely accurate account of the artistic work process by which the individual work acquires form; an account which, however, can be read as the soothing murmur of common sense:

> To give form to the product of beautiful art . . . requires merely taste, to which the artist, after he has practiced and corrected it by means of various examples of art or nature, holds up his work, and after many, often laborious attempts to satisfy it, finds the form that contents him.
>
> (Ibid.: 191, §48)

Who would deny (conceptual art aside) that the artistic idea must be actualized in resistant matter? This recognition remains compatible with the belief that genius remains the most important thing in art. The more or less 'materialist' concept of form that Kant evokes in the passage quoted above only occasionally glimmers in his discussion; the actual artwork, the sensible form, that is made by 'mechanical' art is, as such, merely a 'vehicle', a 'manner . . . of presentation' of a concept (ibid.: 191, §48). Genius remains the power by which art reaches the art-transcendent dimension; and this art-transcendent dimension is definitive of arthood (Zammito 1992: 129–47). In this way, the genuine, anxiety-provoking force of the notion that genius, left to itself, produces only formless Stoff and nonsense, appears to be papered over.

Yet Kant's radical insight into the limitations of genius remains. An innate, natural faculty, no matter how 'creative' in some notional sense it might be, cannot be the effective *origin of form* in art; and the formation of form is the fundamental question in the theory of art, the question that divides Romantic and humanistic accounts of art from techne-oriented or at least techne-compatible accounts. If, as Kant says, the origin of form is to be found in the work process guided by artistic techne, then it is techne itself that we must interrogate for insight into the mystery of art. If form cannot be brought forth by an innate faculty, then, as V. N. Vološinov said in his fundamental, and still today essential, critique of Romantic philosophy of language, 'all form comes from outside' – from the social outside, where form-giving technai are historically developed, stored up, and transmitted to individuals who then put them into action (Vološinov 1973: 83–98).

III

Once we have detached the question of the origin of form from that of its ineffable geistlich precedents, we can begin to refine our inquiry into the art-making process along lines suggested by Valéry in the following, much noticed, remarks:

> It takes two to invent anything. The one makes up the combinations; the other chooses, recognizes what he wishes and what is important to him in the mass of things that the former has imparted to him. What we call genius is much less the work of the first one than the readiness of the second one to grasp the value of what has been laid before him and to choose it.[4]

Valéry's formulation is in a clear line of descent from Kant's division of art making into two stages for which two distinct faculties are responsible, but he adds two decisive new articulations to this division.

First, Valéry suggests that the function of production and that of critical judgement are so distinct that they could be carried out by two distinct persons. This notion, which is devastating to traditional concepts of genius, is strongly validated by the case of the paradigmatic poem of modernism. As is well known, Eliot's original production that became *The Waste Land*, *He Do the Police in Different Voices*, was twice as long as the poem that resulted from Pound's intervention, and was, in Eliot's own judgement – a judgement that has never been seriously challenged – a formless mess. In despair, Eliot gave it to Pound, who cut out half of it, rearranged some, added hardly anything and amazed Eliot, and subsequently the world, with the result. Reading the facsimile of the original is a peek into the lumber room of creation; there are passages so bad that it is hard to imagine Eliot could not independently recognize their badness; but he did, fortunately, recognize that the whole thing was formless. *The Waste Land* is permanently ensconced in the modern canon, a work of genius if anything is, but who or what is the genius responsible for it as a successful aesthetic form?

Second, Valéry redefines the productive faculty as bringing forth not *formless material* but 'combinations', a term that throws us back (or ahead) onto structuralist ground. Valéry does not specify what the combinations are combinations of; but, since, on this model, the critical faculty's only power is the ability to recognize and choose the more valuable combinations among the mass of worthless or less valuable ones, they would necessarily have to be combinations of the constitutive elements of the art in question (words, sentences, metres and so forth in the case of poetry). Hence, the mass of combinations from which the critical faculty selects would constitute not an absolutely formless raw material but the protoforms of art. And this in turn implies that the agent or faculty that brings forth the combinations is one that already commands the elements of the art; which in turn presupposes that the agent involved has undergone the rigorous apprenticeship in the relevant art that is necessary to attain such command. On this account, then, the productive, 'creative' faculty itself is already not, as Kant held, a natural faculty that brings forth in a way that is independent of prior models and conventions, but a preliminary stage of the operation of techne; otherwise its materials cannot be *rich* for the imposing of final form.

In this preliminary stage, a skilled artist generates or identifies combinations that are more than nonsense but which, if they possess any value at all as art, do so only as a sort of proto-value or potential value, which the second faculty has to 'grasp' and 'choose' in order to actualize its potential. The proto-forms already possess potential value because they already possess form, qua combinations at their level of combination; let us say, in the example of *The Waste Land*, that the combination in question is a line of verse, which is on its face reasonably well-formed as a line. Now this line has to be integrated into a passage of verse, and if this is, on the face of it, successfully achieved, the line, which remains the same words in the same order as before, has moved up one level towards the realization of its potential value as a form. The final level of integration of combinations is the whole, finished poem, and it is on the basis of an anticipatory feeling around for this finished form that the critical faculty recognizes the (proto)value of the combinations which it selects from the mass of proto-forms. Now that I have introduced the notion of a *feeling around for the form of the whole* as the basis of the critical faculty, it becomes, perhaps, easier to swallow Valéry's claim that this is where genius resides; but, as Kant was sharply aware, form making 'is not a matter of inspiration or a free swing of the mental powers' (Kant 2000: 191, §48) but a matter of work that is informed by a knowledge of the techne in question.

The notion that this work is merely mechanical and cannot generate the new without the intervention of some higher power is a mere superstition, akin to the notion (to the shreds of which Kant still clings) that only a Designer could be responsible for the cunning forms of biological life. The true techne-standpoint on this issue is summed up sharply by Rilke, who, it should be noted, learned about techne in Rodin's studio. Rilke observes that 'In art, you can only stay within the "well done", and by your staying there, it increases and surpasses you again and again'. Even 'the "ultimate intuitions and insights"', according to Rilke, 'will only approach one who lives in his work and remains there' (Rilke 1985: 8). Art *increases and surpasses* the artist again and again when she stays within the limits of skilled practice. New rhythms are born out of old rhythms; new forms out of old forms;

this is the normal process that produces art from the most conventional to the most radical.

IV

It is, however, exceedingly difficult to put to rest the doubts concerning the account of art as techne. We are so much under the spell of Romanticism that it seems as though the *most essential thing* is being left out of this account; as though art were being 'reduced' to a simulacrum of itself. If the productive stage of which Valéry speaks is already informed by techne, does not this simply mean there must be another, more primordial stage behind this one at which the real work of 'creation' gets done? Yes, Homer was the heir of an ancient, highly sophisticated techne of poem making, but surely the emergence of the Homeric poems can only be explained in terms of the new, original inspiration that Homer brought to it! And in any case there must have been a proto-Homer who lived hundreds or thousands of years earlier and who started the whole poetry thing, and who had to do so without the benefit of a pre-existent techne. Doesn't Aristotle in the *Poetics* say so? The art of poetry, he says, started in 'improvisation'. And if the original proto-Homer could create out of nothing, then it follows that Homer could, too.

No doubt everything, traced back far enough, does originate in improvisation; the question is whether the product of pure improvisation is 'art'. (There are today, of course, various technai of improvisation, in which one can be trained, but these are not relevant here; I am using the term in its more innocent sense.) If we define art as techne, by definition, the only works of art are those produced by art; it is one of the main virtues of this definition that it renders the notion of artworks not *made by* art meaningless; the original proto-Homer, then, could by definition only create a sort of proto-art, and not even of the kind that counts as 'combinations' in Valéry's account. But is this a just definition? How are Mozart and Rimbaud possible on the techne hypothesis? How could 'Kubla Khan' have sprung full-blown out of Coleridge's head?

The answers are straightforward. When we systematically understand art as techne, prodigies like Mozart and Rimbaud, who might seem to be 'spontaneous artists', show up simply as early starters who devote themselves to their techne and master it like any other artist, only at an untypically early age, and with unusual aptitude; their works remain as much a product of techne as those of anyone else. There are mathematical prodigies who can perform enormously complex calculations intuitively, but it is inescapably the techne of *mathematics* that provides them with all the resources by which they produce their results; no amount of mathematical genius will produce an intuition of prime numbers in a culture that has not yet developed mathematics. Why, apart from our theology of art, should we think the case is any different with artists? Even if we did not know that Mozart's father was a well-known music pedagogue who gave his son intensive training from infancy, it is self-evident that the art of the symphony, at however early an age, or by whatever means Mozart might have picked it up, was painstakingly evolved over centuries by generations of musicians, and that Mozart had somehow to internalize this art in order to serve as the medium by which it could give birth to new creations. Mozart in a Neolithic tribe would have had not the slightest inkling even of the dodecaphonic scale, much less a symphony. As for the case of 'Kubla Khan': it is recognizably a very well done Romantic lyric, a poem that could not possibly have been written in the Renaissance or in the Romantic period by anyone who was not already a master of the technai of Romantic poetry. Neither how young the artist was nor how fast the work was done, whether consciously or unconsciously, proves anything at all about the nature of art.

There is, no doubt, a beginning in biology of the ability to create form; art, however, does not arise from some innate formative urge but from a long process of cultural evolution by means of which the form-bestowing powers of human beings are developed and enhanced in specific cultural traditions that across time accumulate the know-how required for this power. The form-bestowing power is coded by the long process of cultural evolution into the tools and know-how of social practices, from which it is picked up by individual practitioners (sometimes with uncanny aptitude, but there is a differential in aptitudes for all human practices) and without which, no matter how much aptitude they might have, they would be entirely helpless to bestow form.

V

It is true that well-informed scholars, whether formalists or contextualists, have always been aware of, and sometimes well informed about, the productive technai behind art works; but information about techne is commonly held in art discourse in a kind of colloidal suspension, along with particles of all sorts of other information (the artist's biography and psychology, the ideological factors involved in the production of art and so forth) from which only a rigorous theory of techne would be able to filter it.

As the concept of techne is, in a strong sense, *formalist* – the formal study of a highly specific slice of the evolution of social practices – nothing has interfered more with the development of the theory of techne, after the promising beginning made by the Russian Formalists, than the various confused notions of formalism that subsequently developed and which have cemented in the critical consciousness the notion that formalist method is concerned with the art object 'in itself', in static, empiricist isolation (Staten 2010). The Russian group clearly and consistently defined their object of investigation not as the 'verbal icon' but as the productive literary technology by means of which literary works are made. In recent decades, by contrast, the concern with the productive process has been relegated either to materialist approaches that range over the whole scale of social determinants of art-production, and fail to define the specific techne-aspect of this production, or to 'intentionalist' approaches that treat biographical persons as the primary agents of art and are in principle hostile to any kind of formalism, whether historical or not.

For techne formalism, as I have been arguing, form is the trace or index of the form-bestowing power/knowledge of art as techne. This know-how, when properly transmitted to new practitioners by a functioning techne-community, gives birth to individual art projects, which then give birth to particular works. Because the entire art project of an individual or collective artist-subject is the essential mediation between the level of 'tradition' (the techne as carried forth by a techne community) and that of the particular work, such a project is the basic unit of the study of techne. However, the specific techne-aspect of a specific art tradition, or of an individual artist's project as a whole, can be held consistently in view only if investigation works dialectically between, on one side, these higher levels of analysis and, on the other , precise formal analysis of individual works in the particularity of their forms as a whole. It is the very point of the technai we call art that they aim at works that are marked by particularity or, more precisely, by what Derek Attridge (2004) has called 'singularity', and the techne-oriented critic has to follow in the track of this aim.

As techne theory adopts the standpoint of the artist towards art making, despite its formalism, it is also in a sense intentionalist. But techne coincides with artist's intention only to the degree that artist's intention coincides with *it*. The fact that Kandinsky believed colours to be a mystical language, for example, and that this belief in some sense guided his painting practice, is no more relevant to the understanding of his art as techne than would be the belief that extraterrestrials were dictating his paintings to him. The techne of his paintings is that which can be analyzed and judged in relation to the techne of other contemporary abstract painters, to the history of the unfolding of his own painting practice as evidenced in his pictures and to the history of abstraction. Kandinsky himself, when he talked shop with other painters who did not share his beliefs about the colour-language, would have had to 'talk techne' with them in a way that was mutually intelligible, on pain of being thought a mere eccentric. Yeats's private symbolism is similarly irrelevant, or only marginally relevant, to the understanding of his art, and the failure to understand this has driven even very good critics to produce some startlingly obtuse readings of the poems.

VI

Both the interests and the competence of the critic or theorist differ from those of the artist; the theorist's toolbox and techne are transformations, not duplications, of the artist's; but these transformations should be based on as close a knowledge of the artist's toolbox and techne as possible, and would ideally involve training in the specific art involved, even when the critic has no intention of becoming an artist. At the limit I am speaking of the training of scholars, yet the ordinary viewer too would benefit from education, however limited, in the techne standpoint. Children should be taught the methods and materials of art not with an eye to unleashing their own creativity (something that, if they are equipped with the appropriate techne, will happen of itself, where there is any creativity to unleash), but as a flashlight into the penetralia of the mystery of art and thus as a way of cutting down to size the mismatch that Gell describes between the spectator's sense 'of his own powers as agent' and his sense of 'the powers of the artist'.

No doubt the ordinary spectator's enjoyment of art of a modern type is often clouded, not by the sense of her own feebleness as agent, compared with the genius of the artist, but by the opposite feeling, that she could do something this good, and that art is 'anything whatever', as long as it can somehow get certified by 'the artworld'. This kind of thinking was given philosophical respectability in the 1970s and 1980s by Arthur Danto (1964, 1981), who argued, initially on the basis of his experience of Warhol's Brillo Box, that, given two or more perceptually indistinguishable objects, one might be art and the other not. Thus, he concluded, there is nothing about the object itself that 'makes it art'. Arthood must, rather, be bestowed by some factor in the environing artworld – for example, a *theory* of art that declares A, but not (perceptually indistinguishable) B to be art.

Nothing better illustrates the conceptual havoc wrought by the focus on the art product than Danto's conundrum. *Of course*, there is nothing about the object itself that makes it 'art'. Only the fetishism of the art object – the abstraction of the perceptual experience of an art object, when framed as art by the artworld, from the productive process that brought it forth – would make one think so. Even if Danto's false assertion that Warhol's hand-crafted wooden box is perceptually indistinguishable from a manufactured Brillo carton were true, it would still remain that Warhol's box is of an entirely different type from the manufactured object because, regardless of how it looks, it was produced by an entirely different kind of techne – just as a copy of a Rembrandt perceptually indistinguishable from the original is an entirely different kind of object from a Rembrandt, because it is produced by the forger's, not the painter's, art (a fact that vividly illustrated by new methods of microscopic analysis showing that, among other things, forgeries have many more brush strokes than do originals).

The fact that Warhol's box is handcrafted does not, however, mean that it should be judged by the skill of hand it displays (any more than we judge a forgery, which can display tremendous skill of hand, in that way); the point, rather, is that the way this object was made is an essential clue to the kind of art making that Warhol was then engaged in and to the kind of intervention into the dialectic of forms in the artworld that it constituted within the overall logic of his art project.

Duchamp's 'Fountain', by contrast, manifests only in the most minimal way the intervention of an artist's hand, and none of these interventions is of a craft type. Thus 'Fountain', and the kind of neo-Dadaist work for which it and Duchamp's other readymades prepared the way, might seem to show that if art was ever techne, it is not anymore. But it is not at all clear that this is the case. As my discussion of Warhol has already indicated, the concept of techne is rooted in, but not limited to, the model of handicraft. Techne means both skill of hand and the knowledge that guides it; but the knowledge is the fundamental thing, and knowledge of one techne might guide other approaches to the making of works, including purely conceptual approaches. On the techne conception, an artist is one who practices a historically evolved (and perpetually mutating) techne or technai in a way that commands the respect of some significant subset of the community of its or their practitioners, *or that could, if brought to their attention, do so.* The fundamental, and fully evident, fact about the works of both Duchamp and Warhol is that their makers were consummate artists, not because they said they were or because the artworld so proclaimed them, but because of the way they shaped sustained, intensively pursued techne–projects that can only be understood as such in terms of the environing contexts of art practice. On the techne view, if they had worked in total obscurity they would, nonetheless, have been artists, and their works would have been works of art, not because of their intrinsic qualities but because of the deep art-cunning evidenced in the sustained art practices that brought them forth.

The 'neo-Dadaists' understood 'Fountain' as licensing the notion that 'anything whatever' can be baptized art by mere naming and framing; but this interpretation misses 'Fountain's' deep art-cunning because it takes the work out of the context of Duchamp's sustained art practice. Within this overall project, 'Fountain' has a significance that is quite limited compared to the exquisitely worked 'Large Glass', a work to which, having conceived it in 1912, 5 years earlier than 'Fountain', Duchamp devoted many preparatory studies and 11years, and which might, if Rhonda Roland Shearer is right, shed more light on 'Fountain' and the other purported 'readymades' than anyone had suspected. Based on meticulously detailed research into the physical characteristics of the presumptive urinal in the famous Stieglitz photograph, Shearer *et al.* (2004) argue that this object *never existed*, having been photographically 'composed' according to the principles of 'a single geometric system' – possibly the new and mathematically rigorous '"rehabilitated perspective" geometry Duchamp spoke about in interviews', and which is instantiated far more fully in the 'Large Glass'. Duchamp scholars have suggested that Shearer's research, if true, would impugn Duchamp's standing as an artist; from the techne standpoint, however, it would show Duchamp to be an even greater artist than anyone had thought.

To take the products of conceptual visual art and its analogues in other art genres at the value of the labels and frames that denominate them as 'art', and to fail to reinscribe them in the context of the specific techne-history from which they derive, is to enter a frictionless, zero-gravity realm in which we can only flail at the question of value. When art is defined as techne, and form as the result of work informed by techne, we jettison the notion, which continues to grip the imagination of our time, and which is at the root of our theology of art, that the authentic origin of artistically valuable form is something beyond culture; but we also reject the notion, formulated in reaction to this theologization of art, that the value of the work of art is a matter of some cultural formation's mere say-so. It remains true that there are better and worse artists, and some who are so good at what they do that they deserve to be awarded prizes and laurel wreaths and so forth.

This is not to deny that there is a much larger history within which techne itself, when it has been understood as such, must be reinscribed; and then a new, more sophisticated dialectic of analysis would be required, one in which we work back and forth between the formal elements of techne, as these elements are grasped in the final instance in formal analysis of individual works, and the formative action on these elements of historical forces that are not of a techne type. I claim for techne formalism only that *relative* autonomy that Leon Trotsky (1960: 178–80), in his famous attack on the Russian Formalists (still, in my view, the best brief statement of the relative claims of formalism and history), amply conceded.

Notes

1 Aristotle developed the fullest Greek articulation of the concept of techne, and my account here follows Aristotle's.
2 The ineffable quality of grazia is a product of Renaissance art theory; but the notion of art as techne was not thrown into the background until our own era, and it is this later, fuller development that I am referring to as the 'Romantic' theory.
3 That Borges is not a 'postmodernist' master of the 'play of the signifier' has been shown by the recent work of Díaz Pozueta (2007, 2009).
4 I do not know the precise source of this quotation, which has been widely reproduced based on the quotation in Hadamard (1945: 30). Hadamard says only that the passage appeared in the *Nouvelle Revue Française*.

Bibiliography

Attridge, D. (2004) *The Singularity of Literature*, London: Routledge.
Coote, J. and Shelton, A. (1992) *Anthropology, Art, and Aesthetics*, Oxford: Clarendon Press.
Danto, A. (1964) 'The Artworld', *Journal of Philosophy*, 61.19: 571–84.
Danto, A. (1981) *The Transfiguration of the Commonplace*, Cambridge, MA: Harvard University Press.
de Duve, T. (1996) *Kant after Duchamp*, Cambridge, MA: MIT Press.
Díaz Pozueta, M. (2007) *Image, Form, and Death: Borges's Anti-intellectual Project*, unpublished dissertation, University of Washington, DC.
Díaz Pozueta, M. (2009) 'From Idealism to Ideology in "Tlön, Uqbar, Orbis Tertius" and "Deutsches Requiem"', *CR: The New Centennial Review*, 9.3: 209–28.
Dickie, G. (1984) *The Art Circle: A Theory of Art*, New York: Haven.
Firth, R. (1951) *Elements of Social Organization: Josiah Mason Lectures Delivered at the University of Birmingham*, London: Watts & Co.
Firth, R. (1992) 'Art and Anthropology', in J. Coote and A. Shelton (eds) *Anthropology, Art and Aesthetics*, Oxford: Clarendon Press. 15–39.
Gell, A. (1992) 'Technology and Enchantment', in J. Coote and A. Shelton (eds) *Anthropology, Art and Aesthetics*, Oxford: Clarendon Press. 40–66.
Gell, A. (1998) *Art and Agency: An Anthropological Theory*, Oxford: Clarendon Press.
Hadamard, J. (1945) *An Essay on the Psychology of Invention in the Mathematical Field*, Princeton, NJ: Princeton University Press.
Kant, I. (2000) *Critique of the Power of Judgment*, ed. P. Guyer, trans. P. Guyer and E. Matthews, Cambridge: Cambridge University Press.
Rilke, R. M. (1985) *Letters on Cezanne*, trans. Joel Agee, New York: Fromm International Publishing Corporation.
Shearer, R. R., with Alvarez, G., Slawinski, R., Marchi, V. and text box by Gould, S. J. (2004) Updated 3 01-05. 'Why the *Hatrack* is and/or is not Readymade'. *Toutfait.com. The Marcel*

Duchamp Studies Online Journal. Online. Available HTTP: http://www.toutfait.com/ online_journal_details.php?postid=1100 (accessed 26 October 2009).

Staten, H. (2010) 'Art as Techne, or The Intentional Fallacy and the Unfinished Project of Modernism', in G. L. Hagberg and W. Jost (eds) *A Companion to the Philosophy of Literature*, Chichester: Wiley-Blackwell. 420–35.

Trotsky, L. (1960) *Literature and Revolution*, Ann Arbor: University of Michigan Press.

Valéry, P. (1958) 'Poetry and Abstract Thought', in *The Art of Poetry*, trans. D. Folliot, Vol. 7 of *The Collected Works of Paul Valéry*, ed. J. Mathews, New York: Pantheon Books.

Vološinov, V. N. (1973) *Marxism and the Philosophy of Language*, trans. L. Matejka and I. R. Titunik, New York: Seminar Press.

Zammito, J. H. (1992) *The Genesis of Kant's Critique of Judgment*, Chicago: University of Chicago Press.

16

LITERATURE AFTER THEORY, OR: THE INTELLECTIVE TURN

Laurent Dubreuil

The duplication implied by the title of this volume led me to write a twofold article. The two parts of this text say almost the same thing, although the very fact of saying something twice would be enough to alter each utterance and the thing that is said.[1]

I

'Theory' names a scholarly discourse that focuses *on the constructible* and *on language*, with recourse to a *philosophical syntax and vocabulary*.

At least, this is what I mean today by 'theory', and *theory*, *théorie*, *Theorie* or *théôria* would obviously produce other meanings. 'Theory', or 'T' by convention, would refer to an experience of thought one could exemplarily find in the works of Deleuze, Derrida, Foucault, Lacan, Fanon or Lyotard etc. This group of 'T'-authors already sounds extremely heterogeneous. Including most literary theorists (beginning with Wellek), psychoanalysts (Freud and afterwards) and the so-called Continental philosophers in 'theory' is another possibility. But in that case, I believe, we would be speaking about *theory* in general, and – at best – we would be attempting to delimit a discursive field governed by a form of resistance to the empirical (dogmatic empiricism being just a way of controlling the ineffability and unpredictability of experience through rational ordering). As I read it, the syntagm *theory after 'theory'* does not point to the renewal of the *theoretical* (vs. the practical or the empirical) after the end of the historical sequence called 'French Theory'. If I had to conform, even fugitively, to the title of the present collection, my own question would be about the undone job of 'Theory'. The insistence on the constructible and on language does not have to be moderated. I do not think it is time to stop caring about language and to *restore* the privilege of the given, of facts or of nature. Should we 'radicalize' the old 'theory', as some suggest? It is true that illustrious 'T' authors ended up holding theses somehow rebellious to decision making (think of neo-Pyrrhonism in Derrida's later works) or potentially more in phase with mainstream individualistic societies (see Foucault's neo-Stoicist promotion of the self). However, it is pointless to consider 'theory' as a body of discourse, which should be kept and perfected. This is the usual gesture of all academicism, which consists of an attempt at salvation of the maxims of the Master, be it at the price of losing the value of what should be kept and sophisticated. As a matter of fact, if we want to elaborate some theory after 'theory', we need not *radicalize the doctrines* of our 'glorious ancestors', but *maximize the effects* and procedures of their intellective attitude. Contrary to what the consensus asserts, 'theory' did not go too far, and it is up to those who believe they come *after* it to show how far we still need to go. In this perspective, the experience of literature has a lot to teach us, because literary *oeuvres* always come *after* other speeches (Dubreuil 2007): and their response to the discursive disciplines of knowledge is all the more manifest, since theory's flourishing. In the economy of the present essay, literature is going to play a crucial role, 'after' other (and parallel) considerations on the philosophical. For any possible renewal of theory, radicalism becomes one, secondary, option; if turned into a goal, it is merely a solid pre-conception, thus escaping the critique of the constructible by virtue of a juxtaposed *a priori*, and crippling in advance one of the stakes of 'theory'. Maximalism strikes me as a better way to continue 'T' beyond its usual field, as long as a dogmatic statement on the (im)possibility of reaching the maximum is not formulated.

I believe that the dependence on *philosophical* grammar in 'theory' has not been discussed enough. This idea might strike readers as very difficult to maintain, or even irrelevant. After all, the institutional *doxa* of 'analytic philosophy' is precisely that Lyotard, Foucault, Derrida, Deleuze and the like had absolutely nothing to do with philosophy. On a more fundamental level, all such 'theoreticians' have direly put to the test the usual claims and techniques of their own discipline of origin. Nevertheless, I hold that, *in fine*, the most extreme critiques of philosophy have still been organized by the rules of rationality associated with *philosophia* in the (post-) Greek tradition, especially the tenability of the concept, the laws of non-contradiction and the immanently metaphysical structure of language. Certainly, Derrida contested the omnipotence and purity of *Begriff* and he tried to do justice to contradictions in thought, but he always attempted to avoid any unwilling self-contradiction and he insistently posited the possibility of a preliminary indeconstructible. From there, he constantly referred to the concept, say, of hospitality, as something that is not only produced by discourse, but as a sort of predetermination haunting language. Deleuze wanted to get rid of the presumably inherent *logic* of *logos* through an appeal to the senses or schizophrenia, and he attacked ordinary approaches to rationality, but the aim was still to construct concepts in order to continue afresh the *oeuvre of philosophy*. Among more contemporary authors of theory or 'theory' after 'T', Alain Badiou represents the idle return to the positivity of the positive and, while he situates his work in the wake of Lacan and (on a minor scale) Deleuze, his agenda is clearly the restoration of the old dignity of Philosophy. Giorgio Agamben or Jacques Rancière would certainly not make such a goal their own mission, and they have explicitly called for something other than 'just' philosophy. Rancière has recently put his scholarship under the sign of *indis-ciplinarity* (Rancière 2006).[2] Agamben closes his 2008 essay on method with his desire to abandon the ontological anchorage of the human and social sciences, that is, to de-philosophize the disciplines. Can I confess that I am unconvinced here? As I have shown elsewhere (Dubreuil 2006, 2007), both Agamben and Rancière read and write history from the site of the concept: *bios* and *zoē*, *belles-lettres* and *literature*, etc. Instead of holding a sort of eternal impassibility of the concept, Agamben and Rancière opt for a transitory disposition where consistency is assured by historicity. They do not modify the logic of rational conceptuality, but rather give an abridged version of it. Such *theory* (even 'after "theory"') is still *oriented* by the reigning protocols of philosophy.

The epistemic site of 'theory' is not only deduced from the practice called philosophy, it also justifies the latter as the necessary base for an arch-discourse. We only really begin to be *after 'theory'* when one contests not only the institution of philosophy or its self-celebrating rhetoric, but also its most necessary protocols and tools. In short, the 'theory' I would like to see taking place afterwards needs to inquire into the constructible, to consider its place inside language as an empirical summation, even to examine the possibility of the non-constructible, and, from there, to bypass its own philosophical grammar. There is little doubt to me that 'T' authors did not effectively perform this last task. Moreover, the scope of 'theory' was philosophical through and through, and self-contradiction continued to be perceived as the worst possible sin. Even Derrida had to introduce a kind of prag-matic relativism according to which the distinction between philosophy and lit-erature was not clear-cut. I would agree, but first, Derrida did not say that both discourses were the same (this is a deconstructive vulgate exhibiting a weird oblivion of difference), and furthermore, the absence of obvious and/or objective separations does not automatically imply that we should renounce using categories. Even if the line is blurred, the distinction can still be operative. Taking advantage of the difficulty (or the impossibility) of definition to prevent the critique of the philosophical is a clever strategy, though nothing more than a strategy. Hence, it might be conceived and judged on the basis of its effects and consequences (namely, here, re-conducing the philosophical against Philosophy). Another legacy of the logic of rational conceptuality is the face-to-face with philosophy: philoso-phy and literature, and history, and social sciences, and . . . Yes, there are good rea-sons to believe that what is called philosophy developed a highly efficient way of reasoning. Inferring from this the supremacy of philosophy is more awkward. The site has to be changed. Though I believe in utopias, I am afraid there is no absolute non-place for us. As a result, we can dream of being totally off the ground, but in all likelihood we can only try to deterritorialize our thought as much as possible, with-out being perpetual nomads. As long as I shall write books and articles or give talks, it appears to me that, at least, my possible ground is language. When we all become telepaths, the situation might be different. Until that day, there is a high probability for the site of any theory after 'theory' to be *lingual*, even when it analogically refers to the non–constructible (under the names of Nature, Being or the Real). 'That is to say' that the concern for language, which I identified as an important feature of 'theory', would be continued in another (maximized) form, and for another purpose.

If they are acknowledged, the inabilities of language – in particular the inadequacy for conceptuality as well as the excess and contradiction of the process of signification – often lead philosophers to scepticism, relativism or cynicism. In search of solid foundations, others might try to find a new, stable, base in the solidity of the non-verbal; God and mathematics serving as the most usual refuges. The dominant tradition simply denies the opacity of language. After several decades, this last position being more difficult to maintain directly, it is now conjoined with a (justified) reappraisal of the sciences and a (vain) bracketing of the discursiveness of thought.[3] To me, once we revoke the pious conservation of a 'theoretical' inheritance, the urgent question is definitely not 'how could we go back to a more positive tone?' Our task should rather be the production of an affirmative thought *in spite of* its inevitable defectiveness. Then, the critical consideration of the limits of language will be absolutely necessary, though it does not have to be the necessary absolute of scholarship. It should be clear that I chose to emphasize this aspect in this article, because I find the current obsession with the real misleading as well as misguiding so long as it does not take lingual negativity into account.

Had the critique of language been articulated before the advent of 'theory?' Yes, actually. It is conveyed by language itself and is pervasive in discursive reasoning. It appears each time a slippage, an inadequacy, a contradiction is expressed. The 'critique' merely organizes the negativity inherent to language and through which signification is paradoxically produced. Our speeches are made of this, and we tend to avoid, forget or neutralize such defects. But literature is precisely the name for discursive practices whose lingual failure is a condition of success. Whereas conceptual disciplines are supposedly marred by their lingual and rational inabilities, whereas the *parole* of power prescribes opposite behaviours as the multiple facets of unitary conformity, a literary event consists in the fragile affirmation of a singular signification (the oeuvre) in spite of its intense negativity and obvious contradictions. Literature is a constantly renewed *mise en scène* of human intellective failure by the means of semantic lacks. It goes without saying (yes, by the way, rhetorical preteritions are other evidence of the slippage of *dictum*) that I take *literature* here for a category to be constructed, and that I mark strong differences between the literary and other types of discourses. I usually say that literature, which is much more than storytelling, style or verbal invention, is the *warrant of signification in language*. That is, it does not try to conceal, to suspend, to cover or to prevent the defect of meaning. Rather, literary oeuvres exhibit this defect by responding to other forms of speech, including the most theoretical ones, and thus by questioning their alleged efficiency (be it rationality, political ordinance, action, etc.). And this is how literature thinks *nevertheless*. Such a disposition is just a dramatization of the lingual process of signification. *Literature enacts the defectiveness of logos*. From there, literary texts are apt to develop ideas and arguments, or theories, if you really want to use this word, and every one of these may then in turn be submitted to critical (or hypercritical) inquiries. Such theories generally tend to express minor positions because of literature's affinities with non-rational thought; they aggregate quasi (or ruined) concepts with spoken formulas, life fragments with poetics, and they should not be read as pure content or pure form. What interests me in this essay is less the singularity of such notions than the singularity of these singularities, namely the literary. However, it should be admitted that a better understanding of literature also inspects the way each oeuvre reconfigures literature in the process of its creation.

So returning to language requires us to take literature into account. It should not come as a real surprise that a description of the 'T' phenomenon and of its aftermath includes a consideration of the literary. In my own evocation of 'theory', the function of literary studies was manifestly (and intentionally) missing. We can now suggest that the peculiar coincidence between 'theory' and literary criticism was neither a simple consequence of haphazard circumstances nor merely the result of social constraints. Undoubtedly, inside the American academy, the main channel for 'theory' has been literature departments, especially because of the antagonism of positive philosophy. In addition to this institutional factor, the paradigmatic role devoted to literature in French 'high culture' and education in the largest part of the twentieth century also explains why philosophers, psychoanalysts, historians or sociologists tended to write on poetry, novels or drama. The role of artistic avant-gardes might also be quoted, given that Surrealism served as a (counter) model for movements such as *Tel Quel* or *l'Internationale situationniste*. Of course. But the convergence between 'theory' and the study of literature is also epistemic, or, better, *intellective*. Literature is properly an art, an artifice, a construct by the means of language. It has been presented by the dominant philosophical tradition as rebellious or impervious to rationality or concepts. Xenophanes of Colophon, a pre-Socratic, already mocked Homer and Hesiod for representing gods in contradiction with their essential definition. When 'theory' offered a critique of the majority philosophy, focusing on literature was an obvious choice: since the end of Sophistic thinking, poetry has been the favourite inner enemy of post-Greek philosophers. But even in classical Athens, as Plato put it, this was an *ancient controversy* (*palaia diaphora*; Plato 1937: 607b). The noun *diaphora* could also be rendered as *difference*, *différend*, or *dissensus*. One would have noticed that these three possible translations equally refer to words and concepts that are crucial (respectively) in Derrida, Lyotard and Rancière. With or without a nominative trace such as in these three cases, 'theory' used the *palaia diaphora* to alter philosophy. It might be noted that other solutions are philosophically possible in regard to literature (e.g. ancillary inclusion in Aristotle, deliberate oblivion in Wittgenstein). The mark of 'theory' was to approach the literary as the minor part *of* philosophy. By doing so, a formidable renewal and displacement was made possible. At the same time, the legend of a particular dialogue between philosophy and literature was once again promoted, to the detriment of the other epistemic responses literary oeuvres could bring and of entire textual continents, often including (post)colonial *parole*. Perhaps more importantly, literature was tacitly subdued to a certain philosophical order. In trying to free *poièsis* from the tyranny of interpretation, Deleuze puts it outside the realm of thinking. In holding that concepts are inherent to words (while, in my view, they are only, and defectively, produced by meaning in language), Derrida reattaches literary critique of metaphysics to metaphysics itself or celebrates literature for its alleged arch-originary source. And, in isolating forms of anti-philosophy in literature, Badiou, contrary to some of his claims, simply duplicates the Platonic gesture (praise and banishment).

If there is a time for theory after 'theory', we need to obtain a better understanding of intellective construction, by renouncing the *a priori* supremacy of philosophical rationality, which includes the belief in a ready-made conceptuality conveyed by words. Contrary to the Analytic tradition, I hold that language – as the inevitable matter of discursive scholarship – is not better understood in its 'everyday' form, but that literary texts that condense and criticize other manners of speaking maximally operate the process of signification. From this point, we should be able to read and touch more disciplines and issues than those taken into account by 'theory'. Though the task is daunting, it should not be the *end* of theory in any sense, but rather the meta-theoretical condition for renewed ways of thinking beyond.

II

Do we need another 'turn' in scholarship? I doubt it, and I have always been a bit troubled by the intersections of research and marketability. But, just in case, here is a new one: *the intellective turn*. Since it is devoted to thought itself, it is not authentically 'new', if anything 'authentically new' ever existed, and it is barely a *turn*. We all pay attention to what we think and say; or at least, we are supposed to, especially when we pretend to be scholars. If theory names the inquiry on the intellective, I take it to be something as urgent as it is heteronomous. I have to admit, though, that this concern is not terribly popular among scholars of my generation (or just a bit older than I, to be more authentically autobiographical). If we leave aside the soft conformism of standard scholarship, as well as the debates on the only correct interpretation of yesterday's doctrines, the trend in what might be identified as theory (after 'theory') is, rather than any given turn, a *return* to the positive. The two main hypostases are the renewed interest in the *real* (the thing, the fact, the pre- or non-verbal), and the focus on the *political*. What is 'positive,' in both cases, is not the real or the political themselves, but the claim that, by studying them, we might find something more tangible, more unitary or truer than by going in other directions. This is why Alain Badiou's work is so often referred to among exponents of 'speculative realism' or of politicalism, because his philosophy is nomothetic while appearing historically as linked to cutting-edge 'theory'. This is also why the theoretical return to the positive is intrinsically *institutional*: it seeks to re-anchor solidly (in the *thing*, in *science*, in the *fact*, in the *revolution*) what seems to have been shattered in the last few decades. Let me be Pythian for one second: these new realists or ultra-radical political thinkers are still marginal now, but I have no doubt that they will succeed in creating a scholarly orthodoxy, for, perhaps against their desires, they are obsessed with the restoration of the norm, and they should be rewarded for this service by the powers in place.

That said, the problems that such attempts pose are not so easily dismissible. Beyond their social agendas and postures, the proponents of neo-positive theory are right in stating, for instance, that reality is not reducible to its human construction, or that the thing and the thing in language might differ. However, how could they *state* this without or outside language? Non-verbal and a-semantic soul communication, pre-lingual neuronal cognition, absolutely formal equations might be acceptable methods. I just fear that, if such means exist, their description by a treatise could entrap them into discursive thought. The will to touch the thing itself, if it supports theoretical developments, cannot neutralize language. Pretending to do so creates exactly the opposite situation: by saying that language is *no-thing*, one is unable to undo it and one paradoxically, but effectively, takes it for all the real. Philosophically, the discursive 'suspension' of language in the name of reality seems to ratify the necessary becoming-verbal of the non-verbal. It also makes language properly *in-discussable* and so ratifies its omnipotence at the moment it would like to forget or annul it. In other terms, as long as we use words, we need to pay attention to them and to what they allow and forbid us to think. This is the intellective condition of any discursive apprehension of the non-lingual. Philosophical realism is more entrapped in language than 'theory', for it is merely unable to apprehend the part of reality that is its own discourse.

Here, the study of literature becomes a *sine qua non*. Not because the literary would be superior to anything else, but because it refers to a complex art of rearranging previous speeches, helping us situate what is at stake in language. Through this displacement, words suddenly signify differently than what our habits, common sense or dictionaries would have indicated, syntax is both weird and valid, ready-made discourses are transpierced by new events of *paroles*, the idioms of the disciplines are re-arranged so that their patient constructions strangely crumble while continuing to make sense. On the one hand, literature comes *after* other speeches: it is not oracular, ante-predicative, arch-originary, since it precisely consists in saying differently what has already been uttered (and this obviously includes other literary texts). On the other hand, literature shows us what language is able to do: more than just describing or prescribing, more than following all usages and grammars, less than allowing a firm, stable and perennial edifice of ideas, less than taking us directly to the thing (the real, the concept) itself. The simple fact that a rational fragment or maxim can be transplanted into a poem and then acquire a meaning that is now irreducible to the values it first had exhibits how language works: with an excess of meaning, that is, just temporarily tamed by ordinary communication, power or rationality, and with a defect of consistency. The experience of the literary invites us to violently reconsider how, and why, we speak and think. Furthermore, the oddity of this afterwards implies that literature is both theoretical and post-theoretical, inasmuch as it at least does and undoes what makes theory. Hence, literary oeuvres come after all theories, succeeding them and chasing their principles or axioms. This approach to literature is certainly at odds with most critical dogmas based on the sensible, the imaginary, on technique or on truth. Since I hold that even concepts are opened and fissured by the literary process of signification, I also diverge from a philosophizing method of reading, which seeks in a poem or a play the very performance of an idea. But, more problematically, I could appear to be in total contradiction with what is exactly said by numerous literary texts. As might become clear, avoiding self-contradiction is not my major concern, for I believe in a non-rational regime of thought. Besides, I guess that this contradiction is precisely a literary effect. Writers not only disassemble the logic of other discourses, they also undo their own stances or positions; and this is what makes an oeuvre.

Literature is both a singular and a collective noun. As I described in the previous pages, it could be treated as a collection of practices; it should concurrently be studied at the textual level. There is a gap between these two renderings of the literary, and it would be useless to attempt to fill it with a transcendental category. Close readings are not very popular anymore, though they are less a question of choice than a necessity, all the more if we stress defectiveness and seek to eschew the illusion of the positive that generalizing accounts traditionally produce. I will end this article with a brief commentary of one of D. H. Lawrence's *Last Poems*, 'Anaxagoras'. I hope that my reasons for choosing this text will gradually appear in the next pages. At this point, suffice it to say that while Lawrence's poetry often expresses contrapuntal differences with philosophy, it also makes the case against intellectualism. Any theoretical conjecture should confront its possible counter-examples, so if we want to reflect on literature and the intellective part of our thought, we should begin with the most difficult; and here, Lawrence is a wonderful start.

Here is the first stanza of 'Anaxagoras':

> When Anaxagoras says: Even the snow is black!
> he is taken by the scientists very seriously
> because he is enunciating a 'principle,' a 'law'
> that all things are mixed, and therefore the purest white snow
> has in it an element of blackness.
>
> (Lawrence 1932: 41)

In this text, Lawrence precisely responds to the pre-Socratic philosopher Anaxagoras, while more generally condemning 'mental conceit'. In this regard, the word 'scientists' matters. The term rightly associates Anaxagoras with the Greek tradition of writings devoted to *Physics* – that is, on the constitution of nature – at the intersection of 'science' and philosophy. With a slight anachronism then, I would say that Lawrence refers to the theoretical apparatus of thought. In parallel, *scientists* is linked with *knowledge* in general (*scientia*). In many other poems by Lawrence one finds a certain disdain for knowledge, or rather a disqualification of its omnipotence. For instance, the text entitled 'Know-all' asserts 'Man knows nothing / Till he knows not-to-know' (ibid.: 74). Such statements are not so far from what Georges Bataille was beginning to develop at the same time on *non-knowledge*. They could also be compared with the textual tradition of the wise, to be found in the Bible, in Socrates or in French *moralisme*. I am recalling such examples to emphasize that Lawrence's trial of *scientia* is not, in itself, a perfectly isolated theme. One of the impressive peculiarities of Lawrence is his way of bypassing the ready-made form of the paradox (whose paradigm would be *I know that I know nothing*), as when he writes about 'centres . . . / where we may cease from knowing, and, as far as we know, / may cease from being' ('Temples', ibid.: 76). The desire is to *cease* from knowing, or oblivion is 'the end of all knowledge' ('Know-all', ibid.: 74). Then, going 'as far as we know' is precisely the interruption of knowledge. However, nothing assures us that such a journey would be accomplished once and for all, meaning that we constantly need to know until we do not know. As a result, waiting for oblivion would not be the best option. We also need to forget what we know and to distance ourselves from the constitution of forever valid 'laws' or 'principles'.

Of course, there is in Lawrence a kind of impossible nostalgia, a primitivist fascination for the purity of nature, for a real untouched by human thought. In 'Anaxagoras', one reads that 'pure snow is white to us / white and white and only white / with a lovely bloom of whiteness upon white' (ibid.: 41). This appeal to the constitution of reality for us is opposed to Anaxagoras's doctrine that 'all things are mixed' (ibid.: 41). By judging from the fragments of his books, Anaxagoras held the existence of 'one world', where the contraries could not be separated as with 'an axe' (Diels and Kranz 1934: §59, B8–12). Nevertheless, Anaxagoras, as it seems, did not exactly contest dichotomies; he used them to show their irrelevance at the level of the world. In his response to the pre-Socratic, Lawrence deliberately takes the party of common sense. He even aggravates it in some sense with the repetition of *white*, culminating in the trochaic tetrameter 'white and white and only white' whose final catalexis rhythmically marks the absolute limit of *white*. So, here, Lawrence sounds like an adversary of 'mentalism' or 'intellectualism', to the profit of an enjoyment of (or participation in) the simple experience of the senses and life. In a different poem from the same period, one reads another attack against the 'conceit of being immune' and 'the puerility of contradictions / like saying that snow is black, or desire is evil' ('Kissing and Horrid Strife', Lawrence 1932: 42–3).

There is certainly a profound disdain in Lawrence for what he considers to be 'mystification' or religious-like estrangement from life. We could go further and infer from all this that Lawrence posits poetry against knowledge, that the aim of his literature (and potentially of most powerful literary oeuvres) is to focus on the *percept* by short-circuiting conceptual sophistication. This Deleuzean reading would undermine the role of Anaxagoras in the process. Instead of bluntly celebrating life or perception, Lawrence quotes a philosopher and confronts his discourse to what 'scientists' would elaborate. In other terms – the ones I use – he effectively aims to *respond* to philosophical doctrines and maxims. As a result, the text is not simply on another plane than conceptual discourse, and the encounter with philosophy is not just an 'intersection'. Rather, Anaxagoras, as a cited textual construction, is a point of departure for the development of the poem. Could it be (in a more Derridean fashion this time) that Lawrence, in spite of all, actually remains imprisoned in very traditional metaphysical dispositions, in his description of *pure* snow, in his contempt for *contradiction*? It is possible that the poet does not totally perform what he attempts to do. Nonetheless, it should first be noted that the last stanza of 'Anaxagoras' suddenly adds 'And in the shadow of the sun the snow is blue, so blue-aloof' (ibid.: 41). As much as 'Anaxagoras' funeral black' is still rejected, the white *white* of snow *is* blue 'in the shadow of the sun' (ibid.: 41). Lawrence is not the advocate of the identity principle; it is not because 'A is A' that he refuses the proposition of the pre-Socratic, but according to an idiosyncratic desire for the joy of bliss, as snow (or desire) allows it. Along the same lines, all 'contradictions' are not marked by 'puerility', but only *some* of them. It would be difficult, I think, to generalize Lawrence's statements as remnants of a metaphysical or conceptual structure without presupposing that the latter is inherent to language. But if we consider concepts as constructed through discourse and speech, then the possibilities of a purity other than *purity*, of a contradiction other than *contradiction* are open.

Now, though our reading might benefit from taking the poem as a response to fragments of rational and conceptual thought, Lawrence's demonstration on the bliss of life against mental conceit does not seem strikingly in support of what I coined as the intellective turn of theory. One easy, but uncommon, way to avoid the difficulty would be asserting that we might show little concern for what authors say, or, more 'seriously', that we could disagree with the empirical contents (here: the poem's dictum) and advance a bigger, or more fundamental, truth without being too troubled by 'aberrant' results. This para-scientific attitude is not thoroughly irrelevant. As a matter of fact, we can admire without adhering; and I believe critique to be a part of literary criticism. However, taking for nothing positions that sound foreign or hostile to our own is merely *too* easy. The usual way of solving the problem is to insist on appearances or facticity: yes, we have at least a *porte-à-faux* here, but 'in a final analysis', or 'more fundamentally' or 'in reality', etc., we can neglect what is said to the profit of what we say it says. This 'solution' is heavily used in the dialectic tradition, including post-Marxism. Unfortunately, it just undermines the status of the literary. We could prove that something else is at stake in the poem than what we said (and I am going to do it), *but* the discrepancies and contradictions are precisely what form the oeuvre, so they should not be reduced.

Lawrence's poems *say* something. That language is not divine, as is argued in a text on the beginning of the world ('Let There Be Light!', ibid.: 297), or that it serves 'the conceit that kills us' ('Conceit', ibid.: 282) does not mean it does not exist or that its value is univocal. 'Even snow is black!' is what 'Anaxagoras <u>says</u>' or '<u>enunciat[es]</u>'. And Lawrence says something back. He reiterates the philosopher's discourse, he not only quotes it, but he literally includes it in the body of his text (erasing the typographical marks), in such a way that the conceit, once uttered, is fractured by the very fact of being expressed, differently. There is no need to conceal that the poetic postulation towards 'communion' or 'oblivion', that the rejection of mechanical spiritualism sometimes cross in Lawrence a distrust for language as well, as a possible vector of fatal self-consciousness. But there is no way to ignore the lingual form that is used here, and clearly underlined by the text itself. When he named this type of poem *pansies*, Lawrence was also exposing his project of re-establishing *thoughts* (*pensées*) by emulating Blaise Pascal's fragmented manner, in healing (*panser*) the wounds made by conceits, in taking these thoughts as concrete flowers (*pansies*) then gathering them into a real *antho-logy*. By doing so, *he was maximizing the abilities of language*, exhibiting the indefinite instead of a word definition. 'Anaxagoras' is a text about the necessary dissolution of mental mystification, a response to a given doctrine and a demonstration of the process of signification. Instead of being neutralized by its performative contradiction, the text makes sense. Ideas and doctrines are shown as nothing else than *flatus vocis*, but only sentences and words can mean it. This difficulty should not be described as a simple paradox, or a weird aporia. Rather, it locates the intellective function of language, or how we think and speak: defectively.[4]

Or: As long as we speak and write, we should be aware of the unavoidable opacity of language as our intellective site. Minimizing discursive defectiveness is the paradoxical triumph of circular logology, for it ratifies the built-in illusion of language as no thing. The truth is, there is no absolute truth in my speech, but I can affirm a thought nevertheless – as literature shows, with much more intensity than 'ordinary language'. On the condition that the process of signification will be understood from the site of its literary maximum, the future of theory after 'theory' could finally be post-theoretical.

Notes

1 I thank Laurent Ferri, Ioana Vartolomei and the editors for their comments.
2 Before that see the title of Pasquier 2004 (*Jacques Rancière l'indiscipliné*) and Esposito (1999: VII).
3 In this sense, Meillassoux's remarkable 2006 book is nothing more than a *metaphorical rendition* of the absolute: it is simply unable to keep the promise made of the 'great outdoors'.
4 May I add, too rapidly, that a contemporary of Lawrence, Alfred Tarski, while reflecting on snow and language, concluded that natural idioms are unable to say, or establish, the truth? Tarski's logical and mathematical essays maintained that only *formal* languages could be true, in a strict and positive redefinition of the category, and under the laws and principle of what he called the 'T-convention' (see Tarski 1986). As Quine said, however, even mathematicians happen to use natural idioms and the link between equations and word sentences is once again problematic (Quine 1960: §33, 56).

Bibliography

Diels, H. and Kranz, W (eds.) (1934) *Die Fragmente der Vorsokratiker*, Berlin: Weidmann.
Dubreuil, L. (2006) 'Leaving Politics', *Diacritics*, 36.2: 83–98.
Dubreuil, L. (2007) 'What is Literature's Now?', *New Literary History*, 38.1: 43–70.
Esposito, R. (1999) *Categorie dell'impolitico*, 2nd edition, Bologna: Il Mulino.
Lawrence, D.H. (1932) *Last Poems*, Florence: Orioli.

Meillassoux, Q. (2006) *Après la finitude: Essai sur la nécessité de la contigence*, Paris: Seuil.

Pasquier, R. (ed.) (2004) *Jacques Rancière l'indiscipliné*, special issue of *Labyrinthe. Atelier interdisciplinaire* 17.

Plato (1937) *Plato in Twelve Volumes*, vol. 2, *The Republic*, trans. P. Shorey, Cambridge, MA: Harvard University Press; Heinemann.

Quine, W.v.O. (1960) *Word and Object*, Cambridge, MA: Technology Press of the MIT.

Rancière, J. (2006) 'Thinking Between the Disciplines: An Aesthetics of Knowledge', *Parrhesia*, 1-1: 9–12.

Tarski, A. (1986) 'The Concept of Truth in Formalized Languages', in *Collected Papers*, vol. 2, Basel: Birkhaüser.

17

THE LIBERAL AESTHETIC

Amanda Anderson

In the past couple of decades, there have been a number of attempts within literary studies to return, in one way or another, to aesthetics. A major impetus for this tendency has been dissatisfaction with ideological criticism, both for its inattention to aesthetic value and for its subordination of the aesthetic to ideological functions such as the display of cultural capital or forms of mystification. Some of these reconsiderations of aesthetics focus on the singularity and importance of aesthetic experience; others aim to reconfigure the relation between ideology and aesthetics so as to give more emphasis to aesthetic experience and value, or to aesthetic form's active engagement with political thought and experience (Armstrong 2000; Attridge 2004; de Bolla 2001; Levine 1994; Scarry 1999). In what follows, I will be pursuing this second avenue in relation to an ideological formation that has been a key target of theoretical work in the humanities: liberalism. As a political formation, liberalism is not favoured within an academic context in which radical politics are privileged, and as an aesthetic, liberalism is seen as narrowly focused on temperament and harmonious diversity, rather than the formally and conceptually challenging modes associated with radicalism. The purpose of this essay is to move beyond these default positions, and to propose a framework for rethinking literary engagements with liberal thought, one that is attentive both to the complexities of philosophical liberalism and to the history of literary form. This approach therefore is committed to a defence of liberalism and seeks to reconceptualize what a liberal aesthetics might mean in a context of a renewed understanding of liberal thought. I will be particularly concerned to draw out the ways in which nineteenth-century realism might serve as the basis for a renewed understanding of the liberal aesthetic, but I should stress that the liberal aesthetic as I conceive it is broadly applicable to many forms of literary and extra-literary experience.

Commonly associated with ideas of human perfectibility and assured progressivism, philosophical liberalism is often contrasted not only with radical philosophies that call for wholesale transformation, but also with a conservative tradition that claims a monopoly on tragic, pessimistic and 'realistic' conceptions of humanity, and of the forms of political response appropriate to that condition. From this perspective, liberalism is seen as naively optimistic, failing to attend to structural inequities or economic, psychological and political realities. Moreover, as a theory characterized as 'thin' or abstract, liberalism has been seen as failing to register the existential density, and affiliation-prompting intensity, that other belief systems – especially systems more at home with religious and nationalist rhetoric – have been able to offer. This concern has been central to the influential communitarian critique of liberalism. Some commentators see the problem as endemic to liberalism since its inception; others see a falling away from earlier and more robust forms of civic, welfare or social democracy (Brinkley 2007).

These critical frameworks typically fail to credit liberalism for the genuineness of its predicaments, and the seriousness and complexity of its engagement with them. It must be acknowledged, of course, that very real ideological differences and political commitments undergird the division between the radical and the liberal left, and between conservatism and liberalism, both within and without the academy. But liberalism has a more complex and 'thick' array of attitudinal stances, affective dispositions and political objectives than the conventional contrasts admit. Throughout its history, liberalism has engaged sober and even stark views of historical development, political dynamics and human and social psychology. This is strikingly evident in American liberalism of the thirties and forties, when liberalism was articulated as a refusal of communism on the one hand (whose utopianism was seen as entailing grave dangers) and fascism on the other. More current theoretical discussions of liberalism have tended to misrepresent liberalism's considered engagements with negative social and historical forces.

The complexity of liberal thinking is evident across a spectrum of writing that engages philosophical liberalism, by writers as diverse as Alexis de Tocqueville, John Stuart Mill, Isaiah Berlin, Hannah Arendt, Richard Hofstadter, Reinhold Niebuhr, Lionel Trilling, Judith N. Shklar and Jürgen Habermas. The work of these writers brings into view a number of undercurrents or persistent perceptions within liberal aspiration: the intractability of liberal vices and recalcitrant psychologies, the limits to argument, the exacting demands of freedom amidst value-pluralism, the tragedy of history and the corruptibility of procedure. Properly assessed, liberalism can be seen to encompass and not simply occasionally to disclose the psychological, social and economic barriers to its moral and political ideals. Liberalism is best understood, that is, as a philosophical and political aspiration conceived in an acute awareness of the challenges and often bleak prospects confronting it. Only once we admit this fuller understanding of political and philosophical liberalism can we approach any renewed appreciation of aesthetic engagements with liberal thinking.

To isolate one central example from nineteenth-century liberalism, John Stuart Mill's thinking importantly combined a faith in the ideal of self-development on the one hand and a sociological assessment of the dangers associated with mass opinion on the other. This type of split within liberal thinking – its inclusion of both a moral and a sociological perspective – can be attributed in part to the fact that it emerged concomitant with the evolutionary or historical view of social development characteristic of much nineteenth-century European thought. Importantly, the double view promotes a variety of attitudinal stances, not only forms of progressive confidence but also, as in this case, irony and pessimism. John Burrow (1988) dates the double-vision structure back to the eighteenth century and to Adam Smith pre-eminently, though of course Mill's version is a kind of reverse Smithism. In place of the gap between the invisible hand and the self-interested individual, that is, we find a gap between the moral agent and darker sociological tendencies: the malevolent hand. Alert to many variations of this double-vision, Burrow memorably describes it at one point as a persistent disjunction, at the intellectual level, between 'what we morally admire and what we sociologically discern' (Burrow 1988: 51). Liberals do not have a monopoly on this split view, but it tends to cause them more angst, since there is an ideal of reflective enlightenment in liberalism that cannot rest easily with a gap between a sociological condition seen to characterize what the masses do and believe, and its own progressive ideals.

Liberalism's commitment to the ideal of reflective enlightenment is often expressed not as a mere investment in neutrality or principle, but precisely as a kind of existential challenge. The liberal tradition is characterized by a devotion to the examined life in its many dimensions, including the rigorous scrutiny of principles, assumptions and belief systems; the questioning of authority and tradition; the dedication to argument, debate and deliberative processes of legitimation and justification; and the commitment to openness and transparency. Turning these principles and practices into a way of life, or infusing them into political institutions, has typically been seen as a challenge for liberalism, certainly not as a simple matter. Acknowledging the philosophical complexities and existential predicaments attending liberal thought allows us to begin to conceptualize, and to disclose, a richer tradition of liberal aesthetics. As I will argue, the realist novel often can be seen to engage liberal thought through its own version of the dual perspective (the first- and third-person perspectives) and to grapple in diverse ways with the difficulty of living the examined life, or successfully enacting political or philosophical ideals. And while realism will be my prime example, it is the premise of this analysis that it could be extended and adapted to a broad range of modern and contemporary literature and other artistic media.

The critique of liberalism in contemporary literary and cultural studies takes several distinct forms (Anderson 2006). For the purposes of the present discussion, the key context is the rise of theory beginning in the sixties, though it should be noted that a longer genealogy of anti-liberal and anti-democratic critique would need to take account of the tradition of organicist cultural critique extending from Coleridge, Carlyle and Arnold, and up through F. R. Leavis in Britain and the Southern Agrarians in the United States. In both their theoretical premises and their political commitments, the dominant forms of literary scholarship have taken their distance from liberalism and in a key sense have constituted liberalism as an assumed stable target of critique. Anti-humanist critiques of Enlightenment, including structuralist, post-structuralist and ideological criticism, have sought to dismantle the primacy of the liberal humanist subject and to identify the ideology of liberalism as a function of capitalist interests or, in the case of Foucault, modern disciplinary power. Collateral critiques have been waged from the vantage point of communitarianism (which essentially extends the organicist tradition mentioned above), feminism (with its critique of rationality and neutrality) and queer theory (with its focus on normativity as normalization). More recently, the critique of liberal modernity has come to focus on proceduralism and state politics, partly in response to the aftermath of 9–11 (specifically, the abrogation of civil liberties in the so-called 'war on terror', and the expansion of executive power). While on the one hand, the current geopolitical situation has promoted a closer consideration of proceduralism, on the other hand, the negative judgement of liberalism has essentially not changed. Indeed, the reconsideration of proceduralism has been framed by theories of the state of exception, which read violations of the rule of law and democratic procedure as unavoidable features of modern constitutionalism, rather than departures from a progressive democratic norm that merits strong constitutional and philosophical defence.

Giorgio Agamben's work, which draws on the theories of Carl Schmitt as well as Foucault's concept of biopower, has been central to this renewed critique of liberalism. Agamben insists on the enduring importance of sovereignty (as opposed to disciplinary power), and he argues that the state of exception and the politicization of what he calls bare life are at the heart of the horror of modernity, and lead inexorably to the Nazi death camps as the paradigmatic political topos in a world in which the state of exception has become the norm. Crucially, Agamben sees the politicization of life as encompassing both the rise of liberal democracy and the emergence of totalitarianism. Like Foucault in his late-middle period, Agamben has a sinister view of liberalism and the freedoms it pretends to promote, seeing those rights and freedoms as indissolubly linked to the production of more subtle and pervasive forms of power:

> It is almost as if, starting from a certain point, every decisive political event were double-sided: the spaces, the liberties, and the rights won by individuals in their conflicts with central powers always simultaneously prepared a tacit but increasing inscription of individuals' lives within the state order, thus offering a new and more dreadful foundation for the very sovereign power from which they wanted to liberate themselves.
>
> (Agamben 1998: 121)

By abandoning the resources of the liberal democratic tradition, and by assimilating it to a modernity in which a Holocaust-hue covers all of political life, Agamben's theory further entrenches the longstanding anti-liberal and anti-proceduralist commitments of much of contemporary literary theory.

Agamben's position has of course not stood uncontested, and there have also been some important broader critiques of the academic left's failure adequately to address, and think through, democratic institutions and state politics (Brenkman 2007; Brennan 2006; LaCapra 2004; Szalay and McGann 2005). These critiques, it should be noted, tend to include at least two different lines of argument. One is theoretical and political, stressing that the forms of negative critique dominating the field result in anti-normative, anti-procedural and, consequently, anti-statist positions and stances. The second criticism responds to what it sees as a romantic temperament driving the theoretical visions under discussion, one linked to forms of aesthetic thinking or valuation that fundamentally displace the political. LaCapra identifies modes of sublime excess and utopian displacement in Agamben. Brennan faults literary and cultural theorists for aesthetic, poetic and sublime modes of thinking. Szalay and McGann emphasize the symbolic, magical and aesthetic solutions that mark what they also tellingly call 'literary thinking' after the New Left.

We should acknowledge more directly, however, the reasons why the valorization of aesthetic concepts or modes gains ascendancy in the literary field. There is a genuine and deep problem here, one which has to do with the core vocational orientation, on the part of the literary left, towards the values of the aesthetic. Apart from any question of ideological or philosophical tendencies in the field, that is, we should not be surprised that aesthetic values figure prominently within its analytical frameworks. It is worth considering, moreover, how this particular field condition has played out in broader intellectual historical terms. One way to put this is to ask whether and to what extent the aesthetic investments of the field practitioners have influenced broader critical and theoretical frameworks. This will allow us to begin to analyze why there is such difficulty, within the literary field, in apprehending or thinking in distinctly aesthetic terms of political liberalism – its conceptual forms, normative values and institutional practices.

To identify what one means by aesthetic values or investments is of course a potentially difficult task, given the long and varied history of thinking on the aesthetic. Given the coincidence of the development of the field of literary studies with the modern period, I will emphasize a range of values and concepts that derive from that period, and that are also recognizably post-Kantian in their self-understandings and internal differentiations. Let us stipulate, then, that the aesthetic, as a governing orientation of the field, involves a broad spectrum of values associated with complexity, difficulty, variousness, ambiguity, undecidability, hermeneutic open-endedness and threshold experiences – or experiences that prompt or tease one into an apprehension of the new, the unrealized or the buried. While particular readings may assert what may seem to be a finalizing authority or narrow certainty, in general we consider aesthetic objects and especially the complex conceptual forms of literary art to yield an ongoing richness of interpretive possibilities, and we associate what we call the experience of the aesthetic with the values of incompleteness, variousness, complexity, difficulty, excess, ambiguity, aporia. These values shift in emphasis, and can be mapped in relation to familiar oppositions: beautiful/sublime, liberal/radical, human/inhuman. What is salient for the purposes of this analysis, however, is that even in their more tame liberal humanist non-sublime forms, these aesthetic values jar with the cathexes and investments of normative liberal philosophy, democratic proceduralism and the mundane aspects of participatory and state politics. There is a kind of temperamental aversion within literary and cultural studies, across the liberal and radical camps, to certain key values of normative philosophy and procedural theory – most especially, normative explicitness, reason-giving argument, transparency. Against these, the aesthetic temperament values the implicit, the tacit, paradox and a rich opacity.

Thus, apart from the real ideological commitments driving the critique of liberalism, commitments whose explanatory relevance I in no way intend to dismiss or demote, it is also the case that there is a temperamental affinity at play that favours the forms of critique that target liberalism. Theories and modes of analysis that manage to play out – either conceptually or formally – an aesthetic resistance to the values of liberalism and proceduralism are often given pride of place. For perhaps the most overt instances of this broader tendency, one needs only look to the influential theoretical readings of Kafka's fable, 'Before the Law'. Kafka's short text describes an encounter between a man from the country and a gatekeeper who stands 'before the law', barring entry yet also speaking as though entry is simply being deferred – not yet may the man enter. The man remains waiting, his entreaties to enter endlessly put off by the gatekeeper, until his death. Just as death approaches he asks the gatekeeper why no one else has approached to try to enter. The gatekeeper responds: 'No one else could ever be admitted here, since this gate was made only for you. I am now going to shut it' (Kafka 1978: 184). Jacques Derrida reads the fable as demonstrating the incessant deferral of the decision as to whether the man can pass through the door; in this way, we see the law as 'a nothing that incessantly defers access to itself' (Derrida 1992: 208), and the subject as always before the law, before an incessantly deferred judgement. And importantly, the law is fundamentally subordinated in Derrida's analysis to the more primary conditions of language and literature. For Derrida, while the law is always trying to project an authority that lies beyond or outside of narrative or history, it inevitably partakes of the same condition of possibility of literature, the fundamental linguistic conditions of *différance* and undecidability. It is crucial, therefore, that in Kafka's text, the law projects its authoritative power and originary status within a fable. In a later and equally influential text, 'Force of Law: The "Mystical Foundation of Authority"', Derrida juxtaposes law's calculability to the incalculability of justice, arguing for the necessity of acts of decision within a kind of impossible aporia. The law in its calculability is a degraded and limited form, associated with a fundamental violence; justice as a kind of ideal stands above and beyond it to show its limits and conditioned aspect. It is very hard in this sort of framework to talk in any way about a viable procedural politics, since it will on the one hand fall beneath the level of the romanticized decision, and on the other will be squarely within the realm of the calculability of the law.

In *Homo Sacer*, Agamben differentiates his reading of Kafka's fable from Derrida's, as part of a broader and longer critique of deconstruction's tendency to rest in aporias. For Agamben, the parable is not an account of an event that never happens, or happens in not happening, but rather a description of 'how something has really happened in seeming not to happen': the virtual state of exception becomes real in the eventual closing of the door (Agamben 1998: 57). The indeterminacy of contemporary politics, evident in the many 'zones of indistinction' he identifies, is not an absolute condition of political existence but precisely what needs to be at once diagnosed and overcome. Whether this methodological distinction ultimately amounts to a difference that makes a difference is of course open to debate. Revealingly, Agamben acknowledges only a limited value to a proceduralist approach, and that is a diagnostic one that will refuse the pieties and misguided humanism of a liberal response:

> The correct question to pose concerning the horrors committed in the camps is, therefore, not the hypocritical one of how crimes of such atrocity could be committed against human beings. It would be more honest and, above all, more useful to investigate carefully the juridical procedures and deployments of power by which human beings could be so completely deprived of their rights and prerogatives that no act committed against them could appear any longer as a crime.
>
> (Ibid.: 171)

Crucially for our purposes, Agamben's negative critique of liberal modernity is combined with a call to move entirely beyond the logic of modernity: what is really called for is the possibility of thinking the relation between potentiality and actuality differently, or, as he puts it cryptically, 'to think ontology and politics beyond any figure of relation' (ibid.: 47). Liberal and procedural modernity are themselves beyond redemption.

By anatomizing the approach Derrida and Agamben take to the analysis of law in modernity, one can see why critics emphasize the suspicious displacement of state and institutional politics by romantic, aesthetic and mystical values and modes. However, as I have suggested, it is a self-limiting response to simply identify and reject a pattern of 'aestheticizing'. One can certainly point out, remaining at the level of the theory, that the move from a diagnostic-critical mode which analyzes the procedural history of the state of exception to a call to think beyond any relation is, at best, obscure and, at worst, evasive and messianic. But we need a better understanding of the relation of this work, and its influence, to the history and conditions of the field. If we wish to propose an alternative that will be effective and influential within literary studies, we need to remain responsive to the field's values and methods, which are, in a word, inescapably oriented towards the aesthetic. And it needs to be stressed that this is not merely a practical or instrumental consideration: the history of liberalism, as both a philosophy and a literary topos, is richer, and more amenable to interpretive challenges and complexity, than many of the current oppositional frameworks allow.

It must be conceded that thinkers within the liberal tradition have in some sense contributed to the problem at hand. Indeed, to the extent that self-identified liberal thinkers have implicitly or explicitly taken up the question of liberalism's relation to the aesthetic, there has been a tendency to refuse or at least evade the development of a liberal aesthetic that encompasses the forms and practices of political liberalism itself. In the work of thinkers and critics such as Lionel Trilling, Richard Rorty and Stefan Collini, for example, a certain humanist emphasis on creative richness ('variousness', to use Trilling's term) and aesthetic temperament has set the terms for what many anti-liberal thinkers view as an easily discernible (and dismissible) liberal aesthetic. Trilling and Rorty, moreover, emphasize and help to entrench a certain gulf between political liberalism and liberal aesthetics (Collini 2004; Rorty 1989; Trilling 1950). In his influential essay 'Private Irony and Liberal Hope', Rorty argues that we should accept and even cultivate a productive division between private and public life, one which precisely turns on the modes, temperaments and values suitable to each. In opposition to the notion, put forward by Habermas, that postmodernism has been destructive of social hope, Rorty claims that one can be an ironist in private, endlessly re-elaborating one's self-descriptions and one's frameworks of understanding, without jeopardizing the role one needs to adopt in public in order to honour the values and practices of the procedural public sphere, or liberal democracy. Here a kind of generative self-fashioning and playful aesthetic mode is given full force in the private realm, and then curtailed or muted in public. It is true that Rorty's position involves complex understandings of the ways in which private irony might actually generate better forms of understanding and practice in the public sphere, where one is constantly needing to negotiate different standpoints and different sets of interests. And his position shifts over time towards a discussion of the ways various aesthetics might animate public discourse (Rorty 1993). But 'Private Irony and Liberal Hope' insists on a division not only between the private and public spheres, but also, it is clear, between aesthetics and politics. And importantly, even though Rorty stresses irony as opposed to, say, tolerance and appreciation of diversity, his emphasis on individual self-fashioning falls within the broader rubric of the creative liberal individualism that stretches back to John Stuart Mill's emphasis on 'experiments in living'.

Rorty's position is anticipated by Lionel Trilling, a thinker deeply interested in the relation between liberalism and literature. In *The Liberal Imagination*, Trilling offers the observation that readers in a liberal democratic culture like his own, most value works by writers who are actually antagonistic to the culture's social and political ideals (he invokes, as valued writers, Yeats, Eliot, Proust, Joyce, Lawrence and Gide). He also observes that to the extent that contemporary American literature is politically liberal in orientation, it is not of lasting interest. Trilling's larger point here is that there is a serious aesthetic deficiency in the ideas of political liberalism. There is not any insistence that this need be the case for all time, but there is a sense that liberalism cannot generate a profound literature, one to which we would return or with which we would live, as Trilling puts it, 'in an active reciprocal relation' (Trilling 1950: 286). 'It is by no means true', Trilling writes, 'that the inadequacy of the literature that connects itself with a body of ideas is the sign of the inadequacy of those ideas, although it is no doubt true that some ideas have less affinity with literature than others' (ibid.: 287).

In the Preface to *The Liberal Imagination*, Trilling expresses his project as an internal critique of liberalism, one which will '[recall] liberals to a sense of variousness and possibility' (ibid.: 10). Trilling's conception of political liberalism is broad, it should be noted, including both what we think of as democratic liberalism in the United States and other forms of progressive politics, from social democracy to communism (Teres 1996: 260–61). The danger of political liberalism in all its forms is its tendency, according to Trilling, to 'organize the elements of life in a rational way':

> [W]hen we approach liberalism in a political spirit we shall fail in critical completeness if we do not take into account the value and necessity of its organizational impulse. But at the same time we must understand that organization means delegation, and agencies, and bureaus, and technicians, and that the ideas that can survive delegation, that can be passed onto agencies and bureaus and technicians, incline to be ideas of a certain kind and of a certain simplicity: they give up something of their largeness and modulation and complexity in order to survive. The lively sense of contingency and possibility, and of those exceptions to the rule which may be the beginning of the end of the rule – this sense does not suit well with the impulse to organization.
>
> (Trilling 1950: 9–10)

Trilling's argument parallels more recent claims of literature's superiority to philosophy when it comes to capturing living ideas (Nussbaum 1990), but he offers a more specific claim about the poverty of political liberalism as an existential and aesthetic mode of thought. Also evident is the distinction between liberalism as a temperament and liberalism as a body of ideas or a practical orientation towards institutions and the larger political system. The former is enabling for literature and, through literature, for politics: it is the true promise of liberalism. The latter is a threat or problem for vital literary art.

The examples of Rorty and Trilling reveal what is actually a broader and quite consequential phenomenon – an odd gap, often actively elaborated and reflectively endorsed, between political liberalism and liberal aesthetics. Such thinkers, while broadly liberal in political orientation, tend to disavow systematic political thought in general. Reinforcing the effects of this phenomenon is the fact that more systematic liberal philosophers such as John Rawls and Jürgen Habermas have not tended to pay sustained attention to matters aesthetic. Moreover, certain approaches that may appear to overcome or refuse the split in liberalism between the political and the aesthetic registers (the 'creative democracy' of John Dewey [1976], the 'democratic aestheticism' of George Kateb [2000]), tend by and large to reinforce a liberal humanism oriented to the aesthetic register of the beautiful and to ethico-political virtues associated with harmonious diversity. Missing from such visions are the intractable energies of those moods of scepticism, despair and difficulty that frequently accompany the commitment to liberal democratic principles and modes of life. From this perspective, the motivating scepticism of Trilling and Rorty can be seen as both an important acknowledgement of the specificity of institutional and procedural politics (the distance between those forms of politics and common conceptions of the liberal imagination) and as a symptom of an entrenched way of thinking about liberal aesthetics. What is required, however, is an angle of sight that makes it possible to discern the productive difficulty and excess that attend rich literary engagements with liberal political forms such as argument, procedure and the rule of law, and with the broader values of philosophical modernity that subtend them. Also crucial is the development of an approach that can acknowledge the importance of the long view, or the systems perspective, to liberal thought, without exiling it to an extra-literary realm of politics or sociology.

Some key work in the literary field has importantly identified and elevated a submerged or underappreciated liberal tradition, most notably in relation to the theory of the public sphere (Morris 2004; Plotz 2000; Warner 1990). Additionally, some recent work on nineteenth- and twentieth-century American and British literature has turned its lens on the importance of the state and its institutions, and this work could be seen as an accompaniment to the more polemical interventions of critics such as Brennan, and Szalay and McGann. Moving away from the Foucauldian model of disciplinarity and surveillance, which productively engaged earlier critics of power such as Miller (1988) and Armstrong (1987), these studies have insisted on a more differentiated understanding of state power, and some have taken a less suspicious look at forms of social democracy and the welfare state (Goodlad 2003; Robbins 2007; Szalay 2000). All these critics explore modes of experience that issue from specific engagements with institutions of the state. My aim, however, is to expand the field of inquiry to include explorations of when, where and how specific literary forms engage some of the shaping principles of liberal political thought as well as the enduring challenges of liberal democratic institutions. This approach promises to yield significant insights in relation to the formal economy of the realist tradition. Sometimes a writer who appears detached from, or even cynical about, institutional politics may at the same time be engaging some of the key concepts or challenges associated with democratic and liberal practice and belief.

It is also helpful to shift attention away from any goal of identifying a liberal canon, which can produce a limiting framework and yield. Rather than showing the ways in which literary texts exemplify or champion liberalism, one might explore the ways in which certain literary texts exemplify the problem of exemplifying liberalism or, to put it in terms that resonate with Trilling's immanent critique of liberalism, exemplify the problem of how to think about the claims of argument and liberal critique given the complexity of existence and specific historical conditions and constraints. Literature whose politics, whether radical or liberal, are too direct and legible – committed literature in the sense that Adorno (1980) complained of – is often precisely not work that resonates aesthetically and with which, to invoke Trilling, we would live in an active and reciprocal relation. But there is nothing about liberalism that needs to be less capable of being given complex aesthetic treatment. Indeed, there are interesting elements within the realist tradition that provide the occasion for complex enactments of enduring liberal challenges. Overall, the novelistic tradition, especially in its more intellectualist formations, is often itself interested in the relation between ideas and life, or how one might live theory. Coming at the same historical juncture as the rise of liberalism, the nineteenth-century novel takes up some of the same issues that exercise liberalism itself: imagining the rigorous critique of custom and convention as a way of life; mediating between the moral life of individuals and a long sociological or historical view of communities and societies; and engaging the relation between existence and doctrine, or life and theory.

Obviously, one would need to move past simple analogies between the formal characteristics of realist works and the structuring challenges of liberalism. The persuasiveness of the analysis in each case would depend on how compellingly the aesthetic features of a work or author seemed to dovetail with the philosophical and political terrain of liberalism. While it is not the purpose of this essay to provide extended literary analysis of individual works, the approach I am proposing can provide fresh angles of interpretation on writers such as George Eliot, Charles Dickens and Anthony Trollope. To invoke one central example, Dickens's *Bleak House* displays a powerful working through of the relation between a bleak systems view (in the third-person narrative) and the aspirations of a socially minded moral participant (in Esther's first-person narrative). Eliot's ongoing engagement with liberal thought, by contrast, resides chiefly in her powerful representations of morally and intellectually charged relations between doctrinaire figures and striving, ardent idealists: it is in the treatment of highly-personalized argument that one sees the significance for Eliot of the task of attempting to live one's theory. And interestingly, Trollope's project centrally explores the complexities of sincerity and liberal critique in relation to a world where forms of ethos, especially the ethos of tacit gentlemanliness, are paramount. His work manages to show the strains on manners at a time of increasing liberal challenge to entrenched privilege, even as his own ideological position remains, like Eliot's, complicated. It bears underscoring that we risk missing the important elements of realism's engagement with liberalism if we simply seek to assign authors to ideological positions. Trollope is deeply engaged by questions having to do with argument, sincerity, and the relation between psychology and principle; this is less an active promotion of liberal ideology or the importance of the liberal state than a dynamic engagement with core ideas of liberalism (Anderson 2007).

A renewed attention to realism's complex enactment of liberal ideas would also have implications for understandings of the relation between realism and modernism, and this consequence is especially important in light of the fact that theoretical tendencies have worked in tandem with established literary histories to interpret the relation between realism and modernism in light of an antinomy between bourgeois and aesthetic modernity, the latter associated with Baudelaire, Nietzsche and Wilde. As Robert Pippin (1999) argues, a pivotal alliance between the critique of bourgeois modernity and the promotion of aesthetic modernity has defined and shaped a certain bias in the modern academy. This tendency downplays the internal divisions and self-criticisms of Enlightenment modernity (which is dismissed as bourgeois), divisions which included an awareness of the many forms of finitude that threaten the ideals of the Enlightenment. A rethinking of this framework is crucial to any renewed assessment of liberalism, in both its philosophical and literary forms.

As an alternative to the misunderstanding of realism fostered by the privileging of aesthetic modernity, Pippin brings to a progressive liberal framework an emphasis on Hegelian narrative, just as Lukács asserted the importance of realism, via Marxism, against what he saw as a subjective modernism that was merely reflecting the alienated experience of reification under capitalism. Of course one wants to refuse the reductive opposition in Lukács between a realism associated with a critical view of the social totality, and a modernism that is fundamentally symptomatic. As Adorno points out, one of the key problems in Lukács is a failure to properly understand the aesthetic specificity of art works, his tendency to imagine the novel as a kind of social science, thereby neglecting the primacy of aesthetic form. It should be possible to acknowledge a tradition of political modernity in the novel without setting in place, as both Lukács and Pippin do, a primary evaluative distinction between realism and a deficient aesthetic modernity. Such attempts to divide the aesthetic field in an evaluative way, and to elevate realism as more historically rich or sociologically comprehensive, risk limiting the understanding of realism and liberalism, insofar as they prescribe the form of realism's aesthetic complexity, stabilizing and framing its liberal imagination. In this regard, I would advocate a return to Trilling, but with a greater emphasis on ways in which political liberalism finds more complex and resonant expression in the literary tradition than he allows. The liberal tradition is not as prosaic, rule-governed and simply hopeful as its critics seem to suppose; certain kinds of aspirations and threshold experiences, certain energies at once negative and utopian, are as vital within the liberal aesthetic tradition as they are in the Marxist aesthetics of someone like Adorno. Liberal aesthetics are formally and conceptually fraught, just as political liberalism is existentially challenging.

Bibliography

Adorno, T. (1980) 'Commitment', trans. F. McDonagh, in T. Adorno *et al.*, *Aesthetics and Politics*, London: Verso.

Agamben, G. (1998) Homo Sacer: *Sovereign Power and Bare Life*, trans. D. Heller-Roazen, Stanford, CA: Stanford University Press.

Anderson, A. (2006) *The Way We Argue Now: A Study in the Cultures of Theory*, Princeton, NJ: Princeton University Press.

Anderson, A. (2007) 'Trollope's Modernity', *ELH* 74: 509–34.

Armstrong, I. (2000) *The Radical Aesthetic*, Oxford: Basil Blackwell.

Armstrong, N. (1987) *Desire and Domestic Fiction: A Political History of the Novel*, New York: Oxford University Press.

Attridge, D. (2004) *The Singularity of Literature*, New York: Routledge.

Brenkman, J. (2007) *The Cultural Contradictions of Democracy*, Princeton, NJ: Princeton University Press.

Brennan, T. (2006) *Wars of Position: The Cultural Politics of Left and Right*, New York: Columbia University Press.

Brinkley, A. (2007) 'Liberalism and Belief', in N. Jumonville and K. Mattson (eds), *Liberalism for a New Century*, Berkeley: University of California Press.

Burrow, J. (1988) *Whigs and Liberals: Continuity and Change in English Political Thought*, Oxford: Clarendon Press.

Collini, S. (2004) 'On Variousness and On Persuasion', *New Left Review* 27: 65–97.

de Bolla, P. (2001) *Art Matters*, Cambridge, MA: Harvard University Press.

Derrida, J. (1990) 'Force of Law: The "Mystical Foundation of Authority"', *Cardozo Law Review* 11: 919–1045.

Derrida, J. (1992) 'Before the Law', in D. Attridge (ed.), *Acts of Literature*, New York: Routledge.

Dewey, J. (1976) 'Creative Democracy: The Task Before Us', in J. Boydston (ed), *John Dewey: The Later Works, 1925–1953*, vol. 14, Carbondale: Southern Illinois University Press.

Goodlad, L.M.E. (2003) *Victorian Literature and the Victorian State: Character and Governance in a Liberal Society*, Baltimore, MD: Johns Hopkins University Press.

Kafka, F. (1978) 'Before the Law', in *Wedding Preparations and Other Stories*, trans. W. and E. Muir, Harmondsworth: Penguin. [Reprinted in Derrida 1992.]

Kateb, G. (2000) 'Aestheticism and Morality: Their Cooperation and Hostility', *Political Theory* 28 (1): 5–37.

LaCapra, D. (2004) *History in Transit: Experience, Identity, Critical Theory*, Ithaca, NY: Cornell University Press.

Levine, G. (ed.) (1994) *Aesthetics and Ideology*, New Brunswick, NJ: Rutgers University Press.

Miller, D. A. (1988) *The Novel and the Police*, Berkeley: University of California Press.

Morris, P. (2004) *Imagining Inclusive Society in Nineteenth-Century Novels: The Code of Sincerity in the Public Sphere*, Baltimore, MA: Johns Hopkins University Press.

Nussbaum, M. (1990) *Love's Knowledge: Essays on Philosophy and Literature*, New York: Oxford.

Pippin, R. (1991, 2nd edn 1999) *Modernism as a Philosophical Problem: On the Dissatisfactions of European High Culture*, Oxford: Blackwell.

Plotz, J. (2000) *The Crowd: British Literature and Public Politics*, Berkeley: University of California Press.

Robbins, B. (2007) *Upward Mobility and the Common Good: Toward a Literary History of the Welfare State*, Princeton, NJ: Princeton University Press.

Rorty, R. (1989) *Contingency, Irony, Solidarity*, Cambridge: Cambridge University Press.

Rorty, R. (1993) 'Human Rights, Rationality, and Sentimentality', in S. Shute and S. Hurley (eds), *On Human Rights: The Oxford Amnesty Lectures*, New York: Basic Books.

Scarry, E. (1999) *On Beauty and Being Just*, Princeton, NJ: Princeton University Press.

Schmitt, C. (2005) *Political Theology: Four Chapters on the Concept of Sovereignty*, trans. G. Schwab, Chicago: University of Chicago Press.

Szalay, M. (2000). *New Deal Modernism: American Literature and the Invention of the Welfare State*, Durham, NC: Duke University Press.

Szalay, M. and McGann, S. (2005) 'Do You Believe in Magic?: Literary Thinking After the New Left', *Yale Journal of Criticism* 18 (2): 435–68.

Teres, H. (1996) *Renewing the Left: Politics: Imagination, and the New York Intellectuals*, New York: Oxford University Press.

Trilling, L. (1950) *The Liberal Imagination: Essays on Literature and Society*, New York: Doubleday.

Warner, M. (1990) *The Letters of the Republic: Publication and the Public Sphere in Eighteenth-century America*, Cambridge, MA: Harvard University Press.

PART VI

Philosophy after theory

18

THE ARCHE-MATERIALITY OF TIME

Deconstruction, evolution and speculative materialism

Martin Hägglund

The last decade of developments in 'theory' has been marked by a turn away from questions of language and discourse, in favour of a renewed interest in questions of the real, the material and the biological. If Ferdinand de Saussure and linguistics were once an obligatory reference point, Charles Darwin and evolutionary theory have increasingly come to occupy a similar position. Alongside this development, the status of deconstruction has been downgraded. Derrida's work is largely seen as mired in the linguistic turn or as mortgaged to an ethical and religious piety that leaves it without resources to engage the sciences and develop a materialist philosophy.

Such an assessment of deconstruction is, however, deeply misleading. One does not have to look farther than *Of Grammatology* to find Derrida articulating his key notion of 'the trace' in terms of not only linguistics and phenomenology but also natural science (Derrida 1976). Indeed, Derrida defines the trace in terms of a general co-implication of time and space: it designates the becoming-space of time and the becoming-time of space, which Derrida abbreviates as spacing (*espacement*). In my book *Radical Atheism: Derrida and the Time of Life*, I argue that the necessity of spacing can be deduced from the philosophical problem of succession (Hägglund 2008). Succession should here *not* be conflated with the chronology of linear time, but rather accounts for the constitutive delay and deferral of any event. Without succession nothing will have happened, whether retrospectively or prospectively, and Derrida analyzes this structure of the event in terms of a necessary spacing. Spacing is thus the condition for anything that is subject to succession, whether animate or inanimate, ideal or material.

It is important to underline, however, that Derrida does not generalize the trace structure by way of an assertion about the nature of being as such. The trace is not an ontological stipulation but a *logical structure* that makes explicit what is implicit in the concept of succession. To insist on the logical status of the trace is not to oppose it to ontology, epistemology or phenomenology, but to insist that the trace is a metatheoretical notion that elucidates what is entailed by a commitment to succession in either of these registers. The logical structure of the trace is expressive of *any* concept of succession – regardless of whether succession is understood in terms of an ontological, epistemological or phenomenological account of time.

By the same token, one can make explicit that the structure of the trace is implicit in scientific accounts of how time is recorded in biological processes and material structures. For reasons that I will specify, the structure of the trace is implicit not only in the temporality of the living but also in the disintegration of inanimate matter (e.g. the 'half-life' of isotopes). The logic of the trace can thereby serve to elucidate philosophical stakes in the understanding of the relation between the living and the non-living that has been handed down to us by modern science.[1] I will here seek to develop this line of inquiry by demonstrating how the logic of the trace allows one to take into account the insights of Darwinism. Specifically, I will argue in favour of a conceptual distinction between life and non-living matter that nevertheless asserts a continuity between the two in terms of what I call the 'arche-materiality' of time.[2]

My point of departure is a critical engagement with the work of Quentin Meillassoux. The rapidly growing interest in Meillassoux after the English translation of his first book *After Finitude* (2008), and the announcement of the movement of 'speculative realism' in its wake, is perhaps the most striking instantiation of the turn from linguistic to ontological concerns in contemporary theory. Furthermore, the rationalist argumentative style of Meillassoux may seem to be at the furthest remove from the supposed literary excesses of Derridean deconstruction. For precisely this reason, however, it is instructive to confront the logic of Meillassoux's arguments with the deconstructive logic of the trace that I seek to pursue, beyond any linguistic or pious version of Derrida's thinking.

Meillassoux targets nothing less than the basic argument of Kant's transcendental philosophy, which holds that we cannot have knowledge of the absolute. Against all forms of dogmatic metaphysics, which lay claim to prove the existence of the absolute, Kant argues that there can be no cognition without the forms of time and space that undercut any possible knowledge of the absolute. The absolute would have to be exempt from time and space, whereas all we can know is given through time and space as forms of intuition. As is well known, however, Kant delimits the possibility of knowledge in order to 'make room for faith'. By making it impossible to prove the existence of the absolute Kant also makes it impossible to refute it and thus rehabilitates the absolute as an object of faith rather than knowledge.

In contrast, Meillassoux seeks to formulate a notion of the absolute that does not entail a return to the metaphysical and pre-critical idea of a necessary being. He endorses Kant's critique of dogmatic metaphysics, but argues that we can develop a 'speculative' thinking of the absolute that does not succumb to positing a necessary being. According to Meillassoux,

> it is absolutely necessary that every entity might not exist. This is indeed a speculative thesis, since we are thinking an absolute, but it is not metaphysical, since we are not thinking any *thing* (any entity) that would *be* absolute. The absolute is the absolute impossibility of a necessary being.
>
> (Meillassoux 2008: 60)

The absolute in question is the power of *time*. Time makes it impossible for any entity to be necessary, since the condition of temporality entails that every entity can be destroyed. It is precisely this destructibility that Meillassoux holds to be absolute: 'only the time that harbours the capacity to destroy every determinate reality, while obeying no determinate law – the time capable of destroying, without reason or law, both words and things – can be thought as an absolute' (ibid.: 62). Armed with this notion of the absolute, Meillassoux takes contemporary philosophers to task for their concessions to religion. By renouncing knowledge of the absolute, thinkers of the 'wholly other' renounce the power to refute religion and give the latter free reign as long as it restricts itself to the realm of faith rather than knowledge. As Meillassoux puts it with an emphatic formulation: '*by forbidding reason any claim to the absolute, the end of metaphysics has taken the form of an exacerbated return of the religious*' (ibid.: 45).

Although Meillassoux rarely mentions him by name, Derrida is clearly one of the intended targets for his attack on the idea of a 'wholly other' beyond the grasp of reason. As I demonstrate in *Radical Atheism*, however, Derrida's thinking of alterity cannot be aligned with any religious conception of the absolute (Hägglund 2008). For Derrida, alterity is indissociable from the condition of temporality that exposes every instance to destruction. Consequently, Derrida's notion of the 'absolutely' or 'wholly' other (*tout autre*) does not refer to the positive infinity of the divine but to the radical finitude of every other. Every finite other is absolutely other, not because it is absolutely in itself but, on the contrary, because it can never overcome the alterity of time and never be in itself. Far from consolidating a religious instance that would be exempt from the destruction of time, Derrida's conception of absolute alterity spells out that the subjection to the violent passage of time is absolutely irreducible.

Nevertheless, there are central and decisive differences between the conception of time proposed by Meillassoux and Derrida respectively. For Meillassoux, the absolute contingency of time (the fact that anything can happen) has an ontological status which entails that the advent of the divine is possible and that life may emerge *ex nihilo*, independent of preceding material conditions.[3] In contrast, I will show that the conception of time as dependent on the structure of the trace provides a better model for thinking temporality and contingency than the one proposed by Meillassoux. Contrary to what Meillassoux holds, time cannot be a virtual power to make anything happen, since it is dependent on a spatial, material support that restricts its possibilities. My argument proceeds by demonstrating how the structure of the trace can be deduced from the philosophical problem of succession. The structure of the trace entails the arche-materiality of time, which is crucial for thinking the relation between the animate and the inanimate, while undermining Meillassoux's notion of the virtual power of time.

Articulating his conception of time, Meillassoux proceeds from the empirical phenomenon of what he calls *arche-fossils*, namely, objects that are older than life on Earth and whose duration it is possible to measure: 'for example an isotope whose rate of radioactive decay we know, or the luminous emission of a star that informs us as to the date of its formation' (2008: 10). Such arche-fossils enable scientists to date the origin of the universe to approximately 13.5 billion years ago and the origin of life on Earth to 3.5 billion years ago. According to Meillassoux, these 'ancestral' statements are incompatible with the basic presupposition of transcendental philosophy, which holds that the world cannot be described apart from how it is given to a thinking and/or living being. The ancestral statements of science describe a world in which *nothing was given* to a thinking or living being, since the physical conditions of the universe did not allow for the emergence of a life or consciousness to which the world could be given. The ensuing challenge to transcendental philosophy 'is not the empirical problem of the birth of living organisms, but the ontological problem of the coming into being of givenness as such' (ibid.: 21). Rather than being able to restrict time to a form of givenness for consciousness, we are confronted with an absolute time 'wherein *consciousness* as well as *conscious time* have *themselves emerged in time*' (ibid.: 21).

Meillassoux is well aware that he could here be accused of conflating the empirical with the transcendental. Empirical bodies emerge and perish in time, but the same cannot be said of transcendental conditions. The transcendental subject is not an empirical body existing in time and space, but a set of conditions through which knowledge of bodies in time and space is possible. Thus, a scientific discourse about empirical objects or the empirical universe cannot have purchase on the transcendental subject, since the latter provides the condition of possibility for scientific knowledge.

In response to such an objection, Meillassoux grants that the transcendental subject does not exist in the way an object exists, but insists that the notion of a transcendental subject nevertheless entails that it must *take place*, since it 'remains indissociable from the notion of a *point of view*' (ibid.: 25). The transcendental subject – as both Kant and Husserl maintain – is essentially *finite*, since it never has access to the world as a totality but is dependent on receptivity, horizon, perceptual adumbration and so on. It follows that although transcendental subjectivity is not reducible to an objectively existing body, it must be incarnated in a body in order to be what it is. Without the incarnation in a body there would be no receptivity, no limited perspective on the world, and hence no point of view. As Meillassoux puts it: 'That the transcendental subject has *this* or that body is an empirical matter, but that *it has* a body is a non-empirical condition of its taking place' (ibid.: 25). Consequently, when scientific discourse 'temporalizes and spatializes the emergence of living bodies' it also temporalizes and spatializes the basic condition for the taking place of the transcendental (ibid.: 25). Thus, Meillassoux argues that the problem of the ancestral 'cannot be thought from the transcendental viewpoint because it concerns the space-time in which transcendental subjects went from not-taking-place to taking-place – and hence concerns the space-time anterior to spatiotemporal forms of representation' (ibid.: 26). Far from confirming the transcendental relation between thinking and being as primordial, the ancestral discloses 'a temporality within which this relation is just one event among others, inscribed in an order of succession in which it is merely a stage, rather than an origin' (ibid.: 10).

Despite highlighting the problem of succession, however, Meillassoux fails to think through its logical implications (2008: 71). Meillassoux argues that the principle of non-contradiction must be 'an absolute ontological truth' for temporal becoming to be possible. If a contradictory entity existed it could never become other than itself, since it can already contain its other within itself. If it *is* contradictory, it can never cease to be but would rather continue to be even in not-being. Consequently, the existence of a contradictory entity is incompatible with temporal becoming; it would eliminate 'the dimension of alterity required for the deployment of any process whatsoever, liquidating it in the formless being which must always already be what it is not' (ibid.: 70). This argument is correct as far as it goes, but it does not consider that the same problem arises if we posit the existence of a non-contradictory entity. A non-contradictory entity would be indivisibly present *in itself*. Thus, it would remove precisely the 'dimension of alterity' that is required for becoming. Contrary to what Meillassoux holds, the movement of becoming cannot consist in the movement from one discrete entity to another, so that 'things must be this, *then* other than this; they are, *then* they are not' (ibid.: 70). For one moment to be succeeded by another – which is the minimal condition for any becoming whatsoever – it cannot *first* be present in itself and *then* be affected by its own disappearance. A self-present, indivisible moment could never even begin to give way to another moment, since what is indivisible cannot be altered. The succession of time requires not only that each moment be superseded by another moment, but also that this alteration be at work from the beginning. Every moment must negate itself and pass away *in its very event*. If the moment did not negate itself there would be no time, only a presence forever remaining the same.

This argument – which I develop at length in *Radical Atheism* – does not entail that there *is* a contradictory entity that is able to contain its own non-being within itself. On the contrary, I argue that the constitution of time entails that there cannot be any entity (whether contradictory or non-contradictory) that contains itself within itself. The succession of time implies that nothing ever is *in itself*; it is rather always already subjected to the alteration and destruction that is involved in ceasing-to-be.

It follows that a temporal entity cannot be indivisible but depends on the structure of the trace. The trace is not itself an ontological entity but the logical structure that explains the becoming-space of time and the becoming-time of space. A compelling account of the trace therefore requires that we demonstrate the necessary co-implication of space and time. The classical distinction between space and time is the distinction between simultaneity and succession. The spatial can remain the same, since the simultaneity of space allows one point to co-exist with another. In contrast, the temporal can never remain the same, since the succession of time entails that every moment ceases to be as soon as it comes to be and thus negates itself. By the same token, however, it is clear that time is impossible without space. Time is nothing but negation, so in order to be anything it has to be spatialized. There is no 'flow' of time that is independent of spatialization, since time has to be spatialized in order to flow in the first place. Thus, everything we say about time (that it is 'passing,' 'flowing,' 'in motion' and so on) is a spatial metaphor. This is not a failure of language to capture pure time but follows from an originary *becoming-space of time*. The very concept of duration presupposes that something remains across an interval of time and only that which is spatial can remain. Inversely, without temporalization it would be impossible for a point to *remain* the same as itself or to exist *at the same time* as another point. The simultaneity of space is itself a temporal notion. Accordingly, for one point to be simultaneous with another point there must be an originary *becoming-time of space* that relates them to one another.[4] The structure of the trace – as the co-implication of time and space – is therefore the condition for everything that is temporal. Everything that is subjected to succession is subjected to the trace, whether it is alive or not.

The arche-materiality of time follows from the structure of the trace. Given that every temporal moment ceases to be as soon as it comes to be, it must be inscribed as a trace in order to be at all. The trace is necessarily spatial, since spatiality is characterized by the ability to persist in spite of temporal succession. Every temporal moment therefore depends on the material support of spatial inscription. Indeed, the material support of the trace is the condition for the synthesis of time, since it enables the past to be retained for the future. The material support of the trace, however, is itself temporal. Without temporalization a trace could not persist across time and relate the past to the future. Accordingly, the persistence of the trace cannot be the persistence of something that is exempt from the negativity of time. Rather, the trace is always left for an unpredictable future that gives it both the chance to live on and to be effaced.

Let me emphasize again, however, that the deconstructive notion of the trace is logical rather than ontological. Accordingly, my argument does not assume the form of an unconditional assertion ('being is spacing, hence arche-materiality') but rather the form of a conditional claim ('if your discourse commits you to a notion of succession, then you are committed to a notion of spacing and hence arche-materiality'). The discourse in question can then be ontological, epistemological, phenomenological or scientific – in all these cases the logic of the trace will have expressive power insofar as there is an implicit or explicit commitment to a notion of succession.

The logical implications of succession are directly relevant for the main argument in *After Finitude*, which seeks to establish the necessity of contingency. As Meillassoux formulates his guiding thesis: 'Everything is possible, anything can happen – except something that is necessary, because it is the contingency of the entity that is necessary, not the entity' (2008: 65). This notion of contingency presupposes succession, since there can be no contingency without the unpredictable passage from one moment to another. To establish the necessity of contingency, as Meillassoux seeks to do, is thus also to establish the necessity of succession.

Meillassoux himself, however, does not theorize the implications of succession, and this comes at a significant cost for his argument. In a recent essay, Aaron F. Hodges has suggested that Meillassoux's critique of the principle of sufficient reason is potentially damaging for my notion of radical destructibility, which holds that everything that comes into being must pass away (Hodges 2009: 102–3). In fact, however, it is rather my notion of radical destructibility that allows us to locate an inconsistency in Meillassoux's argument. Let me quote in full the passage from Meillassoux to which Hodges calls attention:

> To assert . . . that everything must necessarily perish, would be to assert a proposition that is *still* metaphysical. Granted, this thesis of the precariousness of everything would no longer claim that a determinate entity is necessary, but it would continue to maintain that a determinate situation is necessary, viz., the destruction of this or that. But this is still to obey the injunction of the principle of reason, according to which there is a necessary reason why this is the case (the eventual destruction of X), rather than otherwise (the endless persistence of X). But we do not see by virtue of what there would be a reason necessitating the possibility of destruction as opposed to the possibility of persistence. The unequivocal relinquishment of the principle of reason requires us to insist that both the destruction and the perpetual preservation of a determinate entity must equally be able to occur for no reason. Contingency is such that anything might happen, even nothing at all, so that what is, remains as it is.
>
> (Meillassoux 2008: 62–3)

While emphasizing that a necessary entity is impossible, Meillassoux maintains that it is possible for nothing to happen, so that the entity remains as it is. As soon as we take into account the intrinsic link between contingency and succession, however, we can see that the latter argument is untenable. If nothing happened and the entity remained as it is, there would be no succession, but by the same token there would be no contingency. An entity to which nothing happens is inseparable from a necessary entity. In order to be subjected to succession – which is to say: in order to be contingent – the entity must begin to pass away as soon as it comes to be and can never remain as it is. Consequently, there *is* a reason that necessitates destruction, but it does not re-import the metaphysical principle of reason. On the contrary, it only makes explicit what is implicit in the principle of unreason that Meillassoux calls the necessity of contingency. Contingency presupposes succession and there is no succession without destruction. If the moment were not destroyed in being succeeded by another moment, their relation would not be one of succession but of co-existence. Thus, to assert the necessity of contingency is to assert the necessity of destruction.

For the same reason, Meillassoux's opposition between destruction and persistence is misleading. Persistence itself presupposes an interval of time, which means that nothing can persist unscathed by succession. The destruction that is involved in succession makes any persistence dependent on the *spacing* of time, which inscribes what happens as a spatial trace that remains, while exposing it to erasure in an unpredictable future. The erasure of the spatial trace is indeed a *possibility* that is not immediately actualized, but it already presupposes the *necessity* of destruction that is operative in succession. Given that nothing can persist without succession, destruction is therefore at work in persistence itself.

Meillassoux's response would presumably be that his notion of time does not depend on succession, but designates a 'virtual power' that may leave everything as it is *or* subject it to succession. To posit such a virtual power, however, is not to think the implications of time but to posit an instance that has power *over* time, since it may stop and start succession at will. In contrast, I argue that *time is nothing in itself*; it is nothing but the negativity that is intrinsic to succession. Time cannot, therefore, be a virtual power. Given that time is nothing but negativity, it does not have the power to *be* anything or *do* anything on its own. More precisely, according to my arche-materialist account, time cannot be anything or do anything without a spatialization that constrains the power of the virtual in making it dependent on material conditions.

We can clarify the stakes of this argument by considering the example of the emergence of life, which for Meillassoux is a 'paradigmatic example' of the virtual power of time (Meillassoux 2007: 73). His way of formulating the problem, however, already reveals an anti-materialist bias. According to Meillassoux, 'the same argumentative strategies are reproduced time and time again in philosophical polemics on the possibility of life emerging from inanimate matter':

> Since life manifestly supposes, at least at a certain degree of its evolution, the existence of a set of affective and perceptive contents, either one decides that matter already contained such subjectivity in some manner, in too weak a degree for it to be detected, or that these affections of the living being did not pre-exist in any way within matter, thus finding oneself constrained to admit their irruption *ex nihilo* from that matter – which seems to lead to the acceptance of an intervention transcending the power of nature. Either a 'continuism,' a philosophy of immanence – a variant of hylozoism – which would have it that *all* matter is alive to some degree; or the belief in a transcendence exceeding the rational comprehension of natural processes.
>
> (Ibid.: 79–80)

It is striking that a philosopher with Meillassoux's considerable knowledge of science would present such an inadequate description of the actual debates about the emergence of life. A materialist account of the emergence of life is by no means obliged to hold that all matter is alive to some degree. On the contrary, such vitalism has been thoroughly debunked by Darwinism and its most prominent philosophical proponents. For example, what Daniel Dennett analyzes as Darwin's dangerous idea is precisely the account of how life evolved out of non-living matter and of how even the most advanced intentionality or sensibility originates in mindless repetition (Dennett 1995). Rather than vitalizing matter, philosophical Darwinism devitalizes life. For Meillassoux, however, life as subjective existence is something so special and unique that it requires an explanation that is refractory to materialist analysis.[5] In Dennett's language, Meillassoux thus refuses the 'cranes' of physical and biological explanation in favour of the 'skyhook' of a virtual power that would allow for the emergence of life *ex nihilo*.

To be sure, Meillassoux tries to distinguish his notion of irruption *ex nihilo* from the theological notion of creation *ex nihilo*, by maintaining that the former does not invoke any transcendence that would exceed rational comprehension, but rather proceeds from the virtual power of contingency that Meillassoux seeks to formulate in rational terms (2007: 73). In both cases, however, there is the appeal to a power that is not limited by material constraints. Symptomatically, Meillassoux holds that 'life furnished with sensibility' emerges '*directly* from a matter within which one cannot, short of sheer fantasy, foresee the germs of this sensibility'. As Meillassoux should know, this is nonsense from a scientific point of view. Life furnished with sensibility does not emerge directly from inanimate matter, but evolves according to complex processes that are described in detail by evolutionary biology. If Meillassoux here disregards the evidence of science it is because he univocally privileges logical over material possibility.[6] Contingency is for him the virtual power to make anything happen at any time, so that life furnished with sensibility can emerge without preceding material conditions that would make it possible. This idea of an irruption *ex nihilo* does not have any explanatory purchase on the temporality of evolution, however, since it eliminates time in favour of a punctual instant. Even if we limit the notion of irruption *ex nihilo* to a more modest claim, namely, that the beginning of the evolutionary process that led to sentient life was a contingent event that could not have been foreseen or predicted, there is still no need for Meillassoux's concept of contingency as an unlimited virtual power to explain this event. Consider, for example, Dennett's Darwinian argument concerning the origin of life:

> We know as a matter of logic that there was at least one start that has us as its continuation, but there were probably many false starts that differed *in no interesting way at all* from the one that initiated the winning series. The title of Adam is, once again, a retrospective honour, and we make a fundamental mistake of reasoning if we ask, *In virtue of what essential difference* is this the beginning of life? There need be no difference at all between Adam and Badam, an atom-for-atom duplicate of Adam who just happened not to have founded anything of note.
>
> (Dennett 1995: 201)

The beginning of life is here described as a contingent event, but notice that the contingency does not depend on a punctual event of irruption but on what happens successively. There is no virtual power that can determine an event to be the origin of life. On the contrary, which event will have been the origin of life is an effect of the succession of time that can never be reduced to an instant. Consequently, there is no need for Meillassoux's skyhook of irruption *ex nihilo* to explain the emergence of life. The emergence of life is certainly a contingent event, but this contingency cannot be equated with a power to make anything happen at any time. Rather, the emergence is dependent both on preceding material conditions that restrict what is possible and on succeeding events that determine whether it will have been the emergence of anything at all.

Thus, I want to argue that the notion of time as *survival* – rather than as virtual power – is consistent with the insights of Darwinism. The logic of survival that I develop in *Radical Atheism* allows us to pursue the consequences of the arche-materiality of time, as well as the general co-implication of persistence and destruction. If something survives it is never present in itself; it is already marked by the destruction of a past that is no longer while persisting for a future that is not yet. In its most elementary form, this movement of survival does not hinge on the emergence of life. For example, the isotope that has a rate of radioactive decay across billions of years is *surviving* – since it remains and disintegrates over time – but it is not alive.

Consequently, one can make explicit a continuity between the non-living and the living in terms of the arche-materiality of time. The latter is implicit not only in our understanding of the temporality of living processes but also in our understanding of the disintegration of inanimate matter. On the one hand, the disintegration of matter answers to the *becoming-time of space*. The simultaneity of space in itself could never allow for the successive stages of a process of disintegration. For there to be successive disintegration, the negativity of time must be intrinsic to the positive existence of spatial matter. On the other hand, the disintegration of matter answers to the *becoming-space of time*. The succession of time could not even take place without material support, since it is nothing in itself and must be spatialized in order to *be* negative – that is, to negate anything – at all. The notion of arche-materiality thereby allows us to account for the minimal synthesis of time – namely, the minimal recording of temporal passage – without presupposing the advent or existence of life. The disintegration of matter records the passage of time without any animating principle, consciousness or soul.

Accordingly, there is an asymmetry between the animate and the inanimate in the arche-materiality of the trace. As soon as there is life there is death, so there can be no animation without the inanimate, but the inverse argument does not hold. If there were animation as soon as there is inanimate matter, we would be advocating a vitalist conception of the universe, where life is the potential force or the teleological goal of existence. The conception of life that follows from the arche-materiality of the trace is as far as one can get from such vitalism, since it accounts for the utter contingency and destructibility of life. As Henry Staten formulates it:

> the strong naturalist view, from which Derrida does not deviate, holds that matter organized in the right way brings forth life, but denies that life is somehow hidden in matter and just waiting to manifest itself. . . . Life is a

possibility of materiality, not as a potential that it is 'normal' for materiality to bring forth, but as a vastly improbable possibility, by far the exception rather than the rule.

(Staten 2008: 34–5)

What difference is at stake, then, in the difference between the living and the non-living? The radioactive isotope is indeed surviving, since it decays across billions of years, but it is indifferent to its own survival, since it is not alive. A living being, on the other hand, cannot be indifferent to its own survival. Survival is an unconditional condition for everything that is temporal, but only for a living being is the *care* for survival unconditional, since only a living being cares about maintaining itself across an interval of time. The care in question has nothing to do with a vital force that would be exempt from material conditions. Rather, the care for survival is implicit in the scientific definition of life as a form of organization that of necessity is both open and closed. On the one hand, the survival of life requires an *open* system, since the life of a given entity must be able to take in new material and replenish itself to make up for the breakdown of its own macromolecular structures. On the other hand, the survival of life requires a certain *closure* of the system, since a given entity must draw a boundary between itself and others in order to sustain its own life. It follows that the care for survival is inextricable from the organization of life. Neither the openness to replenishment nor the closure of a boundary would have a function without the care to prevent a given life or reproductive line from being terminated.

The distinction between matter and life that I propose, however, is not meant to settle the empirical question of where to draw the line between the living and the non-living. Rather, it is meant to clarify a *conceptual* distinction between matter and life that speaks to the philosophical stakes of the distinction. With regard to the philosophical stakes of the relation between matter and life, then, the notion of arche-materiality can be said to have two major consequences.

First, the notion of arche-materiality undercuts all idealist or speculative attempts to privilege temporality over spatiality. The constitutive negativity of time immediately requires a spatial, material support that retains the past for the future. Contrary to what Meillassoux holds, the contingency of time cannot be a pure virtuality that has the power to make anything happen. The virtual possibilities of temporality are always already restricted by the very constitution of time, since the material support necessarily places conditions on what is possible. The spatiality of material support is the condition for there to be temporality – and hence the possibility of unpredictable events through the negation of the present – but it also closes off certain possibilities in favour of others.

Second, the notion of arche-materiality allows for a conceptual distinction between life and matter that takes into account the Darwinian explanation of how the living evolved out of the non-living, while asserting a distinguishing characteristic of life that does not make any concessions to vitalism. The care for survival that on my account is co-extensive with life does not have any power to finally transcend material constraints but is itself a contingent and destructible fact. Without care everything would be a matter of indifference *and that is a possibility* – there is nothing that necessitates the existence of living beings that care. The fact that every object of care – as well as care itself – is destructible does not make it insignificant but is, on the contrary, what makes it significant in the first place. It is *because* things are destructible, because they have not always been and will not always be, that anyone or anything cares about them. Far from depriving us of the source of vitality, it is precisely the radical destructibility of life that makes it a matter of care.

Notes

1 I want to thank Joshua Andresen, Ray Brassier and Henry Staten for a set of incisive questions that forced me to clarify the status of 'the trace' in my argument. My understanding of the logical, rather than ontological, status of the trace is also indebted to conversations with Rocío Zambrana and to her work on Hegel's *Logic*. See Zambrana (2010).
2 Several respondents to *Radical Atheism* have pointed out that I equivocate between describing the structure of the trace as a general condition for everything that is temporal and as a general condition for *the living*. The precise relation between the temporality of the living and the temporality of non-living matter is thus left unclear in *Radical Atheism*. See Brown (2009), Egginton (2009), Haddad (2009) and Hodges (2009). I am grateful for these responses to my work, which have led me to elaborate how the relation between life and non-living matter should be understood in terms of the logic of the trace.
3 For a radical atheist critique of Meillassoux's 'divinology', see Hägglund (2010), where I further develop the implications of my arguments in this essay.
4 See Derrida's argument that 'simultaneity can appear *as such*, can be simultaneity, that is a *relating* of two points, only in a synthesis, a *complicity*: temporally. One cannot say that a point is *with* another point, there cannot be an *other* point with which, etc., without a temporalization' (Derrida 1982: 55).
5 See Meillassoux's lecture 'Temps et surgissement ex nihilo,' where he explicitly rejects Dennett's materialist analysis of the emergence of life. The lecture is available online at http://www.diffusion.ens.fr/index.php?res=conf&idconf=701
6 See also Peter Hallward's astute observation that Meillassoux tends to treat 'the logical and material domains as if they were effectively interchangeable' (Hallward 2008: 56).

Bibliography

Brown, N. (2009) 'To Live Without an Idea', *Radical Philosophy* 154: 51–3.
Dennett, D. (1995) *Darwin's Dangerous Idea*. New York: Simon & Schuster.
Derrida, J. (1976) *Of Grammatology*. Trans. G. Spivak. Baltimore, MD: Johns Hopkins University Press.
Derrida, J. (1982) *Margins of Philosophy*. Trans. A. Bass. Chicago: University of Chicago Press.
Egginton, W. (2009) 'On Radical Atheism, Chronolibidinal Reading, and Impossible Desires', *CR: The New Centennial Review* 9.1: 191–208.
Haddad, S. (2009) 'Language Remains', *CR: The New Centennial Review* 9.1: 127–46.
Hägglund, M. (2008) *Radical Atheism: Derrida and the Time of Life*. Stanford, CA: Stanford University Press.

Hägglund, M. (2010) 'Radical Atheist Materialism: A Critique of Meillassoux', in L. Bryant, G. Harman and N. Srnicek (eds) *The Speculative Turn: Continental Materialism and Realism*, Melbourne: Re: press. 114–29.

Hallward, P. (2008) 'Anything is Possible', *Radical Philosophy* 152: 51–7.

Hodges, A. F. (2009) 'Martin Hägglund's Speculative Materialism', *CR: The New Centennial Review* 9.1: 87–106.

Meillassoux, Q. (2007) 'Potentiality and Virtuality', *Collapse* II: 55–81.

Meillassoux, Q. (2008) *After Finitude: An Essay on the Necessity of Contingency*. Trans. R. Brassier. London: Continuum.

Staten, H. (2008). 'Derrida, Dennett, and the Ethico-political Project of Naturalism', *Derrida Today* 1.1: 19–41.

Zambrana, R. (2010) 'Hegel's Hyperbolic Formalism', *Bulletin of the Hegel Society of Great Britain* 60/61: 107–30.

19

CONCEPTS, OBJECTS, GEMS

Ray Brassier

1. The question 'What is real?' stands at the crossroads of metaphysics and epistemology. More exactly, it marks the juncture of metaphysics and epistemology with the seal of conceptual representation.

2. Metaphysics understood as the investigation into *what* there is intersects with epistemology understood as the enquiry into how we *know* what there is. This intersection of knowing and being is articulated through a theory of conception that explains how thought gains traction on being.

3. That the articulation of thought and being is necessarily conceptual follows from the Critical injunction, which rules out any recourse to the doctrine of a pre-established harmony between reality and ideality.[1] Thought is not guaranteed access to being; being is not inherently thinkable. There is no cognitive ingress to the real save through the concept. Yet the real itself is not to be confused with the concepts through which we know it. The fundamental problem of philosophy is to understand how to reconcile these two claims.

4. We gain access to the structure of reality via a machinery of conception which extracts intelligible indices from a world that is not designed to be intelligible and is not originarily infused with meaning. Meaning is a function of conception and conception involves representation – though this is *not* to say that conceptual representation can be construed in terms of word–world mappings. It falls to conceptual rationality to forge the explanatory bridge from thought to being.

5. Thus the metaphysical exploration of the structure of being can only be carried out in tandem with an epistemological investigation into the nature of conception. For we cannot understand *what* is real unless we understand what 'what' *means*, and

we cannot understand what 'what' means without understanding what 'means' *is*, but we cannot hope to understand what 'means' is without understanding what 'is' *means*.

6.   This much Heidegger knew.[2] Unlike Heidegger however, we will not conjure a virtuous circle of ontological interpretation from the necessary circularity of our pre-ontological understanding of *how* things can be said to be. The metaphysical investigation of being cannot be collapsed into a hermeneutical interpretation of the being of the investigator and the different ways in which the latter understands things to be. Although metaphysical investigation cannot be divorced from enquiry into what meaning *is*, the point of the latter is to achieve a metaphysical circumscription of the domain of sense which avoids the phenomenological equivocation between meaning and being.

7.   If we are to avoid collapsing the investigation of being into the interpretation of meaning, we must attain a proper understanding of what it is for something to *be* independently of our conceiving, understanding, or interpreting its being. But this will only be achieved once we possess a firm grip on the origins, scope and limits of our ability to conceive, understand and interpret *what* things are.

8.   The metaphysical desideratum does not consist in attaining a clearer understanding of what we mean by being or what being means for us (as the entities we happen to be because of our natural and cultural history), but to break out of the circle wherein the meaning of being remains correlated with our being as enquirers about meaning, into a properly theoretical understanding of what *is* real regardless of our allegedly pre-ontological understanding of it – but not, please note, irrespective of our ways of conceiving it. Such a non-hermeneutical understanding of metaphysical investigation imposes an epistemological constraint on the latter, necessitating an account that explains how sapient creatures gain cognitive access to reality through conception.

9.   Meaning cannot be invoked either as originary constituent of reality (as it is for Aristotelian essentialism) or as originary condition of access to the world (as it is for Heidegger's hermeneutic ontology): it must be recognized to be a conditioned phenomenon generated through meaningless yet tractable mechanisms operative at the sub-personal (neurocomputational) as well as supra-personal (sociocultural) level. This is a naturalistic imperative. But it is important to distinguish naturalism as a metaphysical doctrine engaging in an ontological hypostasis of entities and processes postulated by current science, from naturalism as an epistemological constraint stipulating that accounts of conception, representation and meaning refrain from invoking entities or processes which are in principle refractory to any possible explanation by current or future science. It is the latter that should be embraced. Methodological naturalism simply stipulates that meaning (i.e. conceptual understanding) may be drawn upon as an epistemological *explanans* only so long as the concomitant gain in explanatory purchase can be safely discharged

at a more fundamental metaphysical level where the function and origin of linguistic representation can be accounted for without resorting to transcendental skyhooks (such as originary sense-bestowing acts of consciousness, being-in-the-world or the *Lebenswelt*). The Critical acknowledgement that reality is neither innately meaningful nor inherently intelligible entails that the capacities for linguistic signification and conceptual understanding be accounted for as processes within the world – processes through which sapient creatures gain access to the structure of a reality whose order does not depend upon the conceptual resources through which they come to know it.

10.   The junction of metaphysics and epistemology is marked by the intersection of two threads: the epistemological thread that divides sapience from sentience and the metaphysical thread that distinguishes the reality of the concept from the reality of the object. Kant taught us to discern the first thread. But his correlationist heirs subsequently underscored its significance at the expense of the metaphysical thread. The occultation of the latter, following the liquidation of the in-itself, marks correlationism's slide from epistemological sobriety into ontological incontinence.[3] The challenge now is to hold to the metaphysical thread while learning how to reconnect it to the epistemological thread. For just as epistemology without metaphysics is empty, metaphysics without epistemology is blind.

11.   Kant underscored the difference between knowing, understood as the taking of something *as* something, classifying an object under a concept, and sensing, the registration of a somatic stimulus. Conception is answerable to normative standards of truth and falsity, correctness and incorrectness, which develop from but cannot be collapsed into the responsive dispositions through which one part of the world – whether parrot or thermostat – transduces information from another part of the world – sound waves or molecular kinetic energy. Knowledge is not just information: to know is to endorse a claim answerable to the norm of truth *simpliciter*, irrespective of ends. By way of contrast, the transmission and transduction of information requires no endorsement; it may be adequate or inadequate relative to certain ends, but never 'true' or 'false'. The epistemological distinctiveness of the former is the obverse of the metaphysical ubiquity of the latter.

12.   Critique eviscerates the object, voiding it of substance and rendering metaphysics weightless. Tipping the scale towards conception, it paves the way for conceptual idealism by depriving epistemology of its metaphysical counterweight. Conceptual idealism emphasizes the normative valence of knowing at the cost of eliding the metaphysical autonomy of the in-itself. It is in the work of Wilfrid Sellars that the delicate equilibrium between a critical epistemology and a rationalist metaphysics is restored.[4] Re-inscribing Kant's transcendental difference between *noesis* and *aisthesis* within nature, Sellars develops an inferentialist account of the normative structure of conception that allows him to prosecute a scientific realism unencumbered by the epistemological strictures of empiricism.[5] In doing so, Sellars

augurs a new alliance between post-Kantian rationalism and post-Darwinian naturalism. His *naturalistic rationalism*[6] purges the latter of those residues of Cartesian dogmatism liable to be seized upon by irrationalists eager to denounce the superstition of 'pure' reason. Where the prejudices of metaphysical rationalism hinder reason in its struggle against the Cerberus of a resurgent irrationalism – phenomenological, vitalist, pan-psychist – Sellars' account of the normative strictures of conceptual rationality licenses the scientific realism that necessitates rather than obviates the critical revision of the folk-metaphysical categories which irrationalism would consecrate.[7]

13.   Ultimately, reason itself enjoins us to abjure supernatural (i.e. metaphysical) conceptions of rationality. An eliminative materialism that elides the distinction between sapience and sentience on pragmatist grounds undercuts the normative constraint that provides the cognitive rationale for elimination. The norm of truth not only provides the most intransigent bulwark against the supernatural conception of normativity; it also provides the necessary rationale for the elimination of folk metaphysics.

14.   Unless reason itself carries out the de-mystification of rationality, irrationalism triumphs by adopting the mantle of a scepticism that allows it to denounce reason as a kind of faith. The result is the post-modern scenario, in which the rationalist imperative to explain phenomena by penetrating to the reality beyond appearances is diagnosed as the symptom of an implicitly theological metaphysical reductionism. The metaphysical injunction to know the noumenal is relinquished by a post-modern 'irreductionism' which abjures the epistemological distinction between appearance and reality the better to salvage the reality of every appearance, from sunsets to Santa Claus.[8]

15.   Irreductionism is a species of correlationism: the philosopheme according to which the human and the non-human, society and nature, mind and world, can only be understood as reciprocally correlated, mutually interdependent poles of a fundamental relation. Correlationists are wont to dismiss the traditional questions that have preoccupied metaphysicians and epistemologists – questions such as 'What is X?' and 'How do we know X?' – as false problems, born of the unfortunate tendency to abstract one or other pole of the correlation and consider it in isolation from its correlate. For the correlationist, since it is impossible to separate the subjective from the objective, or the human from the non-human, it makes no sense to ask what anything is in itself, independently of our relating to it. By the same token, once knowledge has been reduced to technical manipulation, it is neither possible nor desirable to try to understand scientific cognition independently of the nexus of social practices in which it is invariably implicated. Accordingly, correlationism sanctions all those variants of pragmatic instrumentalism which endorse the primacy of practical 'know-how' over theoretical 'knowing-that'. Sapience becomes just another kind of sentience – and by no means a privileged kind either.

16.   The assertion of the primacy of correlation is the condition for the post-modern dissolution of the epistemology-metaphysics nexus and the two fundamental distinctions concomitant with it: the sapience-sentience distinction and the concept-object distinction. In eliding the former, correlationism eliminates epistemology by reducing knowledge to discrimination. In eliding the latter, correlationism simultaneously reduces things to concepts and concepts to things. Each reduction facilitates the other: the erasure of the epistemological difference between sapience and sentience makes it easier to collapse the distinction between concept and object; the elision of the metaphysical difference between concept and object makes it easier to conflate sentience with sapience.

17.   The rejection of correlationism entails the reinstatement of the critical nexus between epistemology and metaphysics and its attendant distinctions: sapience/sentience; concept/object. We need to know *what* things are in order to measure the gap between their phenomenal and noumenal aspects as well as the difference between their extrinsic and intrinsic properties. To know (in the strong scientific sense) what something is to conceptualize it. This is not to say that things are identical with their concepts. The gap between conceptual identity and non-conceptual difference – between what our concept of the object is and what the object is in itself – is not an ineffable hiatus or mark of irrecuperable alterity; it can be conceptually converted into an identity that is not *of* the concept even though the concept is *of* it. *Pace* Adorno, there is an alternative to the negation of identity concomitant with the concept's failure to coincide with what it aims at: a negation of the concept determined by the object's non-conceptual identity, rather than its lack in the concept. *Pace* Deleuze, there is an alternative to the affirmation of difference as non-representational concept (Idea) of the thing itself: an affirmation of identity in the object as ultimately determining the adequacy of its own conceptual representation. The difference between the conceptual and the extra-conceptual need not be characterized as lack or negation, or converted into a positive concept of being as Ideal difference-in-itself: it can be presupposed as already-given in the act of knowing or conception. But it is presupposed without being posited. This is what distinguishes scientific representation and governs its stance towards the object.[9]

18.   What is real in the scientific representation of the object does not coincide with the object's quiddity as conceptually circumscribed – the latter is what the concept *means* and what the object *is*; its metaphysical quiddity or essence – but the scientific posture is one which in there is an immanent yet transcendental hiatus between the reality of the object and its being as conceptually circumscribed. The posture of scientific representation is one in which it is the former that determines the latter and forces its perpetual revision. Scientific representation operates on the basis of a stance in which something in the object itself determines the discrepancy between its material reality – the fact *that* it is, its existence – and its being, construed as quiddity, or *what* it is. The scientific stance is one in which the reality of the object determines the meaning of its conception, and allows the discrepancy between that reality and the way in which it is conceptually circumscribed

to be measured. This should be understood in contrast to the classic correlationist model according to which it is conceptual meaning that determines the 'reality' of the object, understood as the relation between representing and represented.

19.   The distinction between the object's conceptual reality and its metaphysical reality has an analogue in the scholastic distinction between objective and formal reality. Yet it is not a dogmatic or pre-Critical residue; rather, it follows from the epistemological constraint that prohibits the transcendentalization of meaning. The corollary of this Critical constraint is the acknowledgement of the transcendental difference between meaning and being, or concept and object. Contrary to what correlationists proclaim, the presupposition of this difference is not a dogmatic prejudice in need of critical legitimation. Quite the reverse: it is the assumption that the difference between concept and object is always internal to the concept – that every difference is ultimately conceptual – that requires justification. For to assume that the difference between concept and object can only be internal to the concept is to assume that concepts furnish self-evident indexes of their own reality and internal structure – that we know *what* concepts are and can reliably track their internal differentiation – an assumption that then seems to license the claim that every difference in reality is a conceptual difference. The latter of course provides the premise for conceptual idealism, understood as the claim that reality is composed of concepts – precisely the sort of metaphysical claim which post-Kantian correlationism is supposed to abjure. Yet short of resorting to the phenomenological myth of an originary, self-constituting consciousness (one of the many variants of the myth of the Given, denounced by Sellars[10]), the same critical considerations that undermine dogmatism about the essence and existence of objects also vitiate dogmatism about the essence and existence of concepts (whether indexed by signifiers, discursive practices, conscious experiences, etc.) Consequently, it is not clear why our access to the structure of concepts should be considered any less in need of critical legitimation than our access to the structure of objects.[11] To assume privileged access to the structure of conception is to assume intellectual intuition. But this is to make a metaphysical claim about the essential nature of conception; an assumption every bit as dogmatic as any allegedly metaphysical assertion about the essential nature of objects.

20.   Thus, even as it declares its metaphysical agnosticism, correlationism constantly threatens to collapse into conceptual idealism. The latter begins by assuming that knowledge of identity and difference in the concept is the precondition for knowledge of identity and difference in the object, before going on to conclude that every first-order difference between concept and object must be subsumed by a second-order conceptual difference, which must also in turn be conceptually subsumed at a higher level, and so on all the way up to the Absolute Notion. But unless it can be justified by the anticipation of a conceptual Absolute retrospectively enveloping every past difference, the subordination of every difference to the identity of our current concepts is *more* not less dogmatic than the transcendental presupposition of an extra-conceptual difference between concept and object.

21.   More often than not, this idealist premise that every difference must be a
difference in the concept underwrites the argument most frequently adduced by
correlationists against metaphysical (or transcendental) realism. This argument
revolves around a peculiar fallacy, which David Stove has christened 'the Gem'.[12]
Its *locus classicus* can be found in paragraph 23 of Berkeley's *Treatise Concerning the
Principles of Human Knowledge*, where Berkeley challenges the assumption that it is
possible to conceive of something existing independently of our conception of it
(we will disregard for present purposes the distinction between conception and
perception, just as Berkeley does):

> But, say you, surely there is nothing easier than for me to imagine trees, for
> instance, in a park, or books existing in a closet, and nobody by to perceive
> them. I answer, you may so, there is no difficulty in it; but what is all this, I
> beseech you, more than framing in your mind certain ideas which you call
> books and trees, and the same time omitting to frame the idea of any one
> that may perceive them? But do not you yourself perceive or think of them
> all the while? This therefore is nothing to the purpose; it only shews you
> have the power of imagining or forming ideas in your mind: but it does not
> shew that you can conceive it possible the objects of your thought may exist
> without the mind. To make out this, it is necessary that you conceive them
> existing unconceived or unthought of, which is a manifest repugnancy.
> When we do our utmost to conceive the existence of external bodies, we
> are all the while only contemplating our own ideas. But the mind taking no
> notice of itself, is deluded to think it can and does conceive bodies existing
> unthought of or without the mind, though at the same time they are appre-
> hended by or exist in itself. A little attention will discover to any one the
> truth and evidence of what is here said, and make it unnecessary to insist on
> any other proofs against the existence of material substance.
>
> (Berkeley 1988: 61)

22.   Berkeley's reasoning here is instructive, for it reveals the hidden logic of every
correlationist argument. From the indubitable premise that 'One cannot think or
perceive something without thinking or perceiving it', Berkeley goes on to draw the
dubious conclusion that 'Things cannot exist without being thought or perceived.'
Berkeley's premise is a tautology: the claim that one cannot think of something
without thinking of it is one that no rational being would want to deny. But from
this tautological premise Berkeley draws a non-tautological conclusion, namely, that
things *depend* for their existence on being thought or perceived and are *nothing apart
from* our thinking or perceiving of them. Yet Berkeley's argument is clearly formally
fallacious, since one cannot derive a non-tautological conclusion from a tautological
premise. How then does it manage to exude its modicum of plausibility? As Stove
points out, it does so by equivocating between two senses of the word 'things': things
as conceived or perceived (i.e. *ideata*), and things *simpliciter* (i.e. physical objects). This
is of course the very distinction Berkeley seeks to undermine; but he cannot deny it

from the outset without begging the question – the negation of this distinction and the metaphysical claim that only minds and their *ideata* exist is supposed to be the consequence of Berkeley's argument, not its presupposition. Yet it is only by substituting 'things' in the first and tautological sense of *ideata* for 'things' in the second and non-tautological sense of physical objects that Berkeley is able to dismiss as a 'manifest absurdity' the realist claim that it is possible to conceive of (physical) things existing unperceived or unthought. For it would indeed be a manifest absurdity to assert that we can conceive of physical things without conceiving of them. But it would be difficult to find any metaphysical realist who has ever endorsed such an absurdity. Rather, the realist claims that her conception of a physical thing and the physical thing which she conceives are two different things, and though the difference is perfectly conceivable, its conceivability does not render it mind-dependent – unless of course one is prepared to go the whole Hegelian hog and insist that it is conceptual differences all the way down (or rather, up). But then it will take more than the Gem to establish the absolute idealist claim that reality consists entirely of concepts; indeed, once the fallacious character of the Gem has been exposed, the absolute idealist claim that everything is conceptual (there are no things, only concepts) has little more to recommend it than the vulgar materialist claim that nothing is conceptual (there are no concepts, only things).

23. The difficulty facing the proponent of the Gem is the following: since the assumption that things are only *ideata* is every bit as metaphysical ('dogmatic') as the assumption that *ideata* are not the only things (that physical things are not ideas), the only way for the idealist to trump the realist is by invoking the self-authenticating nature of her experience as a thinking thing (or mind) and repository of ideas. But this she cannot do without invoking some idealist version of the myth of the Given (whose dubiety I take Sellars to have convincingly exposed). So in this regard, the alleged 'givenness' of the difference between concept and object would be no worse off than that of the identity of the concept (qua self-authenticating mental episode). Obviously, this does not suffice to vindicate metaphysical realism; what it does reveal however is that the Gem fails to disqualify it. It is undoubtedly true that we cannot conceive of concept-independent things without conceiving of them; but it by no means follows from this that we cannot conceive of things existing independently of concepts, since there is no logical transitivity from the mind–dependence of concepts to that of conceivable objects. Only someone who is confusing mind-independence with concept-independence would invoke the conceivability of the difference between concept and object in order to assert the mind-dependence of objects.

24. The paradigmatic or Berkeleyian version of the Gem assumes the following form:

> You cannot conceive of a mind-independent reality without conceiving of it. Therefore, you cannot conceive of a mind-independent reality.

Note that, *pace* Berkeley, the Gem does not entail that there is no mind-independent reality; it merely states that it must remain inconceivable. This is of course the classic correlationist claim. But as we have seen, it is predicated on a fundamental confusion between mind-independence and concept-independence. To claim that Cygnus X-3 exists independently of our minds is not to claim that Cygnus X-3 exists beyond the reach of our minds. Independence is not inaccessibility. The claim that something exists mind-independently does not commit one to the claim that it is conceptually inaccessible. By implying that mind-independence requires conceptual inaccessibility, the Gem saddles transcendental realism with an exorbitant burden. But it is a burden which there is no good reason to accept.

25. That one cannot conceive of something without conceiving it is uncontroversial. But the tautological premise in a Gem argument need not be so obvious. All that is necessary is that it exhibit the following form:

> You cannot do X unless Y, some necessary condition for doing X, is met.

Thus a Gem is any argument that assumes the following general form:

> You cannot X unless Y, a necessary condition for Xing things, is met. Therefore, you cannot X things-in-themselves.

One gets a Gem by substituting for X and Y:

> You cannot experience/perceive/conceive/represent/refer to things unless the necessary conditions of experience/perception/conception/representation/reference obtain. Therefore, you cannot experience/perceive/conceive/represent/refer to things-in-themselves.

Of course, having distinguished Xed things from things-in-themselves and relegated the latter to the wastes of the inconceivable, the pressure soon mounts to dispense with the in-itself altogether and to shrink all reality down to the confines of the 'for us' (the phenomenal). Thus, although it is only supposed to secure correlationist agnosticism about the in-itself rather than full-blown conceptual idealism, the Gem invariably heralds the slide towards the latter.

26. But the Gem is better viewed as an argument for correlationism rather than for full-fledged conceptual idealism. For there are any number of human activities besides thinking or conceiving that can be substituted for X, thereby yielding an equally wide assortment of non-idealist anti-realisms: pragmatism, social constructivism, deconstruction, etc. Thus, it comes as no surprise that the Gem should have proved the trusty adjutant for almost every variety of late twentieth-century correlationism, from Goodman and Rorty at one end to Merleau-Ponty and Latour at the other. But unfortunately for correlationism, no amount of inventiveness in

substituting for X and Y can suffice to palliate the fallaciousness of the Gem, which Stove (1991: 147) understandably dismissed as 'an argument so bad it is hard to imagine anyone ever being swayed by it'.

27.   In light of this argumentative paucity, it is somewhat perplexing to see Quentin Meillassoux, the philosopher who has done more than anyone in recent years to challenge the hegemony of correlationism, declare his admiration for 'the exceptional strength of this [correlationist] argumentation, apparently and desperately implacable [. . .It is] an argument as simple as it is powerful: No X without a givenness of X, no theory about X without a positing of X' (Meillassoux 2007: 409). What Meillassoux is entreating us to admire here is the high transcendentalist variant of the Gem, where 'givenness' and 'positing' stand for the conditions of receptivity and reflection respectively, and X is the object whose necessary conditions they provide. In order for X to be given, the necessary conditions of givenness must obtain (transcendental affection). In order for there to be a theory of X, the necessary conditions of positing must obtain (transcendental reflection). Meillassoux has Fichte rather than Kant in mind here.[13] For as he points out, it is not Kant but Fichte who is the veritable architect of the correlationist circle, understood as the abolition of the Kantian dualism of concept and intuition. Fichte overcomes the Kantian duality of active conception and passive affection through his notion of the *Tathandlung*, which is at once the positing of the given and the giving of the posited. By construing the correlation as a self-positing and thereby self-grounding *act*, Fichte seals the circle of correlation against any incursion of dogmatically posited exteriority – in other words, he eliminates the thing-in-itself. For Fichte, the non-I through which the I is affected is merely the posited residue of the absolute I's free and spontaneous act of self-positing. Thus, it is Fichte who uncovers the full idealist potency of transcendental reflection by tracking the power of positing back to its source in the unobjectifiable activity of the absolute ego.

28.   Meillassoux underlines the extent to which Fichte's radicalization of transcendental reflection seems to preclude any possibility of metaphysical realism. Reflection as condition of objectification (representation) is precisely what cannot be objectified (represented); thus, Meillassoux argues, one cannot defeat correlationism merely by positing an unobjectifiable real as the allegedly mind-independent condition of objectification, for in doing so one is effectively contradicting oneself, since the non-posited status of the reality that is the content of one's thought is effectively contradicted by the act of thinking through which one posits it. Thus, transcendental realism understood as the positing of what is allegedly non-posited becomes self-refuting. According to Meillassoux, one is merely dogmatically *seceding* from rather than rationally *refuting* Fichtean correlationism if one thinks that positing an un-posited reality suffices to exempt one from the circle of transcendental reflection. By emphasizing what he takes to be the exceptional rigour of Fichtean correlationism, Meillassoux reasserts his conviction that correlationism can only be overcome from within: since Fichte has disqualified the possibility of positing the

absolute as an object, the only non-dogmatic alternative to Fichte's transcendentalization of reflection consists in absolutizing the contingency of the correlation; that is, the inability of positing to ground its own necessity, which Meillassoux sees exemplified by Fichte's characterization of the *Tathandlung* as a *free* act – in other words, something that is contingent rather than necessary:

> We choose whether or not to posit our own subjective reflection, and this choice is not grounded on any necessary cause, since our freedom is radical. But to say this is just to recognize, after Descartes, that our subjectivity cannot reach an absolute necessity but only a conditional one. Even if Fichte speaks abundantly of absolute and unconditional necessity, his necessity is no longer a dogmatic and substantial necessity, but a necessity grounded in a freedom that is itself ungrounded. There can be no dogmatic proof that the correlation exists rather than not.
>
> (Meillassoux 2007: 430, translation modified)

29.   Meillassoux is surely right to identify Fichte as the veritable founder of strong correlationism (as opposed to weak or Kantian correlationism, which continues to postulate the existence of the in-itself). But transcendental realists may be forgiven for remaining unmoved by the claim that the free act of positing reflection disqualifies every invocation of a non-posited reality. For the Fichtean distinction between objectification and reflection hardly ameliorates correlationism's rational credibility once we realize that the attempt to indict realism of performative contradiction is simply an elaborately camouflaged version of the Gem. Consider:

> One cannot posit Saturn unless the conditions of positing (the free and unobjectifiable activity of the absolute ego) obtain.

> Therefore, one cannot posit Saturn as non-posited (existing independently of the free and unobjectifiable activity of the absolute ego).

Here once again, the sleight of hand consists in the equivocation between what should be two distinct functions of the word 'Saturn'. (We will use 'Saturn' when mentioning the word and **Saturn** when designating the concept for which the word stands). For the premise to be safely tautological (rather than an outrageously metaphysical begging of the question), the word 'Saturn' must be understood to mean *sense* (or 'mode of presentation') of the concept **Saturn**. But, in order for the conclusion to be interesting (as opposed to blandly tautological), the word 'Saturn' must be understood to mean the *referent* of the concept **Saturn**. Once this is understood, it becomes clear that the considerations that make it true to say that **Saturn** cannot be posited independently of the conditions of its positing (i.e. the conditions for the proper use of the concept) do not make it true to say that Saturn cannot be posited as non-posited (i.e. that Saturn cannot exist unless there are conditions for the proper use of **Saturn**).

30.   When I say that Saturn does not need to be posited in order to exist, I am not saying that the meaning of the concept **Saturn** does not need to be posited by us in order to exist – quite obviously, the concept **Saturn** means what it does because of us, and in this sense it is perfectly acceptable to say that it has been 'posited' through human activity. But when I say that Saturn exists un-posited, I am not making a claim about a word or a concept; my claim is rather that the planet which is the referent of the word 'Saturn' existed before we named it and will probably still exist after the beings who named it have ceased to exist, since it is something quite distinct both from the word 'Saturn' and the concept **Saturn** for which the word stands. Thus the 'Saturn' that is synonymous with 'correlate of the act of positing' (i.e. **Saturn** as the sense of the word 'Saturn') is not synonymous with the Saturn probed by Cassini-Huygens. To say that Saturn exists un-posited is simply to say that Cassini-Huygens did not probe the sense of a word and is not in orbit around a concept.

31.   It might be objected that we need **Saturn** to say *what* Saturn is; that we cannot refer to Saturn or assert *that* it is without **Saturn**. But this is false: the first humans who pointed to Saturn did not need to know and were doubtless mistaken about what it is: but they did not need to know in order to point to it. To deny this is to imply that Saturn's existence – *that* it is – is a function of *what* it is: that Saturn is indissociable from **Saturn** (or whatever else people have believed Saturn to be). But this is already to be a conceptual idealist. Even were the latter to demonstrate that the conditions of sense *determine* the conditions of reference, this would still not be enough to show that the *existence* of the referent depends upon the conditions of reference. To do that, one would have to show that 'to be' means 'to be referred to'; an equation tantamount to Berkeley's equation of 'to be' with 'to be perceived'. Yet it would require more than another Gem to dissolve such a fundamentally normative distinction in meaning. Of course, this distinction can be challenged by questioning the nature of the relation between sense and reference and interrogating the relation between words and things.[14] The more sophisticated varieties of anti-realism have done so in interesting and instructive ways. But the claim that the difference between what things are and *that* they are is not ultimately conceptual cannot be challenged by wilfully conflating the sense of a word with the referent of its concept, as the Fichtean argument above does. Fichte notwithstanding, there would seem to be good cognitive grounds for distinguishing words from things and meanings from objects. One can of course contest this cognitive conviction by alleging that it is a rationally indefensible dogma; but confusing **Saturn** with Saturn is not the way to do it. It is tautologically true to say that one cannot posit something without positing it; but it no more follows from this that the posited X is nothing apart from its positing than that **Saturn** is the same thing as Saturn.

32.   Fichte's putative refutation of transcendental realism rests on an equivocation between the necessary or *formal* conditions for the structure of cognitive activity

and the *real* conditions for the being of its correlate. The correlationist conceit is to suppose that formal conditions of 'experience' (however broadly construed) suffice to determine material conditions of reality. But that the latter cannot be uncovered independently of the former does not mean that they can be circumscribed by them. Since Fichte's purported disqualification of transcendental realism relies entirely on this conflation, there is no reason for us to lend it any more credence than we accord to Berkeley's 'proof' of the impossibility of conceiving independently existing material objects.

33.   The problem of objective synthesis (or what Laruelle calls 'philosophical decision') is basically that of how to adjudicate the relationship between conceptual thought and non-conceptual reality. But, that we have a concept of the difference between **Saturn** and Saturn does not entail that the difference is a difference in the concept: *concept of difference ≠ conceptual difference*. The acknowledgement of this non-equivalence is the basic premise of transcendental realism, which cannot be subverted simply by equivocating, in the manner of strong or Fichtean correlationism, between the conditions of positing and the being of the posited. For as Laruelle points out, even this equivocation cannot but invoke the absolute reality of the *Tathandlung* or act of self-positing: the Fichtean cannot help but be a realist about her own positing activity. Realism is uncircumventable, even for the most stubborn anti-realist. The problem is to identify the salient epistemological considerations so that the question of what to be a realist about may be rationally adjudicated. In this regard, the sorts of phenomenological intuition about conscious activity resorted to by Fichteans and other idealists remain a dubious source of authority. More fundamentally, the question is why those who are so keen to attribute absolute or unconditional reality to the activities of self-consciousness (or of minded creatures) seem so loath to confer equal existential rights upon the unconscious, mindless processes through which consciousness and mindedness first emerged and will eventually be destroyed.

34.   Kantians rightly charge dogmatic metaphysicians with ignoring the problem of cognitive access: this is the Critical problem of the relation between representation and reality. Yet far from resolving the access problem, strong correlationism simply dissolves it by abolishing the in-itself. Acknowledging the autonomy of the in-itself, transcendental realism faces the problem of determining what is real. This cannot be addressed independently of scientific representation. For those of us who take scientific representation to be the most reliable form of cognitive access to reality, the problem is one of granting maximal (not, please note, incorrigible) authority to the scientific representation of the world while acknowledging that science changes its mind about *what* it says there is. Accordingly, the key question becomes: how can we acknowledge that scientific conception tracks the in-itself without resorting to the problematic metaphysical assumption that to do so is to conceptually circumscribe the 'essence' (or formal reality) of the latter? For we want to be able to claim that science knows reality without rehabilitating the

Aristotelian (i.e. pre-Modern) equation of reality with substantial form. This is to say that the structure of reality includes but is not exhausted by the structure of discretely individuated objects. Indeed, it is the nature of the epistemological correlation between individuated concepts and individual objects that is currently being investigated by cognitive science. Here again, Sellars' work provides an invaluable starting point, since his critique of the Given shows that we require a theory of concepts as much as a theory of objects. Indeed, folk psychology is itself a proto-scientific theory of mind which can be improved upon. The science of objects must be prosecuted in tandem with a science of concepts, of the sort currently prefigured by Sellarsian naturalists such as Paul Churchland – although we cannot follow the latter in maintaining that pragmatic-instrumentalist constraints provide a secure epistemological footing for the connection between concepts and objects.

35.   Of course, recognizing this does not resolve or answer any of the profound epistemological and metaphysical difficulties which confront us in the wake of science's remarkable cognitive achievements. But it may help us realize that these difficulties cannot be circumvented, as both correlationists and dogmatic metaphysicians seek to do, by dispensing with those hard-won dualisms that have helped clarify what distinguishes scientific representation from metaphysical fantasy. Dualisms such as those of meaning and being, knowing and feeling, concept and object, are not relics of an outmoded metaphysics; they are makeshift but indispensable instruments through which reason begins to be apprised both of its continuity and its discontinuity with regard to what it is still expedient to call 'nature'.

Notes

1   The use of the capitalized 'Critical' is intended to signal the author's endorsement of the anti-dogmatic spirit of Kant's project but not the letter of its doctrine, specifically, transcendental idealism.
2   See Heidegger (1962): Introduction.
3   For an account of correlationism, see Meillassoux (2008).
4   See in particular, Sellars (1968).
5   Sellars' inferentialist account of rationality has been developed and expanded by Robert Brandom, the contemporary philosopher who has probably done most to draw attention to the significance of Sellars' philosophical achievement. See Brandom (1994, 2000).
6   Or 'rationalistic naturalism': straddling as it does the divide between post-Kantian rationalism and post-Darwinian naturalism, Sellars' philosophical project is susceptible to very different interpretations depending on whether one emphasizes its rationalistic or naturalistic aspect. The rationalist component of Sellars' legacy has been developed by Robert Brandom. By way of contrast, its naturalistic dimension has influenced such uncompromising philosophical materialists as Paul Churchland, Daniel Dennett and Ruth Garrett Millikan. Although Brandom's 'neo-Hegelian' interpretation of Sellars has dominated recent discussion of the latter's legacy – arguably to the detriment of his naturalism, and particularly his commitment to scientific realism – the importance accorded to the scientific image in Sellars' 'synoptic vision' has been emphasized by James O'Shea (2007).

O'Shea's work provides a much-needed corrective to the dominant neo-Hegelian appropriation of Sellars' legacy.

7   See Sellars (1968: 173). The concept of 'folk metaphysics', understood as the set of default conceptual categories in terms of which humans make sense of the world prior to any sort of theoretical reflection, is beginning to play an increasingly important role in cognitive science. Faces, persons, bodies, solid objects, voluntary motion, cause and effect, are examples of folk-metaphysical categories in this sense.

8   Bruno Latour has written a manifesto for irreductionism: see his *Irreductions*, Part Two of Latour (1993).

9   This is one of the most valuable insights in the mid-period work of François Laruelle (which he refers to as *Philosophie II*): see in particular Laruelle (1991). Unfortunately, its importance seems to diminish in Laruelle's subsequent work.

10 See Sellars (1997).

11 The signal merit of Paul Churchland's work, following Sellars', is to challenge the myth that the nature of concepts is intuitively accessible. See Churchland (1989).

12 See Stove (1991). 'Gem' is of course a sardonic moniker for a particularly egregious argumentative fallacy. Stove's capitalization here is intended to underscore the surprising popularity of this particular philosophical fallacy. Stove is a curious figure: a philosophical writer of outstanding analytical acumen and scathing wit, he is too acerbic to be respectable but too brilliant to be dismissed as a crank. No doubt his noxious political views (maniacal anti-communism coupled with not-so-thinly veiled racism and sexism) prevented him from gaining the recognition his work might have won had he been of a more benign temper. Some will cite his reactionary opinions as reason enough to dismiss him; correlationists in particular are liable to conclude from the fact that Stove, who defended realism, was racist and sexist, that realism entails racism and sexism.

13 Interestingly, a good case can be made for the claim that Kant's work is far less indebted to the Gem than that of many Kantians. This is a point made by James Franklin (2002). Among the many merits of the Sellarsian reconstruction of Kant is that it gives us a Gem-free Kant: it suggests that transcendental philosophy can and should be dissociated from transcendental idealism, and that Kant's transcendental distinction between concepts and intuitions can and should be dissociated from his arguments for the ideality of space and time.

14 Sellars for one does not believe that meaning can be understood in terms of a set of relations between words and things (whether mental or physical). His 'conceptual role' semantics require that we cease to construe 'reference' as a relation between language and extra-linguistic reality. However, Sellars has a fascinating account of the way in which the rule bound regularities that are constitutive of semantic functioning supervene upon causal regularities between organisms and their environment. Thus, for Sellars, the superstructure of rule governed symbol behaviour is anchored in the infrastructure of 'tied behaviour', or what Brandom calls 'reliable differential responsive dispositions.' Sellars' account is far too intricate to be addressed here, but suffice it to say that he remained committed to a naturalistic scientific realism, and that his philosophy of language provides no warrant for the sort of anti-realism we have been considering.

Bibliography

Berkeley, G. (1988) *Principles of Human Knowledge and Three Dialogues*, ed. R. S. Woolhouse, St. Ives: Penguin.

Brandom, R. (1994) *Making it Explicit: Reasoning, Representing and Discursive Commitment*, Cambridge, MA: Harvard University Press.

Brandom, R. (2000) *Articulating Reasons: An Introduction to Inferentialism*, Cambridge, MA: Harvard University Press.

Churchland, P. (1989) *A Neurocomputational Perspective: The Nature of Mind and the Structure of Science*, Cambridge, MA: MIT.

Franklin, J. (2002) 'Stove's Discovery of the Worst Argument in the World', *Philosophy* 77: 615–24.

Heidegger, M. (1962) *Being and Time*, trans. J. Macquarrie and E. Robinson, Oxford: Blackwell.

Laruelle, F. (1991) *En tant qu'un. La non-philosophie expliquée au philosophes*, Paris: Aubier.

Latour, B. (1993) *The Pasteurization of France*, trans. A. Sheridan and J. Law, Cambridge, MA: Harvard University Press.

Meillassoux, Q. (2007) 'Speculative Realism' in *Collapse: Philosophical Research and Development*, vol. III: 408–35.

Meillassoux, Q. (2008) *After Finitude: An Essay on the Necessity of Contingency*, trans. R. Brassier, London: Continuum.

O'Shea, J. (2007) *Wilfrid Sellars: Naturalism with a Normative Turn*, Cambridge: Polity.

Sellars, W. (1968) *Science and Metaphysics: Variations on Kantian Themes*, London: Routledge and Kegan Paul.

Sellars. W. (1997) *Empiricism and the Philosophy of Mind*, ed. R. Brandom, Cambridge, MA: Harvard University Press.

Stove, D. (1991) 'Idealism: A Victorian Horror Story (Part Two)', in *The Plato Cult and Other Philosophical Follies*, Oxford: Blackwell.

20

PHARMACOLOGY OF SPIRIT

And that which makes life worth living

Bernard Stiegler

TRANSLATED BY DANIEL ROSS

1. 'So many horrors could not have been possible without so many virtues'

In his 1919 essay 'The Crisis of Spirit [or the Mind]', Paul Valéry emphasises more than anything else the *fundamental ambiguity* of this spirit – of the science, reason, knowledge and even the moral elevation that made possible so much ruination, death and devastation throughout Western Europe, beyond what any previous historical epoch could ever have imagined:

> So many horrors could not have been possible without so many virtues. Doubtless, much science was needed to kill so many, to waste so much property, annihilate so many cities in so short a time; but *moral qualities* in like number were also needed. Knowledge and Duty, then, are suspect.
>
> (Valéry 1971: 24; trans. modified)

Valéry, like Husserl a little later, and like so many thinkers who were overwhelmed during the interwar period, thus described the way in which the First World War revealed that Spirit is always composed of two contrary sides: it is a kind of *pharmakon* – *at once* a good *and* an evil, *at once* a remedy *and* a poison, as Plato said about writing, which is the technology of the rational mind, that is, of Western spirit.

The evidence for this pharmacology, for this ambiguity and hence for this fragility of spirit, imposes itself on Valéry and on his contemporaries in the form of a series of interconnected crises – military, economic and spiritual[1] – through which science is 'dishonoured' (ibid.).

2. Anamnesis and transindividuation

Whether it is a matter of the critique of sophistic logography according to Plato, or the critique of the Hollywood-style artificial imagination according to Horkheimer and Adorno, the stakes are the relation to the *pharmakon*, that is, finally, to technics. But Horkheimer and Adorno do not apprehend technics pharmacologically – or else they only see in the *pharmakon* its poisonous character, which means that they do not see it *as pharmakon*.

Furthermore, in the twentieth century, pharmacology became industrial, that is, also, technoscientific: as rationalisation, the *pharmakon* is henceforth constituted *through science itself*, and it is as such a product of *anamnesis* – excepting the fact that it can be contested whether science is still anamnesic (which is precisely the question Husserl asked in *Crisis of the European Sciences*).

Anamnesic memory, which for Plato was the source of all knowledge, all ontologically founded *episteme*, all *mathesis* and all learning (*apprentissage*), is that which constitutes the pure autonomy of thinking for oneself. As such, it could be called transcendental memory. Plato constitutes this 'transcendental memory' by opposing it to hypomnesic memory, that is, artificial memory, the *pharmakon*. Likewise, Kant devalues the image–object by subordinating it to the scheme, which he thus proposes as a transcendental absolute (an a priori concept) founding an ontology.

Logos is always a *dia-logos* within which those who enter the dialogue co-individuate themselves – trans-form themselves, *learn* something – by dia-loguing. This co-individuation can result in disagreement, in which case each participant is individuated *with* the other, but *against* the other – as occurs, for example, in a tennis match or a game of chess. But co-individuation can also result in agreement, in which case it enables the *production of a concept* that is shared by the interlocutors, who thus together produce a *new locution* through which they agree on a meaning (*signification*) – that which, in Platonic doctrine, must be produced in the form of a *definition* responding to the question *ti esti*?

In the language of Simondon, this meaning constitutes the 'transindividual'. The transindividual is the outcome of what I analyse as a process of transindividuation, in which circuits of transindividuation are produced, circuits which form networks, which are more or less long, through which circulate intensities (of desires: circuits of transindividuation are always circuits of desire[2]), and which can be short-circuited.

An *anamnesic circuit* is a *long circuit co-produced by those through whom it passes*: this is what Plato calls 'thinking for oneself', and it is only in this way that a *mathesis* can be formed into an *episteme*. A hypomnesic circuit can short-circuit this long circuit through which a soul is trans-formed and through which it learns, and it can come to de-form the soul by causing it to interiorize a circuit which it has not itself produced – by obliging it to *adapt* itself to a *doxa*, that is, to dominant ideas which have not been produced and conceived by those who merely submit to them, rather than share in them. This is what is produced by the entire system of proletarianization.

3. Pharmacology of the scapegoat

It was Jacques Derrida who opened up the pharmacological question – within which the hypomnesic appears as that which constitutes the condition of the anamnesic. I have striven in various works to establish how the noetic movements through which a soul is trans-formed are always arrangements of primary and secondary retentions, arrangements themselves conditioned by tertiary retentions, that is, by hypomnesic systems and thus to show that everything which consists in *opposing* the anamnesic to the hypomnesic, such as transcendental memory or transcendental imagination, leads to an impasse.

The fact remains that there is an historical and political necessity at the origin of such oppositions: Plato struggles against that sophistic which had caused the spirit of the Greek city to enter into crisis through its misuse of the *pharmakon* – by short-circuiting thought, that is, anamnesis, thus depriving the souls of citizens of the knowledge that founds all citizenship (all autonomy). In this regard, the *pharmakon* constitutes a factor in the proletarianization of spirit (in the loss of knowledge) just as the machine-tool would later be a factor in the proletarianization of the bodies of producers, that is, of workers (depriving them of their *savoir-faire*). Likewise, it is a system of proletarianization of spirit that Horkheimer and Adorno denounce in the Hollywood-style imagination machinery of the citizen-become-consumer (yet which they did not analyse in these terms).

Nothing is more legitimate than these philosophical struggles against what, in technics or technology, is toxic for the life of the spirit. But faced with that which, in the *pharmakon*, constitutes the possibility of a weakening of the spirit, these struggles choose as well to ignore the originarily pharmaco-logical constitution of this spirit *itself*. They choose to ignore the *pharmacology of spirit* by taking the *pharmakon* in general as a *pharmakos*: a scapegoat – like those found in the sacrificial practices of polytheistic ancient Greece, or equally in Judea, practices in which this *pharmakos* is laden [*chargé*] (as Christ will be) with every fault, before being led 'to an inaccessible region' (Leviticus XVI: 22).

4. Pharmacology of the transitional object and default of interiority

Regression consists here in posing that tertiary retention is a poison which destroys interiority, because in fact there *never was* any interiority – if one understands by that an originally virgin source of all affection. Interiority is what is constituted *through the interiorization* of a *transitional* exteriority that precedes it, and this is as true for anthropogenesis as it is for infantile psychogenesis: *the transitional object constitutes the infantile stage of the pharmacology of spirit*, the matrix through which transitional space is formed in transductive relation to the 'good mother', that is, the provider of care.

This relation of care constituted by the transitional object, that is, by the first *pharmakon*, forms the basis of what becomes, as transitional space, an intermediate area of experience where objects of culture, of the arts, of religion and of science are formed.

> Of every individual that has reached the stage of being a unit with a limiting membrane and an outside and an inside, it can be said that there is an *inner reality* . . . but is it enough? . . . the third part of the life of a human being, a

part that we cannot ignore, is an intermediate area of *experiencing*, to which inner reality and external life both contribute.

(Winnicott 2005: 3)

Spirit is the *après-coup* interiorization of this non-interiority (as *revenance*), what Winnicott (2005: 55) also calls potential space, and this interiorization is what presupposes care, that is, a process of learning (*apprentissage*) through which an art of interiorization is developed – an art of living – that Winnicott calls creativity, the *pharmakon* here taking the name of transitional object.

Within pharmacological space, which can only become therapeutic insofar as *pharmaka* form transitional objects of all kinds, autonomy is not what *opposes* heteronomy, but that which *adopts* it as a necessary default (*un défaut qu'il faut*) and is that 'which makes the individual feel that life is worth living' (ibid.: 87).

What Winnicott calls the self ('the interior') is constituted from the *primordial default of interiority* as adoption (as creativity, i.e., as individuation) of transitional space, interiorization being a co-individuation of this space itself (transitional space thus being constituted as a process of transindividuation in which circuits form).

Pharmacologically, transitional space becomes poisonous (i.e., in the language of Winnicott, a form of 'illness') when it installs

a relationship to external reality which is one of compliance, the world and its details being recognised but only as something to be fitted in with or demanding adaptation. Compliance carries with it a sense of futility for the individual and is associated with the idea that nothing matters.

(Ibid.)

A pharmacology of care would completely re-evaluate the psychoanalytic question with regard to the clinical analyses of Winnicott.

The thought of non-interiority is without doubt what, in a thousand ways, characterises not only philosophical thought in the twentieth century, in Europe as in America, but also, as we have just seen, in an essential area, psychopathology. There is no doubt that this constitutes the common ground of what is called 'French theory'. What, however, remains at worst ignored, but at best a site that has barely been opened – which thus constitutes, and this is my thesis, the major site for a *new critique* – is the pharmacological and therapeutic question constituted by the transitional space of those transitional objects that are *pharmaka*.

This site remains *barely* opened because pharmacology presupposes organology, itself including and necessitating a history of the process of grammatization (which grammatology, as logic of the supplement, was insufficient for thinking).

5. The pharmacological critique of the unconscious

If 'critical theory' is unsatisfying precisely on this point, where it lacks that which constitutes the condition of any critique (of which anamnesis is for Plato the model), namely the *pharmakon*, that which *also* makes possible the short-circuit of any critique, it nonetheless remains the case that in *Dialectic of Enlightenment,* Horkheimer and Adorno identify the unfolding of a process in which the culture industries become the central element, and it remains necessary in our time to reopen this question by honouring the lucidity of these thinkers, as well as certain others – in particular Marcuse – while nevertheless analysing their limits (which is the only way of honouring a philosophy).

To analyse their limits is to lose oneself in, and try and feel one's way around in, shadows: in what their illuminations *owe* to shadows, if it is true that what is lucid is that which brings light, and if it is true that there is no light without shadows – if not blindness. This task imposes itself today, as it always does, and does so as the reopening of the question of reason, at the very moment when rationalisation, and the resulting domination of the irrational, now constitutes a systemic stupidity – lying at the heart of what one believes must before anything else be described and delimited as a systemic crisis of global finance.[3]

Systemic stupidity is engendered by *generalised proletarianization*, from which there is no escape for *any* actor within the consumerist industrial system, prole-tarianization proceeding precisely from a pharmacological development, where the *pharmakon* short-circuits those whom it inscribes in the circuit of production, con-sumption and speculation, and does so by destroying *investment, that is, the desiring projection of imagination.*[4]

The question is not, however, as Horkheimer and Adorno believed, the *exteri-orisation of imagination* (there *never* having been any imagination *without* image–objects, i.e., without tertiary retentions of all kinds), but rather the *dysfunctioning of that libidinal economy* that is presupposed by reason, reason being a fruit of a libidinal economy that constitutes it as *projector of shadows as well as light* – of powers (*puis-sances*) of the unconscious constituting the depth of field of consciousness.

Revisiting the questions of critical theory, a new critique is required by the originarily pharmacological situation of spirit: a pharmacological critique *of the unconscious* – and here 'of' evidently involves a double genitive. If reason has always been *opposed* to passion, to *pathos*, both of these themselves confounded with affect and desire, nevertheless for Plato desire is the condition and the *necessary default (le défaut qu'il faut)* of philosophy – while for Aristotle, whose *Peri psukhes* is the horizon of Spinoza's *Ethics*, desire (as movement towards the prime unmoving mover, object of all desire) is the condition of all forms of life: vegetative, sensitive or noetic.

What still lies before us, when it comes to reason understood first of all as motive, as the most elevated modality of desire (i.e. of movement, of e-motion), is to identify the role of *pharmaka* in the formation of desire in general, and in the formation of reason in particular – in the formation of consciousness as attention, in the sense both of psychic attention and social attention, that is, moral consciousness – such that it then constitutes the therapeutic of this pharmacology.

This is the point of departure for a new critique, which is necessarily as such a critique of the unconscious: the *pharmakon*, in all its forms, is before anything else a support for the projection of fantasies, that is, a sort of fetish. As such, it is always susceptible to causing desire to regress to a purely drive-based stage. From out of the critique of the unconscious, and as *practice* of the *pharmakon* as a transitional object, a new critique of consciousness becomes possible, a new theory that can only be a *political economy of the spirit* as formation of attention, itself conditioned by the play of primary and secondary retentions, a play of retentions that the *pharmakon*, as tertiary retention, authorises.

6. The *pharmakon* as *automaton*

Knowledge is always constituted in a pharmacological *après-coup*, and *as* this *après-coup*: it constitutes a *deferred time* of the *pharmakon*, and opens the play *of its différance*.

Nevertheless, industrial pharmacology is that which, through digital syntheses of understanding, enabling comprehension functions to be delegated to machines and apparatus, develops technologies of what in the 1960s began to be called 'real time', establishing the pharmacology of *light-time*. It is in this context that the question appears of what Derrida ventured to call the 'absolute *pharmakon*': that of the atomic era, that is, of an age structurally turned towards the possibility of its nuclear auto-apocalypse.

With the military infrastructure devoted to the unleashing of nuclear fire, constituted by missile pads, output terminals of digital computer networks for which the inputs are the radars and other strategic surveillance apparatus guided by calculation systems synthesising the functions of understanding – themselves connected to a network of networks the architecture of which is the origin of the internet – the question is posed of a *pharmakon* become *pure automaton*.

Moreover, the *industrial* pharmacological age is *essentially* that of automation. This begins with Vaucanson and spreads progressively as the proletarianization of the various strata that form circuits of transindividuation. When this reached nuclear armament, a threshold was clearly crossed: it ended in the *structural* proletarianization of the politico-military commander-in-chief himself and, with him, of the sphere of politics as such – it ended in the liquidation of the political body and of the regime of psychic and collective individuation that is specific to it, through the destruction of political knowledge,[5] to which the telecratic becoming of democracy equally leads.

Paul Virilio (1986) introduced this question in *Speed and Politics* by showing how the stakes of the 1962 Cuban crisis and, 10 years later, of the negotiations between Nixon and Brezhnev, which aimed officially, if not for denuclearisation, at least for the limitation of nuclear weapons, had as their genuine stake the preservation of the possibility of human decision, and of avoiding a total automation of the military pharmacological systems – that is, a total proletarianization.

Beginning with the simulation systems for the radar/missile systems of both East and West, however, military technologies rapidly migrated towards management, then towards markets and the most everyday social practices, as real-time interactive systems, first in the spheres of the stock market, entertainment and banking, and eventually to be found nearly everywhere, especially with the development of digital networks from the time of the Arpanet, which became the Internet, weaving the fabric that is the *world wide web*, a new pharmacological milieu if ever there was one, and within which carbon-time gave way to light-time.

This is why what Cornell University called *nuclear criticism*, referring to a colloquium in which Jacques Derrida participated in April 1984, carried to its apocalyptic extremes, and as a pharmacology of nuclear fire, a much more general question of the *pharmakon* of which the stake is speed:

> Are we having today *another* experience of speed? Is our relation to time and to motion becoming qualitatively different? Or, on the contrary, can we not speak of an extraordinary, although qualitatively homogeneous, acceleration of the same experience? And on what temporality are we relying when we put the question that way? It goes without saying that we can't take the question seriously without reelaborating all the problematics of time and motion, from Aristotle to Heidegger by way of Augustine, Kant, Husserl, Einstein, and Bergson.
>
> (Derrida 2007: 388)

7. The spatialized time of the *pharmakon* and the step beyond

If it is nevertheless true that the thinking of work and of its relation to capital essentially passes, since Marx, through the question of time and its measurement, without convoking this philosophy here, in this meditation on the questions opened by the nuclear age and by the hypotheses of nuclear criticism, does this not lead to a major geopolitical and economico-political choice – and a choice very prejudicial to the crossing of a necessary *step beyond*?

Because finally, the 'absolute *pharmakon*' that provokes these questions extends to the *totality* of social relations the Marxist question of the *measurement of time by its technical spatialization* (by what I describe as a tertiarization, which is a grammatization). Daniel Bensaïd, for example, repeats Augustine's question from books XXI and XIV of the *Confessions* – 'If it is by time that we measure the movement of bodies, how can we measure time itself?' (Bensaïd 1995: 96) – thus recalling that capitalism solves this question *factually*, through the technical *abstraction of labour time*, an abstraction lying within the principles of capitalism as the short-circuit of the time of noetic souls, that is, the short-circuit *of the right and the duty of individuation*, and of what Canguilhem or Winnicott named creativity or normativity:

> In order that such measurement could become conceivable, we had to suspend that which ceaselessly 'transforms and diversifies itself,' standardise the diversity of movement, spatialise duration . . . capital reduces the particular time of *savoir-faire* . . . to abstract social time.
>
> (Ibid.)

This time of *savoir-faire* is that of desire, including in the smallest work activity *insofar as it is not reducible to employment*, that is, insofar as a *savoir-faire* is creatively cultivated through it (this is precisely what constitutes *savoir-faire*), and as contribution to the individuation of a world constituting an associated milieu – whereas proletarianization consists precisely in a process of dissociation, that is, of social sterilization.

It is thus desire and its proteiform transformations, that is, too, *all forms of will*, which find themselves short-circuited by the technologies of temporal measurement that characterise the industrial age of the *pharmakon*. These short-circuits traverse society through and through when

> the nuclear age *gives us to think* this aporia of speed starting from the limit of absolute acceleration, such that in the uniqueness of an ultimate event, of a final collision or collusion, the temporalities called subjective and objective, phenomenological and intra-worldly, authentic and inauthentic, originary or 'vulgar,' would end up being merged into one another – playing here with Bergsonian, Husserlian and Heideggerian categories.
>
> (Derrida 2007: 390)[6]

Here there is no longer any reference to Aristotle or Einstein, and we can well understand why not. But there is also no longer any reference to Marxist categories, and this is far less comprehensible.

8. Les coups. Living pharmacologically

The remarkably rich developments emerging from this conference, published under the title 'No Apocalypse, Not Now', lead to this conclusion: a *critique* of the nuclear age *is not possible*. If nuclear criticism is necessary, as are new forms of study developed in the United States, what nevertheless makes this new problematic paradigm appear would be the fact that the very category of 'critique' is now outdated. Given that '"Nuclear criticism", like Kantian criticism, is a thinking about the limits of experience as a thinking of finitude', and given that for this Kantian criticism, 'the history of humanity [is the] example of finite rationality', that is, of *intuitus derivativus* in relation to the *intuitus originarius* of a divine and *infinite* intellect,[7] and that it thus 'presupposes the possibility of an *infinite* progress regulated on an idea of reason' (ibid.: 406–7, my emphasis), then nuclear criticism

> would make it possible to think the very limit of criticism. This limit comes into view in the groundlessness of a remainderless self-destruction of the self, auto-destruction of the *autos* itself. Whereupon is shattered the nucleus of criticism itself.
>
> (Ibid.: 407)

But what would enable an advance on such an affirmation? What is it about the *factual* possibility of 'the self-destruction of the very "*autos*"' that makes it *necessary*, that is, *right (en droit)*, to shatter 'the very nucleus of criticism'?

Without doubt, it is the fact that this *autos*, which only claims to constitute itself *by right* (*en droit*) by positing its *absolute autonomy* as a principle, is *in fact* never *constituted* other than through the accidentality of a *pharmakon* that is absolutely empirical, that is, heteronomic – 'autonomy' always having its *provenance* (and this would be a fact which could never be *opposed* to a right) in a primary heteronomy, autonomy being therefore always *relative*: this relative autonomy is a *relational* autonomy, and relational autonomy (i.e., also, dialogical autonomy) is what *composes* with heteronomy; it is what plays creatively with transitional space, as one could also say. It is what invents norms in the enormity of pharmacological pathogenesis, like that child that is time.[8]

But if we can agree here that the primary *epokhe* that provokes all *pharmakon* as short-circuit *may also* constitute itself *après-coup* as a system of care, reconstituting long circuits founded on anamneses, that is, on creative and normative individuation processes providing the feeling that life is *worth* living, that life is *worth the BLOW, the COUP,* of being lived (which is something that can never be proven), for example, as the noetic activity of a *krinein* that might very well have denied its pharmacological provenance throughout its 'metaphysical' history, and as such denied its grammatological constitution, but which in spite of all that was not made in vain, then it remains unclear why 'the very nucleus of criticism' would be condemned to 'shatter'.

Rather, it is *obliged to care for itself*, to *learn to live* pharmaco-logically, that is, normatively, affected and even *wounded* as it is by the infidelity of its pharmacology – of the pharmacology of Spirit, which comes to blows (*heurte de ses coups*) with the spirits of Valéry, Husserl, Freud, Benjamin, Adorno, Horkheimer, Habermas, Anders and so many others – through which its original pathogenetic content is revealed.

'Caring for oneself' here means not renouncing reason, motives for living, that which makes life worth living, namely: not renouncing the noetic, which *transitionally infinitises* its objects, which is what Valéry thus called Spirit; and yet not ignoring all kinds of sublimation processes, which have a phantasmatic essence that can never be isolated, thus which are, in other words, an imaginative activity coming from the unconscious and from *its* critique, in both senses of the genitive, that is, from transitional practices through which it is projected towards the real and via the symbolic, practices that can always be reversed and become their opposite and thus, like fire, become that which, as origin of civilisation, also constitutes the possibility of its negation and of its end – the possibility of apocalypse, that is, of what must and can *remain impossible*.

9. Wanting to deconstruct

The nucleus that nuclear criticism would, according to Derrida, shatter, is the 'transcendental subject' that constitutes the three syntheses of imagination, and the schematism that they prop up, through which the categories of understanding are constituted – that transcendental imagination which, according to Kant, precedes images, that is, precedes the *pharmaka* which always threaten to proletarianize understanding: to draw the subject back to its minority. It was against that threat that the Enlightenment wanted to *conquer* majority *for all*.

Now, *what* does deconstruction *want*, if not to constitute an *ultra-majority* for deconstructors, who would thus no longer be taken in by and no longer themselves repeat the lures of pure autonomy? What could it mean to claim that the nucleus has 'shattered', if not that one will *no longer* be lured by the blinding effects of the *pharmakon*?

But is such a claim not a hyper-criticism? To ask this question is to enter into and to claim to have undertaken a hyper-critique of the limits of deconstruction [this is what I have outlined in 'Derrida and technology' (Stiegler 2001)]: it is to ask if such a programme is pharmacologically sustainable – if it has not always already pharmacologically shattered, while not ceasing to redouble itself in the *après-coup of that which is worthwhile* (*vaut*), that is, of that which is *necessary* (*faut*): the default.

Is it possible to reduce the pharmaco-logy of the *pharmaka*? Evidently not. No-one has said better than Derrida why this is so. It is necessary to 'make do with' (or 'make the most of') – that is, to make do with (or make the most of) the fact that *life is in the end only worth living pharmacologically*, and in particular as deconstruction of the logic of the *pharmakon*, as deluded (*leurrée*) as such an operation can *itself* remain at its 'nucleus', if it is necessary to have an originary point of *absolute singularity* around which such a nucleus is formed.[9]

Because in any case the deconstructor – who regularly claims the gesture of the *Aufklärer* in spite of everything that Derrida asserts *à propos* criticism and critique – would not know how to reduce the pharmacological condition that he deconstructs, which means that he himself projects lures, casts delusions, that he cannot see. These delusions are not necessarily those of a promised or conquered autonomy: they can clearly be 'negative', and in some way hyper-limiting or hyper-inhibitors – nightmares, apocalyptic discourses of all kinds, diverse attacks of acute melancholy, chained to or stuck in absolute heteronomy, the liver exposed. Such is the insurmountable lot of pharmacological beings.

10. The discernment of the lovable (aimable)

What *at the same time* permits the nucleus and its delusions, including those that are 'negative', that is, self-destructive, what permits this point of singularity at the origin of all deconstruction as its self-decomposition in the face of the heterogeneous, is the libidinal economy of an infinite desire for an infinite singularity on the part of a singularity itself infinite, that is, unachieved, but often fatigued by its never finishing, that is, susceptible to regression.

This infinity, which distinguishes justice from the law and the promise from the program – and this is what leads Derrida to regularly venture the term 'quasi-transcendental' – no longer presents itself to us as a Kantian question, but rather as a Freudian question. It is the novelty of this difference that opens the site for a new critique. The consideration of this infinity cannot, however, be contained within

Freudian thought alone: it must pass through Winnicott and through the transitional object, that is, the *pharmakon*.

Derrida affirms that the nucleus of criticism shatters because it equates critical possibility with absolute autonomy and excludes the possibility of a relational criticism. The necessity of initially posing such an equivalence is completely understandable: such is the way that philosophical critique has always been thought, from the question, '*ti esti?*' to the Kantian questions ('What can I know?', 'What must I do?', 'What am I permitted to hope for?', 'What is human?') and beyond. Such an affirmation (that 'the very nucleus of criticism shatters' because criticism *equated* critical possibility and absolute autonomy) presupposes that criticism and critique are *only* conceivable as the noetic acts of a *purely* autonomous subject.

Derrida opposes to this autonomy an automatism of the *pharmakon*. Deconstruction is itself, in effect, a kind of automatic process, beginning by way of a primary suspension, an *epokhal* redoubling:

> Deconstruction takes place, it is an event that does not await the deliberation, consciousness, or organisation of a subject, or even of modernity. It deconstructs itself.... And the 'se' [the self] of 'se deconstruire' [deconstructs itself], which is not the reflexivity of an ego or of a consciousness, bears the whole enigma.
>
> (Derrida 1985: 4)

What is this *automatic reflexivity* outside the self or the ego, without ego, before all ego, if not transitional space become industrial, and the institution, as grammatization, of a *rapidity* such that it leads to the short-circuiting of the psycho-somatic work of transindividuation, that is, to the proletarianizing of everything that thinks and moves?

This automatic reflexivity, this reflexive system, which is obviously also the origin of systemic stupidity, is Freud's 'perfecting of organs' – and the *primary* movement of that *pharmakon* which is always already deconstructing the pathogenetic being. This 'spontaneous' deconstruction – which, when faced with the Derridean 'quasi-transcendental' it would be tempting (wrongly) to call 'quasi-natural' – is accelerated in the industrial age of the *pharmakon* and seems to liquidate the very transitionality of systemically proletarianized pharmacological space.

Neither grammatology nor deconstruction is sufficient to *treat* (*soigner*) this, to take care of this: it requires an organology, that is, a history of the supplement yet to see the light of day, deconstruction having always remained encamped in the undecidable logic of the supplement – as if the *automaton* alone can discriminate or, as Deleuze says, 'bifurcate', if not critique, and through the tremors of its automatic crises.

Now, there is a second moment in this automatic reflexivity. It is not that of a reappropriation, which would be a return to the proper, that is, a purification of the *pharmakon*, the elimination of its poisonous side: it is, rather, the moment of *adoption*, which is utterly to the contrary of adaptation, this being precisely an automatic submission to the *automaton*.

Adoption, which is a process of individuation, the *différance* of a *making do with* (or *making the most of*, or *doing*) *what is worthwhile*, is hyper-pharmaco-logical and constitutes what Derrida names '*exappropriation*': an appropriation always on the way towards the dis-appropriation of its *alteration*, to the extent that *its object is that of its desire*, that is, of its unconscious, and not only of its consciousness. But such an adoption, as struggle against proletarianization – thus as 'deproletarianization' – necessitates a politics: it is a question not only of psychotherapy but of sociotherapy.

Transitional adoption, pharmacological through and through, constitutes the rearming of a relational critical faculty, first as discernment of the lovable – and as the *epimetheia* of contemporary *prometheia*. It is an experience of desire, that is, of a 'proper' and a self (or ego) which always already projects *itself* outside itself, beyond the self and into that which is never absolutely one's own because it is, precisely, one's other.

But such a projection is *also* a reflexivity: a pharmacological and fantasmatic mirror which no longer affirms its pure autonomy, but which, insofar as it treats and takes care of (*soigne*) itself, and which, so doing, takes care of transitional space, always affirms the absolute infinitude of its object: its consistence – its promise.

11. The displacement of the infinite

The question here is the infinite and its interminable *displacement*. The infinite constitutes the horizon of the critical subject, nucleus of criticism. Proletarianization is the death of God, that is, of *this* infinity – as that which projects itself as motive of reason (idea) become *progress to the infinite* for that finite being endowed (or equipped, *doté*) with an *intuitus derivativus*:

> The *intuitus derivativus* of the receptive (that is, perceiving) being, of which the human subject is only one example, cuts its figure out on the (back) ground of the possibility of an *intuitus originarius*, of an infinite intellect that creates rather than invents its own objects.
>
> (Derrida 2007: 406–7)

Now, Husserl breaks with Kant precisely on this point:

> God, the Subject of absolutely perfect knowledge, and therefore also of every possible adequate perception, naturally possesses what to us finite beings is denied, the perception of things in themselves.
>
> But this view is nonsensical. It implies that there is no *essential difference* between transcendent and immanent, that in the postulated divine intuition a spatial thing is a real [*réelles*] constituent, and indeed a lived experience itself, a constituent of the stream of the divine consciousness and the divine lived experience.
>
> (Husserl 1931: 123; trans. modified)

In the Husserlian eidetic, this opposition between the finite and the infinite is 'nonsensical'. The *eidos* of red, 'the' red, which does not exist, is the condition of possibility of any experience of red, is what is *aimed at* in all red experiences, experiences of such and such red, and this inexistence is an infinitude of red that opens the indeterminate possibility of all finite reds. The Husserlian transcendental subject is a projector of infinite objects for practices themselves infinite – painting or geometry, for example. This is why geometry opens the community of a *we*, itself infinite: the *we* of geometry forms a circuit of transindividuation infinite in law, and geometry *is* this law.

In other words, a long circuit is not merely long: it is infinite, that is, open – because it is always oriented towards a consistence that does not exist.

Such an infinitude, which is that of an infinite *play*, presupposes a transitional dimension that is neither on the side of the subject, nor on the side of the object. Geometry, for example, which presupposes 'written expression' (Derrida 1989: 87), 'graphic signs' (ibid.: 89), is a way of living space noetically, that is, such that it is worth the *pharmacological blow* of being lived. Painting, and more generally art, experiences, for example, colour or matter in their necessity, wholly accidental as they can and must be.

Derrida calls this transitional dimension of phenomenology 'spectral' [and 'hauntological' (Derrida 1994: 10)]:

> [T]he radical possibility of all spectrality should be sought in the direction that Husserl identifies, in such a surprising but forceful way, as an intentional but *non-real* [*non-réelle*] component of the phenomenological lived experience, namely the *noeme*. Unlike the three other terms of the two correlations (*noese-noeme, morphe-hule*), this non-reality [*non-réellité*], this intentional but *non-real* inclusion of the noematic correlate is neither 'in' the world nor 'in' consciousness. But it is precisely the condition of any experience, any objectivity, any phenomenality, namely of any noetico–noematic correlation. . . . Is it not . . . what inscribes the possibility of the other and of mourning right onto the phenomenality of the phenomenon?
>
> (Ibid.: 189 n.6)

As strange as this may seem in the first analysis, this experience is also that, primordially, of transitional objects and transitional phenomena of the *infans*, such that they

> belong to the realm of illusion which is at the basis of initiation of experience. . . . This intermediate area of experience, unchallenged in respect of its belonging to inner or external (shared) reality, constitutes the greater part of the infant's experience, and throughout life is retained in the intense experiencing that belongs to the arts and to religion and to imaginative living, and to creative scientific work.
>
> (Winnicott 2005: 19)

In the course of this experience an economy is constituted which is that of *investment in the object*, through which the object can appear, that is, be aimed at and intentionalized:

In object-relating the subject allows certain alterations in the self to take place, of a kind that has caused us to invent the term cathexis [that is, investment]. The object has become meaningful. Projection mechanisms and identifications have been operating.

(Ibid.: 118)

To which Winnicott adds this question: '[I]f play is neither inside nor outside, where is it?' (ibid.: 129).

What Derrida calls the quasi-transcendental opens *this* transitional space of play in which that which does not exist consists:

The chimera becomes a possibility. If there is an art of photography (beyond that of determined genres, and thus in a quasi-transcendental space), it is found here. Not that it suspends reference, but that it indefinitely defers a certain type of reality, that of the perceptible reference. . . . As for the truth of revelation, it not only finds itself exposed, but in the same blow inscribed, situated, organised, as the 'revelatory,' in the system of an optical apparatus. In the process of development. In the functioning of a *tekhne* of which the truth, in its turn, etc.

(Derrida and Plissart 1998: n.p.)

In all this, and in this 'etc.', what appears – and disappears – is an interminable displacement of the question of the infinite.

If it is necessary to contribute to the infinite commentary on Husserl and on so many other geniuses, it is also necessary to draw the consequences on a plane that will enable facing up to life: that will make it worth living pharmacologically. The hauntological, spectral structure, that is, the intentional structure, is that which presupposes a pharmacological transitional space in which the real, redoubled by and in its encounter with the *pharmakon* (for example, for the protogeometer, in the first place as surveying), is symbolically redoubled as the infinitude of the imaginary.

This is only possible insofar as a therapeutic is implemented, making the unconscious speak and *consist* [the unconscious being a condition of what Husserl calls the faculty of reactivation, 'that belongs originally to every human being as a speaking being' (Derrida 1989: 164), and which itself presupposes the anamnesic capacity], and thus, whether it passes through consciousness (like geometry) or does not pass through consciousness (like photography), inventing another epoch of decision, *krisis*, that is, of judgment, *krinon*, of *analusis*, decomposition, etc.: all categories without which there is no critique, and which are themselves only known by passing through critique. Psycho-*analysis* in its Freudian stage is only the beginning of this new critique.

There is, then, as fact then as right, a double critique:

- that which operates the *pharmakon*, unconsciously – which means here outside consciousness, but not through the unconscious, which is a psychic agency (*instance*), and not only a pharmacological one;

- that which operates consciousness from new motives coming from the unconscious, because they have been *made projectable and schematizable* by the redoubling of the critique induced by the *pharmakon* in the first moment.

This second moment is the one that, concerning the *pharmakon* of the letter, I have described in *Disorientation* as the process of a *différantial* identification induced by the literalization of utterances and the new relation to the context of utterances as well as reading in which it results. Because in fact, the unconscious is dialogical, and as such raises what Julia Kristeva, reader of Bakhtin, calls intertextuality. But intertexuality is only a particular case within the pharmacology of the unconscious. It would clearly be necessary to evoke the concept of preindividual milieu put forward by Simondon in order to make these statements more precise.

12. After intoxication – the time of the après-coup

That the time of the *après-coup* has come is neither a fact nor a right bestowed by philosophical decree: it is what is produced in our time, in society, as a new relation of forces – as the new creativity and normativity that make possible a transitional space the characteristics of which in turn make possible the overcoming of the functional opposition between producers and consumers. This is what *Ars Industrialis* has not ceased to describe for the past 5 years, and it is what constitutes the stake of the struggle for free software, the more general philosophy of 'open source', and of 'creative commons', and the numerous unprecedented practices emerging from collaborative technologies, all of which foreshadow what we call an economy of contribution.

Such struggles pose anew the questions of individual and collective investment, of property, of the proper and of exappropriation, and of new forms of psychic and collective individuation – that is, also, of sublimation – elaborated through these struggles. This is why *Ars Industrialis* unconditionally supports free software activists: their struggle engages engineers and technicians first of all, against the proletarianized condition which has been imposed by the cybernetic division of their labour, which thereby ceases to be work and becomes merely a job (that of 'developer', i.e., a producer of code – within the process of digital grammatization, and as its first *coup*).

Through their struggles and the carrying out of these struggles, through which there is reconstituted an individuation, that is, a *self*, they are engaged in the age of deproletarianization – which is a sort of disintoxication.

Today we all know that humankind in its totality, constituted by pharmacological beings, must disintoxicate itself. Many examples could be cited: the struggle to ban smoking in enclosed public places (and where the sale of cigarettes was methodically promoted by marketing on the basis of the analyses of Bernays, himself inspired by his uncle Sigmund Freud); the removal of asbestos from buildings, a material that until recently was systematically used in construction; the establishment of new regimes of healthy eating, in order to struggle against that pathology which has become so important in industrialised countries, that is, obesity; as well as in a thousand other areas, and first of all the consumption and production of energy, the methods of agricultural production, the size of the carbon footprint involved in the transportation of goods, the huge attentional disequilibriums that affect infantile psychic apparatuses etc. – in all these cases, attempts are made to find new models capable of freeing people from the poisonous explosion of *pharmaka*.

Now, humankind is an *irreducibly* pharmacological being. Human beings will *never* be rid of the threat that is constituted by every *pharmakon*, and which is symbolised by fire as both technics and desire. This is why the condition of all forms of possible disintoxication is the establishment of a new relation to *pharmaka* as the *après-coup of intoxication* and the *process of spreading disintoxication*, aiming no longer at a transcendental nucleus of criticism, but at the *everyday or ordinary capacity for discernment of the extra-ordinary* that supports the individuation of those who, each one ensconced within the mystery of their skill or their craft, their *métier*, have creative and normative access to transitional space, and who thus learn – for themselves and for others – why and how life is worth living.

Notes

1 The military crisis may be over. The economic crisis is still with us in all its force. But the intellectual crisis, being more subtle . . . this crisis will hardly allow us to grasp its true extent, its *phase*.

(Valéry 1971: 25)

2 I have developed this point in Stiegler (2005).
3 But this does not only take hold of the financial system, because this fact will be imposed on the *totality* of social relations.
4 See Stiegler (forthcoming).
5 What is accomplished here in the strategic field is lost in the social field, something I try to describe in Stiegler (2006).
6 *Translator's note*: the published English translation of this text differs from the French version, lacking the precise phrase to which Stiegler draws attention, concerning 'Bergsonian, Husserlian and Heideggerian categories'.
7 This is how Kant characterises the finitude of the critical subject: contrary to divine understanding, its intuition is not creative but receptive, and the objects of its intuition cannot be given through experience.
8 'Time is a child playing draughts, the kingly power is a child's' (Heraclitus, fragment 52).
9 See Derrida (2003: 9).

Bibliography

Bensaïd, D. (1995) *Marx l'intempestif*, Paris: Fayard.
Derrida, J. (1985) 'Letter to a Japanese Friend', in D. Wood and R. Bernasconi (eds), *Derrida and Différance*, Warwick: Parousia Press. 1–6.
Derrida, J. (1989) *Edmund Husserl's Origin of Geometry: An Introduction*, trans. J. P. Leavey, Jr., Lincoln, NE: University of Nebraska Press.
Derrida, J. (1994) *Specters of Marx*, trans. Peggy Kamuf, New York: Routledge.

Derrida, J. (2003) *Chaque fois unique, la fin du monde*, Paris: Galilée.

Derrida, J. (2007) 'No Apocalypse, Not Now', in *Psyche: Inventions of the Other*, vol. 1, Stanford, CA: Stanford University Press. 387–409.

Derrida, J. and Plissart, J.-M. (1998) *Right of Inspection*, New York: Monacelli Press.

Horkheimer, M. and Adorno, T. W. (1991), *Dialectic of Enlightenment* (1944), trans. J. Cumming, New York: Continuum.

Husserl, E. (1931) *Ideas: General Introduction to Pure Phenomenology*, trans. W. R. Boyce Gibson, New York: Macmillan.

Husserl, E. (1970) *The Crisis of European Sciences and Transcendental Phenomenology: An Introduction to Phenomenological Philosophy* (1954), trans. D. Carr, Evanston, IL: Northwestern University Press.

Kant, I. (1929) *Critique of Pure Reason*, trans. N. K. Smith, Hampshire: Macmillan.

Stiegler, B. (2001) 'Derrida and Technology: Fidelity at the Limits of Deconstruction and the Prosthesis of Faith', in T. Cohen (ed.), *Jacques Derrida and the Humanities*, Cambridge: Cambridge University Press. 238–70.

Stiegler, B. (2005) *De la misère symbolique 2. La catastrophè du sensible*, Paris: Galilée.

Stiegler, B. (2006) *La télécratie contre la démocratie*, Paris: Flammarion.

Stiegler, B. (2009) *Technics and Time 2: Disorientation*, trans. S. Barker, Stanford, CA: Stanford University Press.

Stiegler, B. (forthcoming) *Pharmacology of Capital and Economy of Contribution*.

Valéry, P. (1971) 'The Crisis of the Mind', in *The Collected Works of Paul Valéry: History and Politics*, vol. 10, trans. D. Folliot and J. Mathews. Princeton, NJ: Princeton University Press.

Virilio, P. (1986) *Speed and Politics: An Essay on Dromology* (1977), New York: Semiotext(e).

Winnicott, D. (2005) *Playing and Reality*, Abingdon, UK: Routledge.

INDEX

Abel, Marco 11
Achebe, Chinua 164, 174
Adorno, Theodor: the aesthetic 11, 24;
    differentiation 54; history 26; identity
    282; liberalism 258; *pharmakon* 294,
    295, 296, 298, 302; philosophy of
    history 27, 28; rational will 93; realism
    and liberalism 260; restoration of
    philosophy 23; theory's evolution 3
the aesthetic: art as techne 223–5, 231–2,
    234–5; human life 70; judgement
    122, 123, 125; liberalism 249–61;
    philosophical grammar of theory
    237–48; theorization of 10–12
affect 11, 105
Afghanistan 83
African National Congress (ANC) 90
Agamben, Giorgio: the aesthetic 12;
    animality 70; 'bare life' 9, 145;
    hedonism of spectacle 69; liberalism
    252, 253, 254, 255; philosophical
    grammar of theory 238–9; potentiality
    106, 107, 117; role of theory 34;
    theory's evolution 3, 14; voluntarism 94
agencements 109
agency 150, 153, 156–60
AIDS (acquired immune deficiency
    syndrome) 68
Alberts, D.S. 84, 86, 88
alienation 136, 137, 140–2, 144
Alizart, M. 30
Althusser, Louis 19, 21, 23, 93, 107, 118,
    140–2, 147

analytic philosophy 43, 238
anamnesis 295, 296, 297, 302
Anand, Mulk Raj 175
'Anaxagoras' 244–7
Anderson, Amanda 3, 12, 249–61
Anderson, P. 112
apartheid 90
Appiah, K.A. 165
Aquinas, Thomas 188
Arcades Project 24, 30
arche-fossils 267–8
Arendt, Hannah: judgement 120–31;
    liberalism 250; life 70; natality 10, 196,
    198, 199, 201; political judgements 8;
    politics 65; theory's evolution 3, 4; will
    93, 95
Aristide, Jean-Bertrand 96, 101
Aristotle: anti-essentialist contextualization
    39; art as techne 224, 235; art of
    poetry 230; collective behaviour
    184; concept of life 182–3; desire
    298; ethics of care 199; law and
    philosophy 59; ontology of life
    189–92; philosophy and literature 241;
    subjectivity 209; time 300
Armah, Ayi Kwei 165
Armstrong, Isobel 11, 14, 249
Armstrong, N. 258
Arnold, Matthew 251
Arpanet 300
Arquilla, J. 77, 79, 87, 183
Arrow of God 174
ars oratoria 126

art: art-making process 225–30; conceptual
art 233–4; critique of the aesthetic
11, 12; Frankfurt School 24; genius
223, 228, 229; human life 70; infinite
play 306; literature 241; mediatized
reflexivity 136–41, 144; natality 196;
postcolonial theory 175; scientific
research 43; techne theory 223–5,
231–2, 234–5
Artaud, Antonin 145
artificial life 181
artificial people 211
attention 76, 77, 81
Attridge, D. 70, 232, 249
augmented intelligence 84, 85
Augustine, Saint 95, 300
automation 299, 304
autonomy 195, 199, 211, 295–7, 302,
304, 305
Avatar 67

Bachelard, Gaston 147
Badiou, Alain 12; antihumanism 66;
metaphysics 22; philosophical
grammar of theory 238; philosophy
and literature 242; philosophy of
history 30; theory's evolution 3, 14;
will 93, 94, 98, 99
Bakhtin, Mikhail 308
'bare life' 9, 10, 145
Barthes, Roland 11, 138, 147
Bataille, Georges 245
BattleSwarm 183
Baudelaire, Charles 259
Bazin, André 144, 145
The Beautiful Ones Are Not Yet Born 165
de Beauvoir, S. 93, 98, 99, 100, 101
'Before the Law' 254
Beiner, Ronald 121, 122, 131
Benjamin, Walter 24, 26–30, 135, 136–40,
142–7, 302
Benny's Video 145
Bensaïd, Daniel 300
Benveniste, Emile 216
Bergson, Henri 42, 69, 182, 184, 185,
217, 300
Berkeley, G. 284, 285, 286, 289, 290
Berlin, Isaiah 250
Bernays, Edward 308
Bernstein, J.M. 14
Bhabha, Homi 163–5, 167–72
Bichat, Xavier 207
Bierce, Ambrose 192
bios theoritikos 65, 67

biotechnology 181
birth 196, 199
The Black Cloud 192
Black Easter 185
Blanchot, Maurice 10, 11, 31, 147, 216
Bleak House 259
Blish, James 185
The Blob 192
body 65, 69, 81–2, 207–8, 210–12,
213, 215
Bolivia 92, 97
Borges, Jorge Luis 227, 235
Boyle, Danny 68
Braidotti, Rosi 31
Brandom, Robert 291, 292
Brassier, Ray 2–4, 13, 14, 66, 278–93
Brecht, Bertolt 3, 9, 135–8, 139–47
Brenkman, J. 253
Brennan, T. 253, 258
Bretton Woods 110, 154
Brezhnev, Leonid 299
Brinkley, A. 250
Brown, John 95, 98
Brown, N. 276
Brown, W. 118
Brunner, O. 53
Buck-Morss, Susan 93
Burke, Edmund 96, 101
Burke, Kenneth 35
Burrow, John 251
Bush, George W. 75, 76
Butler, Judith 22, 24, 65, 196, 198

Caché 146
Camazine, S. 183
Cameron, James 67
Canguilhem, Georges 94, 217, 300
capitalism 47, 50, 66, 101, 151, 154,
260, 300
care 195, 196, 198, 200, 202, 203, 296, 297
Carlyle, Thomas 251
Catholicism 206
causality 120, 121
Cavarero, Adriana 3, 10, 194–204
Cavell, Stanley 121
Cebrowski, A. 80, 87
Chakrabarty, Dipesh 8, 151, 152, 154–5,
156, 157, 159
Chambers, Ross 176
Chatterjee, Partha 159, 160
Cherniavsky, Eva 2, 4, 8–9, 149–62
Chiesa, L. 31
Chow, Rey 2–4, 9, 135–48, 155, 161
Christianity 94, 208

Churchland, Paul 291, 292
cinema *see* films
civil society 159, 160
Cixous, Hélène 31
Clarke, Andy 36
class 64, 98, 107, 115
von Clausewitz, C. 83, 84
climate change 67, 68, 70
cogito 30
cognitive science 5, 35, 37
Cohen, G.A. 63
Cohen, Hermann 59
Cold War 68, 78
Colebrook, Claire 2, 4–6, 9, 62–71
Coleridge, Samuel Taylor 230, 251
collective behaviour 182–5
Collini, Stefan 256
colonialism 8, 110, 156, 172–3, 174, 176
Commonwealth Literature 169, 170, 171
communism 250
communitarianism 252
complexity 83, 84
computer science 183, 205
Comte, Auguste 207
'Conceit' 246
conceptual art 139, 143, 223, 233–4
consciousness 36, 207, 268, 298, 307, 308
constructivism 37, 40
Cooper, Lane 225
'corporate university' 35, 44, 45, 47
Corral, W.H. 14
correlationism 13, 280–4, 286–8, 290
counter-memory 69
Cremonini, Leonardo 140
Critchley, S. 22
critical theory 5, 19–20, 22–4, 56–8, 107, 116–17
criticism 22, 232, 301–4
critique 22, 23, 107
cultural studies 11, 34, 35, 46, 47, 254
culture 12, 114
Cussett, F. 19

Damasio, Antonio 35
Dante, A. 10, 186, 187, 188
Danto, Arthur 233
Darwin, Charles 265, 272
Darwinism 266, 272, 273, 274, 275
Das, V. 118
Davidson, Donald 41
The Day After Tomorrow 68
The Day the Earth Stood Still 69
De Anima 189, 190, 191
de Bolla, P. 249

de Duve, T. 223
de Maistre, Joseph 102
De Malo (On Evil) 188
de Man, Paul 66, 147, 166, 167, 170, 173
death 106, 108, 117
death of the author 226
Debord, Guy 143, 147
decolonization literature 163–5, 170, 172–6
deconstruction 20, 70, 158, 265, 266, 303, 304
Defense Advanced Research Projects Agency (DARPA) 76
DeLanda, Manuel 36
Deleuze, Gilles: the aesthetic 12; automata 304; boundaries of the organism 69; concept of life 182, 192; destruction 29; disavowal of philosophy 22; French and German theory 25–7; heyday of 'Theory' 1, 237; identity 282; life 66; personalism 217, 218; philosophical grammar of theory 238; philosophy and literature 242; philosophy of history 30; potentiality 7, 105, 106, 107, 117; pragmatism 42; repetition 76; theory's evolution 3, 4; will 94, 96
democracy 57, 159, 196
demonology 185–9
Dennett, Daniel 272, 273, 276, 291
dependency 195, 196, 200, 204
depersonalization 206, 211
Derrida, Jacques: the aesthetic 11; conception of time 265, 266, 267, 276; deconstruction 70; heyday of 'Theory' 1, 237; inhuman forces of writing 69; language 6; law 254, 255; life 66; literature 67; the 'messianic' 24; *pharmakon* 295, 299, 300, 301, 302–7, 309; philosophical grammar of theory 238, 239; philosophy and literature 241; postcolonial theory 166, 176; scientific research 44, 45, 46, 47; scientific turn 5; subaltern studies 155; theatre of cruelty 145; theory's evolution 3; trace-structure of time 13; will 94, 96
Descartes, René 95–6, 210
desire 298, 299, 301
destruction 29, 271–2, 274
determinative judgements 122, 124, 127
Le Devoir de violence 165
Dewey, John 257
dialectical voluntarism 7, 91

diaphora 241
Díaz Pozueta, M. 235
Dickens, Charles 259
Dickie, G. 227
Diels, H. 245
différance 6, 254, 299, 305
difference 28, 65, 169–71, 241, 283
differentiation 52, 53
digital media 63, 69
disability studies 14, 63
disaster epics 68
discourse 38
Döblin, Alexander 146
Dollimore, J. 22
Doré, Gustav 187
Dosse, F. 30
Dostal, Robert 126
drama 137, 138, 139, 140, 142
Draper, H. 97
Du Bois, W.E.B. 101
Dubiel, H. 23
Dubreuil, Laurent 12, 237–48
Duchamp, Marcel 12, 223, 233, 234
Dunayevskaya, R. 98
Duns Scotus, J. 95

Eagleton, Terry 11, 14
education 232
Efuru 174
Egginton, W, 276
ego 194, 210, 304
Einstein, Albert 300
Eisenstein, Sergei 138
Eliot, George 259
Eliot, T.S. 228, 256
embodiment 37
empiricism 36, 38, 47
Engelhardt, Hugo 212
Engels, Friedrich 21, 23, 91, 97, 100
Enlightenment 6, 56, 149, 153, 260
epic theatre 9, 135, 136, 138, 139, 143
epistemological warfare 77, 79
epistemology 278, 280, 282
erotic art 144
Esposito, Roberto 3, 4, 10, 69, 200,
    205–19, 247
ethical substance 107, 117
ethics 9–10, 22, 69, 195, 198, 200
Euripedes 201, 202
the event 4, 6, 7, 75
evil 186, 188, 201–3
evolutionary theory 265, 273
examples 127, 128
exemplary validity 128

facts 39
Fanon, F. 95, 97, 101, 172, 173, 237
fascism 50, 57, 93, 94, 250
Faust 185
feminism: colonialism 8; domestication of
    theory 34; ethics of care 195, 196, 198,
    199, 201; film studies 141; liberalism
    252
Feuerbach, L. 28
Feyerabend, Paul 38
Ffrench, P. 26
Fichte, Johann Gottlieb 13, 50, 92, 96, 98,
    100, 287–9
films: demonology of swarms 185; end of
    human life 67, 68, 69, 192; mediatized
    reflexivity 137, 138, 141, 142, 145, 146
Firth, Raymond 225
Fish, Stanley 39
fog of war 83, 84, 85
forgery 233
formalism 231, 232, 235
Foster, H. 14
Foucault, Michel: counter-memory 69;
    genealogy of theory 35; heyday of
    'Theory' 1, 237; history of thought 21;
    liberalism 31, 252; neoliberalism 110;
    personalism 217, 218; philosophical
    grammar of theory 238; philosophy of
    history 26, 27; potentiality 107, 118;
    power 6, 94; space 147; subjectivity
    210; theory's evolution 3
'Fountain' 233, 234
Frank, Adam 37
Frankfurt School 20, 22–3, 24, 25, 56
Franklin, James 292
freedom: judgement 120, 121, 122, 123,
    125; liberalism 252; political practice
    6; postcolonial theory 172; reflexivity
    143; theory's evolution 14; will 95, 96,
    98–100
Freire, Paolo 90, 98, 99
French revolution 91, 92, 94, 96, 100
French theory 19–20, 22, 24–7, 65, 237,
    297
Freud, Sigmund 10, 25, 96, 213–14, 237,
    302–4, 308
functional differentiation 52, 53, 54
Funny Games 145
future 27

Gaius 208, 210, 212
Galileo 120
Gallagher, C. 63
Galloway, A. 193

García Linera, A. 97
Garrett, Ruth 291
Garstka, J. 80, 87
Gasché, Rodolphe 11, 20
Gaskell, I. 14
Gather, Darkness! 185
Gauthier, F. 101
Gaza 92
Gell, Alfred 224, 225, 226, 233
the Gem 284, 285, 286, 287, 289
gender 37, 63, 199, 200
genealogy 27, 35
genius 223, 227, 228
geometry 306
German theory 20, 22–3, 24, 27
Giap, V.N. 90
Gide, André 256
Gikandi, Simon 4, 9, 163–78
Gilligan, Carol 195, 198, 200
Glassman, D. 30
globalization 47, 83
Goethe, Johann Wolfgang von 185
Goodlad, L.M.E. 258
Goodman, Nelson 286
Gordon, Deborah 183
Graff, Gerald 166
A Grain of Wheat 165, 175
Gramsci, A. 92, 100
grand narratives 63
Grassi, Ernesto 129
Gray, Russell 35
great politics 213
Greenblatt, S. 63
Griffiths, Paul 36
Grossberg, Lawrence 14
Guaraldo, O. 194
Guattari, Félix 30, 31, 66, 69, 192
Guevara, Che 95, 98
Guha, Ranajit 156, 157, 160, 161

Habermas, Jürgen: Frankfurt School 23,
    24, 25, 56; judgement 121, 122, 123;
    liberalism 250, 256, 257; *pharmakon*
    302; postcolonial theory 165
habit 76, 81, 82
Hacking, Ian 40
Hadamard, J. 235
Haddad, S. 276
Hägglund, Martin 2, 13, 265–77
Haiti 90, 91, 92, 100
Hales, Steven D. 51
Hallward, Peter 2–4, 7, 14, 90–104, 276
Hamacher, Werner 170
Hampson, N. 102

Haneke, Michael 9, 145, 146
Hansen, Mark 36, 37, 38, 41, 42, 43
haptic dimension 11
Hardt, Michael 66, 69, 70
Harman, Graham 67
Harvey, D. 118, 154
Hayes, R.E. 86, 88
Hayles, Katherine 36
Hegel, G.W.F.: freedom 143; French
    and German theory 21, 23, 25, 30;
    philosophy of history 26–9; reason 50;
    trace-structure of time 276; will 92,
    93, 95, 98, 100
hegemony 150, 154, 158
Heidegger, Martin 25, 27–9, 93, 94, 101,
    127, 279, 291, 300
Held, V. 198
Heraclitus 309
Hesiod 241
high art 11
historicism 167, 168, 173, 174
history 26–9, 29, 98, 101, 167, 169, 173,
    239
Hobbes, Thomas 96, 210, 211
Hodges, Aaron F. 271
Hodgson, William Hope 192
Hofstadter, Richard 250
Homer 202, 230, 241
Honneth, A. 24
hope 105, 116–17
Horkheimer, Max 23, 54, 93, 294, 295,
    296, 298, 302
horror 182, 185, 191–2, 201–2, 203
A House for Mr Biswas 170
Howard, John 108, 111, 112
Hoyle, Fred 192
The Human Condition 199
human life 65, 66, 206, 208, 209
human rights *see* rights
humanities 43–7
humanity 63, 64, 66–70, 100, 128, 207
Hume, David 96, 210
Husserl, Edmund 69, 268, 294, 295, 300,
    302, 305–7
hyper-determination 93

iconicity 160
identity: class 64; colonialism 8; conceptual
    identity 282; extinct theory 70;
    personalism 206, 210, 214, 217;
    philosophy of history 28; scientific
    research 35; social structure 55;
    subaltern studies 149, 155, 156, 159
ideology 57, 140, 141, 158

imagination 126–7, 128, 298
immanent critique 105, 106, 107, 112, 116, 117
improvisation 230
indetermination 93
India 153, 156, 157, 175
Indigenous people 108–13, 113–16, 117, 225
individuation 217
infanticide 201, 203
Inferno 10, 186, 187, 188
infinite 305, 306, 307
information 84, 85
information technologies 47, 84
installation art 139, 143
intellective turn 242, 246
interdependency 195, 196, 204
interiority 296, 297
l'Internationale situationiste 241
Internet 205, 300
The Interpreters 165
intersubjective validity 123
intertextuality 308
The Invasion 68
Ion 225
iPhone 143
Iraq 83, 84
Irigaray, Luce 31
irony 9, 167, 171, 172, 174, 175, 256
irreductionism 281

Jameson, Fredric 3, 34, 135, 140, 147
Jordan, A. 98
Joughin, J. 14, 70
Joughin, Martin 42
Jowett, Benjamin 225
Joyce, James 256
judgement 8, 120–32
Judt, Tony 110

Kafka, Franz 216–17, 254
Kandinsky, Wassily 232
Kant, Immanuel: the aesthetic 11; art as techne 223, 226, 227, 228, 229; correlationism 287; epistemology 280; genius 227, 228; judgement 120, 122–8, 130, 131; moral philosophy 198; *pharmakon* 295, 300, 302, 305, 309; philosophy of history 28, 30; reason 49, 50, 62; speculative realism 13; swarms 185; transcendental philosophy 266, 268, 291, 292; will 92, 95, 96, 98, 100, 101
Kateb, George 257

Kemal, Salim 14, 124
Kierkegaard, Søren 23, 76
'Kissing and Horrid Strife' 245
Klein, N. 87
Knapp, Steven 34, 64, 70
knowledge: art as techne 233; personalism 218; perspectivism 51; *pharmakon* 299; scientific research 40, 42, 43, 44, 47; truth 280; warfare 86
Kogacioglu, D. 111
Kojève, A. 98, 100
Korsgaard, C.M. 63
Koselleck, Reinhard 53
Kosik, Karel 28
Kourouma, Ahmadou 165
Kranz, W. 245
Kristeva, Julia 11, 31, 308
'Kubla Khan' 230, 231

La Boétie, Etienne 101
labour 184, 300
Lacan, Jacques: the aesthetic 11; heyday of 'Theory' 237; life 66; oblativity 202; philosophical grammar of theory 238; psychoanalysis 21; subjectivity 6, 140; theory/philosophy divide 30; theory's evolution 3
LaCapra, D. 253
Lambert, Gregg 44, 47
Lamming, George 164–5
language: the aesthetic 12; human life 70; judgement 129; law 254; philosophical grammar of theory 237, 239–43; poetry 246, 247; political practice 6; postcolonial theory 166, 167, 168
'Large Glass' 234
Larrabee, M.J. 198
Laruelle, François 290, 292
late liberalism 109–11, 113, 114, 116
Latour, Bruno 14, 38, 286, 292
law: liberalism 254, 255; personalism 208–9, 210, 213, 215, 218; and philosophy 59, 60; social structure 56
Lawrence, D.H. 12, 244, 245–7, 256
learning 151, 152, 159, 160
Leavis, F.R. 168, 169, 170, 251
Lecourt, D. 21
Leiber, Fritz 185
Leibniz, G.W. 209
Lenin, V.I. 97, 98
Leonardo da Vinci 196–9, 200, 201, 203, 204
Leroi-Gourhan, André 37
'Let There Be Light!' 246

Levinas, Emmanuel 14, 22, 155, 203
Levine, G. 14, 249
Lewis, M.G. 185
liberalism: and aesthetics 12, 249–61; late liberalism 7, 109–11, 113, 114, 116; neo-pragmatism 39; role of theory 47
Libet, Benjamin 86
life: art as techne 229; bare activity 82; 'bare life' 9, 10; biopolitics 69; human life 65, 66, 206, 208, 209; naturalism 70; personalism 206–9, 217, 218; potentiality 106; scientific turn 5, 6; theory's evolution 14; time 266, 272–6
linguistics 21, 265
literary criticism 141, 166–70, 241
literary theory 67, 166–7, 170, 237, 251, 253–5, 258
literature: the aesthetic 12; art as techne 226, 231; human life 67, 70; liberalism 254, 256, 258, 259, 260; mediatized reflexivity 138, 140–2; personalism 216; philosophical grammar of theory 237–48; postcolonial theory 163–5, 167, 168, 170, 173, 174, 176; *Tel Quel* 21
Little Children Are Sacred 111, 112, 116
Locke, John 210, 212
Locusts: The 8th Plague 185
Loesberg, Jonathan 11, 14
Longuenesse, Béatrice 130
Loraux, N. 201, 202
love 105
Lovecraft, H.P. 10, 191
Luhmann, Niklas 3, 5, 51–60
Lukács, G. 92, 97, 155, 260
Lyotard, Jean-François 1, 11, 126, 155, 166, 237, 238, 241

McCarthy, Cormac 68
McGann, S. 253, 258
Machado, Antonio 90
Macherey, Pierre 141, 142, 147
Machiavelli, N. 95
Malpas, S. 14, 70
manga 192
Marcuse, Herbert 147, 298
Maritain, Jacques 206, 214
Marrati, P. 26
Marx, Karl: capital 80; dialectical voluntarism 91; differentiation 53; French and German theory 21, 23, 25; measurement of time 300; philosophy of history 27; reason 50; 'self-sufficient philosophy' 22; swarms 184; will 92, 97, 98, 100

Marxism: domestication of theory 34; French and German theory 20, 21, 24, 25; genealogy of theory 35; *pharmakon* 300–1; philosophy of history 28; realism 260; subaltern studies 150, 151, 157; voluntarism 97
Massumi, Brian 4, 7, 9, 10, 14, 36, 75–89, 106, 116
materialism 36, 41, 42, 47
maternity 196, 197, 198, 199, 202
mathematics 183, 230
Maturana, Humberto 38
Medea 201, 202, 203
media 116, 145, 146
mediatization 9, 146
Mei Lan-fang 137
Meillassoux, Quentin: antihumanism 67; conception of time 266–75, 276; correlationism 287, 288, 291; language 247; speculative realism 3, 13, 31, 266; theory's evolution 3, 14
memory 75, 76, 84, 210, 217, 295
Merleau-Ponty, Maurice 69, 217, 286
metaphysics 278, 279, 280, 282
Metzinger, Thomas 37
Michaels, Walter Benn 34, 39, 64, 70
military operations 7, 76, 77, 80, 82–5, 183, 299
Mill, John Stuart 212, 250, 256
Miller, D.A. 258
Millikan, Ruth Garrett 291
mimesis 4, 9, 165, 166, 170, 172–6, 224
The Mist 192
Mitchell, Stanley 137, 146, 147
Mitchell, Timothy 173
Mitchell, W.J.T. 14
modernism 27, 165, 228, 259, 260
modernity 28, 29, 52–4, 56–8
Moffat, J. 87
Mohanty, Chandra 8, 161
money 80
The Monk 185
montage 138, 143
Montesquieu, C. de 96, 101, 102
Moore-Gilbert, Bart 151, 157
moral philosophy 198
Morales, Evo 97
Morris, P. 258
mothers 199, 200, 201, 202, 204, 296
Motluk, A. 87
Mounier, Emmanuel 206, 214
Mozart, Wolfgang Amadeus 230–1
multiculturalism 110
Mulvey, Laura 141, 142

Munster, Anna 36
music 226, 230–1
Musil, Robert 216

Naipaul, V.S. 165, 170–2
Nancy, Jean-Luc 25
Narayan, R.K. 164, 175, 176
natality 10, 196, 199, 200, 201
natural people 210, 211
naturalism 70, 279
Nazism 206, 207, 212, 214, 215, 252
Nedelsky, Jennifer 123
Negri, Antonio 27, 34, 66, 69, 70, 80, 94
neo-pragmatism 39
neoliberalism 7, 108, 109, 110, 113, 116
Nesbitt, N. 101
neuroscience 5, 35, 36, 37, 42
New Historicism 11
Ngai, Sianne 11
Ngugi wa Thiong'o 165, 171, 175
Niebuhr, Rienhold 250
Nietzsche, Fredrich: aesthetic modernity
    259; destruction 29; end of human life
    68; French and German theory 25;
    perspectivism 51, 55; philosophy 31;
    philosophy of history 27; reason 50;
    repetition 76; sciences and humanities
    43; will 93, 94, 96; will to power 213
The Night Land 192
nihilism 50, 60
9/11 68, 252
Nixon, Richard 299
norms 57, 58, 60, 126
novels: demonology of swarms 185;
    liberalism 259, 260; postcolonial
    theory 167, 169, 170–2, 174, 175–6
nuclear age 299, 300, 301
nuclear criticism 300, 301, 302
Nussbaum, M. 257
Nwapa, Flora 165, 174–5

Obama, Barack 76
obesity 309
objectivity 43, 44, 46, 125, 217
objects 13, 283, 284, 285, 287, 290, 291
observation 51, 52, 54, 55, 57
ontology: concept of life 182; ego 194,
    195; ethics of care 196, 198, 202;
    intersubjectivity 10; logic of life
    189, 190, 191; perspectivism 51, 52;
    scientific research 43
open source 308
Orientalism 8, 167
Osborne, Peter 5, 11–13, 19–33

O'Shea, James 291, 292
other 194, 195, 198, 199, 200
Ouologuem, Yambo 165
Outbreak 68

painting 142, 232, 306
Pakistan 83
pandemics 68
paradoxes 60
Pascal, Blaise 247
Pasquier, R. 247
Patai, D. 14
Pataki, George 75, 76, 77
performativity 65
personalism 10, 206, 208, 212, 215
perspectivism 51, 52, 58
Petito, J. 70
Phaedrus 13
pharmakon 13, 294–9, 300–4, 307–9
phenomenology 27, 35, 67, 70
PhotoShop 143
Pippin, Robert 259, 260
Plato 13, 49, 50, 59, 65, 241, 294–8
pleasure 107, 128, 142
Plissart, J.-M. 307
Plotz, J. 258
plurality 121, 122, 124, 125
poetry 12, 168, 224–5, 228–32, 241, 243–7
poiesis 224, 242
positivism 63
postcolonial theory 8, 9, 163–78
postmodernism 163, 165, 256
poststructuralism: domestication of theory
    34; freedom 6; French theory 20;
    military operations 7; postcolonial
    theory 164; reflexivity 9, 139;
    subaltern studies 149, 150, 155;
    theory's evolution 4
potentiality 7, 105–7, 113, 116, 117,
    120, 255
Pound, Ezra 228
Povinelli, Elizabeth 4, 7, 105–19
power: liberalism 252; personalism 213,
    217, 218; political practice 6; warfare
    86; will 94, 96, 98
pragmatism 22, 27, 39, 40, 42, 43
Prakash, Gyan 150, 156, 157
proceduralism 252, 254
prodigies 230
proletarianisation 295, 296, 298, 299,
    301, 305
proof 124, 125
Protevi, John 36, 37, 41, 42, 43
Proust, Marcel 256

psukhē 189, 190, 192
psychoanalysis 21, 24, 34, 214, 297, 307
public sphere 153, 160, 258

queer theory 1, 14, 63, 252
Quine, W.v.O. 247
Quinlan, Karen 106, 108

race 8, 63
racism 206, 207, 213
Rajan, Tilottama 34, 46, 47
Ramachandran, V.S. 35
Ramchand, Kenneth 169, 171
Rancière, Jacques 3, 11–12, 14, 31, 93–4,
    147, 238–9, 241
Rasch, William 3, 5, 49–61
Rawls, John 257
Raymond, J.E. 86
Readings, Bill 44
realism: correlationism 284–90; liberalism
    249, 251, 258–60; postcolonial theory
    165, 167, 168, 171–3; scientific
    research 36, 38–43, 47
reason: irreductionism 281; judgement 122,
    124, 126, 127; law and philosophy 59,
    60; *pharmakon* 298; reduction of 50;
    science 49; will 96
reciprocity 196
Redfield, M. 14
reflective enlightenment 251
reflective judgement 122, 125, 127, 128
reflexivity 135–48, 304, 305
relativism 40
religion 29, 59, 60, 94, 267
repetition 76, 77
representation 8–9, 14, 75, 158, 224
research 44, 45, 47, 48
rhetoric 126, 166
Ricoeur, Paul 28, 206
rights: liberalism 252; personalism 10, 206,
    208, 209, 215, 216, 218; revolutions
    92; social order 57
Rilke, R.M. 229
Rimbaud, Arthur 230
Robbins, B. 258
Robespierre, M. 95, 97, 99, 100, 102
Roman law 208–9, 210, 215
Romanticism 223, 228, 230, 231
Ronfeldt, David 77, 79, 87, 183
Rorty, Richard 5, 38–45, 47, 256, 286
Rousseau, J.-J. 3, 90, 92, 95–100, 101, 102
Rumsfeld, Donald 79, 87
Rushdie, Salman 9, 164, 176, 177
Russian Formalism 231, 235

Said, Edward 8, 167, 176, 177
St. John, M. 87
Saint-Just, L.A. de 96, 97, 100
*Sant'Anna, la Madonna e il bambino con
    l'agnello* 196, 197, 203–4
Sarkar, Sumit 149, 160, 161
Sartre, J.-P. 91, 93, 94, 95, 98, 100
Saussure, Ferdinand de 21, 265
Scarry, E. 249
Schleicher, August 207
Schmitt, Carl 252
Schopenhauer, Arthur 93, 207
science: concepts and objects 290, 291;
    conceptual reality 282; emergence
    of life 272; *pharmakon* 295; and
    philosophy 244, 245; project of theory
    36; reason 49; reflexivity 142; research
    35, 42–8; scientific realism 38–40;
    transcendental subject 268
science fiction 182, 185
scientific turn 3, 5
Searle, John 43
Segwick, Eve 37
self 41, 42, 199–200
self-determination 90, 91, 93, 94, 95
Sellars, Wilfred 280, 281, 283, 285,
    291, 292
semantics 52–8
Sen, Amartya 110
senses 11, 142, 143
sensus communis 125, 126, 128, 130
sexual abuse 111, 112
Shapiro, K.L. 86
Shearer, Rhonda Roland 234
Shklar, Judith N. 250
Shklovsky, Victor 136, 137, 144, 146, 147
Sieyès, E.J. 95, 97
Simondon, Gilbert 42, 217, 295, 308
Singer, Peter 212
singularity 232
slavery 208, 210, 215
Slavin, J.P. 96
Sloterdijk, Peter 25
Smith, Adam 251
Smith, Barbara Herrnstein 38, 40, 41,
    44, 45
smoking ban 308
Social Darwinism 207
social order 57, 58
social structure 52, 53, 54, 55, 56
Socrates 19, 225
soft power 77, 78
software 308
Les soleils des indépendances 165

South Africa 90
sovereignty 121, 172, 210, 211, 213, 252
Soyinka, Wole 165
space 30, 139, 142, 265, 269–70, 274
spectacle 143
spectrality 306, 307
speculative realism 3, 6, 13, 242, 266
speech 13
Spencer, Herbert 183
Spillers, Hortense 156, 161
Spinoza, Baruch 60, 96, 105, 116, 182, 298
spirit 294, 297, 302
Spivak, Gayatri 8, 149–59, 163, 177
Stafford, Barbara 36, 37, 41, 42
staging 141, 142, 143, 145
StarCraft 185
Staten, Henry 12, 223–35, 231, 274–5
Steigler, Bernard 13, 37
Stein, Edith 206
Steinberger, P. 130
Stengers, I. 62, 83
stereotypes 199, 200, 201, 202
Stiegler, Bernard 294–310
Stieglitz, Alfred 234
Stove, David 284, 287, 292
strategic essentialism 152
stratification 53
Strauss, Leo 58, 59, 60
structuralism 20, 43, 226, 227, 228
subaltern studies 8, 9, 110, 149–62
subjection 210, 211, 217
subjective validity 125, 126
subjectivity: freedom 6; human life 70;
    personalism 206, 210, 217; reason
    50; sciences 44; scientific realism 41;
    subaltern studies 150, 155; theory's
    evolution 14; will 98
subjects 209–12, 213
succession 265, 269–72
Sunshine 68
supernatural horror 191–2
surplus–value 80
Surrealism 241
survival 274, 275
The Swarm 185
swarms 10, 182–9, 185–9
Szafranski, R. 84
Szalay, M. 253, 258

tableau 135, 136, 138, 143
Tarski, Alfred 247
taste 124, 125, 126
techne 12, 223–6, 228–32, 234–5
technology 218, 299, 308

Tel Quel 21, 241
Teres, H. 257
terror 99–100
terrorism 68, 70, 77
Thacker, Eugene 4, 10, 181–93
theatre 137, 138, 140, 141
theatre of cruelty 145
Them! 185
Things Fall Apart 174
Thompson, Evan 36
Tihanov, Galin 144, 147
time: emergence of life 272–6; history 26,
    27; perception 76; *pharmakon* 300,
    301; philosophy of history 28, 30;
    speculative realism 13, 266; succession
    265, 269–72; trace-structure 13,
    265–7, 269, 270, 272, 276;
    transcendental philosophy 266,
    268; warfare 86
Time 205
Tocqueville, Alexis de 96, 250
Toer, Peamoedya Ananta 164
Tolstoy, Leo 49, 50, 141, 144
Toscano, Alberto 13, 31
trace-structure of time 13, 265–7, 269, 270,
    272, 276
transindividual 295
transitional objects 297, 304
Trilling, Lionel 3, 250, 256, 257, 258, 260
Trollope, Anthony 259
Tronto, Joan 195, 196, 198
Trotsky, Leon 235
28 Days Later 68
28 Weeks Later 68

Ullman, H.K. 77, 78, 79, 80, 87
uncertainty 83
unconscious 207, 214, 297–9, 307, 308
United Democratic Front 90
Universal Declaration of Human Rights
    206, 208
universities 44, 45, 46, 47
Untouchable 175
Uzumaki 192

Valéry, Paul 225, 228, 230, 294, 302, 309
validity 123, 124, 125, 128
values 57, 58, 124
Varela, Francisco 36, 38
video games 185
Viego, Antonio 161
Villa, D. 130
violence 145, 201–2, 203
Virgin Mary 196, 197, 198, 201, 203

Virilio, Paul 78, 299
Virno, Paolo 94
virtuality 6, 113
virtue 99
viruses 68
vis existendi 105, 107, 109
Vo Nguyen Giap 95
Vološinov, V.N. 228
voluntarism 93, 94, 95, 96

Wade, J.P. 77, 78, 79, 80, 87
Wahnich, S. 100, 101
Waiting for the Mahatma 175–6
Wallerstein, I. 118
war 76–86, 212
war on terror 7, 68, 75, 76, 252
Warhol, Andy 233, 234
Warner, M. 160, 258
The Waste Land 228
Weber, Max 49, 50, 55, 56, 57, 60
Weber, S. 24
Weil, Simone 3, 10, 214–15
weird fiction 191–2
Wellek, René 237
Wellmer, A. 24, 123

Welshon, Rex 51
West Indies 169, 170, 171
Wheeler, William Morton 183
Wiggershaus, R. 20
Wild, R. 112
Wilde, Oscar 259
will to power 213
Wilson, E.O. 183
Winnicott, D. 297, 300, 304, 306, 307
Wittgenstein, L. 8, 55, 96, 122, 125, 241
Wolfe, Cary 2, 3, 4, 5, 9, 34–48
women 141, 158, 196–9, 200
writing 13, 294

X: The Unknown 192
Xenophanes of Colophon 241

Yeats, W.B. 232, 256
Young, R. 177

Zambrana, R. 276
Zammito, J.H. 228
Zerilli, Linda 2–4, 7–8, 11, 120–32
Zikode, S. 98
Žižek, Slavoj 24, 30, 34, 94, 96